Strategies of Cooperation

Strategies of Cooperation

Managing Alliances, Networks, and Joint Ventures

JOHN CHILD AND DAVID FAULKNER

OXFORD UNIVERSITY PRESS
1998

Oxford University Press, Great Clarendon Street, Oxford OX2 6DP
Oxford New York
Athens Auckland Bangkok Bogotá Buenos Aires Calcutta
Cape Town Chennai Dar es Salaam Delhi Florence Hong Kong Istanbul
Karachi Kuala Lumpur Madras Madrid Melbourne Mexico City Mumbai
Nairobi Paris São Paolo Singapore Taipei Tokyo Toronto Warsaw
and associated companies in
Berlin Ibadan

Oxford is a registered trade mark of Oxford University Press

Published in the United States
by Oxford University Press Inc., New York

British Library Cataloguing in Publication Data
Data available
Library of Congress Cataloging in Publication Data
Data available
ISBN 0–19–877484–2 (Hbk)
ISBN 0–19–877485–0 (Pbk)

10 9 8 7 6 5 4 3 2 1

Typeset by Hope Services (Abingdon) Ltd.
Printed in Great Britain by
Bookcraft (Bath) Ltd.,
Midsomer Norton, Somerset

PREFACE

The rapidly growing numbers of alliances in the business world today have in recent years captured the attention of academic writers. However, their contributions have so far focused mainly on single issues such as market-entry strategy or the conditions for alliance formation. Also more attention has been devoted to strategic matters than to such factors as how to manage alliances successfully.

In this book we attempt to synthesize the ideas of many contributors as well as those of our own research. The result, we hope, is a more comprehensive guide to the subject than has hitherto been available. In order to make this book a more flexible resource for its readers, each chapter is followed by its own set of references to sources and further reading.

In preparing this book, we have been significantly assisted by the many companies with which we have worked, and the executives who have provided us with so many germane case examples. We have also benefited from the opportunities to pursue research on this subject provided by the Economic and Social Research Council, the Leverhulme Trust, and the Carnegie–Bosch Institute. Members of the Cambridge University M.Phil. in Management Studies classes of 1996/7 and 1997/8 provided valuable comments on an earlier draft of the book. Sally Heavens provided valuable editorial assistance in the preparation of the final manuscript. Last but not least, we could not have completed the task without the forbearance and sympathetic support of our families.

John Child
Cambridge

David Faulkner
Oxford

January 1998

CONTENTS

LIST OF FIGURES

LIST OF TABLES

ABBREVIATIONS

AIDS	acquired immune deficiency syndrome
AMEF	Agit Manufacturing Enterprise Forum
ASEAN	Association of South East Asian Nations
BAT	British American Tobacco
BATNA	Best Alternative to a Negotiated Agreement
C&W	Cable & Wireless
CEO	chief executive officer
CIBAM	Centre for International Business and Management
COCOM	Coordinating Committee for Multilateral Export Controls
COMECON	economic association of Communist countries
DCF	discounted cash flow
DMNC	decentralized multinational corporations
EBRD	European Bank for Reconstruction and Development
EJV	equity joint venture
EVC	Eurovynyl Chloride
FDI	foreign direct investment
GM	general manager
GRIT	graduated reciprocation and tension [reduction]
HRM	human-resource management
IBM	International Business Machines
IBOS	Interbank On-line System
ICI	Imperial Chemical Industries
ICV	international cooperative venture
IDC	International Digital Corporation
IJV	international joint venture
IOR	inter-organizational relationship
ISA	international strategic alliances
IT	information technology
ITRI	International Trade Research Institute
JIT	just in time
JV	joint venture
MBA	make–buy–ally
MCC	Micro-electronics and Computer Technology Corporation

MNC	multinational corporation
MNE	multinational enterprise
MOD	Ministry of Defence
MOE	multi-organizational enterprise
MOFERT	Ministry of Foreign Economic Relations and Trade
MPT	market-power theory
NCFC	Nantong Cellulose Fibers Company
NPV	net present value
PAL	pool resources–ally–link systems
PRC	People's Republic of China
PRV	Peugeot, Renault, and Volvo
PVC	physical value chain
PVC	polyvinyl chloride
R&D	research and development
RBS	Royal Bank of Scotland
SMT	strategic-management theory
TCE	transaction-cost economics
TNC	transnational corporations
TQM	total quality management
UNCTAD	United Nations Conference on Trade and Development
VC	virtual corporation
VVC	virtual value chain
WFOE	wholly owned foreign enterprise

1

Introduction

COOPERATIVE STRATEGY

Cooperative strategy is the attempt by organizations to realize their objectives through cooperation with other organizations, rather than in competition with them. It focuses on the benefits that can be gained through cooperation and how to manage the cooperation so as to realize them. A cooperative strategy can offer significant advantages for companies which are lacking in particular competences or resources to secure these through links with others possessing complementary skills or assets; it may also offer easier access to new markets, and opportunities for mutual synergy and learning.

The distinction is made between competitive and corporate strategy (Bowman and Faulkner 1997), and it is important to see how cooperative strategy relates to them. Competitive strategy is concerned with the question of how a firm can gain advantage over its competitors. There are two broad traditions within thinking about competitive strategy. The first emphasizes how superior profits can derive from the structure of the industry in which a firm is located, and from the pursuit of generic strategies—cost leadership, differentiation, or focus—in ways which suit the conditions of that industry (Porter 1980, 1985). The second tradition draws attention to the competitive advantage that can be gained from a firm's unique competences and resources, which combine to deliver valued products and are difficult to imitate or acquire (Collis 1996). A strategy of cooperation with one or more other firms can be a counterpart to the pursuit of competitive advantage in the ways identified by both these traditions of thinking about competitive strategy. This will become clearer in Chapter 4, which examines the motives behind a cooperative strategy, and Chapter 13, which examines the ability of alliances to enhance a firm's competences through learning.

The ability to maintain both the structure of an industry and a firm's position within it can be enhanced by cooperation with competitors. This could be a primarily defensive alliance against dominant firms, or a more offensive alliance intended to secure a stronger position within the industry and/or reduce opportunities for new entrants. Both these kinds of alliance are currently evident within the global telecommunications industry. The proposed, but abortive, merger in 1996 between British Telecom and Cable & Wireless illustrates an offensive alliance aimed at securing a dominant industry position as the first truly global telecoms operator. Other telecom companies, emerging from protected domestic markets and facing aggressive companies such as AT&T and BT, have formed more defensive joint ventures—an example being GlobalOne formed between Deutsche Telekom and France Télécom.

Sometimes, entry into an industry or regional sector is only feasible in the first place via a partner. The ability to enter some markets, especially in developing countries or those with invisible entry barriers like Japan, may be possible only through cooperation with a local firm. The local firm is able to offer a capability which the foreign partner does not at the time possess. This case leads on to the second tradition of thinking on competitive strategy, which draws attention to the competitive advantage that can be gained from possessing unique capabilities. Valued competences and resources are often available only from a partner, or from sharing their development with a partner. Alliances may enable firms to gain access to partners' advanced technology or share the high cost of developing new capabilities through research and development. Its joint venture with Motorola, for example, has given Toshiba access to the former's microprocessor technology. Cooperation between firms can also permit the pooling of their complementary strengths so as to secure creative synergies. The successful collaboration between Rover and Honda, which ceased only with the decision of Rover's owners to sell it to BMW, was based on identifiable complementarities which gave rise to fruitful synergies. Rover could offer access to a network of component suppliers and subcontractors, spare capacity in its factories, and an understanding of European automobile tastes. Honda was able to offer Rover the quality engineering it badly lacked and models to revitalize its model range (Faulkner 1995).

Competitive strategy tends to focus on the particular industry and product. Many firms, however, are in, or have the capacity to be in, several businesses and various geographical locations. So there are also the questions of what business, market, and locations should a firm be in and how should it run them? This draws attention to the domain of corporate strategy, which is concerned with selecting businesses and operational areas, resourcing, and controlling them (Bowman and Faulkner 1997). It is the ability to make and sustain these strategic decisions which justifies having a corporate function in the first place rather than constituting each business separately.

The issue of cooperation comes within the purview of corporate strategy in several ways. First, it should reflect the mission and objectives which corporate management set for a company. If one objective is to become more innovative, alliances may well be sought which promise access to superior know-how and technology. Secondly, as we have already noted, cooperation may be sought as a means of sharing the resourcing, or its risk, of desired new developments. Thirdly, it may be incumbent on the corporate function to superimpose a controlling and coordinating framework over a firm's different businesses, especially if these are developing through alliances with different partners in a given country where the company has to maintain a cohesive voice *vis-à-vis* governmental authorities. These authorities may, as in China, be the customer for several of the separate businesses. A more fundamental connection between corporate and cooperative strategy stems from the trend for firms to be seeking a global presence and competitive advantage through working within complex networks of cooperative arrangements with other companies. This trend, as Chapter 6 discusses, raises significant questions about the future role of corporate centres.

Cooperative strategy is therefore not an alternative to either competitive or corporate strategies. It amounts to a further domain of policy options whose purpose is to enable firms to compete more effectively. Questions about the configuration and constitution of actual and potential alliances are important items on the agenda of corporate strategy. Fig. 1.1 illustrates how cooperation can exist alongside competition but not without tensions and variable results. The cooperations referred to in the figure are described in more detail in the Appendix.

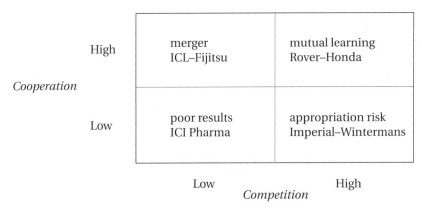

Fig. 1.1. Different combinations of cooperation and competition
Source: adapted from Stiles (1997).

Where cooperation is high and competition low, there will be strong pressures for the partners to merge once the alliance has demonstrated its success over a period of time. Where both competition and cooperation are high, the abiding tensions between the partners will be apparent but both partners will be concerned to learn from each other rapidly, lest its partner defect. Where both cooperation and competition are low, the alliance will cease to engage the minds of top management and is likely to achieve only limited results. However, where competitive forces between the partners are very apparent even after the alliance has been set up, yet actual cooperation is low, the risk of one partner appropriating the skills and knowledge of the other are high.

A KEY THEME

Cooperative strategy has attracted increasing attention over the last decade or so, particularly in the popular management press and the academic journals. Books tackling the subject in a wider and more all-embracing way than is possible in single-theme articles have been less plentiful. A number of coexisting contemporary trends fuel current interest. Companies have looked increasingly to cooperate with each other due to the limitations of coping successfully on their own with a world where markets are becoming global in scope, technologies are changing rapidly, huge investment funds are regularly demanded to develop new products with ever-shortening life cycles, and the economic scene is becoming characterized by high uncertainty and turbulence.

At the same time the economies of the East are showing distinct signs of upstaging those of the West in an increasing number of industries. Despite the West's economic dominance during the nineteenth century and the first half of the twentieth, and its emergence from the Second World War in a position of supreme power, world leadership in automobiles, electronics, shipbuilding, steel, and textiles either has, or arguably is, in the process of passing to the East. If there is one key difference between the West and the East in business philosophies it is that the West is individualistic and competitive right down to an interpersonal level, whilst the East is collective and cooperative within dense networks of relationships. This, many commentators argue, is the basis of its strength. If so, it is important that Western companies understand the philosophy and practice of cooperation, and perhaps adopt those aspects of it that are culturally congruent with our own way of doing things.

The movement away from the traditional concept of the firm is accentuated by the growth of 'federated organizations' (Handy 1992). This concept places a limited life on integrated multinational corporations (MNCs), which often suffer from high overheads, a bias towards the culture of their national headquarters, and low flexibility. The move towards the federated firm is portrayed by Fig. 1.2.

One of the converts to the concept of federation is IBM, one of the most powerful multinational corporations in the world. After experiencing a significant decline in performance, and suspecting a loss of competitive advantage, it decided in 1991 to restructure its operations radically from those of an integrated worldwide firm with a strong single culture, to a federation of fourteen potentially competitive companies. This fundamental change clearly places a premium on the ability of the federated companies to cooperate, where appropriate, whereas previously their activities were coordinated through

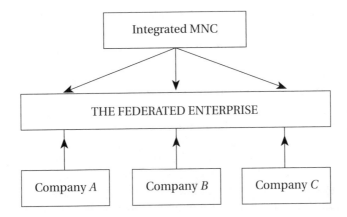

Fig. 1.2. The move towards the federated enterprise

hierarchical channels. The culture shock has been so great, and the immediate results so mixed, that the chief executive has recently resigned, and his successor has come from outside the computer industry. The IBM of the future is likely to be a federated enterprise, although the company has clearly not yet successfully adapted to such a radically changed paradigm.

The concurrent growth of alliances approaches the flexible transnational structure from the other end. In other words, it involves the amalgamation of previously independent resources and competencies in contrast to the federation of previously hierarchically controlled resources and competencies.

Where the traditional concepts of firm, industry, and national economy start to become concepts of declining clarity, and thus to lose their exclusive usefulness as tools for strategic analysis, the need for an adequate understanding of alliances and other cooperative network strategies assumes increased importance.

FOCUS OF THE BOOK

This book attempts to take stock of current thinking on the subject of cooperative strategy. The focus will be on cooperation between firms, though many of the insights into establishing and managing inter-firm cooperation can also be applied to partnerships between other types of organization. Alliances, which are partnerships between firms, are the normal agent for cooperative strategy. They are often 'strategic' in the sense that they have been formed as a direct response to major strategic challenges or opportunities which the partner firms face. Alliances are a means to an end, and consequently they are not necessarily formed with a long-term cooperative relationship in mind. But they may be established with this intention, the more so when the partners invest substantially in them. Once alliances are up and running, partners may also perceive unanticipated benefits from cooperation, such as mutual learning, which lead them to re-evaluate it positively.

However, alliances can also be formed with shorter-term objectives in view. A firm may, for example, intend to use an alliance as a means of appropriating competences and knowledge from its partner, which it continues to regard as an actual or potential competitor. Or a firm may enter into an alliance as a way of taking out an option for the future in conditions of uncertainty—for example, entering an unfamiliar national market. Once it has mastered the uncertainty, it may no longer attach much value to continuing the cooperation.

Whatever the underlying motivation for its formation, any alliance requires an ability to manage cooperation in order to generate returns to the partners. The ever-growing prevalence of alliances, and the need to understand the basis for their successful management, provides the main justification for the present book. It is informed by John Child's work on joint ventures in China and to a lesser extent Eastern Europe, and David Faulkner's work on strategic alliances between companies in developed nations. It also attempts to integrate what the authors believe to be the salient ideas of other writers on cooperative strategy in tackling some of the key issues currently under debate in the field.

A number of important ideas emerge from the writers' efforts in this endeavour which are perhaps worth capturing before the reader embarks on the task of a detailed reading of the book.

1. Cooperative strategy is not new; it has always been with us. It means what it suggests, namely the achievement of an agreement and a plan to work together; not the giving of orders down hierarchies. Firms embarking upon alliances with other firms need to keep this in the forefront of their consciousness when devising systems and controls, and activating them in the joint enterprise. This book, whilst concentrating on perhaps the pre-eminent form of cooperation—namely, the various forms of strategic alliance—encompasses other forms of cooperation as well that are met in business activity, even down to the humble distributor or supplier agreement.

2. Commitment and trust are the key attitudes most strongly associated with success in alliances. No amount of energy and clear direction will compensate for their absence. And it should be noted that commitment can exist without trust and vice versa, but both are necessary for a lasting and stable relationship.

3. Strategic alliances, including joint ventures, collaborations, and consortia, are at base all about organizational learning, and should be structured towards that end. However, many other types of cooperation, such as networks or virtual corporations, are primarily about skill substitution—i.e. company *A* cooperates with company *B* because it sees that its partner can exercise a particular skill better than it can.

4. Other forms of cooperative strategy, such as virtual organizations, networks, outsourced corporations, are about capability substitution. Their strength lies in their specializations, their adaptability and flexibility, but not necessarily in the learning opportunities they afford.

5. Cooperative enterprises do not do away with the need for intelligent purpose, a brain, and a central nervous (information) system if they are to achieve competitive advantage in relation to integrated corporations which more self-evidently have these characteristics.

6. To cooperate does not mean to allow all proprietary information to pass unchecked to the partner. As Richardson (1972) warns: 'Firms form partners for the dance but, when the music stops, they can change them.'

7. Issues of control need to be addressed, but more subtly than in hierarchies, as too great a degree of control in cooperative enterprises stifles innovation and motivation.

8. A successful alliance is one that evolves into something more than was perhaps foreseen at the outset. Conscious attempts must be made to cause the alliance to develop if it is to attract the best people, and contribute most to the partner companies.

9. The interface between the two (sometimes more) company cultures is the crucible of potential achievement. Sensitivity to each other's cultures is vital to effective joint operation. Its absence leads to a failed alliance, however great the potential economic synergies between the partners.

10. Information technology makes the task of coordinating cooperative strategy that much easier, but it cannot and must not be allowed to substitute for bonding between cooperating company executives.

ORGANIZATION OF THE BOOK

These and other key lessons from the research behind this book are developed in more detail in the chapters that follow (see Fig. 1.3).

Part I is concerned with the nature of cooperation and its role in strategy. Chapter 2 outlines the main perspectives that contribute to an understanding of cooperative strategy. The theory of cooperative strategy is related to contributions from economics—market-power theory, transaction-cost economics, agency theory, and increasing-returns theory—as well as to game theory, strategic-management theory, and contributions from organization theory on resource dependence and modern organizational forms. This chapter summarizes the relevance of these theories and draws out the complementarities between them.

Cooperation depends on trust between partners. Chapter 3 presents the insights into trust which can be derived from psychological and sociological research. This identifies the factors on which trust can be based and through

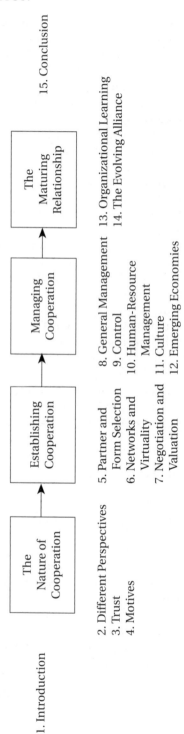

Fig. 1.3. Alliance development, as traced through the book

which it can develop. The first step is to find a basis on which the risks of depending on partners become mutually acceptable. As the partners get to know more about each other, this improved understanding should breed further mutual confidence. Eventually, the cooperation may become firmly established on the basis of genuine personal friendships between the key participants. These elements in trust development can support the phases through which cooperation within an alliance can develop. The chapter closes with guidelines for developing trust within cooperative relationships between firms.

Chapter 4 discusses the principal motives behind a cooperative strategy. The most common reasons for setting up a collaborative activity with a competitive or complementary firm are considered. The various different types of resource and skill deficiency are rated in relation to their importance as stimuli to cooperative activity. It is emphasized that it is not only competence vulnerabilities, but also the desire to spread risk, and the need to reach markets fast, whilst 'windows of opportunity' last, that drive organizations to set up cooperative arrangements. Strategic, transaction-cost-reducing and organizational learning motives for cooperative activity are compared and contrasted (Kogut 1988).

The chapters in Part II are concerned with how cooperation between firms is established and the various forms it can take. Chapter 5 considers the criteria to be highlighted in selecting a partner and deciding upon the appropriate form the alliance should take. Once a collaborative activity has been decided upon, it is necessary to find an appropriate partner. This chapter attempts to operationalize the strategic-fit/cultural-fit matrix. It emphasizes that the possible achievement of synergies through the use of complementary assets and competences underlies the concept of strategic fit (Geringer 1991). It also draws the reader's attention to the need for inter-cultural sensitivity if the alliance is to succeed. The second half of the chapter considers the question of collaborative forms, and considers which one to select. The key characteristics of the various forms of cooperative activity are considered, as well as the circumstances in which each form is most appropriately adopted. In addition to the major strategic alliance forms of the joint venture, the collaboration and the consortium, the flexible nature of collaborative networks is discussed.

Chapter 6 looks at the strengths and limitations of network forms in greater detail. It considers the varied types of network that form the basis of much cooperative strategy. Networks are the loosest form of alliance between companies. At their weakest they represent a well-developed communication system within an industry that enables companies operating in that industry to keep abreast of developments. They are often crystallized in trade associations. In a stronger form they represent a ready-made band of would-be cooperating companies willing to tackle commercial opportunities together without setting up formal links that may compromise the individuality of networking firms. Dominant-partner and equal-partner networks are compared and contrasted. The information technology-based Virtual Corporation is then considered. The 'Virtual Corporation' is the name for the network and IT-orientated form of organization based around centres of excellence in particular competences. It can be created very rapidly to meet specific sometimes transitory sets of circumstances, and can equally easily be dismantled and reformed as circumstances and profit opportunities change. This new concept is discussed and its strengths and limitations assessed. Many strategic alliances demonstrate characteristics of the virtual corporation.

Chapter 7 addresses the question of how to negotiate in an alliance situation, and how to value your partner's and your own prospective contributions to the enterprise. The chapter emphasizes that, whereas in a takeover situation, the negotiators are single-mindedly concerned to achieve the best price for their company—the highest or lowest price depending on the side of the negotiating table—this is not the case in an alliance. Unless both partners are concerned that the other has a good deal, the alliance will not prosper over time. A so-called win–win situation is sought. The problem of contribution valuation, however, is truly more an art than a science.

In Part III of the book different aspects of the management of cooperative activity are reviewed. Chapter 8 looks at the general and overall management of alliances. This chapter emphasizes that the management of alliances differs in its essential nature from that of integrated companies. The ability to give instructions is replaced by the need to seek areas of mutual agreement and to develop constituencies behind a course of action (Kanter 1989). It is noted that appropriate management styles will differ, particularly in the circumstances of a joint venture, which can be treated much like an ordinary company, and a collaboration, where a sensitive boundary-spanning mechanism is necessary.

Chapter 9 looks at control as an issue in cooperation. It recognizes both that control is not possible in a complete sense in alliances, because of the consensual nature of alliance activities, but also that some control by each partner is necessary if the partners are not each going to feel themselves to be in the hands of total uncertainty. The importance therefore is to specify controls that are at once clear yet flexible.

Chapter 10 addresses the specific management area of human resources. Some of the key human resource issues that arise when personnel from different countries and different cultures are brought to work together in a new collaborative environment are considered. The building of local management teams, the nature of training, and the role of the international manager are discussed.

Chapter 11 addresses the culture problem. It is now widely recognized that one of the most common reasons for the failure of alliances is the clash of the partners' contrasting company cultures. Yet there is evidence to suggest that the issue of congruent cultures is not one high on the checklist of companies seeking partners. The nature of cultural differences, the barriers to performance and to bonding that such differences provide, and the attitudes necessary to overcome such problems are discussed. Every company's unique cultural web is considered. The chapter deals in particular with two distinct forms of potential cultural problem—that between two partners from the developed world, and that between a developed world company and a partner from the developing world such as China, Central and Eastern Europe, and Latin America. In discussing these collaborative configurations, the 'culture problem' will be assessed in its broader institutional context identified in work such as that by Whitley (1992) on comparative business systems.

Chapter 12 looks more specifically at how to manage cooperative strategy in relation to emerging economies. Cooperation between companies in developed and emerging economies is a particularly fast-expanding feature of world trading relationships. This chapter discusses this issue with particular reference to China and Brazil and seeks to identify ways in which such collaborations differ from those between firms that are both in developed countries.

Part IV of the book addresses the question of how cooperative activity can be brought to maturity and made more permanent between partners. Organizational learning is the subject of Chapter 13. The role of organizational learning in all its aspects as a primary driver in cooperative activity is discussed. Single- and double-loop learning (Argyris 1992) is applied to alliances. The analysis of learning into technical, systemic, and strategic components (Child and Rodrigues 1996) is also described and its application to strategic alliances considered. The different forms of learning are also discussed, including opportunity learning, technology transfer, and tacit learning. Attention is given to the mechanisms and policies which help promote and transmit learning within alliances.

Chapter 14 emphasizes the importance of the role of evolution in the success of alliances. This implies the growth of the alliance in terms of new projects and new responsibilities. It is maintained that all alliances suffer potentially from entropy (Thorelli 1986), and that, unless the bonds brought about by the creation of the cooperative activity are constantly attended to and strengthened, there is an ever-present risk that the alliance will decline in importance to the partners, attract mediocre staff, and steadily become marginalized in the partners' priorities.

The conclusion, Chapter 15, attempts to draw together the threads of the arguments advanced throughout the book, and looks ahead to future developments. The analysis must of necessity relate to the changing nature of the international business context, which is one in which complexity is becoming inherently less predictable and dynamic disequilibrium the norm.

COMPARISON WITH OTHER BOOKS

The summary of chapter contents just presented indicates how this book offers a comprehensive coverage of its subject, with a strong emphasis on the managerial challenges in operating a cooperative strategy. There are relatively few other books on the subject of cooperative strategy and strategic alliances which bring together in one place the many issues and themes which can be found scattered in articles and case studies. It will be helpful to mention what we consider to be the other major relevant books at the time of writing, and how the present one compares with them.

Lorange and Roos, *Strategic Alliances: Formation, Implementation and Evolution* (1992), has become a standard text during the past few years. Their book contains valuable material on the formation and management of alliances, though as a whole it is quite loosely structured. There are several issues addressed in the present book to which Lorange and Roos pay little attention, including non-joint venture forms of cooperation, the role of trust and learning, and cooperative strategy in transitional economies.

In 1993 Bleeke and Ernst edited a set of papers by McKinsey consultants entitled *Collaborating to Compete: Using Strategic Alliances and Acquisitions in the Global Marketplace.* The editors are strongly in favour of cooperative strategy for the global marketplace: 'Collaboration is the value of the future. Alliances are the structure of the future' (p. 269). Their book offers stimulating examples and the results of in-house studies drawn from various parts of the developed world. It does not, however, extend to emerging or transitional economies. Nor are the various contributions integrated and ordered into a framework which would take the reader through the issues involved and enable conclusions to be drawn.

A significant and more recent text is Yoshino and Rangan, *Strategic Alliances: An Entrepreneurial Approach to Globalization* (1995). This has the virtue of being analytically a tighter book than the two mentioned so far. It provides the reader with useful 'road maps' and other frameworks. It is also illustrated with examples from large corporate alliances. Yoshino and Rangan give space to globalization and global networking as the context for many major alliances. They also provide a good treatment of alliance formation and general management. On the other hand, they either ignore or treat very briefly the more human side of cooperation between firms in terms of negotiation, trust, learning, human resource management, and culture. Nor does their global focus extend in any depth to transitional economies—it is quite heavily focused on US and Japanese firms.

In 1996 Gomes-Casseres published his *The Alliance Revolution: The New Shape of Business Rivalry.* This book provides an analysis of why alliances are formed for competitive advantage, and the impact this is having on industrial organization and the nature of global business competition. It focuses on alliance strategy rather than on its implementation, and takes its examples primarily from those industries where alliances are now common—automobiles, biotechnology, electronics, global airline services, and pharmaceuticals. It is a book that informs managers of the alliance context in which they now operate rather than being concerned with questions of how to manage the alliances themselves.

Finally, mention should be made of two edited books which, although not integrated texts, are important sources of relevant articles. The first is *Cooperative Strategies in International Business* (1988) edited by Contractor and Lorange. The second is the three-volume *Cooperative Strategies* (1997) edited by Beamish and Killing, with one volume on 'North American Perspectives', the second on 'European Perspectives' and the third on 'Asian Pacific Perspectives'.

REFERENCES

Argyris, C. (1992), *Organizational Learning* (Cambridge, Mass.: Blackwell).

Beamish, P. W., and Killing, J. P. (1997) (eds.), *Cooperative Strategies: North American Perspectives, European Perspectives, Asian Pacific Perspectives* (3 vols., San Francisco: New Lexington Press).

Bleeke, J., and Ernst, D. (1993) (eds.), *Collaborating to Compete: Using Strategic Alliances and Acquisitions in the Global Marketplace* (New York: Wiley).

Bowman, C., and Faulkner, D. (1997), *Competitive and Corporate Strategy* (London: Irwin).

Child, J., and Rodrigues, S. (1996), 'The Role of Social Identity in the International Transfer of Knowledge through Joint Ventures', in S. R. Clegg and G. Palmer (eds.), *The Politics of Management Knowledge* (London: Sage), 46–68.

Collis, D. (1996), 'Organizational Capability as a Source of Profit', in B. Moingeon and A. Edmondson (eds.), *Organizational Learning and Competitive Advantage* (London: Sage), 139–63.

Contractor, F. J., and Lorange, P. (1988) (eds.), *Cooperative Strategies in International Business* (New York: Lexington Books).

Faulkner, D. (1995), *International Strategic Alliances: Co-operating to Compete* (Maidenhead: McGraw-Hill).

Geringer, J. M. (1991), 'Strategic Determinants of Partner Selection Criteria in International Joint Ventures', *Journal of International Business Studies*, 22: 41–62.

—— and Hebert, L. (1989), 'Control and Performance of International Joint Ventures', *Journal of International Business Studies*, 20: 235–54.

Gomes-Casseres, B. (1996), *The Alliance Revolution: The New Shape of Business Rivalry* (Cambridge, Mass.: Harvard University Press).

Handy, C. (1992), 'Balancing Corporate Power: A New Federalist Paper', *Harvard Business Review* (Nov.–Dec.), 59–72.

Kanter, R. M. (1989), *When Giants Learn to Dance* (London: Simon & Schuster).

Killing, J. P. (1988), 'Understanding Alliances: The Role of Task and Organizational Complexity', in F. J. Contractor and P. Lorange (eds.), *Cooperative Strategies in International Business* (New York: Lexington Books), 55–67.

Kogut, B. (1988), 'Joint Ventures: Theoretical and Empirical Perspectives', *Strategic Management Journal*, 9: 319–32.

Lorange, P., and Roos, J. (1992), *Strategic Alliances: Formation, Implementation and Evolution* (Oxford: Blackwell).

Porter, M. E. (1980), *Competitive Strategy: Techniques for Analyzing Industries and Competitors* (New York: Free Press).

—— (1985), *Competitive Advantage: Creating and Sustaining Superior Performance* (New York: Free Press).

Richardson, G. B. (1972), 'The Organization of Industry', *Economic Journal*, 82: 883–96.

Stiles, J. (1997), 'Managing Strategic Alliance Success: Determining the Influencing Factors of Intent within the Partnership', paper presented to the Fourth International Conference on Multi-Organizational Partnerships and Cooperative Strategy, Oxford, July.

Thorelli, H. B. (1986), 'Networks: Between Markets and Hierarchies', *Strategic Management Journal*, 7: 37–51.

Yoshino, M. Y., and Rangan, U. S. (1995) *Strategic Alliances: An Entrepreneurial Approach to Globalization* (Boston, Mass.: Harvard Business School Press).

Whitley, R. D. (1992), *Business Systems in East Asia* (London: Sage).

I

THE NATURE OF COOPERATION

Part I of the book starts in Chapter 2 by looking at cooperative strategy from a number of different perspectives commonly found in the academic literature, as it concedes that there is no universally accepted theory of cooperation at a meta level acceptable to economist, sociologist, and anthropologist alike.

The views of the economist are discussed first as they are met in market-power theory, transaction-cost analysis, game theory, agency theory, and increasing-returns theory. Strategic choice is highlighted in the perspective of the strategic-management theorist, and the importance of both strategic and cultural fit between partners if the alliance is to be successful. The key contribution of the organizational theorist is seen as the so-called resource-dependency perspective, in which partners seek out in each other the resources that they themselves most lack.

Chapter 3 turns to the importance of the attitudes of partners to each other in cooperative relationships. It emphasizes the pivotal role of trust in such relationships, and breaks this concept down into three aspects—calculative trust, that is, the trust that is necessary to set up an alliance when the partners' synergies are clear to see, predictive trust, which develops as both partners prove to be as good as their word, and bonding trust, which may develop as they come to enjoy working together.

Chapter 4 considers the motives for setting up alliances, and, whilst noting that these are contingent upon specific circumstances of time and place, it suggests that there always needs to be an external driver and an internal felt need in response. In the 1990s the most commonly cited external drivers are the trends towards globalization of markets and technologies, and the fast-changing nature of the economic world that require large amounts of capital to deal with ever shortening product life cycles. Internally the resource-dependency perspective comes into play, as do transaction-cost minimization, the perceived need to spread risk, and the requirement to achieve speed to market. Greater opportunities for achieving scale and scope economies are also frequently cited motives for setting up alliances.

2

Different Perspectives

One looks in vain for a unified theory or approach to provide the basis for understanding cooperative strategy. Useful, but partial, insights can be drawn from economics, game theory, strategic-management theory, and organization theory. As Parkhe (1993a: 229) has remarked, 'An overarching theme is required to cohesively pull together the theoretical advances into a unified theory addressing the nature of the [cooperative] . . . relationship.' Although that unified theory is not yet available, it is possible to offer a systematic overview of the main perspectives which contribute to our understanding of the subject and to draw some comparisons between them.

ECONOMICS

There are four main perspectives in economics which contribute to the understanding of cooperative strategy. These are (1) market-power theory (MPT), (2) transaction-cost economics (TCE), (3) agency theory, and (4) increasing-returns theory.

Market-power theory

Market-power theory (MPT) is concerned with the ways in which firms can improve their competitive success by securing stronger positions in their markets. Michael Porter, in his book *Competitive Strategy* (1980), argued that the relative position which firms occupy within their industry's structure determines the generic strategies which are the most viable and profitable for them. A cooperative strategy may offer a mutually advantageous opportunity for collaborating firms to modify the position which they occupy within their industry. In other words, it may enable them to increase their market power.

This chapter has been valuably informed by Lu (1996) and Simard (1996).

Hymer (1972) was one of the first to apply MPT to the study of cooperative strategy when distinguishing offensive from defensive coalitions.

Offensive coalitions are intended to develop firms' competitive advantages and strengthen their position by diminishing other competitors' market share or by raising their production and/or distribution costs. A recent example is the alliance between American Airlines and British Airways which has been fiercely opposed by other operators because, they claim, it will give the two partners an unfair competitive advantage especially on North Atlantic routes and hence provide the basis for conservative and restrictive behaviour. Porter and Fuller (1986), in fact, qualified Hymer's argument by indicating that offensive coalitions can have a negative effect through reducing the partners' adaptability in the long run. Defensive coalitions are formed by firms to construct entry barriers which are intended to secure their position and stabilize the industry so as to increase their profits. Defensive coalitions may also be sought by firms that have a weak position in the market in order to defend themselves against a dominant player.

There may also be cooperation between a partner which has a defensive intent and another with an offensive purpose for entering the alliance. Rover entered into collaboration with Honda in order to secure new model designs and engineering capabilities without which it could no longer survive. Honda's main interest in the collaboration was more offensive, seeing Rover as providing a bridge into the European market. Moreover an alliance which starts off with primarily defensive intentions can become offensive in nature if it is successful in the market.

Porter (1985) subsequently introduced the concept of the 'value chain'. This distinguishes between primary activities ('inbound logistics', operations, 'outbound logistics', marketing and sales, after-sales logistics) and support activities (the firm's infrastructure, technology development, human resource management, and procurement). The value-chain concept has been used to distinguish between cooperative strategies according to the type of resources pooled by the partners (Porter and Fuller 1986; Root 1988; Lorange and Roos 1992). One type of strategy is for partners to bring together similar resources to generate economies of scope, rationalize capacity, transfer knowledge, or share risk. This strategy has variously been termed 'additive', 'scale', 'scope' and 'symmetrical'. One example is the alliance between Ciba-Geigy and Chiron, which pooled teams of scientists to develop synthetic vaccines (Lorange and Roos 1992: 36). The intention to secure economies of scope and increase market share can be seen in the various alliances between companies in related businesses which have created Cap Gemini Sogeti as Europe's largest computer services and consulting company (Elfring 1994).

Another type of cooperative strategy, that of forming 'complementary' alliances, refers to situations where partners contribute different value-chain activities, which allow them to build on their respective strengths and competitive advantages. This latter strategy 'links' different activities to form a new value chain which realizes complementarities and gives the alliance a greater competitive advantage. One company, for example, may have a unique tech-nology and associated range of products which it wishes to market globally. Rather than investing in its own sales and distribution network, it could seek to enter an alliance with partners who already control market networks. One example is the alliance between Chrysler and Fiat, where a joint venture imported and distributed the Alfa Romeo 164 in the USA. This car was marketed through a select number of Chrysler dealers to add upstream complementar-ity to Chrysler's own product line (Lorange and Roos 1992: 37). Another instance from the same industry is the alliance between Honda and Rover, in which the former sought to learn how to access the European market, espe-cially through appropriate model designs, and Rover sought both the finance and the know-how to develop new models in the lower-medium part of its model range (Faulkner 1995).

MPT provides several insights into cooperative relationships. One is that greater market power, with consequentially enhanced returns, can be attained through cooperative strategies. Cooperation may be a quicker and cheaper way to gain market power. All-out competition is not the only option. At the same time, the choice between competitive and cooperative strategies describes what is often an uneasy balance of partner calculation. One of the reasons for the breakdown of alliances is when one partner decides that it can in future gain more from resuming competition than from continuing the cooperation.

MPT does not, however, take into account the trust which collaboration may engender between the partners and which may progressively offset any inclination to dispense with the alliance. It is in this respect a fairly determin-istic perspective, which does not readily accommodate the way in which evolving relationships between firms can alter the rationalities and strategic visions held by their policy-makers. MPT therefore has some difficulty in deal-ing with the processes through which cooperative strategies evolve over time. It concentrates on how contextual features—national, industrial, and organi-zational—constrain and shape cooperative relationships at a particular point in time, rather than on how partners might use their collaboration proactively within that context. For instance, MPT assumes that the structure of the industry and national environment in which a firm is located dictates its most appropriate generic strategy—cost leadership, differentiation, or focus in Porter's (1980) terms. The process of forming cooperative alliances is in this way subsumed within an analysis of industrial and national structural deter-minants.

A further major contribution of MPT lies in the concepts and analytical techniques which it offers for understanding the links between cooperative strategies and national and industrial contexts. The value chain concept and the identification of different competitive strategies are particularly helpful for demonstrating where, and for what purpose, an ally might be needed.

Transaction-cost economics

The perspective on strategic alliances offered by transaction-cost economics (TCE) views them as potentially cost-reducing methods of organizing international business transactions. In particular, writers such as Buckley and Casson (1985) have applied the TCE perspective to explain how the internalization of production through foreign direct investment, including alliances, enables multinational enterprises 'to replace the market or alternatively augment it' (p. 9).

Transaction costs are those which are incurred in arranging, managing, and monitoring transactions across markets, such as the costs of negotiation, drawing up contracts, managing the necessary logistics, and monitoring accounts receivable. TCE regards the basic choice in organizing economic transactions as being between effecting these through market exchanges and internalizing them within a single firm where they are governed by hierarchical relationships embedded in organization structures.

Oliver Williamson has been the main proponent of TCE. In his 1975 version of TCE, Williamson identified five factors which are relevant for the choice between internalizing the governance of transactions within firms as opposed to effecting them through market exchanges. These are opportunism, bounded rationality, small numbers, uncertainty and complexity, and information impactedness. Opportunism refers to behaviour that is self-interested and deceptive. The notion of bounded rationality recognizes that there are informational and other limits to the exercise of rationality. Williamson regards these features as the two human factors which pose a problem for the governance of transactions because they respectively identify a major source of risk and limitations on the means for dealing with it. Williamson argues that, when two or more parties transact recurrently under conditions where (1) there are limited numbers of partners to choose between (small numbers), (2) market conditions are uncertain and/or complex, and (3) accurate and adequate information relevant to the transaction(s) is known to one or more parties but not to others without their incurring considerable costs (information impactedness), then the more vulnerable partner is likely to benefit from internalizing the transaction or activity within its own more immediate managerial control.

In his 1985 analysis, Williamson gives more attention to asset specificity as a point of reference for choosing between transactions governance structures. Asset specificity refers to durable investments that cannot readily be redeployed to other uses and which are made in support of particular transactions. The commitment of such assets locks the partners concerned into the given type of transaction. Contractual and/or organizational safeguards are therefore called for to protect the investor in specific-use assets against the risks arising from opportunism, bounded rationality, and uncertainty. A contemporary example is the concern for legal safeguards against opportunistic infringement of intellectual property rights demanded by foreign companies (with the support of their national governments) investing technology in China, where their ability to control its use directly on location can often be limited.

According to Williamson, the attributes of a transaction, especially the degree of asset specificity, should play a key role in the choice of an appropriate governance structure. When transactions are one-off, of relatively short-term duration, and where the assets involved are non-specific, market-based transactions are deemed to be suitable. Under such conditions, the market itself backed by the law of contract, should provide effective safeguards to the transacting parties. By contrast, when transactions are recurrent, have highly uncertain outcomes which may take a long time to mature, and require unique or transaction-specific investments, they should be conducted more effectively within organizations ('hierarchies'). The main legal basis for these unified governance structures is the employment contract, which provides for a structure of authority and command.

Williamson (1985) also recognizes that two possibilities lie between these two extremes. Both involve assets of mixed specificity, the first case where transactions are occasional and the second case where they are recurrent. In the first case, he suggests that market contracting backed by third-party assistance, such as arbitration and litigation, is an appropriate mode of governance. In the second case, he suggests that relational contracting and bilateral governance should prevail. Relational contracting involves a long-term investment in building relationships between the parties. Bilateral governance, however, can be implemented by the parties making mutual investments of specific assets which generate mutual dependence and serve as hostages against opportunism.

Relational contracting and bilateral governance admit the possibility of hybrid governance structures, intermediate between markets and hierarchies. Hybrids, such as joint ventures, are characterized by bilateral dependency between the partners, in that they mutually commit equity and assets, and agree on how costs and profits are to be divided between them. In contrast to hierarchies in which one set of owners and/or managers have unilateral authority, the partners to hybrids share rights to control and monitor activities, thus potentially weakening the control each can exercise. To overcome this problem, the partners have to rely on features such as long-term contracts, the offering of mutual hostages such as assets specific to the collaboration, and the development of mutual trust. Although hybrids offer advantages that TCE identifies—namely, avoidance of the high uncertainty caused by market failure and the high overhead costs of establishing hierarchies (Kogut 1988a; Williamson 1993)—their uneasy position with regard to control lends them an inherent instability (Buckley and Casson 1988; Kogut 1988b).

TCE analysis has been used to address a wide range of topics related to cooperative strategy and strategic alliances. These include modes of entry into foreign markets (Anderson and Gatignon 1986), the selection and structuring of alliance forms (Hennart 1988, 1991; Parkhe 1993*b*), and the formation of new ventures (Oviatt and McDougall 1994). Much of the empirical research conducted within a TCE framework has pointed out that equity joint ventures (EJVs) are used to bypass the inefficiencies of intermediate markets in respect of providing raw materials and components, tacit knowledge, loan capital, and distribution systems (Simard 1996: 19). For instance, a major international company producing industrial ink-jet and laser printers recently formed an EJV with another diversified transnational firm as a basis for undertaking product assembly and more extensive marketing in China. The latter firm has over ten years experience in China and can provide access to its distribution system, to managers who are competent in the local environment, and to its knowledge of how best to deal with government agencies.

Parkhe's (1993*b*) research on 111 inter-firm alliances having at least one US partner tested several propositions drawn from TCE. He found that alliances buttressed by non-recoverable mutual investments are more likely to be high performers, and this supports the argument that the incorporation of deterrence against opportunism is beneficial in partnerships. However, many of the alliances studied were still relatively new, and Parkhe found at the same time that the perception of opportunism among other partners was reduced by a previous history of cooperation between them and by the anticipation of higher future pay-offs from the cooperation.

TCE contributes important insights into the governance forms that alliances may take in the light of the circumstances in which they are formed. The TCE perspective on cooperative relationships throws new light on the relevance of the partners' motives, the nature of the investments they commit to the collaboration, and the specific character of their transactions. Whereas MPT emphasizes motives for cooperative strategy which relate to market power and profit attainment, TCE stresses the efficiency and cost-minimizing rationales for cooperation. An alignment of the two perspectives draws attention to cases where a particular mode for governing transactions is preferred on the grounds of market power rather than efficiency alone; indeed Williamson has been criticized for ignoring the role of power in the choice between market and hierarchy (Francis *et al.* 1983).

Moreover, while TCE provides a sound framework for exploring the choice between market and hierarchy as governance modes, it does not take account of how the relational aspects of cooperation evolve over time and which, as Parkhe (1993*b*) suggested, affect the nature of the transactions themselves. TCE always emphasizes the rational aspects of transacting from a static non-evolutionary stance, in a way that does not take account of how growing trust and bonding between partner firms can reduce opportunism, and possibly reduce the boundedness of rationality through a growing willingness to share information. It deals only in terms of efficiency, and has little to say about questions of fairness or trust in the management of transactions. The qualitative history of business relationships, and the value placed on relationships *per se*, is relegated to the background in most TCE analyses.

This leads to another limitation of TCE in that it ignores those modes of economic organization which are not highly codified (as both markets and hierarchies are in their own ways), and where transactions are governed by more implicit understandings. As Boisot and Child (1988, 1996) point out, the hierarchy-market dimension, even when it allows for intermediate positions such as relational contracting, fails to account for how transactions are governed in societies such as those of East Asia on the basis of tacit trust-based cooperative relationships. Such modes of governance, which are certainly not unknown in Western societies, offer important insights for the management of alliances which are intended to evolve and strengthen over the long term.

Agency theory

Agency theory is concerned with the ability of 'principals' to ensure that their 'agents' are fulfilling their objectives. Much of the work within this perspective has focused on the special case of the principal–agent relationship between the owners and managers of large public corporations (Berle and Means 1932). Other writers have, however, extended the principal–agent framework to other relationships such as that of employer to employee, client to lawyer, and buyer to supplier.

Agency theory is concerned with the governance mechanisms which limit the agent's self-serving behaviour, including various control and incentive mechanisms (Jensen and Meckling 1976; Arrow 1985; Barney and Ouchi 1986; Eisenhardt 1989). Eisenhardt (1989), in her review, identifies the contract between a principal and an agent as the central unit of analysis for agency theory. She points out that agency theory contains a number of assumptions about the nature of human behaviour, organizations, and information. It assumes that human behaviour is self-interested, subject to bounded rationality, and risk adverse. It assumes that organizations contain a degree of conflict between the goals of their members, that there is an asymmetry of information between principals and agents (with agents possessing specific information about what they are doing and relevant contextual conditions), and that efficiency is the criterion of effectiveness. It also assumes that information is a purchasable commodity, so that, for example, principals can choose to spend more in order to secure better information about the conduct of their agents.

Given these assumptions, the focus of agency theory has been on determining the most efficient contract governing the relationship between principal and agent. More precisely, the question becomes one of whether a behaviour-oriented contract is more efficient than an outcome-oriented contract. Behaviour-oriented contracts include those which offer a salary in return for being available to work during stated hours, or in given circumstances, and under the authority of a hierarchical superordinate (i.e. hierarchical governance). Outcome-oriented contracts include commissions, stock options, and having rewards or returns subject to performance within a market place.

Agency theory has reintroduced the importance of self-interest and incentives in thinking about organizations. More specifically, it draws attention to the implications of risk aversion for contractual behaviour under conditions of uncertainty. It also brings to the fore the importance of information for the ability of principals to exercise control over their agents, and hence the role of systems which are designed to provide principals with suitable information.

Within the range of structures through which a cooperative strategy may be pursued, a principal–agent relationship is most clearly established when joint ventures are formed whose managers are accountable to their partner owners. Agency theory would regard the relationship between the partner owners and joint venture managers as a problematic one. The situation becomes more complicated if and when the partner companies themselves have different risk and time preferences. For example, one partner may be more risk adverse and have a shorter time preference than the other, in which case they are likely to disagree over the scale of their shared investment and on whether to distribute or reinvest returns on it. Such disagreement could result in a failure to establish mutual trust between them. If situations like these give rise to mixed signals being sent to joint venture managers (the agents), there is a danger of agency costs rising (Buckley and Chapman 1993). The problem becomes even more complex when there are more than two principals and, possibly, multiple agents running the joint venture such as two general managers. Hennart (1993), using TCE analysis, has pointed out that the headquarters of multinational firms could use different control levers over their subsidiaries—either hierarchical command or price mechanisms. This choice could also apply to the control by partner companies of their joint ventures. Geringer and Hebert (1989) argue that more study should be undertaken into the control strategies adopted by joint-venture partner owners, although, as Chapter 9 indicates, subsequent investigations have enhanced our understanding of this issue.

The implications of agency theory extend to forms of cooperative strategy other than joint ventures, for, in one sense, a cooperative relationship is one in which each partner becomes an agent for the other(s). There is a risk that one partner will engage in self-seeking opportunistic behaviour at the expense of the other, and this raises the question of what monitoring may be appropriate within a cooperative partnership. In Chapter 13 we note how one partner in some alliances has exploited the cooperation as an opportunity to acquire new technology and enhance its competence, and how it has dissolved the partnership once that objective has been achieved. Game theory, discussed in the next section, reminds us that in any cooperation a partner may maximize its own returns at the expense of the other partner, albeit that this is a high-risk strategy and one unlikely to succeed repetitively.

The practical implication of agency theory is therefore that, just as a principal is advised to put in place a combination of incentives and monitoring mechanisms to ensure that an agent's behaviour remains consistent with the principal's objectives, so the partners to a cooperative venture would be advised to make clear to each other the basis on which each will share the returns from effective cooperation, and to put into place the systems for information to be shared between them. These provisions should reduce suspicion between the partners and so provide a basis for mutual trust to develop through their working relationship. As and when the partners do trust each other more, so the monitoring mechanisms emphasized by agency theory can become less prominent.

Increasing-returns theory

Economic theory has traditionally operated on the assumption that after a certain point there are diminishing returns to factor inputs. Such an assumption leads to the predictability of an ultimate equilibrium in markets and to the possibility of 'efficiency' in factor allocation, if contingent distortions can be eliminated from markets.

Economists such as Arthur (1989), however, have observed that increasingly, in knowledge-based industries in particular, the phenomenon of continuing increasing returns has manifested itself. In such circumstances companies able to get a large share of the market early on may lock in their consumers, with the result that these companies are able ultimately to dominate the market without decreasing returns setting in. The phenomenon of Microsoft is evidenced as an illustration of this characteristic. Its Windows product is regarded by technical experts as not necessarily the best product, but it is nevertheless the dominant one in the PC software market since it has enormous installed capacity and sunk costs, very low variable costs to produce, and an army of consumers trained in its use. In such conditions it would be very difficult indeed to dislodge it from its market dominance, and it is able to achieve increasing returns, perhaps until it corners the whole market. In an earlier case the QWERTY typewriter keyboard achieved a similar dominance although not for one company.

The existence of this characteristic of increasing-returns markets leads companies to develop dense technological networks, and to form alliances to achieve sufficient critical mass to be a major player in the market and to become first mover, lest they be pre-empted by rivals. As Arthur (1996: 106) says: 'if technological ecologies are now the basic units for strategy in the knowledge-based world players compete not by locking in a product on their own but by building webs—loose alliances of companies organized around a mini-ecology—that amplify positive feedback to the base technology'.

Bettis and Hitt (1995: 10) confirm this phenomenon of knowledge-based industries in particular. They claim that, 'In industries with a high knowledge content, as opposed to natural resource-based industries, it is uncommon for diminishing returns to occur; instead positive feedback is present where returns continue to increase. . . . The optimum scale may be the entire market and first mover advantages or an early lead in market share may be quickly magnified into market dominance.'

Achieving such a position is of course the key challenge, and this frequently leads to alliances: 'the increasing number of strategic alliances has changed the dynamics within and across industries. For example, alliances formed to develop new technology, such as research consortia . . . change the incentives and dynamics within an industry, whereas stakeholder alliances can change the dynamics across industries' (Bettis and Hitt 1995: 13).

In the new competitive landscape, therefore, companies form alliances first to develop new technology and secondly to fight off foreign competitors or at least to achieve parity in global markets. This applies to knowledge-based industries primarily, but may also extend elsewhere—perhaps, for example, to some service industries.

GAME THEORY

Game theory is concerned with the prediction of outcomes from 'games', which are social situations involving two or more actors (players) whose interests are interconnected or interdependent (Zagare 1984: 7). The nature of a game might be sporting (as with poker), financial (as with bargaining over pay and other contracts), or military. Game theory is concerned with the strategies adopted by the players to a game and the effects these have on the game's outcome. Its insights should therefore be of direct relevance for the understanding of cooperative strategy.

The types of game that can be played vary in complexity. Components of this variation include the number of players (2-person vs. n-person), their interests (conflict, coincide, or both), the information to which they have access (perfect vs. imperfect, complete vs. incomplete), the number of times the game is played, and whether the players are allowed to communicate and make promises, commitments, or threats (Rapoport 1961).

Two-person games are the most elementary, and serve to highlight the dilemma which may attend the choice between a competitive and a cooperative strategy. While game theory assumes that players are self-interested, it does not go on to the further assumption that competitive behaviour necessarily follows. The dilemma is that, while cooperation will maximize joint interest, it does not maximize self-interest—at least for a particular transaction at a particular moment of time. In addition, if one player cooperates while the other defects from the cooperation, the latter will gain at the expense of the former. If neither party cooperates, they will both lose though not to the extent of the loss incurred by the non-defecting party when the other reneges.

These possibilities are contained in the so-called 'prisoner's-dilemma' game, which has two versions relevant to the choice between competitive and cooperative strategies. The traditional version describes situations in which players are logically condemned to defect. This derives from a model first developed in 1951 by Merrill Flood of the Rand Corporation and later termed the prisoner's dilemma by Albert Tucker. It addresses the issue of how we individually balance our innate inclination to act selfishly against the collective rationality of individual sacrifice for the sake of the common good. John Casti (1992: 198) in his book *Paradigms Lost* illustrates the difficulty effectively:

In Puccini's opera Tosca, Tosca's lover has been condemned to death, and the police chief Scarpia offers Tosca a deal. If Tosca will bestow her sexual favours on him, Scarpia will spare her lover's life by instructing the firing squad to load their rifles with blanks. Here both Tosca and Scarpia face the choice of either keeping their part of the bargain or double-crossing the other. Acting on the basis of what is best for them as individuals both Tosca and Scarpia try a double-cross. Tosca stabs Scarpia as he is about to embrace her, while it turns out that Scarpia has not given the order to the firing squad to use blanks. The dilemma is that this outcome, undesirable for both parties, could have been avoided it they had trusted each other and acted not as selfish individuals, but rather in their mutual interest.

Analytically there are two parties and both have the options of cooperating or defecting. If the maximum value to each of them is 3 (a positive benefit with no compromise involved) and the minimum value 0, then the possible outcomes and values for A are as shown below:

- A defects and B cooperates: A scores 3 (and B scores 0; total 3). Tosca gets all she wants without making any sacrifices. This would have happened if Tosca had killed Scarpia, and Scarpia had loaded the rifles with blanks thus enabling Tosca's lover to escape.
- A cooperates and B cooperates: A scores 2 (and B scores 2; total 4). Tosca, although saving her lover's life, has to submit sexually to Scarpia in order to do so, which it is presumed represents a sacrifice for her. Similarly Scarpia's compromise involves not killing Tosca's lover.
- A defects and B defects: A scores 1 (and B scores 1; total 2). This is what happened. At least Tosca has killed the evil Scarpia, but he in turn has killed her lover. Not a successful outcome for Tosca or Scarpia, however, but marginally better for her than the fourth possibility.
- A cooperates and B defects: A scores 0 (and B scores 3; total 3). This is the worst outcome from Tosca's viewpoint. She has surrendered herself to Scarpia, but he has still executed her lover. This is the 'sucker's pay-off', and to be avoided if possible at all costs.

The dilemma is that, since Tosca (A) does not know what Scarpia (B) will do, she is likely rationally to defect in order to avoid the sucker's pay-off. Thus she may score 3 if Scarpia is as good as his word and she can make him the sucker. She will at least score 1. However, if both cooperate they will each score 2, which is the best joint score available. Yet in the absence of trust it is unlikely to be achieved.

In the situation of a strategic alliance, the optimal joint score can be achieved only through genuine trusting cooperation; yet this may be difficult to achieve if both parties in the alliance are overly concerned not to be the sucker, and are thus reluctant to release their commercial secrets, for fear that their partner will defect with them. This was the problem that Robert Axelrod (1984) set out to examine through an interesting set of experiments. The issues he addressed were:

1. How can cooperation get started in a world of egoists?
2. Can individuals employing cooperative strategies survive better than their uncooperative rivals?
3. Which cooperative strategies will do best?

Axelrod invited a number of academics to participate in a contest pitting different strategies against one another in a computer tournament. Each participant was to supply the proposed best strategy for playing a sequence of prisoner's-dilemma interactions in a round-robin tournament. The winning strategy was the simplest—namely, Anatol Rapoport's strategy of tit-for-tat. It had two rules only:

1. cooperate on the first encounter;
2. hereafter do what your opponent did on the previous round.

Such a strategy was a forgiving one, which implied a willingness both to initiate and to reciprocate cooperation. If both partners did indeed cooperate on the first round, then cooperation would continue. However, if only one cooperated on the first round and the other defected thus creating a sucker in the first round, then the cooperator would defect in the second round to show the defector the error of its ways and the penalty for defection. The results were confirmed in a second tournament. The conclusions were that to be cooperative and forgiving was the key, and to retaliate when appropriate but without being vindictive. As Axelrod (1984: 112) summed up:

Tit-for-tat won the tournaments not by beating the other player but by eliciting behaviour from the other player that allowed both to do well. . . . So in a non-zero sum world, you do not have to do better than the other player to do well for yourself. This is especially true when you are interacting with many different players . . . The other's success is virtually a prerequisite for doing well yourself.

This second version of the prisoner's-dilemma game provides for the essence of cooperative strategy. Applied to strategic alliances this series of experiments suggests a number of things:

1. The rational strategy of defection (competition) applies on the assumption of a zero-sum game, and a non-repeatable experience. That is, it applies if you are in business only for a single trade, such as buying a souvenir in a bazaar in Morocco. In this situation, defection is a rational strategy for you to pursue.
2. As soon as the game becomes non-zero-sum, possibly because cooperation is starting to provide economies, and/or it is known that the game will be played over an extended time period, the strategy of defection is likely to become suboptimal. To cooperate and keep your bargain is a

better strategy for both players. If you do not, it will at the very least harm your reputation. You will become known as a player not to be trusted.

3. In these circumstances, forgiving cooperative strategies are likely to prove the most effective.

For example, a partner who defects (say, steals secrets) in an alliance will find his gains short-lived as the alliance founders, and the existence of available future partners becomes somewhat limited, because his reputation for defection goes before him. A good cooperator, however, will develop the opposite reputation, and will experience attractive partnership propositions.

Although the short-term dominant strategy can be shown as defection in a one-shot prisoner's-dilemma game, this does not apply in a multi-shot game with an indeterminate end. Nor does it apply if the penalty for defection is made very high. Thirdly, it does not apply if the partners value working together and care about their reputation in the wider business community. A strategic-alliance partner who is seen to defect would find it very difficult to attract future partners.

The trouble with tit-for-tat is that in the real world the first defection often leads to breakdown, and also as a strategy it is powerless against the persistent defector. Ridley (1996) suggests two alternative strategies that in real life have been found to be more effective than tit-for-tat. They are Pavlov and Firm-but-Fair. Pavlov posits players who, in roulette terms, stick to red if they win on red, and if they lose try black next time. Ridley claims this to be the basis of both dog-training and child-rearing. We are trained to continue to do things that are rewarded and to stop doing things that are punished. However, Pavlov is also powerless against continual defectors. In Firm-but-Fair, actors act successively and can communicate with each other, unlike in the strict prisoner's-dilemma model. This leads them to cooperate with cooperators, return to cooperating after mutual defection, and punish a sucker by further defection, but it assumes that they continue to cooperate after being a sucker in the previous round, which neither tit-for-tat nor Pavlov do. Thus the motivation to cooperate and to continue to cooperate in an alliance is even in game-theory terms very strong if the alliance is set up in the right way.

Iterated versions of the prisoner's-dilemma game have in these ways been used to analyse how cooperation evolves when the players have a possibility of meeting again and therefore have a stake in their future interaction. Axelrod (1984) refers to this as the future casting a shadow over the present situation. When this is the case, Axelrod argues that cooperation *as a social process* can develop in three stages. First, it may commence, even in a context where unconditional defection is the norm, with small clusters of individuals who base their cooperation on reciprocity and have a sufficient proportion of their interactions together. Next, a strategy based on reciprocity can thrive along-side other strategies. Thirdly, once firmly established and accepted on the basis of reciprocity, cooperation can protect itself from invasion by less friendly strategies, such as tit-for-tat, so long as the collaborators retaliate in response to a first defection. However, while this approach works well in computer simulations, it is rarely found in real life, where defection generally leads to the break-up of the collaboration as trust dissipates.

Iterated games also suggest that the probability of cooperation may be improved initially by providing mutual hostages and then progressively reinforced by the benefits it is seen to provide. This is an important insight which directly parallels the conclusion that may be drawn from theories about the ways in which trust between partners can develop over time through continued interaction between them (discussed in Chapter 3). Indeed, Gulati *et al.* (1994) stress the significance of partners making unilateral commitments. They conclude from research on seventeen companies engaged in alliances that one shortcoming of the prisoner's-dilemma framework lies in the way it underestimates the importance of partners acting unilaterally to make commitments that enhance the possibility that all the partners will cooperate. They conclude that such unilateral commitments can be vital to the success of alliances.

Parkhe (1993*b*: 799) summarizes the process whereby cooperation is reinforced through iterations, under conditions postulated by game theory:

Experimental evidence suggests that although noncooperation emerges as the dominant strategy in single-play situations, under iterated conditions the incidence of cooperation rises substantially. . . . Similarly, in strategic alliances, cooperation is maintained as each firm compares the immediate gain from cheating with the possible sacrifice of future gains that may result from violating an agreement. . . . The assumption here seems intuitively reasonable: broken promises in the present will decrease the likelihood of cooperation in the future. By the same token, cooperation in the current move can be matched by cooperation in the next move, and a defection can be met with a retaliatory defection. Thus, iteration improves the prospects for cooperation by encouraging strategies of reciprocity.

Nalebuff and Brandenburger (1996) draw from game theory the message that companies need to weigh up the consequences of cooperative and competitive behaviour. They warn against aggressive strategies that can backfire, citing as an example the fact that the US airline industry lost more money in its price wars of 1990–3 than it had previously made in all the years since the Wright brothers. Nalebuff and Brandenburger argue that game theory is a way of thinking—a tool for analysis—that is well suited to assessing the likely consequences of competitive and cooperative behaviours in conditions where the benefits to one player depend on what the others do, and where in a complex world there are many interdependent factors so that no decision can be made in isolation from a host of other decisions. The central tenet of their book is that business has to recognize the duality between cooperation and competition, a way of thinking that may be more novel for Western managers than for their counterparts in regions such as East Asia.

Kay (1993: 152–3) distinguishes between two categories of strategic alliance— the 'common-objective' alliance and the 'mutually beneficial-exchange' alliance. The former is typically one in which the partners possess distinctive capabilities which complement each other. A classic example was the cooperation between Rover and Honda. The latter is an alliance in which each partner possesses expertise, information, or skill which is of value to the other, an example being General Motors' cooperation with Toyota on lean production manufacturing in the USA which benefited the latter's access to the American market. Applying the logic of game theory, Kay concludes that, in a common-objective alliance, cooperation is a dominant strategy for both partners—it pays both partners to put the maximum effort into attaining the common objective. In the case of a mutually beneficial-exchange alliance, however, the dominant strategy for both partners is to hold back—in other words, to get as much as possible while giving as little as possible. This is the prisoner's-dilemma situation, in which self-interest is not maximized by cooperation even though joint interest may be. The longer the alliance holds, the more likely it is that a recognition of the mutual benefit from cooperation will prevail, but paradoxically the initial pursuit of self-interest is likely to bring an alliance to an early demise.

Game theory, then, makes a valuable contribution to the analysis of cooperative strategy by pointing to situations in which this strategy may be rewarding and also the conditions under which it may be undermined. In its present forms, game theory relies on a number of simplifying assumptions which distance it from reality, without, however, necessarily undermining its essential insight. Among the features of reality which cannot readily be encompassed by the game-theory framework are the personalities of the players, their social ties, verbal communication between the players (and the emotional and norm-building consequences of such communication), uncertainty about what the other player actually did at previous points in the game, and the social conventions and institutional rules in which the players and their interactions are embedded. Game theory also reduces firms to single actors and has difficulties in coping with the differentiation of roles, perceptions, and interests within them. Nevertheless, it continues to have tremendous potential for advancing our understanding of the intrinsic nature of business cooperation.

STRATEGIC-MANAGEMENT THEORY

The perspective on cooperative strategy offered by strategic-management theory (SMT) draws attention to the need for prospective partners to achieve a fit between their respective strategies, so that an alliance between them makes a positive contribution to the attainment of each party's objectives. SMT has also been concerned, though to a lesser degree, with the desirability of achieving another area of fit—namely, that between the organizational and national cultures which the partners bring to their cooperation. The burgeoning literature on strategic management contains a number of key, overlapping, themes that are relevant to cooperative strategy. These concern (1) the motives for forming alliances, (2) the selection of partners so as to achieve compatibility between their goals, and (3) the need to achieve integration between partner cultures and systems. Later chapters treat each one of these themes at greater length. Chapter 4 examines the motives behind cooperative strategy. Chapter 5 looks at partner selection. Several chapters in Part III, especially Chapters 10 and 11, consider how a cultural and operational fit can be developed through successful alliance management. In this last area, contributions from SMT join with those from organization theory.

Much of the emphasis within SMT has focused on the motives for forming strategic alliances. Many scholars have depicted alliance formation as an essentially rational and analytical process (e.g. Harrigan 1988). Tallman and Shenkar (1994), for example, develop a rational managerial decision model for international cooperative venture formation by multinational enterprises (MNEs). Contractor and Lorange (1988: 9) identify seven 'more or less overlapping objectives' for the formation of various types of cooperative arrangement:

1. risk reduction;
2. achievement of economies of scale and/or rationalization;
3. technology exchanges;
4. co-opting or blocking competition;
5. overcoming government-mandated trade or investment barriers;
6. facilitating initial international expansion of inexperienced firms;
7. vertical quasi-integration advantages of linking the complementary contributions of the partners in a 'value chain'.

These potential rationales for forming cooperative relationships raise the twin issues of how compatible are the partners' strategic motives for forming an alliance and how transparent are their motives. A lack of openness about motives is likely to limit the chances of trust developing between the partners later on, and may threaten the very survival of the partnership. Of course, as we shall note in Chapter 13, if one partner's motives for forming an alliance are primarily to 'milk' the other's technology and special skills so that the exchange of benefits is one-way and one-off, then long-term survival of the alliance is not likely to figure highly among its goals.

Logically following on from the strategic motives for alliance formation is the question of partner selection. Geringer (1991) examined previous research on the selection of international joint venture partners which he concluded was vague regarding selection criteria. As a clarification, he distinguished between two categories of selection criteria. 'Task-related' criteria are those which 'refer to those variables which are intimately related to the viability of a proposed venture's operations' (p. 45), and include features such as access to finance, managerial and employee competences, site facilities, technology, marketing and distribution systems, and a favourable institutional environment (or a partner's ability to negotiate acceptable regulatory and public policy provisions). By contrast, 'partner-related' criteria refer to those variables which characterize the partners' national or corporate cultures, their size and structure, the degree of favourable past association between them, and compatibility and trust between their top management teams.

A number of strategic observations can be drawn from Geringer's work and that of others on partner selection. The relative importance of a given task-related criterion appears to depend on the partner's perception of how crucial the feature is for the cooperative venture's performance, how strong is the partner's ability to provide or gain access to the feature, and how difficult the partner thinks it will be in the future to compete in terms of the feature. If, for example, a company perceives technology leadership to be crucial for the venture's performance (and indeed its own), but that it cannot provide this on its own, it will logically give high priority to finding a partner with which an alliance will be capable of securing that leadership. Secondly, the selection criteria applied by partners to an alliance between firms from developed and less developed countries tend to differ quite clearly. The former are generally oriented towards market access and accommodation to governmental regulations which may restrict that access to firms which invest directly in the country. Low-cost production and access to scarce materials are also sometimes priority criteria for firms from developed countries. The latter group normally seek access to technology, know-how, managerial expertise, capital, and international markets.

The identification of partner-related criteria brings us to the third key theme within the SMT perspective. This has been expressed in terms of the need to secure a 'cultural fit' between cooperating partners in order that they can work together effectively and have a sound basis on which mutual confidence can develop (Bleeke and Ernst 1993; Faulkner 1995). According to Faulkner, the requirement is for the partners to have sufficient awareness and flexibility to be able to work together constructively; in other words, to be able to learn from each other's cultural differences and to be able to bring together their respective management systems, capitalizing on the strengths of each. Although this theme is receiving more attention within both the strategic-management literature and alliance practice, it is still underdeveloped and under-recognized. It raises the important question of how much autonomy a cooperative unit, such as a joint venture, should enjoy from its parent partners in order to have the freedom to develop a good cultural fit in terms of its own identity and way of operating (cf. Lyles and Reger 1993).

SMT emphasizes that firms enter into cooperative relations in order to achieve expansion and growth as well as to secure efficiencies of the kind identified by TCE. It draws attention to the external and contextual factors which encourage a cooperative strategy. In so doing, it develops a contingent view on the merits of a cooperative as opposed to a competitive strategy, and on the criteria for selecting a partner. This contingent view is more sophisticated and realistic than the universalistic rationales contained in the MPT and TCE perspectives. It also emphasizes the matching of partners rather than looking at cooperation simply from a single partner's point of view, as again do MPT and TCE. A further contrast with these two major economics perspectives lies in the way that strategic management theory brings the actor into play. Rather than positing that situational contingencies determine which cooperative strategies will be successful, SMT allows for the exercise of strategic choice by the actors who are deciding on firms' policies (Child 1972).

ORGANIZATION THEORY

Organization theory embraces a range of perspectives which offer insights on three main aspects of cooperative strategy. First, there is the significance of resource provision and scarcity in cooperative strategies and relationships. The *resource-dependence* perspective is of central importance here, and can inform both the general issue of why inter-organizational cooperation is sought as well as the more specific question of how the investments partners make in alliances bear upon the control they can exercise over the management of the alliances. Secondly, there are the ways in which alliances can be appropriately *organized*. This issue is informed by network analysis and work on transnational business organization. The third aspect concerns the nature of *trust* within inter-organizational cooperation, on which there is a growing body of recent research. The first two of these aspects are now considered. The question of trust is so fundamental to cooperation between organizations that it is discussed separately and at length in the next chapter.

Resource dependence

The resource-dependence perspective is concerned with the arrangements which are negotiated between organization managers and the external stakeholders, or organizational partners, who contribute necessary resources in the expectation of receiving valued returns. With its focus on needed resources, this perspective contributes to our understanding of why firms, or other organizations, undertake cooperative strategies. It raises as a strategic issue the problem organizations face of how to deal with uncertainties about their supplies of resources and human competences. It indicates that, when resources and competences are not readily or sufficiently available to firms, they are more likely to establish ties with other organizations.

According to Pfeffer and Salancik (1978), resource scarcity prompts organizations to engage in inter-organizational relationships in an attempt to exert power, influence, or control over organizations which possess the required resources. Pfeffer and Salancik tend to emphasize the conflictual and coercive side of relations between organizations. Resource scarcity may, however, also encourage cooperation rather than competition, so giving rise to relationships based on mutual support rather than on domination. This is likely when the potential partners to an exchange anticipate that the benefits of forming a cooperative inter-organizational relationship will exceed its disadvantages, including the cost of managing the linkage and the diminution of decision-making latitude (Simard 1996).

Consistent with this attention to resource scarcity is recent thinking which emphasizes the competitive importance of a firm possessing a portfolio of core competences and value-creating disciplines (Hamel and Prahalad 1994). Similarly, Hall (1992, 1993) has been concerned with identifying the intangible sources of sustainable competitive advantage associated with the possession of relevant advantages in capability over competitive rivals. These intangible resources encompass assets such as patents, trade marks and data, and human competences such as know-how and learning capabilities. The implication of this 'resource-based' view is similar to the resource-dependence argument—namely, that a strong reason for organizations to collaborate with others lies in their recognition that they lack critical competences which they cannot develop readily, and/or sufficiently rapidly, on their own.

The resource-dependence perspective also contributes to an understanding of the relation between resource provision and control within strategic alliances. The ability of business investors to exercise direction over the firms in which they have an ownership stake is an issue of long-standing concern (cf. Berle and Means 1932). It assumes a new form, however, in those types of cooperation in which the partners take an equity stake, notably equity joint ventures. Unless they are simply portfolio investors adopting the role of sleeping partners, the joint-venture (JV) owners will normally contribute much more than just equity capital. In establishing joint ventures to exploit complementarities between themselves, the owners provide skills and knowledge as well. These are assets in the possession of partner firms. They have intrinsic value and amount to ownership inputs with property rights. They confer powers of control over a joint venture both through the formal terms of any contracts by which they are provided, and through the less formal influence that derives from the partner's possession of scarce expertise and resources (cf. French and Raven 1960; Child et al. 1997). Since an owning company faces the problem of protecting the use and integrity of its investments when collaborating with a joint-venture partner, it has a motive for seeking a certain level of control (Hamel 1991).

In treating the relation between resource provision and control, the resource-dependence perspective builds upon Emerson's (1962) observation that dependency in a social relation is the reverse of power. Pfeffer and Salancik (1978) developed this notion to argue that the ability of external parties to command resources which are vital for the operations of an organization gives those parties power over it. In the case of a joint venture, this means that a parent firm which contributes a resource necessary for the venture's success, and that the other parent cannot easily provide, will gain power relative to the partner and relatively greater control over the joint venture. It also implies that a parent's control will be focused on those activities of the joint venture to which it contributes resources.

Some have suggested that the implications of resource dependence for joint-venture control may be mediated by the bargaining powers of prospective partners (Fagre and Wells 1982; Lecraw 1984). They posit that prospective partners can negotiate for a level of joint-venture control, 'given the assets that they command and perhaps general trends that may or may not be currently in their favour. Equity ownership is seen as an outcome of negotiation, a representation of relative power between participating interests' (Blodgett 1991: 64). While much of the bargaining power available to prospective partners is likely to arise from their command of significant resources in the first place, as the quotation admits, this perspective allows for an element of negotiated indeterminacy in the extent to which the command of resources leads to control.

Reference to bargaining power thus warns against an assumption that the impact of resource provision on control in alliances is entirely deterministic. Pfeffer and Salancik's own analysis allows for the ability of firms to manage and avoid dependence. Similarly, the non-dominant partners of joint ventures may be able to reduce their resource dependency over time—for example, through the superior learning process that Hamel (1991) has documented. There are also reasons to expect that even resource-dominant parent companies may choose to exercise their control over joint ventures selectively, depending on their cost/benefit assessment of assuming responsibility for the various areas of joint-venture activity rather than leaving this either to their partners or to the venture's own management. Such an assessment would compare the strategic importance of securing control over different activities against the costs involved, and it would take into account the net benefit of adopting alternative control mechanisms as well.

The resource-dependence theory, being concerned with the exercise of power, contributes a political perspective. This can be applied both to the relations between partner organizations and to the impact on the internal dynamics of an alliance of dependence on partners or other 'external' parties. While resource dependence's emphasis on the balance between partner or other stakeholder contributions and returns is broadly consistent with the focus of game theory, the processes it uncovers are far more complex and evolutionary than is readily incorporated into game theory. There are dynamics both around the interaction of organizational members with external networks, and around coalitions within the firms themselves. In this respect, the resource-dependence perspective is closely related to strategic-choice analysis, which also draws attention to the intra- and inter-organizational political dynamics overlooked by many other perspectives (Child 1972, 1997).

There is a complementary 'resource-based' perspective which makes a qualitative distinction between human and other types of resource, in stressing the vital contribution which the former makes to a company's performance (Hamel and Prahalad 1994). This perspective breaks with the product/market paradigm followed by market-power theory and many students of strategic management (Simard 1996). It highlights the importance of human competence requirements as a stimulus to embracing a cooperative strategy, as well as to the significance of managing alliances in such a way as to secure motivation and synergy among the staff who are brought together from the previously separate partner organizations.

Organization of alliances

The emergence of strategic alliances presents managers with the practical requirement of how best to organize these entities. They have not as yet received a great deal of guidance from organization theorists, whose conventional assumptions are challenged by the 'hybrid' nature of strategic alliances. Moreover, as Borys and Jemison (1989) point out, the varied forms of alliance make them particularly difficult to analyse. The organizational requirements of alliances on which most attention has so far been directed are (1) the relative importance of structure and process in their management, (2) their network (or quasi-network) character, and (3) issues of control, autonomy, and learning. Later chapters discuss these topics in more detail, and they are introduced only briefly at this point.

The question of how theoretically and practically useful it is to focus on the structure rather than the process of strategic alliances was first raised in respect of decentralized multinational corporations (DMNCs). Doz and Prahalad (1993: 26) have argued that:

Except in advocating a matrix organization, which is another way to acknowledge structural indeterminacy, a structural theory of DMNCs had little to offer. Ones needs a theory that transcends the structural dimensions and focuses on underlying processes. Issues of information and control become essential. More than the formal structure, the informal flow of information matters. So do the processes of influence and power, such as how the trade-offs among multiple stakeholders and multiple perspectives are made.

This argument applies even more to strategic alliances which, being generally shorter-lived and subject to more frequent reconfiguration than multinationals, can rely even less on formal structures. While formal channels for reporting back to parent or partner companies on financial, operational, and technical matters are absolutely necessary, there is a particular need in alliances for effective informal information exchange. This is both to promote the bonding and trust which will lead to a better cultural fit, and to ensure that the alliance is sufficiently adaptive to its environment. In other words, information flow is essential to achieve cultural fit and learning within the alliance. Unless an alliance is managed in a completely asymmetric manner, with one partner dominating all executive functions, it has to rely upon open and effective information flows between the partners, the staff they appoint to their cooperative ventures, and other staff who are recruited specifically for the alliance. There is no other way for it to be organized than as a pluralistic enterprise.

At the same time, however, we are reminded by resource-dependence theory that the processes of influence and power are also inherent in an alliance. Alliance partners may even compete for control over areas such as the management of its technology either to safeguard proprietary knowledge or to acquire such knowledge. The founding of alliances on the logic of exploiting complementarities between the partners may in any case make it sensible for each of them to assume responsibility for certain of its activities and decisions. The alliance must also perform according to certain goals and standards, which in turn require monitoring. These considerations bring the question of control into prominence. The challenge is how to organize an alliance and its links to the partners in such a way as to define their respective roles and, having done so, to build in the required degree of control over the alliance's behaviour and performance.

The organization of cooperative activities can assume many forms. One form is the alliance that is dominated by one partner and structured more or less on the hierarchical lines of a so-called 'conventional' organization. Killing (1983) in his study of equity joint ventures found that this 'dominant'-partner model was associated with superior economic performance, and he therefore recommended its adoption wherever possible. It does not, however, represent a truly cooperative strategy and may forgo some contributions which the non-dominant partner could otherwise offer. At the other end of the spectrum is the network model, which views the collaborating partners as linked together by a variety of relationships (Nohria and Eccles 1992). This model has been applied to organizations in order to convey an understanding of the connectivities and communications between its members, which cannot be captured by organization charts or formal role definitions. In the case of cooperative alliances, the term 'network' can be used to depict a particular organizational form which is characterized by a high sense of mutual interest, active participation by all partners, and open communications (Faulkner 1995).

In this latter sense, the network approach in (inter-)organizational theory provides valuable insights, especially when it is combined with those from other transactional perspectives such as TCE and resource dependence. This combination of perspectives illustrates how firms create and manage alliances among themselves as strategic responses to competitive uncertainties. The biotechnology industry provides a good example. Barley et al. (1992: 317) note that 'the particular constraints and opportunities surrounding commercial biotechnology appear to have compelled organizations to form an elaborate web of formal alliances'. As a result, small firms have had to sacrifice some degree of autonomy in order to gain access to markets with high entry barriers. Powell et al. (1996) argue, with reference to the same industry, that its complex and expanding knowledge base, with widely dispersed expertise, causes the locus of innovation to be found in networks of learning rather than in individual firms. The need for learning has, in other words, promoted cooperative strategies in this industry.

Given that many strategic alliances are established in order to secure advantages of learning and knowledge transfer, more attention is now being paid to how the organization of alliances can assist the learning process (Inkpen 1995). Organizing alliances so as to reconcile their needs for learning and control is one of the most important requirements for a truly cooperative strategy to be implemented successfully (Child *et al.* 1994). These issues are considered in Chapters 9 and 13, but, just to anticipate, one approach which has emerged in response to this challenge is a variant of what Peters and Waterman (1982) called 'simultaneous tight–loose coupling'. This operates clearly prescribed standards for achievement in the core functions of accounting, production, quality, and technological integrity. The performance of the alliance is closely monitored in these areas on a basis agreed between the partners. This constitutes the zone of tight coupling, in which control predominates and learning is either incremental or is planned as with technology transfer. By contrast, the zone of loose coupling tends to be found in the areas of business development, marketing, human-resource management, and external relations. Here, the partners' knowledge is less secure and/or less relevant, and potential 'partner-related' complementarities need to be worked out as well. Learning is therefore at a premium, and it becomes appropriate to encourage flexible roles, local initiative, and an unfettered circulation of information—in other words, a loose-coupling approach. It is, clearly, not a straightforward matter to organize an alliance with different levels and types of coupling running together. It demands both a high degree of understanding from the partners and considerable skill on the part of the alliance's chief executive (Schaan and Beamish 1988).

SUMMARY

An overview of the main perspectives which can be brought to bear on cooperative strategy and the management of alliances indicates that they provide numerous insights. Most of these are still underdeveloped in two respects. First, there are still potential synergies to understanding which could come about from combining some of them. For example, both the iterated form of game theory and work on trust-based relations should, if brought together, offer valuable understandings on how cooperation can be strengthened as a cumulative process over time. In so doing, it would be useful to combine the rational calculative approach of game theory with the more sentient and normative features of social interaction which are given a prominent place in theories of trust. The second area of underdevelopment, which subsequent chapters of this book begin to address, is the drawing-out of practical guidelines from the essentially academic insights offered by the various perspectives. We have seen how such insights bear upon both the formulation of cooperative strategy and its implementation. Market-power theory, transaction-cost economics, game theory, and strategic-management theory are oriented towards cooperation as a strategic choice. Transaction-cost economics and game theory also address certain aspects of ongoing cooperative relationships, which are the primary concern of agency theory and organization theory.

There are several implications for the practice of cooperative strategy which can be drawn from the perspectives reviewed in this chapter.

1. *Economic perspectives*
   - Cooperative strategies can enhance market power.
   - One of the considerations in choosing whether to cooperate with other firms, and the form of that cooperation, is the level of transaction costs involved.
   - In the absence of common interests and mutual trust, an alliance needs to provide each partner with adequate incentives not to take advantage of the other and with systems to monitor their respective contributions.
   - In increasing-returns industries dense ecologies of alliances and technology companies coalesce in the pursuit of first-mover-inspired dominance of markets.

2. *Game theory*
   - There is a need to balance and reconcile cooperation and competition between partners.
   - Highly self-interested behaviour in business relations tends to become self-defeating.
   - If cooperation between partners is established according to clear principles, such as 'Firm-but-Fair', there is a good possibility that their relationship will become progressively self-strengthening.

3. *Strategic management theory*
   - Executives need to be clear about their motives for adopting a cooperative strategy in general and for entering into specific alliances in particular.
   - The selection of a suitable partner is of fundamental importance and likely to have a major bearing on the success of the alliance.
   - It is important for alliance partners to work out a good mutual strategic fit, and then to optimize the process of their cooperation by improving cultural fit.

4. *Organization theory*
   - The ability of a partner to exercise control over an alliance will be significantly determined by its dependence on the other(s) for the provision of non-substitutable resources which are crucial for the alliance's operations. This implies that the formal rights inherent in equity share or contracts may not be sufficient to ensure control.
   - Alliances are hybrid organizations that combine some features of conventional hierarchical management with those of networks. Their organization has to recognize and support a number of dilemmas

which stem from this hybrid nature, such as the tension between the ability to control an alliance and to learn from it.

REFERENCES

Anderson, E., and Gatignon, H. (1986), 'Modes of Foreign Entry: A Transaction Cost Analysis and Propositions', *Journal of International Business Studies*, 17: 1–26.

Arrow, K. J. (1985), 'The Economics of Agency', in J. W. Pratt and R. J. Zechauser (eds.), *Principals and Agents* (Cambridge, Mass.: Harvard University Press).

Arthur, W. B. (1989), 'Competing Technologies, Increasing Returns and Lock-In by Historical Events', *Economic Journal*, 99: 116–31.

—— (1996), 'Increasing Returns and the New World of Business', *Harvard Business Review* (July–Aug.), 100–9.

Axelrod, R. (1984), *The Evolution of Cooperation* (New York: HarperCollins).

Barley, S. R., Freeman, J., and Hayes, R. C. (1992), 'Strategic Alliances in Commercial Biotechnology', in N. Nohria and R. G. Eccles (eds.), *Networks and Organizations* (Boston, Mass.: Harvard Business School Press), 311–47.

Barney, J. B., and Ouchi, W. (1986) (eds.), *Organizational Economics* (San Francisco: Jossey-Bass).

Berle, A. A., and Means, G. C., Jr. (1932), *The Modern Corporation and Private Property* (New York: Harcourt, Brace & World).

Bettis, R. A., and Hitt, M. A. (1995), 'The New Competitive Landscape', *Strategic Management Journal*, 16: 7–19.

Bleeke, J., and Ernst, D. (1993) (eds.), *Collaborating to Compete: Using Strategic Alliances and Acquisitions in the Global Marketplace* (New York: Wiley).

Blodgett, L. L. (1991), 'Partner Contributions as Predictors of Equity Share in International Joint Ventures', *Journal of International Business Studies*, 22: 63–78.

Boisot, M., and Child, J. (1988), 'The Iron Law of Fiefs: Bureaucratic Failure and the Problem of Governance in the Chinese Economic Reforms', *Administrative Science Quarterly*, 33: 507–27.

———— (1996), 'From Fiefs to Clans and Network Capitalism: Explaining China's Emerging Economic Order', *Administrative Science Quarterly*, 41: 600–28.

Borys, B., and Jemison, D. B. (1989), 'Hybrid Arrangements as Strategic Alliances: Theoretical Issues in Organizational Combinations', *Academy of Management Review*, 14/2: 234–49.

Buckley, P., and Casson, M. (1985), *The Economic Theory of the Multinational Enterprise* (London: Macmillan).

———— (1988), 'A Theory of Cooperation in International Business', in F. Contractor and P. Lorange (eds.), *Co-operative Strategies in International Business* (New York: Lexington Books), 31–53.

—— and Chapman, M. (1993), 'The Management of Cooperative Strategies', unpublished paper (University of Bradford Management Centre, June).

Casti, J. (1992), *Paradigms Lost: Images of Man in the Mirror of Science* (London: Scribners).

Child, J. (1972), 'Organizational Structure, Environment and Performance: The Role of Strategic Choice', *Sociology*, 6: 1–22.

Child, J. (1997), 'Strategic Choice in the Analysis of Organizational Action, Structure and Environment: Retrospect and Prospect', *Organization Studies*, 18: 43–76.

——Markóczy, L., and Cheung, T. (1994), 'Managerial Adaptation in Chinese and Hungarian Strategic Alliances with Culturally Distinct Foreign Partners', *Advances in Chinese Industrial Studies*, 4: 211–31.

——Yan, Y., and Lu, Y. (1997), 'Ownership and Control in Sino-Foreign Joint Ventures', in P. W. Beamish and P. J. Killing (eds.), *Cooperative Strategies: Asian Pacific Perspectives* (San Francisco: New Lexington Press), 181–225.

Contractor, F. J., and Lorange, P. (1988), 'Why Should Firms Cooperate? The Strategy and Economics Basis for Cooperative Ventures', in F. J. Contractor and P. Lorange (eds.), *Cooperative Strategies in International Business* (New York: Lexington Books), 3–28.

Doz, Y., and Prahalad, C. K. (1993), 'Managing DMNCs: A Search for a New Paradigm', in S. Ghoshal and D. E. Westney (eds.), *Organization Theory and the Multinational Corporation* (London: Macmillan), 24–50.

Eisenhardt, K. M. (1989), 'Agency Theory: An Assessment and Review', *Academy of Management Review*, 14: 57–74.

Elfring, T. (1994), 'Cap Gemini Sogeti: Building a Transnational Organization', in J. Roos (ed.), *European Casebook on Cooperative Strategies* (Hemel Hempstead: Prentice-Hall), 41–56.

Emerson, R. M. (1962), 'Power-Dependence Relations', *American Sociological Review*, 27: 31–41.

Fagre, N., and Wells, L. T., Jr. (1982), 'Bargaining Power of Multinationals and Host Governments', *Journal of International Business Studies*, 13: 9–23.

Faulkner, D. (1995), *International Strategic Alliances: Co-operating to Compete* (Maidenhead: McGraw-Hill).

Francis, A., Turk, J., and Willman, P. (1983) (eds.), *Power, Efficiency and Institutions: A Critical Appraisal of the 'Markets and Hierarchies' Paradigm* (London: Heinemann).

French, J. R. P., Jr., and Raven, B. (1960), 'The Bases of Social Power', in D. Cartwright and A. Zander (eds.), *Group Dynamics: Research and Theory* (2nd edn., New York: Harper & Row), 607–23.

Geringer, J. M. (1991), 'Strategic Determinants of Partner Selection Criteria in International Joint Ventures', *Journal of International Business Studies*, 22: 41–62.

——and Hébert, L. (1989), 'Control and Performance of International Joint Ventures', *Journal of International Business Studies*, 20: 235–54.

Gulati, R., Khanna, T., and Nohria, N. (1994), 'Unilateral Commitments and the Importance of Process in Alliances', *Sloan Management Review*, Spring: 61–9.

Hall, R. (1992), 'The Strategic Analysis of Intangible Resources', *Strategic Management Journal*, 13: 135–44.

——(1993), 'A Framework Linking Intangible Resources and Capabilities to Sustainable Competitive Advantage', *Strategic Management Journal*, 14: 607–18.

Hamel, G. (1991), 'Competition for Competence and Inter-Partner Learning within International Strategic Alliances', *Strategic Management Journal*, 12: 83–103.

——and Prahalad, C.-K. (1994), *Competing for the Future* (Boston, Mass.: Harvard Business School Press).

Harrigan K. R. (1988), 'Joint Ventures and Competitive Strategy', *Strategic Management Journal*, 9: 141–58.

Hennert, J.-F. (1988), 'A Transaction Costs Theory of Equity Joint Ventures', *Strategic Management Journal*, 9: 361–74.

—— (1991), 'The Transactions Costs Theory of Joint Ventures', *Management Science*, 37: 483–97.

—— (1993), 'Control in Multinational Firms: The Role of Price and Hierarchy', in S. Ghoshal and D. Eleanor (eds.), *Organization Theory and the Multinational Corporation* (London: St Martin's Press), 157–81.

Inkpen, A. (1995), *The Management of International Joint Ventures: An Organizational Learning Perspective* (London: Routledge).

Jensen, M., and Meckling, W. (1976), 'Theory of the Firm: Managerial Behavior, Agency Costs, and Ownership Structure', *Journal of Financial Economics*, 3: 305–60.

Kay, J. (1993), *Foundations of Corporate Success* (Oxford: Oxford University Press).

Killing, J. P., (1983), *Strategies for Joint Venture Success* (New York: Praeger).

Kogut, B. (1988a), 'Joint Ventures: Theoretical and Empirical Perspectives', *Strategic Management Journal*, 9: 319–32.

—— (1988b), 'A Study of the Life Cycle of Joint Ventures', in F. Contractor and P. Lorange (eds.), *Cooperative Strategies in International Business* (New York: Lexington Books), 169–85.

Lecraw, D. J. (1984), 'Bargaining Power, Ownership, and Profitability of Transnational Corporations in Developing Countries', *Journal of International Business Studies*, 15: 27–43.

Lorange, P., and Roos, J. (1992), *Strategic Alliances: Formation, Implementation, and Evolution* (Oxford: Blackwell).

Lu, Y. (1996), 'The Paradoxical Nature of International Strategic Alliances: A Critique of the Literature', unpublished working paper (Judge Institute of Management Studies, Cambridge, Mar.).

Lyles, M. A., and Reger, R. K. (1993), 'Managing for Autonomy in Joint Ventures: A Longitudinal Study of Upward Influence', *Journal of Management Studies*, 30: 383–404.

Nalebuff, B. J., and Brandenburger, A. M. (1996), *Co-opetition* (London: HarperCollins).

Nohria, N., and Eccles, R. G. (1992) (eds.), *Networks and Organizations* (Boston: Mass.: Harvard Business School Press).

Oviatt, B. M., and McDougall, P. P. (1994), 'Toward a Theory of International New Ventures', *Journal of International Business Studies*, 69: 45–64.

Parkhe, A. (1993a), ' "Messy" Research, Methodological Predispositions, and Theory Development in International Joint Ventures', *Academy of Management Review*, 18: 227–68.

—— (1993b), 'Strategic Alliance Structuring: A Game Theoretic and Transaction Cost Examination of Interfirm Cooperation', *Academy of Management Journal*, 36: 794–829.

Peters, T. J., and Waterman, R. H., Jr. (1982), *In Search of Excellence* (New York: Harper & Row).

Pfeffer, J., and Salancik, G. R. (1978), *The External Control of Organizations: A Resource Dependence Perspective* (New York: Harper & Row).

Porter, M. E. (1980), *Competitive Strategy: Techniques for Analyzing Industries and Competitors* (New York: Free Press).

—— (1985), *Competitive Advantage: Creating and Sustaining Superior Performance* (New York: Free Press).

—— and Fuller, M. B. (1986), 'Coalitions and Global Strategy', in M. E. Porter (ed.), *Competition in Global Industries* (Boston, Mass.: Harvard Business School Press), 315–44.

Powell, W. W., Koput, K. W., and Smith-Doerr, L. (1996), 'Interorganizational Collaboration and the Locus of Innovation: Networks of Learning in Biotechnology', *Administrative Science Quarterly*, 41: 116–45.

Rapoport, A. (1961), *Fights, Games and Debates* (Ann Arbor, Mich.: University of Michigan Press).

Richardson, G. B. (1972), 'The Organization of Industry', *Economic Journal*, 82: 883–96.

Ridley, M. (1996), *The Origins of Virtue* (London: Viking).

Root, F. R. (1988), 'Some Taxonomies of International Cooperative Arrangements', in F. J. Contractor and P. Lorange (eds.), *Cooperative Strategies in International Business* (New York: Lexington Books), 69–80.

Schaan, J.-L., and Beamish, P. W. (1988), 'Joint Venture General Managers on LDCs', in F. J. Contractor and P. Lorange (eds.), *Cooperative Strategies in International Business* (New York: Lexington Books), 279–99.

Simard, P. (1996), *The Structuring of Cooperative Relationships* (First-Year Report, Doctoral Programme, Judge Institute of Management Studies, University of Cambridge, June).

Tallman, S. B., and Shenkar, O. (1994), 'A Managerial Decision Model of International Cooperative Venture Formation', *Journal of International Business Studies*, 25: 91–113.

Williamson, O. E. (1975), *Markets and Hierachies* (New York: Free Press).

—— (1985), *The Economic Institutions of Capitalism* (New York: Free Press).

—— (1993), 'Comparative Economic Organization', in S. Lindenberg and H. Schieuder (eds.), *Interdisciplinary Perspectives on Organization Studies* (Oxford: Pergamon), 3–38.

Zagare, F. C. (1984), *Game Theory* (London: Sage).

3

Trust

SIGNIFICANCE OF TRUST

Cooperation between organizations creates mutual dependence between them and requires trust to succeed. Although there are many definitions of trust, they tend to agree that it refers to the willingness of one party to relate with another in the belief that the other's actions will be beneficial rather than detrimental to the first party, even though this cannot be guaranteed (cf. Gambetta 1988; McAllister 1995; Kramer and Tyler 1996; Lane and Bachmann 1998). In the world of business cooperation, this means having sufficient confidence in a partner to commit valuable know-how or other resources to transactions with it despite the fact that, in so doing, there is a risk the partner will take advantage of this commitment.

Partners incur further risks when they sink specific assets into capital-based alliances such as equity joint ventures. Joint ventures between partners in developed and developing countries usually involve a greater investment of specific assets by the developed country partner(s) than by the developing country host partner(s), and in this way the former bears the greater risk. One of the hybrid characteristics of alliances arises from the paradox that they often combine elements of cooperation and competition, or at least the attempt to formulate common goals on the basis of not wholly complementary objectives (cf. Hamel 1991). The combination of mutual reliance between alliance partners with residual or potential elements of competition or conflict between them can set up a game-theoretic dynamic that adds to the risk and precariousness of the cooperation. Trust between the partners is required to help overcome this threat, yet at the same time the source of the threat inhibits the development of trust. The reality of this dilemma would appear to be borne out by surveys which suggest that between 40 and 50 per cent of strategic alliances fail within five years (Bleeke and Ernst 1993). These percentages are, however, inflated by the fact that some alliance terminations should not be judged to be 'failures'; for instance, when the partners agree to part amicably or when one partner agrees to its share being bought out by the other.

Most managers involved in alliances are very aware of the significance of trust, though they also realize it is not an easy thing either to create or to preserve (see Box). The fundamental necessity for trust in alliances has also been recognized in the literature on the subject (e.g. Faulkner 1995). The association between alliance partners takes on a network character, and indeed may form part of a more extensive business network. As Creed and Miles (1996: 30) comment, 'both across the firms within a network and within the various network firms, there is little choice but to consider trust building and maintenance to be as essential as control system building and maintenance are viewed in the functional form'. None the less, despite being one of the most critical concepts in management theory and practice, trust also remains one of the least understood.

Increased trust between alliance partners promises an economic pay-off for each. If they can develop mutual trust, this should reduce the negative effects of bounded rationality, specific investment in the alliance, and the opportunism which would otherwise arise, and so reduce transaction costs (Chiles and McMackin 1996). In other words, trust between partners should make them more willing to share information and so better inform their actions and decisions (reduce bounded rationality). Mutual trust should make it safer for the partners to invest assets in their alliance which cannot readily be used elsewhere (asset specificity). Thirdly, mutual trust should reduce the temptation for either partner to take advantage of the other (opportunism) because of the goodwill it represents. If trust can introduce these positive features into a partnership, it will render the cooperation more genuine, reduce the need to spend time and effort

---

Trust and Cooperation: A Conversation between Two Executives

This is an extract from a conversation between two senior executives of a leading UK software and IT systems services company which is involved in a wide range of strategic alliances.

A. Trust is right up there on top of my list of factors which make cooperation work. No partnership will work without trust and it is one of the most difficult things to achieve.

B. I think it has all sorts of dimensions to it. But essentially the way I think I gained the trust of [one of the company's partners] . . . was that I could make our company do what it said it would do. . . . I could deliver this and that's when they started to trust me.

A. What was interesting was that, when I went in to see them, I asked them about their perceptions of our competencies and capabilities. And if it wasn't the first [thing they mentioned], it was the second, it was about partnering. Which was a quite staggering thing, to me, for them to have said. I mean, because we had to struggle incredibly hard to establish a true trust relationship with them.

Source: John Child, personal research.

checking up on the other partner, and help to direct the partners' attention and energies towards longer-term goals of mutual benefit. This is why so many alliance managers, like those in the Box, consider trust to be essential.

As the conversation in the Box indicates, it is not easy to establish trust between people representing different companies. As we shall see, the process has to develop through a number of stages over time. It becomes a special challenge for *international* strategic alliances (ISAs), because these cross the boundaries of the cultural and institutional systems which support trust through the sharing of a common social identity, norms of conduct and institutional safeguards such as the law. The fact that partners from different countries as a result follow different assumptions of 'what can be taken for granted' places particular difficulties in the way of creating trust-based relationships between them, over and above the tensions which might be expected to arise within strategic alliances in general.

This chapter considers different insights into trust which help us to understand the nature of cooperative relationships. These insights can be applied to the process of strategic alliance development. This in turn makes it possible to examine ways in which trust can be enhanced in alliances. Trust is a theme which runs throughout this book and many of the points introduced here are developed further in later chapters.

TRUST AND COOPERATION

Trust is risky, virtually by definition, because, without some uncertainty regarding the outcome of the relationship or exchange, it would not have to come into play. The trustor's expectations about the future behaviour of the trustee may turn out to be incorrect, possibly owing to unfamiliarity with the trustee or the absence of social and legal mechanisms to contain the risk (Lane and Bachmann 1996: 368). This conditional nature of trust has given rise to enquiry into the grounds on which trust might develop and the foundations on which it can rest.

This enquiry has produced three insights which are particularly relevant to an understanding of cooperative relationships. The first is contained in the distinction between calculation, understanding, and personal identification as bases for trust. The second is an appreciation that cooperative relations can develop over time and that this development may be associated with the deepening of trust based on an evolution of its foundations. The third is a recognition that trust is socially constituted, in that it tends to be strengthened by cultural affinity between people and can be supported by institutional norms and sanctions. The first two of these insights contribute to an understanding of cooperation between alliance partners in general, including those engaged in purely domestic alliances, while the third insight is of particular importance for the case of international alliances.

Bases of trust

Lane (1998) identifies three perspectives on the basis of trust, which darw attention respectively to the role of calculation, understanding and personal identification. The first is *calculative trust*—namely, that 'trusting involves expectations about another, based on a calculus which weighs the cost and benefits of certain courses of action to either the trustor or the trustee'. Lewicki and Bunker (1996) argue that this form of trust is based on the assurance that other people will do as they say because the deterrent for violation is greater than the gains, and/or the rewards from preserving trust outweigh any from breaking it. 'In this view, trust is an on-going, market-oriented, economic calculation whose value is derived by determining the outcomes resulting from creating and sustaining the relationship relative to the costs of maintaining or severing it' (Lewicki and Bunker 1996: 120). Trust based on calculation clearly depends on an availability of relevant information, and in practice there may be significant limits to this. Indeed, some critics of the calculative view of trust have argued that it is when relationships or transactions are initiated under conditions of information *uncertainty* that trust in the proper sense comes into play.

Trust based upon calculation is likely to apply particularly to relationships which are new and hence can only proceed on the basis of institutionalized protection (incorporating deterrence) or the reputation of the partner. It may also be the only form of trust which can apply to arm's-length and hence impersonal economic exchanges. However, if those exchanges become recurrent, such as with repeat mail-order business, then another form of trust may also emerge. This is based on increased mutual knowledge among the partners, which nurtures the realization that they share relevant expectations. As we note below, calculation-based trust is very relevant to the formation phase of strategic alliances, though its withdrawal can also undermine the mutual confidence of partners who have developed other bases for trust as well.

A second potential basis for trust lies in the sharing of cognitions, including common ways of thinking, between the parties concerned. This sharing of cognitions provides a basis for *understanding* the thinking of a partner and for predicting that person's actions. Clearly, some cognitive sharing is necessary for a calculative basis of trust to come into play, but common cognitions provide the further reassurance that one can now reasonably predict other persons on the basis of shared expectations. One can normally only be sure of sharing ways of thinking with others by getting to know them well enough, and an aspect of cognitive trust is what Lewicki and Bunker have termed 'knowledge-based trust'. Knowledge-based trust 'is grounded in the other's predictability—knowing the other sufficiently well so that the other's behaviour is anticipatable. Knowledge-based trust relies on information rather than deterrence' (1996: 121). The assumption of rationality contained in the calculative view of trust is relaxed somewhat in cognitive trust, because the trust here is founded upon both the security and the comfort that the partner is well understood and is known to share important assumptions with you.

A third view of trust is that it is based on people sharing a personal identity. This means they hold common values, including a common concept of moral obligation. As Lane points out, common values and norms of obligation can develop in a long-standing relationship where trust was originally created in an incremental manner. This kind of trust is likely to find a parallel at the more inter-personal level, in what Lewicki and Bunker (1996) call 'identifica-tion-based trust'. Identification-based 'trust exists because the parties effectively understand and appreciate the other's wants; this mutual under-standing is developed to the point that each can effectively act for the other' (p. 122). If friendship develops within a long-term relationship, the emotional bond thereby introduced is likely to provide a mainstay for identification-based trust, because it enables a person to 'feel' as well as to 'think' like the other (p. 123). When people come to like each other, they are encouraged to place themselves voluntarily within the powers of another—this is what Brenkert (1998) calls 'the Voluntarist view' of trust. Trust which is based on people identifying with, and liking, each other therefore derives from what we may call '*bonding*' between them.

Running somewhat parallel to this threefold distinction between trust based on calculation, understanding, and bonding is the broader distinction, made by McAllister (1995) among others, between what he calls 'cognition-based' and 'affect-based' trust. Trust that is cognition-based rests upon the know-ledge people have of others and the evidence of their trustworthiness: 'avail-able knowledge and "good reasons" serve as foundations for trust decisions' (McAllister 1995: 26). McAllister points out that previous organizational researchers have assumed competence, responsibility, reliability and depend-ability to be important sources of cognition-based trust. Brenkert (1998) iden-tifies a 'predictability view', which holds that trust denotes the extent to which one can predict that the person being trusted will act in good faith. While Brenkart argues that such prediction rests on 'a belief that one person has about another', this is consistent with the concept of cognition-based trust because the belief almost certainly rests on a degree of knowledge about the other person which is taken to constitute 'good reasons' for trust, however limited and imperfect that knowledge might be.

By contrast, affect-based trust, according to McAllister (1995: 26), is founded on the emotional bonds between people. These bonds express a genuine con-cern for the welfare of partners, a feeling that the relationships have intrinsic virtue, and a belief that these sentiments are reciprocated. In other words, they incorporate an identification with the other person's wishes and inten-tions. Affect-based trust is clearly a form which is most likely to develop and deepen through fairly intensive relating between people on a person-to-person basis over quite a long period of time. As such, it is facilitated by the ability to communicate well and to avoid, or quickly clear up, misunderstand-ings. So mutual knowledge and the sharing of information between the people concerned remain essential conditions. Cultural and associated language differences tend to impede communication and easy understanding, and may therefore stand in the way of affect-based trust. Perceived conflicts of interest will also make it hard to develop or maintain this kind of trust. In strategic alliances, affect-based trust and cooperation will therefore be difficult to achieve, and if they emerge at all this is only likely after the alliance has been operating successfully, and up to the partners' expectations, over a period of some years.

The distinction between cognition and affect in trust-based cooperative relationships suggests that these are likely to form initially on the basis of essentially cognitive considerations, including calculation, but that as the relationship matures it may increasingly incorporate affect through the development of friendship ties.

Development of trust-based relations

The second insight which it is appropriate to apply to strategic alliances is that cooperative relations can develop over time, supported by a corresponding evolution of trust. As Smith *et al.* (1995) note, several writers have suggested that cooperative relationships develop through a number of stages. There are feedback loops in this process whereby the partners evaluate their experience and decide whether to continue to cooperate and, if so, in what form (Ring and Van de Ven 1994). The distinction between trust based on calculation, understanding, and indentification opens a window on the way that the evolution of trust is integral to this dynamic process of evolving cooperation.

In this vein, Lewicki and Bunker propose a model of 'the stagewise evolution of trust' in which 'trust develops gradually as the parties move from one stage to another' (1996: 124). They argue that trust first develops on the basis of calculation. This is the stage at which people are prepared to take some risk in entering into dependence on others because they are aware of some institutional safeguards or deterrents against reneging. For some relationships, trust may remain of this kind and at this level, as in repeated but arm's-length market transactions between people. Lewicki and Bunker suggest that many business and legal relationships begin and end in calculative trust. Calculative trust approximates to the stage at which people in different organizations decide, often somewhat guardedly, that 'OK, I am prepared to work with you'.

If initial cooperative activities serve to confirm the validity of the calculative trust and thus encourage repeated interaction and transaction, then the parties will also begin to develop a knowledge base about each other. In other words, a process of 'getting to know you' is now under way. The conditions are generated for a transition to trust based on mutual understanding. This is the stage in a relationship at which a person feels comfortable with a partner in the knowledge that he or she has proved to be consistent and reliable, and that the partner shares important expectations about the relationship. As a result, the partner is proving to be predictable. In this way, the parties' experience of a calculative trust relationship (i.e. feedback) is critical for their willingness to undergo the shift to cognitive trust. If the feedback is negative, and trust is broken, they will probably move to terminate the relationship. Even short of fracture, if the experience of relating on a calculative basis is not strongly positive, or if the relationship is heavily regulated, or if the interdependence of the partners is heavily bounded, they will have little cause to develop cognitive (knowledge-based) trust.

A further transition may come when normative trust builds on the depth of knowledge which the parties have acquired of each other and on the mutual confidence they have developed. These outcomes from the relationship may encourage the parties to identify with each other's goals and interests. A certain amount of mutual liking will probably now enter into the relationship, so that this stage is typically one at which the partners have become friends. It is the stage of 'getting to like you'. Lewicki and Bunker believe, however, that, whereas stable cognitive ('knowledge-based') trust characterizes many relationships, trust based on personal identification may be less common especially in business or work transactions where some difference of interest is usually inherent in the relationship.

Certain specifics of Lewicki and Bunker's evolutionary model may require modification. It does not, for instance, appear to allow for the possibility that, in the absence of effective external institutional guarantees, it may be necessary to develop a degree of knowledge about the partner to generate even the minimal level of trust necessary for cooperation to be established. Otherwise an adequate foundation for calculating potential benefits, risks, and so forth will not exist. Nevertheless, despite such detailed qualification, the evolutionary model of trust can contribute very significantly to an analysis of ISA formation and development.

Social constitution of trust

The third insight is a recognition that trust is socially constituted, in that it is necessarily realized, and strengthened, by social interaction, cultural affinity between people, and the support of institutional norms and sanctions. Zucker (1986) argues that trust is socially produced through three main modes, of which the latter two have their bases in socially constituted entities. The first mode is one in which trust develops on the basis of the experience of past exchange or the expectations attached to future exchange. Production of trust in this mode arises through the mutual reinforcement of investments in trust and the quality of the cooperation associated with it, and is consistent with the process of developing and deepening trust-based relations which we have already discussed. The second mode is based on the sharing of common characteristics, such as ethnicity and culture. The third mode is one in which formal institutional mechanisms provide codes (as in medicine) or guarantees (as in financial markets supervision) that transactions will take place as promised.

Regarding the second of Zucker's modes, cooperation is likely to be easier between people who have the same cultural norms. There are a number of reasons for this. People are more likely to trust those who share the same values, because this establishes a common cognitive frame and promotes a sense of common social identity which has a strong emotional element. Differences between cultures in language, symbolism, and meaning can make it very difficult to find a common cognitive basis from which trust can first develop.

It will also be easier for trust-based relationships to develop if the risks involved are reduced by institutional mechanisms—the third mode Zucker identifies. These mechanisms include an effective law to enforce contracts, efficient supervision by government agencies, and a strongly developed moral opprobrium for any violation of the social norms applying to trust. The presence of social and cultural norms which attach a value to trust, define the circumstances under which it should be honoured, and justify sanctions for violation indicate the extent to which trust is a socially constituted phenomenon (cf. Lane and Bachmann 1996).

While the social constitution of trust can support cooperation within the boundaries of a given social unit, such as a nation and to a lesser degree an organization, it clearly presents problems for relationships which cross these boundaries. Those in a domestic strategic alliance cross the boundaries of organizations as social units, whereas those in an international strategic alliance cross both national and organizational boundaries. The development of trust-based cooperative relationships within ISAs is therefore a major challenge, especially in the case of alliances between partners from a developed and a developing society. In this case, the partners involved do not share common cultural characteristics and they cannot rely upon the same system of institutional support, except to the extent that international trade law and arbitration procedures have effect. This means that the development of trust in ISAs will depend heavily upon the process mode of its production—namely, the way that their relationships are established and managed.

TRUST AND ALLIANCE DEVELOPMENT

There is considerable agreement among writers on strategic alliances that their development can be broadly divided into three phases: formation, implementation, and evolution (Lorange and Roos 1992). Formation is the phase during which the future partners conceive an interest in the possibility of forming an alliance, select potential partners, and negotiate an agreement (usually a contract). Implementation is the phase during which the alliance is established as a productive venture and people are appointed or seconded by the partners, systems installed, and operations commenced. Evolution refers to the ways in which the alliance develops further following its establishment. There is a potential for trust to evolve in step with these three phases of alliance development on the basis initially of calculation, then understanding, and finally bonding.

Formation and calculation

Trust based on calculation appears at first sight to be a contradiction in terms. However, if trust rests on a belief that another party's action will be beneficial and reliable rather than the opposite, then calculation can clearly enter into it. A calculation that partners have the ability, competence and motivation to deliver on their promises, and that there are sufficient deterrents based on law and reputation for them not to let you down, is a vital condition for being prepared to cooperate with relative strangers.

Early in the formation process, the future partners will have come to the conclusion that they favour an alliance out of a range of possible alternatives. For example, if one partner's purpose is to enter a new market, it has a range of possibilities for accomplishing this objective: these include exporting into the market using local agents, licensing technology to a local producer, forming an alliance with a local firm (in the form of a collaboration, equity joint venture, or merger), and setting up a wholly owned subsidiary (Root 1994). The choice between these alternatives is likely to be informed by the partner's strategic intentions and previous experience of managing different forms of market entry. It will rest almost entirely on *calculation* concerning the relative costs and benefits of each alternative. At this stage, the calculation has to rely primarily upon business intelligence.

If it is decided to explore the possibilities of forming an alliance, the selection of a partner is also likely to be based importantly upon calculation. During this phase, potential partners are identified and their mutual interest grows sufficiently for them to start exchanging information directly rather than using business intelligence. In principle, the potential partners try to find out as much as they can about each other and then compare the information obtained against a range of selection criteria in order to assess the degree of strategic fit between themselves (Geringer 1991; Faulkner 1995). Strategic fit is discussed further in Chapter 5.

In reality, however, information about prospective partners will be limited, especially that relating to their internal cultures, competences, and values. This means that judgements will have to be made on the basis of the partners' reputations, including those for trustworthiness. This 'information stage' (Möllering 1997), during which the prospective partners try to find out as much as possible about each other, will normally precede their entry into negotiations on a contract. In learning about the other, the partners are also embarking on the processes of 'getting to know' each other.

While the information stage of alliance formation is ostensibly aimed at establishing the nature and degree of 'strategic fit' between potential partners, in the case of a putative *international* strategic alliance the nature of cultural differences between them will also become evident. Cultural differences could inhibit the development of mutual understanding and trust, and jeopardize the process of moving towards a formal agreement. This is a quite realistic possibility when alliances are being discussed between partners from societies which are culturally and institutionally disparate. Particularly at the stage of forming an international alliance, it is not possible to treat strategic fit and cultural fit separately and sequentially, because the exchange of information during this phase depends on an initial development of trust which, in turn, depends on how the relations between the partners are affected by their cultural distance (Möllering 1997). Once the calculative basis for the alliance has been agreed, it may become more feasible to work systematically towards a resolution of the operational problems which continue to result from the cultural differences between the partners (Child 1994).

The process of information-gathering, if sustained, will move into one of negotiation. Negotiation hammers out a calculative framework for the 'strategic fit' and the mix of commitments and safeguards embodied in an alliance contract. It also provides an opportunity for the parties to establish a level of comfort for future cooperation based on a deepening of their mutual knowledge. In other words, in so far as the agreement to cooperate is one to establish a mutual dependency between the partners, but where considerable uncertainty remains, it is an act of trust based primarily upon calculation. While the calculus will take account of legal and other institutional safeguards, it is also likely to be informed by the direct knowledge the partners have gathered about one another.

Smitka (1994: 93) uses the term 'contracting' to refer to the negotiation of, and agreement upon, mutual obligations between potential partners, or 'the framing of the environment for transactions'. The value of this term lies in the way it directs attention to the process of negotiating and agreeing the terms of an alliance relationship. Nor is it assumed that the outcome is all captured in the terms of a formal contract *per se*, which is signed at a particular point in time and supposed to define the relationship thereafter. In other words, 'contracting' may well continue after a formal alliance contract is signed and, as we shall see in the case of Sino-foreign alliances, the expectations of Western and non-Western partners can differ considerably on this point. Different expectations on this issue constitute one of the most significant threats to trust between the partners, because from the Western perspective they can readily be interpreted as signs of the other partner's bad faith on the fundamentals of the alliance.

Implementation and mutual understanding

Following the establishment of a strategic alliance, with the allocation of capital and other resources to it, there is a phase of implementation during which it is commissioned as a productive venture. During implementation, people are appointed, technology and systems installed, and operations commenced. Implementation is of crucial importance for the quality of cooperative relations within the alliance. The people appointed to work together may or may not possess the necessary technical competences for the alliance to succeed, and this is equally the case with their cultural competences. If these competences are lacking and, as a result, the alliance founders, the underlying calculus for the alliance can no longer remain valid.

It is therefore essential to maintain the basis of calculation which initially made the partners willing to enter into a cooperative relationship, with the investment and risk that this involved. However, once the alliance is in the process of being implemented, the people working together from the partner organizations have the opportunity of getting to know each other more intensively than before. The growing ability of each partner's staff to understand and predict the thinking and actions of the other's can provide a further basis for trust between them. This mutual understanding should reduce the sense of uncertainty which partners experience about each other.

The systems which are installed during the implementation phase, particularly those for control and information reporting, are for this reason very significant. The ways they are designed and operated can determine the quality of knowledge that is available to each partner. For example, if one partner's systems for accounting, marketing, operational, and technical information reporting are installed in a joint venture, this adds to the quality of the knowledge available to that partner, but not necessarily to the other. The first partner enjoys a potential for trust to mature which may be denied to the other. Similarly, if the personnel appointed to work together within the alliance are insensitive to each other's cultures, the likelihood of their achieving a close cooperative relationship on an integrated basis will be diminished and the most that can achieved may be a suboptimal segregation between spheres of activity and influence (cf. Child and Markóczy 1993; Tung 1993). In order for mutual understanding to develop between the partners, it is also clearly necessary to find ways of resolving the conflicts that are likely to arise in the course of their working together.

Evolution and bonding

If difficulties such as these can be avoided or overcome, and if the alliance proves to be an economic success, it is likely to mature into an organization with an increasing sense of its own identity and culture. Unless the alliance is established for a one-off or temporary purpose only, or as a stepping-stone for one partner to absorb the other, the partners may well not place any time limit upon its potential life. The very success of an alliance will tend to encourage the partner/parent companies to grant it an increasing measure of autonomy, and also provide the management of the alliance with the legitimacy to take its own decisions (Lyles and Reger 1993).

This evolutionary process permits stable, ongoing relationships to develop, relationships both between people in the partner organizations who have a responsibility for (or interest in) the alliance and between people working on an everyday basis in the alliance's own organization. They are in a position to accumulate knowledge about each other, and this tends to reinforce the relationship. Moreover, the success of the alliance in meeting partner interests means that calculative factors should not threaten their relationships. As relationships develop over time within the context of a successful collaboration, so there is a natural tendency for those concerned to identify increasingly with one another's interests as well as for emotional ties to grow. In this way, *bonding* can form between partners, which Faulkner (1995) has identified as being, in turn, a significant requirement for alliance success. Thus a virtuous cycle may be established, which reinforces both trust and the cooperation which it nurtures. This cycle can, of course, be broken and reversed, as we note shortly.

Fig. 3.1 summarizes the coincidence between strategic-alliance development and the evolution of trust-based relationships, which has been analysed in this section.

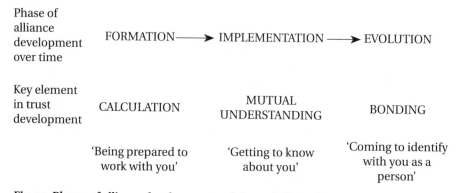

Phase of alliance development over time	FORMATION ⟶	IMPLEMENTATION ⟶	EVOLUTION
Key element in trust development	CALCULATION	MUTUAL UNDERSTANDING	BONDING
	'Being prepared to work with you'	'Getting to know about you'	'Coming to identify with you as a person'

Fig. 3.1. Phases of alliance development and the evolution of trust

It is important to make two further observations in connection with this analysis. First, in reality there will be only certain *individuals* relating with each other across the boundaries of cooperating organizations. Their role in promoting trust between the partner organizations is therefore a key one, and the trust that can be said to exist between the organizations will to a large extent come down to the quality of mutual trust which exists between those individuals. This reminds us that trust is actually an inter-personal phenomenon, upon which the quality of inter-organizational relations is founded. The organizational members upon whom inter-organizational cooperation depends can perhaps be best labelled their 'trust guardians'. The contribution that these trust guardians make to inter-organizational cooperation will depend on (a) the mutual trust they have developed, (b) the influence they enjoy within their respective organizations, and (c) how many there are of them in each organization.

It follows that if there is a frequent turnover of the personnel allocated by the partners to an alliance, the opportunities for developing trust-based cooperation between them will be diminished. Overseas tours of duty for the personnel of a foreign ISA partner are often limited in duration, especially when the other partner is located in a developing country with 'hardship' conditions attached. We shall see that this is a factor inhibiting the development of trust in Sino-foreign joint ventures, especially within the context of a local culture which attaches high value to transactions based upon personal relationships.

The second observation concerns the vulnerability of trust-based cooperation within strategic alliances. As noted earlier, alliances between firms are based on cooperation between partners whose interests do not usually wholly coincide and who, in the case of horizontal alliances, could become competitors at a future point in time. The multi-stage model of trust evolution points to the danger of collapse in an alliance relationship at any stage of its development if the previous bases of trust are withdrawn. In business relationships, given the financial expectations of owners and external stakeholders, bonding cannot sustain trust if one or both of the partners conclude that the calculative or predictive basis of their cooperation has disappeared. Equally, if a problem arises in the basis for a higher level of trust development, such as the emergence of a personal antipathy, it may prove necessary to return to the initial foundations for the relationship in order to rebuild it. For instance, if a personal dislike arises between two inter-organizational trust guardians, it may still be possible to rescue the relationship between the organizations themselves through their leaders recognizing that it continues to retain a basis in mutual economic benefit. A hierarchy of foundations for trust and cooperation is, in effect, being posited here with calculation at the base, prediction in the middle, and bonding at the apex

The fragility of trust in business relationships draws attention to the interdependence between trust and the availability of legal redress, or other institutional support, should cheating occur. The relation between trust and law is, however, still being debated. Does a well-developed legal system offering effective recourse to the courts complement trust-based relations, in providing a baseline support which makes people more prepared to risk offering trust and so set its development in motion? Or is the role of law primarily to act as an alternative framework to trust-based relations for governing the conduct of transactions (Lane and Bachmann 1996; Arrighetti et al. 1997; Deakin and Michie 1997). There is certainly a widespread fear that trust is in decline in business relations and that this is reflected in the growing incidence of disputes being taken to law. This is evident even in countries like China where business people have traditionally relied on the security provided by special trust-based relationships in an otherwise extremely highly risky environment.

DEVELOPING TRUST

The fact that trust in the relations between organizations develops through several stages, and rests upon a number of different foundations, helps us to identify the kind of policies and practical measures which can be taken to develop and promote it.

A basis for mutual benefit

It is clearly vital, when establishing an alliance, to maintain clarity and realism in the commitments that partners promise to make to each other. There are four aspects to this. First, the commitments must be realistic and therefore subject to careful calculation and scrutiny; the partners must be seen to be able to honour those commitments. Secondly, the commitments offered by each partner must together add up to a viable strategic fit. Thirdly, at this early stage, before any significant trust has been established, it is important to research the legal and other institutional safeguards which are available in the event of the other partner reneging on its promised commitments. Last, but not least, an agreement between the partners should be committed to writing, in detail and with the minimum of ambiguity.

All this may appear, paradoxically, to be adopting an untrusting approach. Its relevance lies in the fact that the first basis for developing successful and trusting cooperation between partners is one of calculation. If the calculation is wrong in the first place, the partnership is immediately hostage to blame and recrimination. It is therefore a false economy to rush the process of selecting a partner and negotiating the terms of the agreement. Many potential alliances are with prospective partners whose ability to deliver market access or specific competencies are not well known. This is especially likely with partners from developing countries. In such cases, it is imperative to undertake a thorough appraisal of the prospective partner and the context in which it operates, and not to rely on what the other party itself gives by way of estimates or assurances. It is tempting for a potential partner to promise more than it can realistically deliver when it is keen to achieve the cooperation of another company whose assistance it considers to be a strategic priority.

Predictability and conflict resolution

Conflicts are bound to arise between alliance partners, even if there is very little inherent competition between their underlying business interests. They arise frequently between the units within a single organization and are therefore all the more likely to occur in the cooperation between people from different organizations. There is likely to be a mixture of disputes over 'hard' financial or technological issues and frictions of a 'softer' cultural and inter-personal nature. In each case, it is important to have mechanisms for resolv-ing such conflicts in place from the very outset of the alliance's existence.

Mechanisms for mitigating 'hard' disputes are consistent with the provision of information among alliance members and hence the development of trust based on knowledge and predictability. One example is the arrangement for regular and frequent meetings between the managers and staff seconded or appointed to the alliance by the partners. These meetings should establish the facts of any matters at issue and record the discussion and any solutions pro-posed. The records of such meetings provide a basis on which problems can be addressed at a higher level between the partners, if a resolution is not forth-coming within the alliance organization itself. An important aim of meetings and other formal conflict-resolution mechanisms is to ensure that relatively 'hard' disputes do not get turned into, or mixed in with, interpersonal antipathies. The intention is to depersonalize the issues as far as possible.

Another important approach towards reducing the incidence of 'hard' dis-putes is to invest in a formal specification of rules and guidelines that make matters such as correct financial procedures and the protection of technology clear to the people working within the alliance. It will probably require an investment of time by senior partner managers to agree on this formalization, at a very early stage of the alliance, even before it comes into operation.

Formalization also plays a role in encouraging the sharing of information among the members of an alliance, within any bounds of confidentiality and intellectual property-right-protection that have been agreed in the terms of the cooperation. While formal measures cannot guarantee the amount and quality of information-sharing, procedures such as password access to com-puter networks, the circulation of well-documented material before meetings, and the regular dissemination of data on the alliance's performance can be of considerable assistance. The sharing of information should, over time, con-tribute to a breaking-down of barriers between people who have come from the partners to work together. In so doing, it will help to generate the mutual confidence that takes trust forward beyond a basis of calculation onto one of shared understanding and predictability.

Approaches to reducing conflicts of a 'softer' interpersonal nature within a cooperative relationship will be less formal, but nevertheless also need to be organized. The building of sensitivity about how people coming from the part-ners' organizations perceive each other is central to this effort. There are well-known techniques which Western organizational development consultants have devised for achieving this, and which generally work within that cultural milieu. Other approaches will, however, be necessary for cross-cultural alliances, requiring not the quick 'confrontations' favoured in the USA but a more patient and less personally exposing process of mutual discussion and socializing.

The organizational 'politics of envy' and problems arising from perceived discrimination in the treatment of staff from the alliance partners, have to be tackled systematically as well. For example, serious interpersonal problems can arise within foreign joint ventures established in developing countries over the often quite enormous disparities in pay between foreign and local managers. Local resentment over high expatriate compensation may be eased somewhat by charging this to the foreign partner directly rather than having it as a direct charge on the alliance. However, a more effective solution lies in making the basis for compensation quite clear to all concerned in terms of qualification, performance, market factors, and so forth. This helps to demonstrate the rationale for the compensation system, and also indicates potential channels for betterment that are open to local managers and staff.

It is evident that measures such as these taken to reduce interpersonal conflicts within alliances will, if successful, also help to remove barriers to establishing personal friendships between partners' personnel. Personal friendship is conducive to the third major basis for trust—namely, mutual bonding.

Mutual bonding

There are several practices which facilitate the development of bonding between the people directly involved in cooperation between different organizations. It is extremely important that friendly personal contact is regularly maintained between the leaders of the cooperating organizations. This contact should be visible to all those working under them. This means planning for personal visits between partner chief executives at least once a year, and giving these full publicity. Apart from the intrinsic merit such visits have in ironing out any differences of view between the partners and laying down broad plans for the future, they very importantly set an example and establish a climate of cooperation for the people working further down the alliance. We shall see, later in this book, how visible top-level commitment to cooperation impacts on its success in achieving goals such as mutual learning (Chapter 13).

Careful consideration should be given to the length of appointment or secondment of personnel to an alliance. If this is short, say three years or under, the chances of achieving mutual bonding are reduced. Not only is there personal unfamiliarity to overcome, but, if a language has to be learnt or improved, this clearly takes time as well. Personnel on longer-term appointments are also more likely to invest in establishing relationships within the alliance, for they see it as a more significant part of their overall career path. Western, and especially American, companies tend to attach people to alliances on contracts of four years maximum, whereas Japanese companies tend to attach their people for up to twice as long. Partners in countries where relationship is a requirement for business cooperation commonly complain that personnel assignments to their alliances are too short for any bonding to occur.

The careful selection of people who are to work in an alliance will also assist the prospects of mutual bonding. They should be selected not merely on the basis of technical competence, important though this is, but also on an assessment of their ability to form good relationships with people from other organizational and national cultures. Track records can tell a lot in this respect. Some global companies have, for this reason, now created opportunities for successful alliance and expatriate managers to be able to remain in interorganizational and international assignments without detriment to their long-term advancement within the home corporation. People with open-minded and prejudice-free personalities are likely to be more successful at personal bonding within alliances. These characteristics can be assessed through careful observation and, if appropriate, through systematic personality tests.

The development of personal friendship, and hence normative trust, is further helped by policies intended to avoid the ghetto situations which can easily arise with international alliances where at least one partner's personnel are located in an unfamiliar environment. A ghetto can arise because separate housing of superior quality has to be provided for expatriates, and it can be heavily reinforced if the local language imposes a significant social barrier for the staff and their families. It is important for the alliance to encourage as much socializing between the partners' personnel as possible. Activities such as sports and social events, charitable and sponsorship activities in the local community, and alliance open days, can do a lot to break down social barriers. They help to bring about an acceptance of the alliance within its local community, and a strengthening of its external identity. At the same time they are collective events which help to build up an internal identity within the alliance itself.

It is, of course, not possible to legislate for the development of personal friendship among those working together in a strategic alliance. There is inevitably an element of unpredictability in interpersonal dynamics. Nevertheless, policies such as those just outlined can help a great deal, especially in circumstances where there are no serious commercial or financial differences driving a wedge between the partners. And, once established, personal bonding and a sense of mutual identity between alliance partners can reinforce their determination to solve business problems, if and when they arise.

SUMMARY

Cooperation between organizations creates mutual dependence and requires trust in order to succeed. This comes down to trust between the individuals who are involved in the alliance. Uncertainty about partners' motives, and a lack of detailed knowledge about how they operate, requires that a basis for trust be found for cooperation to get under way in the first place.

We have suggested that there are identifiable stages in the evolution of trust. Calculation, then understanding, and then bonding progressively provide the foundations on which trust can develop. Trust is seen to develop gradually as the partners move from one stage to the next. This is consistent with the view that trust can be strengthened by the partners building up the number of positive exchanges between themselves. As the partners become increasingly aware of the mutual investment they have made in their relationship, the benefits they are deriving from it, and the costs of reneging, they have more incentive to carry it forward. In this sense, the trust between them will benefit from the 'shadow of the future' (Axelrod 1984). The view of trust as an evolving process provides valuable clues about the way in which cooperative relationships can be developed both within and between organizations.

While alliances between firms do sometimes arise on the basis of already-existing personal friendships, they usually start off on impersonal terms. In other words, the partners have to calculate that, under conditions of limited knowledge, the potential benefits of cooperation outweigh the risk of partners' reneging on their commitments. Once an alliance is being implemented, the growing body of shared information and mutual knowledge should enhance trust between the partners, because it increases their ability to understand each other better and hence predict each other's actions. Eventually, the experience of working together may produce a sense of shared identity and personal friendship. In short, the partners develop trust through the repeated experience of working together, making joint decisions and other contacts which generate familiarity and then bonding.

The conclusion that trust between partners can develop over time through continued interaction between them, from an initial basis that is purely calculative, is consistent with the experimental findings from iterated games—namely, that the probability of cooperation may be improved initially by providing mutual hostages and then progressively reinforced by the benefits it is seen to provide. As Chapter 2 noted, the experimental evidence suggests that, although noncooperation emerges as the dominant strategy in single-play (i.e. initial) situations, under iterated conditions the incidence of cooperation rises substantially.

The potential advantages of promoting trust between partners and their employees are considerable, for they offer an opportunity to relieve (though not necessarily resolve) the dilemmas of control, integration, and learning which are inherent in organizing alliances. So far as control is concerned, trust can avoid the managerial costs of second-guessing the other partner's intentions and ways of doing things. It is likely to facilitate agreement on common control and information systems. Trust will break down some of the more intractable barriers to integration between the partners and their personnel, barriers which are usually far more difficult to deal with than, say, differences in technical skills or language. The development of trust should also promote the conditions necessary for a cooperative strategy to achieve its learning objectives, by making its members more willing to share information and ideas.

These insights are fundamental to an understanding of cooperative strategy, its rationale, and its management. They also help to identify the policies and practices which can be taken to promote trust as a condition for effective cooperation. Some policies are geared towards creating a clear calculus for mutual benefit; others are aimed at enhancing shared information, especially to resolve conflicts and to open up communication; while yet others assist the growth of mutual bonding.

REFERENCES

Arrighetti, A., Bachmann, R., and Deaking, Simon (1997), 'Contract Law, Social Norms and Inter-Firm Cooperation', *Cambridge Journal of Economics*, 21: 171–95.

Axelrod, R. (1984), *The Evolution of Cooperation* (New York: HarperCollins).

Bleeke, J., and Ernst, D. (1993) (eds.), *Collaborating to Compete: Using Strategic Alliances and Acquisitions in the Global Marketplace* (New York: Wiley).

Brenkert, G. G. (1998), 'Trust, Morality and International Business', in C. Lane and R. Backmann (eds.), *Trust Within and Between Organizations* (Oxford: Oxford University Press).

Child, J. (1994), *Management in China during the Age of Reform* (Cambridge: Cambridge University Press).

——and Markóczy, L. (1993), 'Host-Country Managerial Behaviour and Learning in Chinese and Hungarian Joint Ventures', *Journal of Management Studies*, 30: 611–31.

Chiles, T. H., and McMackin, J. F. (1996), 'Integrating Variable Risk Preferences, Trust, and Transaction Cost Economics', *Academy of Management Review*, 21: 73–99.

Creed, W. E. D., and Miles, R. E. (1996), 'Trust in Organizations: A Conceptual Framework Linking Organizational Forms, Managerial Philosophies, and the Opportunity Costs of Controls', in R. M. Kramer and T. R. Tyler (eds.), *Trust in Organizations: Frontiers of Theory and Research* (Thousand Oaks, Calif.: Sage), 16–38.

Deakin, S., and Michie, J. (1997), 'Contracts and Competition: An Introduction', *Cambridge Journal of Economics*, 21: 121–5.

Faulkner, D. O. (1995), *International Strategic Alliances: Co-operating to Compete* (Maidenhead: McGraw-Hill).

Gambetta, D. (1988), 'Can We Trust Trust?', in D. Gambetta (ed.), *Trust: Making and Breaking Cooperative Relations* (Oxford: Blackwell), 213–37.

Geringer, J. M. (1991), 'Strategic Determinants of Partner Selection Criteria in International Joint Ventures', *Journal of International Business Studies*, 22: 41–62.

Hamel, G. (1991), 'Competition for Competence and Inter-Partner Learning within International Strategic Alliances', *Strategic Management Journal*, 12: 83–103.

Kramer, R. M.. and Tyler , T. R.(1996) (eds.), *Trust in Organizations: Frontiers of Theory and Research* (Thousand Oaks, Calif.: Sage).

Lane, C. (1998), 'Introduction', in C. Lane and R. Backmann (eds.), *Trust Within and Between Organizations* (Oxford: Oxford University Press).

——and Bachmann, R. (1996), 'The Social Constitution of Trust: Supplier Relations in Britain and Germany', *Organization Studies*, 17/3: 365–95.

————(1998) (eds.), *Trust Within and Between Organizations* (Oxford: Oxford University Press).

Lewicki, R. J., and Bunker, B. B. (1996), 'Developing and Maintaining Trust in Work

Relationships', in R. M. Kramer and T. R. Tyler (eds.), *Trust in Organizations: Frontiers of Theory and Research* (Thousand Oaks, Calif.: Sage), 114–39.

Lorange, P., and Roos, J. (1992), *Strategic Alliances: Formation, Implementation, and Evolution* (Oxford: Blackwell).

Lyles, M. A., and Reger, R. K. (1993), 'Managing for Autonomy in Joint Ventures: A Longitudinal Study of Upward Influence', *Journal of Management Studies*, 30: 383–404.

McAllister, D. J. (1995), 'Affect- and Cognition-Based Trust as Foundations for Interpersonal Cooperation in Organizations', *Academy of Management Journal*, 38/1: 24–59.

Möllering, G. (1997), 'The Influence of Cultural Differences on the Establishment of Trust between Partners in International Cooperation', unpublished paper (Judge Institute of Management Studies, University of Cambridge, Jan.).

Ring, P. S., and Van de Ven, A. H. (1994), 'Developmental Processes of Cooperative Interorganizational Relationships', *Academy of Management Review*, 19/1: 90–118.

Root, F. R. (1994), *Entry Strategies for International Markets* (rev. edn., New York: Lexington Books).

Smith, K. G., Carroll, S. J., and Ashford, S. J. (1995), 'Intra- and Interorganizational Cooperation: Toward a Research Agenda', *Academy of Management Journal*, 38/1: 7–23.

Smitka, M. J. (1994), 'Contracting without Contracts', in S. B. Sitkin and R. J. Bies (eds.), *The Legalistic Organization* (London: Sage), 91–108.

Tung, R. L. (1993), 'Managing Cross-National and Intra-National Diversity', *Human Resource Management*, 32: 461–77.

Zucker, L. G. (1986), 'Production of Trust: Institutional Sources of Economic Structure, 1840–1920', *Research in Organizational Behavior*, 8: 53–111.

4

Motives

BASIC MOTIVES

People have cooperated since the time that evolution enabled them to make decisions and take actions (Ridley 1996). They have also competed and sometimes fought each other to the death. It is important in any examination of cooperative strategy to isolate the conditions that make cooperation more likely; in other words, the motives for cooperation. This chapter examines some of the more salient of these motives.

The process of economic and industrial change in the West since the end of the Second World War has been realized in a number of phases (Chandler 1986). First there was the immediate post-war phase of inherited rigidities from the inter-war period, and the protection of ravaged economies. Then from the 1950s onwards came the dramatic growth of the major multinationals, and of the divisionalized M-form of organization. As Chandler (1986) suggests the multidivisional company replaced the market in many areas in coordinating the distribution of goods and services to the consumer. Ultimately, however, this led to administrative and bureaucratic diseconomies as the multinationals became too large and unwieldy to operate efficiently, and this had to be weighed against the achievement of the clear scale and scope of economies of large-scale operation. As Hrebiniak (1992: 399) puts it: 'Internal expansion, and the inevitable creation of hierarchy can negatively affect flexibility, speed of response to markets, and the free flow of information so desperately needed to implement global strategies.' Thus a third phase manifested itself in the late 1970s and the 1980s when the system 'began to unravel to a degree' (Jorde and Teece 1989). This period saw the growth of the venture-capital-funded entrepreneurial firm with substantial outsourcing of non-key processes, leading previously internalized value-chain activities to be returned to the market place. In many cases this led to the disadvantage of fragmentation of companies, and to their developing resource limitations, particularly in the face of the increasing globalization of markets.

Partly in response to these forces, there has been a dramatic growth of strategic alliances and other forms of cooperative strategy between companies since the late 1980s, particularly in the area of technology and marketing. 'The spectacular growth of international interfirm technical cooperation agreements represents one of the most important and novel developments in the first half of the 80's' (OECD report 1986 cited in Collins and Doorley 1991). And as Gomes-Casseres states (1987: 99): 'Joint ventures may often be instruments providing firms with flexibility in responding to trends that are difficult to predict.' Porter and Fuller (1986: 322) focus on the basic purpose of an alliance when they say: 'Coalitions arise when performing a value chain activity with a partner is superior to any other way. . . . Coalitions can be a valuable tool in many aspects of global strategy, and the ability to exploit them will be an important source of international advantage.'

There are many motivating factors behind the formation of strategic alliances and other cooperative strategies. Most may well fall within the basic need identified for joint ventures by Aiken and Hage so succinctly, in 1968: 'Organizations go into joint ventures because of the need for resources, notably, money, skill and manpower.' Kogut (1988), also dealing with joint ventures, singles out three basic motivations for their formation: (1) that such a form represents the lowest transaction cost alternative; (2) that it enables an improved strategic position to be achieved, and/or (3) it gives an opportunity for organizational learning. These motives may be alternatives, although in some cases all three motivations may apply.

As we noted in Chapter 2, the *transaction-cost* motive deals in particular with situations where there would be small number bargaining, high asset specificity, and high uncertainty over specifying and monitoring performance. Joint ownership largely eliminates the potential costs that arise in such situations, as there is a mutual hostage position through joint commitment of financial or real assets which thereby align partners who otherwise may have potentially conflicting incentives.

The *strategic-behaviour* motive addresses how a joint venture may enable competitive advantage to be developed in the joint venture, that had escaped each of the partners operating alone. This depends then largely on the complementarity of the assets introduced to the joint venture and the synergies that arise as a result of this. 'Whereas the former [transaction cost motive] predicts that the matching should reflect minimizing costs, the latter predicts that joint venture partners will be chosen to improve the competitive positioning of the parties . . . ' (Kogut 1988: 322).

Kogut's third motive, that of capitalizing on an opportunity for *organizational learning*, may depend upon the setting up of a joint venture in order to transfer tacit knowledge (Polanyi 1967). By definition, tacit knowledge cannot be transferred by contractual codified means, and is communicated only by teams working together. A joint venture may be sought in order to achieve this.

Thus the three motives for joint ventures identified by Kogut are claimed by him to be quite distinct although sometimes overlapping. 'Transaction cost analyses joint ventures as an efficient solution to the hazards of economic transactions. Strategic behaviour places joint ventures in the context of competitive rivalry and collusive agreements to enhance market power. Finally transfer of organizational skills views joint ventures as a vehicle by which organizational knowledge is exchanged and imitated . . . ' (Kogut 1988: 323). All three, however, are in fact concerned with the overarching motive of enabling the partners to become more competitive in relation to their rivals in their chosen markets.

Many scholars have depicted alliance formation as an essentially rational and analytical process (e.g. Harrigan 1988). Tallman and Shenkar (1994), for example, develop a rational managerial decision model for international cooperative venture formation by MNEs. Contractor and Lorange (1988: 9) identify seven 'more or less overlapping objectives' for the formation of various types of cooperative arrangement:

1. risk reduction;
2. achievement of economies of scale and/or rationalization;
3. technology exchanges;
4. co-opting or blocking competition;
5. overcoming government-mandated trade or investment barriers;
6. facilitating initial international expansion of inexperienced firms;
7. vertical quasi-integration advantages of linking the complementary contributions of the partners in a 'value chain'.

These potential rationales for forming cooperative relationships raise the twin issues of how compatible are the partners' strategic motives for forming an alliance and how transparent are these motives. A lack of openness about motives is likely to limit the chances of trust developing between the partners later on, and may threaten the very survival of the partnership. Of course, as we shall note in Chapter 13, if one partner's motives for forming an alliance are primarily to 'milk' the other's technology and special skills, so that the exchange of benefits is one-way and one-off, then the long-term survival of the alliance is not likely to figure highly among its goals.

However, the relationships that develop between partners in successful relationships may well be far wider and deeper than the economic perspectives put forward by Kogut and others. As Tallman and Shenkar (1994: 92) also note: 'The decision to form an ICV [international cooperative venture], as well as the selection of cooperative strategies, organizational forms and partners, is not strictly economic, but also a social, psychological and emotional phenomenon. . . . It is no coincidence that ICVs are frequently described using such terms as "trust", "shared visions" and "understanding".'

A particular motive for adopting a cooperative strategy and entering into alliances is provided by the challenge of entering new international markets. Here, the choice is one between (1) exporting, (2) entry via cooperative contracting such as licensing, franchising, counter-trade, and contract manufacture, and (3) investment in the target market through setting up joint ventures with local partners (Young *et al.* 1989; Root 1994). It is possible to identify the most appropriate mode through a contingency analysis which refers to the company's strategic objectives, on the one hand, and to local conditions, on the other. The practical problem is that a company's strategic objectives are seldom fully consistent, and local conditions may not be fully understood (Root 1994: ch. 7).

Thus, although the formation of alliances and joint ventures is presented as typically the result of unitary decisions in the presence of sufficient information to make them, it is more usually the product of a coalition of views in both partners pointing to the possible advantages of such an alliance, when the actual benefits and costs cannot be known until the alliance has been in operation some considerable time. They are, therefore, as much political as economic decisions depending heavily on the internal corporate political power of their champions, and placed at risk if those champions should lose power in their home organizations (Tallman and Shenkar 1994).

Although decisions to set up alliances may be strongly conditioned by political issues and the relative positions of a number of stakeholders, economic arguments will almost certainly be advanced to justify the decisions, and these arguments are likely to be based on either the transaction-cost body of theory, or the resource-dependency perspective. More specifically, the argument will run along the lines that the alliance is the most likely solution to an environmental challenge on the grounds of it showing the best probable excess of probable benefit over cost, that the joint value chains of the partners give competitive advantage where neither did alone.

Before discussing the specific drivers behind cooperative strategy it is worth noting that there are two distinct rationales for such a strategy: (1) learning and (2) skill substitution. In the complexity of an actual cooperative arrangement they may well get muddled but both exist conceptually as distinct rationales and they carry with them different risks.

Thus strategic alliances are generally formed because each partner feels inadequate in a particular area of its activities and wants to learn from the other partner. Clearly this involves risk if total integrity is absent, as one partner may take and not give fully in return. Such partnerships may set up stronger competitors of the other partner. However, even if the alliance ends, the learning has taken place, so mutual benefit will have been obtained.

In skill-substitution arrangements one partner takes over a particular activity because it is the stronger performer. Thus one partner may manufacture, the other market and sell. This is less risky since proprietary information is less likely to be given away, and if the arrangement founders the partners merely need to find another partner. However, little learning may have taken place, so the feeling of failure may be all the greater. Such arrangements are less likely to spawn strong competitors.

Clearly many cooperative arrangements exhibit aspects of both variety of cooperation. Partners in virtual corporations may well also learn, and partners in learning alliances are likely to carry out some activity specialization within the alliance. Rover set out in its cooperation with Honda by seeking a knockdown kit of a Honda car to badge as a Triumph (skill substitution), and ended up in a major exercise of manufacturing-process improvement (learning). The two distinct concepts do exist, however, and are, we believe, helpful as ideas to be borne in mind when one organization is considering entering into a cooperative arrangement with another.

EXTERNAL CHALLENGES

From an economic perspective, the main argument for alliances is that they are usually formed as a result of an external stimulus or change in environmental conditions to which companies respond with a feeling of internal corporate need that they feel is best met by seeking a relationship with another corporation (Nelson 1995).

What might be called an eclectic theory of alliance motivation (cf. Dunning 1974) suggests that all alliances are sparked off by a change in external trading conditions, and that this change reveals an internal resource inadequacy that needs to be corrected if competitive advantage is to be maintained. An alliance will result if both a company and its proposed partner, on analysis, find themselves to have complementary resources and perceived inadequacies. The theory is termed eclectic since there exists a long list of both external and internal conditions, any one of each of which is sufficient to provide the ground motivations for an alliance. For example, the external driver for one company might be the need to achieve scale economies to be able to compete on the world market and the internal need might be to fill underutilized factory capacity. For the other company, the external driver might be a shortened product life cycle, and the internal driver an insufficiently innovative design team, or inadequate investment funds.

Whatever the external and internal drivers, one of both is necessary for each potential partner to provide a strong enough motivation for a strategic alliance. Cooperation between the companies, however, might be motivated unilaterally. DeFillippi and Reed (1991) distinguish here between unilateral arrangements and bilateral agreements (strategic alliances). Unilateral arrangements come about when one company perceives a resource-deficiency need that can be satisfied by another company, but the feeling is not reciprocated by the other company. Thus Rover might have needed Honda's technology skills, at a time when Honda needed nothing from Rover. In this case Honda might have licensed the technology, and provided technical consultancy for a royalty and a consultancy day rate. This is a unilateral arrangement. A resource is transferred in exchange for money. Such arrangements are regularly provided in outsourcing agreements, consultancy studies, and externally provided training courses. These are still cooperative strategies but not strategic alliances. In fact, Rover did require Honda's technology, but Honda for its part required Rover's European styling skills. This provided the conditions for a bilateral agreement—i.e. a strategic alliance.

The External Driving Forces of the Automobile Market

Rover and Honda set up a collaborative alliance in 1979 which lasted in its full form until Rover was bought from its parent British Aerospace in 1993 by BMW, a strong competitor of Honda. Although the motivations for the collaboration were strong and varied on the internal side, there were powerful external stimuli in the automobile industry driving manufacturers towards the conclusion of alliances with their competitors and their 'complementors'. The world automobile industry has become increasingly global over the last decade. It has also exhibited increasing demand turbulence. Economies of scale have increased in its dominant technologies in many areas due in large part to the growing use of robotics. A combination of fast-changing technologies and the growth of fashion demand has led to the continuing shortening of product life cycles, resulting in growing investment requirements which are frequently too onerous for one company to finance alone.

Source: Faulkner (1995).

The conjunction of certain conditions in the structure and nature of the external environment makes alliances more likely at some periods of economic and political history than at others, as illustrated in the Box. Periods of trade protectionism, and of strong anti-trust movements, militate against alliance formation. At such times, cooperative activity between companies tends to be denigrated as anti-competition or as constituting cartels. Correspondingly, during periods when the power of the giant multinational enterprise is perceived as being excessive, but world trade is buoyant, the less threatening nature of the strategic alliance comes into favour, set up as it is to combat the threat of the multinational and frequently giving a competitive chance to smaller more flexible companies.

The growing globalization, and regionalization of markets since the mid-1980s, with the steady reduction of trade barriers, has led to the dramatic growth of cross-border alliances. This has been accompanied by considerable economic turbulence and uncertainty in world markets, and the growth of the free-market ideology in most countries of the world. This is in contrast to the immediately preceding period of economic history, when the ideology of the planned economies of the socialist and communist world stood as an apparently viable alternative economic system to that based on markets. The growth of trade with emerging nations in the Far East and with South America, and in particular with a potential economic colossus like China, leads to a particularly strong external driver for the development of cooperation, since few Western companies possess the cultural knowledge to succeed alone in the East. Chapter 12 will discuss this particular issue in more detail.

Some of the key external driving forces for alliance formation in the 1990s are:

1. turbulence in world markets and high economic uncertainty;
2. the existence of economies of scale and/or scope as competitive cost-reducing agents;
3. the globalization or regionalization of a growing number of industries;
4. the globalization of technology;
5. fast technological change leading to ever-increasing investment requirements;
6. shortening product life cycles.

Turbulence, economic uncertainty, and technological change are often interrelated. This is particularly so at times where the revolutionary phase of the punctuated equilibrium paradigm is at its height (Gersick 1991). According to this concept, the economic phase operates under stable conditions for long periods, and only incrementally changing technologies spawn products with dominant design paradigms which are accepted by the market place. These periods are punctuated, however, by periods of economic ferment in which major technological changes take place, old products are replaced by new, old companies die, and new ones arise. In such circumstances the economic scene becomes very volatile, and the development of networks and alliances provides some security and buffering against external threats to survival. In such a theory, as the new equilibrium develops, the alliances are likely to be converted to mergers, and stability to re-emerge. In reality, of course, such theoretical large-scale environmental determinism may be unduly simplistic. Much anecdotal evidence, however, can be adduced to illustrate the theory—for example, the transistor replacing the valve, expanding applications of the microchip, and so forth.

The external drivers of alliances of technology change, economic uncertainty, and increasing turbulence resonate also with Tushman and Anderson's (1986) identification of competence-enhancing and competence-destroying technological change. They observe that technology evolves through periods of incremental change shaken up by periodic technological breakthroughs that either enhance or destroy the competence of firms in an industry. Illustrations of technological discontinuities that are likely to be competence destroying are jet engines, float glass, or plain paper copying. These relatively rare technological changes trigger a period of technological and product/market volatility which does not cease until a new dominant design paradigm (Teece 1986) emerges. Incremental technological advances enhance and extend the underlying technology and thus reinforce the established technical order. Competence-destroying advances are likely to be developed by new firms (Tushman and Anderson 1989) and disrupt the existing industry structure. Competitive uncertainty is therefore increased and an external environmental driver for alliance creation is brought about.

Not all the above conditions, of course, are necessary to provide the external stimulus for alliance formation at any one time. Most, however, can readily be observed in the economic and political world of the 1990s. Any single strong external factor impelling firms towards alliance formation is sufficient to set the alliance train in motion, without any one specific factor being necessary in itself.

Faulkner (1995) reports that managers in the ten alliances he studied (see Appendix) differed considerably in the external drivers they stated had been relevant for alliance formation. Only managers involved with the Rover–Honda alliance claimed that all the factors we have identified were important external drivers, and those in the ICL–Fujitsu alliance identified all except economic turbulence in their markets. The most common external factor identified was globalization of markets, followed closely by perceived opportunities for economies of scale or of scope, and the need to gear up to fast technological change. All three of these factors were emphasized by executives from the 'Eurobrek', Rover–Honda, ICL–Fujitsu, and Courtaulds–Nippon Paint alliances.

These findings are consistent with the most common explanation of the rapid growth of alliances in recent years, which takes the following form. Technological change has become increasingly rapid, and global in nature. As a result, the difference between regional markets has become smaller (Levitt 1960; Ohmae 1985). Globalization of markets has given major opportunities for companies to realize economies of scale and scope. These factors have lowered unit costs for the firms large enough to take advantage of them. However, a side effect of technological change and globalization has been shortening product life cycles, leading to ever-increasing demand for investment both to install the new technology and to develop new products. Competitive advantage has therefore accrued to the company able to adopt the new technologies, achieve economies of scale and scope, serve global markets, and change its product range regularly. Since few companies have the internal resources and competencies to meet this range of requirements, there has been a widespread resort to strategic alliances and other cooperative arrangements to cope with the needs of the new economic order. These alliances have been termed 'scale' alliances, since the motive for their formation is primarily to achieve economies of scale and/or reduce development costs (Hennart 1988; Garrette and Dussauge 1995).

A significant number of the alliances Faulkner investigated yielded clear evidence to support the above scenario. Eurovynyl Chloride, the joint venture between ICI and Enichem, was set up in response to the globalization of the PVC market. This had led to the growth of modern capacity in the Far East which challenged the older capacity of ICI and Enichem in Europe. The joint venture had the primary purpose of retiring non-economic capacity in a measured way without damaging the market price of the commodity, and hence returning the European units to profit.

Cable & Wireless operates in the strongly global telecommunications market. This market is driven by technology change, demanding the resources of a major global player. A strategy of alliances has therefore proved the natural route for C&W, even where such alliances do not show a short-term profit.

This is the entry fee to being taken seriously in a global market. The company has, with a number of Japanese partners including Toyota and C Itoh, set up an international telecoms consortium in Japan called International Digital Corporation (IDC) with the purpose of developing both the necessary financial strength and market access, as well as exposure to an unfamiliar Japanese market.

A similar argument applies to the ICL–Fujitsu alliance. This case offers a further interesting perspective in respect of Fujitsu's belief that the alliance route gives competitive advantage over the large integrated company with its bureaucratic costs and single view. IBM's recent internal restructuring from a unitary hierarchy to a federal structure gives some credence to the growing currency of this attitude. Fujitsu is in the process of developing a world-wide 'family' as it describes it, so that it can become sufficiently powerful anywhere in the world to compete with IBM. ICL, for its part, lacked the size, reach, and financial muscle to become a world player and could realize these strengths only through a Fujitsu-style partnership, first as an alliance and later as a subsidiary retaining its own legal and corporate identity.

The Courtaulds Coatings and Nippon Paint alliance was initially restricted to the marine paint market, where globalization and technology change are key factors. However, market access is also important, and this made Nippon attractive to Courtaulds, as the Japanese company could guarantee market access in its home country. The alliance was so successful by the mid-1980s that Nippon conceived the ambition to go global independently, thus throwing into doubt the congruency of objectives of the two partners.

The major external forces behind international strategic alliance formation are often inter-related and may stem from varying causes. For example, globalization of markets may lead to technology change, which in turn leads to increased turbulence. Alternatively, the initial driver may be technology change, or even economic turbulence brought about by other possibly political events. The key identifiable current factors, however, seem to be the globalization of markets and technologies, the shortening of product life cycles, and the consequent need for enterprises large enough to take advantage of scale and scope economies, and to be able to access adequate resources and competencies. Other factors exist in specific situations, and these are less generalizable in nature. As with the internal motivations, however, they relate in the main to perceived resource or competency imbalances in the face of the external challenges, threats, opportunities, and competition.

INTERNAL NEEDS

Pfeffer and Nowak (1976) and later Porter and Fuller (1986) suggest several possible reasons for concluding strategic alliances which may be seen from the perspective of internal stimuli:

1. to achieve economies of scale and of learning with one's partner;
2. to get access to the benefits of the other firm's assets, be these technology, market access, capital, production capacity, products, or manpower;
3. to reduce risk by sharing it, notably in terms of capital requirements, but also often in respect of research and development expenditure;
4. to help shape the market—for example, to withdraw capacity in a mature market.

There may also be opportunities through the medium of alliances for the achievement of value-chain synergies (Porter 1986) which extend beyond the mere pooling of assets and include such matters as process rationalization, and even systems improvement.

Resource dependency

Companies are motivated to form alliances for a wide variety of specific reasons, but most come under the heading of perceived resource deficiency (see Chapter 2 on the resource-dependency perspective). Alliances may be of the defensive variety in which the partners collaborate in order to defend their domains in the face of an external threat from a common enemy. Or they may be aggressive, taking advantage of the globalization of their market to realize opportunities to operate with a partner on a global scale. In either case, the motivation for the alliance is resource based. Alone, the potential of each partner's value chains, financial and other resources, core competencies and skills, and networks of contacts is inadequate to achieve its identified objectives, but together the potential synergies from cooperation are perceived as leading to competitive advantage, jointly but not separately available.

A key internal motivation for alliance formation is thus to gain the requisite skills or resources needed to respond to an external challenge or opportunity of some sort. The alliance between ICI Pharmaceuticals and Sumitomo Chemicals provides an illustration (see Box).

The specific needs will vary in nature, but all can normally be classified as feelings of a specific resource, skills, or competency inadequacy or imbalance. Such an imbalance does not need to be skill deficiency. It may, for example, be surplus production capacity, as it was with Rover, which operated with half-empty plants when it first met Honda. Each of the partners in an alliance is likely to seek a different resource or skill compensation from the other. Unless both are able to match their resource or competency needs in a particular partner, then they do not have the right partner. Their options are then to seek a different partner, or alternatively to buy in the skill from the proposed partner, but without providing a complementary skill in return. In this case the deal will be a unilateral exchange and not an alliance.

Bartholomew (1997) illustrates this at a national level in biotechnology research. She notes that German firms typically enter alliances with US firms as a means of operating in a more flexible regulatory regime. Japanese firms,

ICI Pharma

In 1972 ICI Pharmaceuticals (now Zeneca plc) established a joint venture with Sumitomo Chemicals to manufacture and market some of ICI's ethical products in Japan. The joint-venture company was called ICI Pharma and sited in Japan. The internal motivations for this arrangement can be summarized as follows:

(*a*) ICI, although a worldwide chemicals company, was at the time very deficient in business knowledge of Japan. It had few contacts in that part of the world and lacked the ability to market there unaided. The Japanese market was very nationalistic and products made by companies without a Japanese partner did not find ready acceptance. ICI lacked experience in acquiring the necessary pharmaceutical consents and patents to sell its products in Japan. It was also unaccustomed to manufacturing in that country.

(*b*) Sumitomo was able to supply the skills to make up for ICI's deficiencies in these areas. It in turn had its own resource problems. Sumitomo was a very small player in the worldwide pharmaceutical market and lacked a wide range of proprietary products upon which to build a pharmaceutical business. It also lacked ICI's reputation in this area. The respective internal dependency drivers of the companies were therefore complementary.

Source: Faulkner (1995).

however, tend to form alliances with US partners largely in order to gain access to leading-edge research as well as learning how the US research system works. US firms, however, cooperate across borders largely to spread the financial risk of expensive R&D programmes. In all cases the partners tend to get what they want, and it is the provision of skills or resources in which they feel themselves to be limited.

Faulkner (1995) found that its reputation was the strongest internal motivation for choosing the particular alliance partner, coupled with the access to new and strong brand names which the partner could provide. This would suggest a difficulty in forming an effective alliance for companies without either a well established reputation or strong brand names. An alliance of two weak companies leads to a vulnerable alliance. Local knowledge, marketing skills, and distribution channels were other factors commonly cited.

Of other possible resource needs, key labour skills of one type or another were declared as motivating needs by Eurobrek, ICI Pharma, and C&W. In a number of alliances the partner's managerial skills were the attractions. The EVC and Imperial Tobacco alliances were attracted by at least one of the partners' access to raw materials, and C&W identified legal requirements as its basic need in seeking to ally with a consortium of major Japanese corporations.

For an alliance to be formed, it is clear that a mutual resource-dependency perception is often a key internal motivator, and that both partners are likely to have different but complementary resource needs which they perceive their chosen partner can help them to meet. The specific nature of the resource dependencies will of course be contingent on specific circumstances.

There is more than one way of dealing with a perception of resource deficiency. Alternative actions might involve raising further capital in the market, recruiting key personnel in areas of perceived expertise weakness, a merger, or an acquisition, or the development of contractual arrangement to license technology in or distribution out. Resource deficiency, then, is one important condition for alliance formation, but not a necessary one, in the face of the alternative ways of dealing with that deficiency.

Learning

Powell, Koput, and Smith-Doerr (1996) look at the question of alliances and the motivation for forming them from a different perspective. In their view the resource-dependency view, whilst insightful, does not capture the fundamental motives of firms and academics involved in the scientific networks that lead to much breakthrough research in biotechnology. They stress that:

Knowledge creation occurs in the context of a community, one that is fluid and evolving rather than tightly bound or static. The canonical formal organization with its bureaucratic rigidities is a poor vehicle for learning. Sources of innovation do not reside exclusively inside firms; instead they are commonly found in the interstices between firms, universities, research laboratories, suppliers and customers. (Powell *et al.* 1996: 118)

The motivation of firms involved in such innovation is to become part of a community in which new discoveries will be made. The aim is therefore that of learning, a theme that underlies so much of this book. The research conducted by Powell and his colleagues provides strong evidence for the contention that in industries which are complex and expanding, and where the sources of expertise are widely dispersed, innovation will be found mostly in networks of learning firms rather than in individual firms. They suggest, in fact, that the R&D intensity of such an industry is positively correlated with the number of alliances it exhibits. In highly networked industries like biotechnology intense and long-term relationships develop that are fundamentally directed at innovation, and are not one-off arrangements that make up for mutual resource deficiencies. They are dynamic in that they look to the shaping of the industry in the future. Biotech firms, Powell *et al.* found, grow through being connected to rich R&D networks. The most successful biotech firms were those most central in the various networks of research alliances in the industry.

Powell *et al.* also note that the cycle of learning which was visible in the firms researched was path-dependent, but that actual innovations were serendipitous, as they frequently are in scientific research. The complexity, intensity, and variety of alliances were important factors in affording the flexibility to a learning constellation necessary to take advantage of such unexpected discoveries. In their industry,

firms without ties are becoming increasingly rare; the modal firm has multiple partnerships . . . the field is becoming more tightly connected not in spite of, but because of a marked increase in the number of partners involved in alliances with dedicated biotechnology firms . . . We take this increasing connectivity within an expanding universe as further evidence that two processes of learning are occurring simultaneously and recursively. First, firms are increasingly using ties to enhance the inflow of specific information, resources and products. Second, firms are becoming much more adept at and reputed for the general practice of collaboration with diverse partners.   (Powell *et al.* 1996: 142)

Risk limitation

A further factor advancing alliance formation as opposed to the alternatives of merger/acquisition or organic development is the need to limit risk. The spreading of financial risk is frequently cited as a fundamental motivation for the formation of strategic alliances (Mariti and Smiley 1983; Porter and Fuller 1986). It seems also intuitively likely that a company with only moderate financial resources may deal with either an opportunity or a defensive challenge, by seeking an alliance with a partner who can help spread the financial risk. This is particularly prevalent in R&D alliances between medium-sized partners, or between business corporations and academic institutions. Stata (1989) cites collaborative research of this nature as a strong force in bringing about innovation in industry. It is an area in which the Western business world has some catching up to do compared with say Japan or other developed Far-Eastern countries where such collaboration is embedded in the culture (Gerlach 1992).

Speed to market

Another motive behind the conclusion of strategic alliances is the need for speed in reaching the market (Lei and Slocum 1991). In the economic world of the 1990s, first-mover advantages are becoming paramount, and often the conclusion of an alliance between a technologically strong company with new products, and a company with strong market access is the only way to take advantage of an opportunity in time.

Even if a company has sufficient funds to approach an opportunity through organic development, this may not lead to substantial market presence fast enough to take successful advantage of the opportunity. Alliances are the fastest means of achieving market presence to meet an opportunity, if the partners each have strong resources and competencies, but alone insufficient to achieve critical mass. Internal development would take much longer, and acquisition has the disadvantage of the possible demotivating effect of the subsidiary relationship, and the higher level of investment required. Eight out of ten of the cases analysed by Faulkner (1995) claimed speed to market as an important motivating factor in alliance formation.

In increasing-returns industries, speed to market can make all the difference between market dominance and being rapidly marginalized, however superior one's technology. Competition between technologies may have multiple potential outcomes, quite by chance, or through an early lead which locks out competitors. Historical events may indeed lock in an industry to the monopoly of an inferior product. The issue is of path dependence and ultimate single-technology dominance. Such increasing-returns industries are volatile, and have no predictable equilibrium. As Arthur (1989) claims, the adoption of petrol rather than steam for cars seems to have happened largely by chance early in the century, although the automobile industry is not one that would be normally associated with the increasing-returns phenomenon. Speed to market, however, may be a vital key to success, as is an early development of the dominant design.

Cost minimization

The question of the efficiency of the alliance form in meeting a need is a further factor for an organization to consider when deciding whether or not to pursue the alliance route. The efficiency criterion is captured in transaction-costs theory, which holds that companies will form alliances, rather than adopt other strategic options, only if the transaction costs involved in so doing are perceived to be lower than those for the other options. Transaction costs are in many aspects highly judgemental entities, since they involve such basically unquantifiable costs as loss of proprietary expertise to a partner who subsequently becomes a competitor. Although such costs may well be important, they cannot easily be computed, as can costs of production, and it is questionable whether they are considered in detail before deciding to set up an alliance.

It is often suggested by the organizational economics school (Williamson 1985) that an alliance will be set up only if the partners consider that the transaction and other costs involved in the proposed alliance are less than those that would be incurred by alternative strategic actions. This proposition is a difficult one to substantiate, mainly because the decision-takers in the alliances are generally unaware of the concept of transaction costs, and its somewhat sophisticated implications. When it was explained to them in Faulkner's research, no interviewees claimed it had been even an implicit motivating factor in the setting-up of the alliance.

In the literature on strategic alliances, transaction-costs analysis holds a very strong position (e.g. Williamson, 1975, 1985; Barney 1986; Thorelli 1986;

Beamish and Banks 1987; Griesinger 1990; Hill 1990). Chapter 2 has addressed the issue in some detail and it can be seen that, while firms may not consciously calculate transaction costs in deciding whether on not to set up an alliance, if they decide on a course of action in which transaction costs are high they will become uncompetitive and have either to adjust or to fail.

Before adopting the transaction-costs perspective—that is, the efficiency motivation—as a necessary and sufficient criterion for alliance formation, it should be noted that transaction-costs analysis ignores a number of factors which critically influence decision-makers. As Ring and Van de Ven (1994: 93) point out, transaction-costs analysis deals only with costs and hence efficiency, but does not allow equity or fairness to play a part in the decision-making process:

As reflected in transactions cost theory, researchers use efficiency to define the most expeditious and least costly governance structure for undertaking a transaction, given production cost constraints. We assume that an equally important criterion for assessing a cooperative IOR is equity, defined as fair dealing . . . perceptions of equity operate as a lower-bound constraint on efficiency.

Transaction-costs analysis also omits to value the importance of trust in establishing alliances. An alliance may be proposed to minimize transaction costs, but if the partners mistrust each other it is unlikely to be a successful alliance. Trust is a difficult area, since people who may be trustworthy in their private lives may fail to be in their corporate life, if the corporate culture of their employer emphasizes guile and hard bargaining as corporate values (Guitot 1977, cited in Ring and Van de Ven 1994).

Finally, transaction-costs analysis does not take adequate account of the varying levels of risk involved in different governance structures (Faulkner and Bowman 1994). To carry out an activity internally *ceteris paribus* clearly involves less risk than does any other method, since the highest level of employee control is present, and teams within a company have experience of working together. Alliances have in general a fairly high level of risk. They involve less investment than acquisitions or internal development, and only come about after extensive negotiation, but they still involve unfamiliar actors working together across company boundaries. Acquisitions generally carry the highest level of risk.

Motives geared to the reduction of transaction costs can therefore account only partially for alliance formation. The evolutionary economists' argument (Nelson 1995) that natural selection will ultimately leave only the naturally selected lowest-transaction-costs actors in the game is also highly deterministic. As Hannan and Freeman (1989) point out, inertia often prevents transaction costs leading to changes in organizational form, and political and institutional factors are often stronger action determinants than efficiency arguments. Paterson (1992) cites Jacquemin (1989), Litwak and Rothman (1970), and Mariti and Smiley (1983) as advancing arguments to the effect that costs are only one factor in alliance form determination, and not necessarily the most important one. There is little evidence to show that, in computing costs, such factors as the potential cost of opportunism, of impacted information, or of contractual arrangements are taken into account, as they would be in any transaction-costs analysis, although the potential leakage of proprietary information outside the agreement is a common worry. Thus, whereas the low costs of an alliance relative to an alternative form is a positive factor in motivating partners, transaction-costs analysis in its purist sense is neither understood nor calculated even in qualitative terms. It has to be admitted that, even if the concept were fully understood by decision-takers, it is difficult to see how an agreed transaction-cost figure could be arrived at that would quantify such factors as information impactedness, opportunism, or inappropriate proprietary expertise transference.

This is not, however, to dismiss the concept of transaction costs as unimportant in the longer-run 'ecological' sense, since what may not be a strong motivating factor for alliance formation may still exert a powerful influence on ultimate survival.

Current poor performance

Bolton (1993) suggests in her research that a prime motivator for becoming involved in cooperative activity, particularly in innovative R&D, is existing poor performance. This leads the top management of the organization to seek out a means of changing the formula it is presenting to the market. Cooperation is a readily available means of doing this. Poor performers were found by Bolton to be early joiners of R&D collaborations, whereas good performers were late joiners. This is explicable by reference to an implied risk profile. If performance is currently poor, there is little to be lost by finding something different to do in order to improve results. Such an incentive is much weaker when things are currently going well, although an alliance may still be considered to address a deficiency which is thought likely to impact on performance in the longer term.

SUMMARY

In summary, alliances need for their initial stimulus a challenge from a changing external environment. If then an organization develops a feeling of resource deficiency in relation to such an external change, or if it wants to spread risk, or needs to get into a market fast, and believes that the transaction costs of an alliance would be less than those incurred from internal development or acquisition, then the motivation for an alliance exists. If a partner can be found with a similar and complementary motivation, then the circumstances for the conclusion of an alliance are in place.

So runs the economic argument for the establishment of alliances. However, such explanations need to be supplemented by the identification of motivations that stem from political agendas within firms. The economic arguments may be necessary but they are not always sufficient. Ultimately neither transactions costs, the extent of risk, nor future economic benefits can be known at the time the decision is taken to set up an alliance. There must, therefore, also be a political motive for the alliance, perceived by a coalition of the company's key decision-makers. Political agendas are many and varied within a corporation, and, in the absence of corporate champions able to focus such a coalition towards cooperative action, the motives for the formation of strategic alliances may be insufficient to lead to their creation.

Finally the motivation to cooperate remains high even when the alliance has exposed the partners to the temptation to steal each others' secret and run, so long as the alliance is of indeterminate length, the penalties for defection are high, and reputations matter.

REFERENCES

Aiken, M., and Hage, J. (1968), 'Organizational Interdependence and Intra-Organizational Structure', *American Sociological Review*, 33: 912–30.

Arthur, W. B. (1989), 'Competing Technologies, Increasing Returns, and Lock-In by Historical Events', *Economic Journal*, 99: 116–31.

Axelrod, R. (1984), *The Evolution of Cooperation* (New York: HarperCollins).

Barney, J. B. (1986), 'Organization Culture: Can it be a Source of Sustainable Competitive Advantage?', *Academy of Management Review*, 11: 656–65.

Bartholomew, S. (1997), 'National Systems of Biotechnology Innovation: Complex Interdependence in the Global System', *Journal of International Business Studies*, 28: 241–66.

Beamish, R. W., and Banks, J. C. (1987), 'Equity Joint Ventures and the Theory of the Multinational Enterprise', *Journal of International Business Studies*, Summer: 1–15.

Bolton, M. K. (1993), 'Organizational Innovation and Substandard Performance: When is Necessity the Mother of Innovation?', *Organization Science*, 4: 57–75.

Contractor, F. J., and Lorange, P. (1988) (eds.), 'Why Should Firms Cooperate?: The Strategy and Economic Basis for Cooperative Ventures', in F. J. Contractor and P. Lorange (eds.), *Cooperative Strategies in International Business* (New York: Lexington Books), 3–28.

Chandler, A. D. (1986), 'The Evolution of Modern Global Competition', in M. E. Porter (ed.), *Competition in Global Industries* (Boston, Mass.: Harvard Business School Press).

Collins, T., and Doorley, T. (1991), *Teaming Up for the 90's* (Homewood, Ill.: Irwin).

Defillippi, R., and Reed, R. (1991), 'Three Perspectives on Appropriation Hazards in Cooperative Agreements', paper presented to Strategic Management Society Conference, Toronto.

Dunning, J. H. (1974), *Economic Analysis and the Multinational Enterprise* (London: Allen and Unwin).

Faulkner, D. O. (1995), *International Strategic Alliances: Co-operating to Compete* (Maidenhead: McGraw-Hill).

——and Bowman, C. C. (1994), *The Essence of Competitive Strategy* (London: Prentice-Hall).

Garrette, B., and Dussauge, P. (1995), 'Patterns of Strategic Alliances between Rival Firms', *Group Decision and Negotiation,* 4: 429–52.

Gerlach, M. L. (1992), *Alliance Capitalism* (Berkeley and Los Angeles: University of California Press).

Gersick, C. J. G. (1991), 'Revolutionary Change Theories: A Multilevel Exploration of the Punctuated Equilibrium Paradigm', *Academy of Management Review,* 16/1: 10–36.

Gomes-Casseres, B. (1987), 'Joint Venture Instability: Is it a Problem?', *Columbia Journal of World Business,* 22: 97–101.

Griesinger, D. W. (1990), 'The Human Side of Economic Organization', *Academy of Management Review,* 15/3: 478–99.

Guitot, J.M. (1977), 'Attribution and Identity Construction: Some Comments', *American Sociological Review,* 42: 692–704

Hannan, M. T., and Freeman, J. (1989), *Organization Ecology* (Cambridge, Mass.: Harvard University Press).

Harrigan, K. R. (1984), 'Joint Ventures and Global Strategies', *Columbia Journal of World Business,* 19/2 (Summer), 7–16.

——(1988), 'Joint Ventures and Competitive Strategy', *Strategic Management Journal,* 9: 141–58.

Hennart, J.-F. (1988), 'A Transaction Cost Theory of Equity Joint Ventures', *Strategic Management Journal,* 9: 361–74.

Hill, C. W. L. (1990), 'Cooperation, Opportunism, and the Invisible Hand: Implications for Transaction Cost Theory', *Academy of Management Review,* 15/3: 500–13.

Hrebiniak, L. G. (1992), 'Implementing Global Strategies', *European Management Journal,* 10/4 (Dec.), 392–403.

Jacquemin, A. P. (1989), *The New Industrial Economics: Market Forces and Strategic Behaviour* (Cambridge, Mass.: MIT Press).

Jorde, T. M., and Teece, D. J. (1989), 'Competition and Cooperation: Striking the Right Balance', *California Management Review,* 31: 25–37.

Kogut, B. (1988), 'Joint Ventures: Theoretical and Empirical Perspectives', *Strategic Management Journal,* 9: 319–32.

Lei, D. and Slocum, J. W., Jr. (1991), 'Global Strategic Alliances; Payoffs and Pitfalls', *Organizational Dynamics,* 44–62.

Levitt, T. (1960), 'Marketing Myopia', in Levitt, *The Marketing Imagination* (New York: Free Press), 141–72.

Litwak, E., and Rothman, J. (1970), 'Towards the Theory and Practice of Coordination between Formal Organizations', in W. R. Rosengren and M. Lefton (eds.), *Organizations and Clients: Essays in the Sociology of Service* (Columbus, Oh.: Charles E Merrill).

Mariti, P., and Smiley, R. H. (1983), 'Co-operative Agreements and the Organization of Industry', *Journal of Industrial Economics,* 31: 437–51.

Nelson, R. R (1995), 'Recent Evolutionary Theorising about Economic Change', *Journal of Economic Literature,* 33/1: 48–90.

Ohmae, K. (1985), *Triad Power: The Coming Shape of Global Competition* (New York: Free Press).

Paterson, D. (1992), 'Cooperation for Competition: The Formation and Growth of

"Strategic" Networks in the International Motor Vehicle Industry 1959–1988', unpublished Ph.D. dissertation (Notre Dame University, Indiana).

Pfeffer, J., and Nowak, P. (1976), 'Joint Ventures and Interorganizational Interdependence', *Administrative Science Quarterly*, 21: 398–417.

Polanyi, K. (1966), *The Tacit Dimension* (London: Routledge & Kegan Paul).

Porter, M. E. (1986), *Competition in Global Industries* (Boston, Mass.: Harvard Business School Press Press).

—— and Fuller, M. B. (1986), 'Coalitions and Global Strategy', in M. E. Porter (ed.), *Competition in Global Industries* (Boston, Mass.: Harvard Business School Press), 315–44.

Powell, W. W., Koput, K. W., and Smith-Doerr, L. (1996), 'Interorganizational Collaboration and the Locus of Innovation: Networks of Learning in Biotechnology', *Administrative Science Quarterly*, 41: 116–45.

Ridley, M. (1996), *The Origins of Virtue* (St Ives: Viking).

Ring, P. S., and Van de Ven, A. H. (1994), 'Developmental Processes of Cooperative Interorganizational Relationships', *Academy of Management Review*, 19/1: 90–118.

Root, F. R. (1994), *Entry Strategies for International Markets* (2nd edn., New York: Lexington Books).

Stata, R. (1989), 'Organizational Learning—The Key to Management Innovation', *Sloan Management Review* (Spring), 63–74.

Tallman, S. B., and Shenkar, O. (1994), 'A Managerial Decision Model of International Cooperative Venture Formation', *Journal of International Business Studies*, 25: 91–113.

Teece, D. J. (1986), 'Profiting from Technological Innovation', *Research Policy*, 15: 285–305

Thorelli, H. B. (1986), 'Networks: Between Markets and Hierarchies', *Strategic Management Journal*, 7: 37–51.

Tushman, M. L., and Anderson, P. (1986), 'Technological Discontinuities and Organizational Environments', *Administrative Science Quarterly*, 31: 439–65.

Williamson, O. E. (1975), *Markets and Hierarchies* (New York: Free Press).

—— (1985), *The Economic Institutions of Capitalism: Firms, Markets, Relational Contracting* (New York: Free Press).

Young, S., Hamill, J., Wheller, C., and Davies, J. R. (1989), *International Market Entry and Development* (London: Harvester Wheatsheaf).

II

ESTABLISHING COOPERATION

This part of the book deals with those aspects of cooperation that precede the actual business of working together. This is the area that has so far attracted the greatest amount of attention in the literature, and also amongst practitioners.

Once a company has developed the political will to attempt to solve some of its problems through seeking an alliance partner, it has to address a number of issues. It must identify the sort of partner it wants, and form a clear view about what each of them is likely to bring to the relationship. Then, it must work with its proposed partner to agree how these respective contributions can be valued in a fashion that is fair to both partners, taking note of the downside risks and the upside potential. Finally, it must decide upon an alliance form—the structure and systems that are to form the basic framework for bringing the alliances to life. All this needs to be done before the alliance can come into being.

Chapter 5 considers the critical issue of what sort of company would make a good partner. It notes that most companies are able to assess their prospective partners in terms of the complementarity of their assets and skills and the possible synergies that arise as a result of them. Few, however, devote sufficient attention to the cultural compatibility between the partners. Yet this factor is often responsible for the breakdown of alliances. Having dealt with the issue of how to choose a partner, the chapter then deals with the selection of an appropriate form of cooperation.

Chapter 6 develops the question of form in examining two other major cooperative models beyond those specific to alliances. These are the various types of network organization including the so-called virtual corporation.

The subject of Chapter 7 is negotiation and valuation. A cooperative agreement has to be negotiated, even in cases where it remains an informal arrangement rather than one sealed by contract. The partners need to be satisfied that they have a fair and reliable agreement on the contributions and benefits they attach to an alliance in order for their relationship to develop fruitfully. An important element in reaching a fair agreement is the valuation of assets allocated by the partners.

5

Partner and Form Selection

THE ALLIANCE IMPERATIVE

Richardson (1972) in an early article on the importance of cooperation in the organization of industry emphasizes that a major reason for its growing importance is the increasingly specialized nature of needs. Whereas, he suggests, it can safely be left to a market to coordinate supply and demand when large numbers of relatively undifferentiated products are bought and sold by large numbers of economic agents, this is not the case when small numbers of buyers and sellers deal in highly differentiated products. In such cases both buyers and sellers need to match their production and purchasing plans, and this sets the scene for cooperation. As Adam Smith and Alfred Chandler might have agreed, the 'visible hand' replaces the 'invisible hand'. A further need for cooperation comes about in Richardson's view when an economic agent seeks in Ryle's concept (1949: ch. 2) 'knowledge how' as opposed to merely 'knowledge that'. 'Knowledge how' is difficult to communicate through the relationship-less mechanism of the market.

Cooperation then is becoming more and more necessary but how does one select a partner? It follows from what has already been said about the importance of trust, and the bases on which it can be created, that the choice of partner is key to the ultimate success of a joint enterprise. This is an issue which it is difficult to research by means of interviews or questionnaires, since partners in an existing alliance are unlikely to express doubts over their choice of partner, whatever the reality of the situation.

Porter and Fuller (1986) identify six criteria by which they believe the appropriateness of an alliance partner may be judged:

1. *Possession by the partner of the desired source of competitive advantage.* By this Porter and Fuller mean that the partner should have the requisite scale, technology, market access or other contribution to give the coalition the competitive advantage that neither partner possesses alone.
2. *The need for a complementary or balanced contribution from the partner.* Porter and Fuller should perhaps have written 'and' not 'or' before

'balanced', since it is probably necessary that the partners are both complementary in their contributions, but also are roughly similar in size or strength so that the partnership is one of equals and not dominated by one or the other partner.

3. *A compatible view of international strategy.* If one partner is intent on concentrating in one trading area, this must be acceptable to the other. Their attitudes to the international coordination and configuration of their joint enterprise must also be congruent.

4. *There must be a low risk of the partner becoming a competitor.* This criterion is often ignored, however, as many alliances are set up between competitors. Examples are Toyota and GM with their US joint venture NUMMI and, as discussed in Chapter 4, Rover and Honda. Clearly such potential future competitiveness does not preclude the possibility of a successful alliance. It does, however, make the ever-present tension between the need to cooperate and the urge to defect and fight one's erstwhile ally more of a problem to the establishment of trust and commitment than it would be in an alliance between partners cooperating at different points in the value chain. As Chapter 2 noted, the dilemma of cooperation versus competition can be elucidated by game theory.

5. *The partner has pre-emptive value in relation to rivals.* Setting up an alliance with the partner would thus undermine the range of apparent strategies of competitors.

6. *The partners' organizational compatibility is high.* This criterion, in Porter's and Fuller's view, reduces the probability of future problems due to cultural conflict.

Lorange and Roos (1992: 30) take a similar view to that suggested by criteria 1 and 2 above:

The business that each party brings into the strategic alliance should also be assessed in terms of its strength relative to its competition. Is it an established leader? Or is it more a follower, behind its competition and in need of catching up? . . . What are the broad readily apparent benefits from this strategic alliance for each partner? How can the two parties complement each other to create common strengths from which both can benefit?

Bleackley (1991: 49) also notes: 'The choice of a partner has to be more than just a good idea: It is imperative that, when evaluating potential partners, companies must consider the reasons why the partner would itself wish to enter into an alliance and how it could enhance the partner's strategic position.'

It is important that both partners not only complement each other, but actually need each other. If this is not the case, the one with the lesser degree of need is likely to become aware of this, and exploit its power to the detriment of the alliance. If the need is all one-way, then the deal is best handled by a unilateral arrangement in which money rather than an alliance completes the transaction. Thus if Company *A* needs Company *B*'s technology but

Company *B* has no matching need for anything Company *A* has to offer, then Company *A* should pay Company *B* a royalty, plus a *per diem* for technological advice to effect the technology transfer, if Company *B* is willing to do business. A key issue is therefore to identify the level and nature of the companies' respective expectations from each other before the alliance is concluded.

Bronder and Pritzl (1992: 417) further extend the questions to be addressed in the partner selection process:

A win-win situation from which both partners benefit is an ideal supposition. . . . What are the risks associated with realizing these potentials within a reasonable time frame? What are the sources of these risks? Is our partner really interested in the alliance or is he planning a hidden take-over? How stable is the business environment and the industry? Can we expect fast changes that might lead to an immediate exit of our partner? What is the influence of parent companies?

Kanter (1994), whilst approving of the complementarities theme, takes a different approach to the partner-selection process. She, like many others before her, likens the process to the personal-relationships courtship ritual. If it is like that, she argues, then it is driven by emotional attachment as much as by cold-blooded analysis. The selection process therefore needs three fundamental factors to fall into place for an alliance to be concluded:

1. *Self-analysis.* Relationships benefit when the partners know themselves. It is also important that they are sufficiently experienced to be able to assess each other's qualities fairly accurately.
2. *Chemistry.* Deals often turn, she stresses, on the rapport between chief executives, and it is equally important that the executives from the two companies further down the hierarchy get on well.
3. *Compatibility.* The courtship process tests companies' cultures, their philosophies, and fundamental ways of doing business. It is vital that these be broadly compatible between the companies, if they are to work closely together.

Geringer (1991), whilst also stressing the importance of the complementarity of assets, provides a more complex view of the appropriate determinants of partner-selection criteria, particularly in relation to international joint ventures. He first distinguishes task- and partner-related dimensions of selection criteria, and argues that 'the relative importance of task-related selection criteria is determined by the strategic content of the proposed International Joint Venture and the parent firms, specifically the critical success factors of the venture's competitive environment and the parents' static and dynamic position in relation to these factors' (Geringer 1991: 45). Geringer examined previous research on the selection of international-joint-venture partners, which he concluded was vague regarding selection criteria. As a clarification, he distinguished between two categories of selection criteria. 'Task-related' criteria are those which 'refer to those variables which are intimately related to the viability of a proposed venture's operations' (Geringer 1991: 45), and include features such as access to finance, managerial and employee competences, site facilities, technology, marketing and distribution systems, and a favourable institutional environment or a partner's ability to negotiate acceptable regulatory and public policy provisions. By contrast, 'partner-related' criteria refer to those variables which characterize the partners' national or corporate cultures, their size and structure, the degree of favourable past association between them, and compatibility and trust between their top management teams.

Geringer's second contribution lies in the development of a contingency-based conceptual scheme for explaining the weighting of task-related selection criteria. Here he advances three criteria associated with a parent firm's strategic intent:

1. the extent to which the dimension is perceived to be critical to the venture's performance;
2. the parent's existing strength in the critical success factor dimension in question;
3. the anticipated future level of difficulty likely to be encountered in internal efforts to achieve a viable competitive position in relation to the critical success factor.

Geringer's empirical research suggested that parent companies' evaluations of selection criteria typically involved analysis of both their firm's current and future competitive position in relation to achievement of a full set of critical success factors relevant to their target area of competition. Geringer thus emphasizes the importance of the critical success factors in the area to be attacked and a partner's specific weakness in relation to some of them as key determinants of the type of partner sought in a joint venture.

A number of observations can be drawn from Geringer's work and that of others on partner selection. The relative importance of a given task-related criterion appears to depend on the partner's perception of how crucial the feature is for the cooperative venture's performance, how strong is the partner's ability to provide or gain access to the feature, and how difficult the partner thinks it will be in the future to compete in terms of the feature. If, for example, a company perceives technology leadership to be crucial for the venture's performance (and indeed its own), but that it cannot provide this on its own, it will logically give high priority to finding a partner with which an alliance will be capable of securing that leadership.

Secondly, the selection criteria applied by partners to an alliance between firms from developed and less developed countries tend to differ quite clearly. The former are generally oriented towards market access and accommodation to governmental regulations which may restrict that access to firms which invest directly in the country. Low-cost production and access to scarce materials are also sometimes priority criteria for firms from developed countries. The latter group normally seek access to technology, know-how, managerial expertise, capital, and international markets.

A useful tool for identifying asset and capability complementarities is the make–buy–ally (MBA) matrix, illustrated in Fig. 5.1 below. This assists a company's management to determine how best it should carry out particular activities. The two axes measure dimensions of the relative competences of firms needing to carry out specific activities, and the strategic importance of particular activities to the competitive success of those firms.

		Low	Medium	High
	High	Ally	Invest and make	Make
Strategic importance of activity	Medium	Ally	Ally	Make
	Low	Buy	Buy	Buy

Competence compared with best in market

Fig. 5.1. The make–buy–ally matrix

The following thinking informs the matrix. All companies, even the largest, have finite and therefore scarce resources. It is therefore critical that available resources are internally deployed on strategically significant activities. Very few companies make their own travel arrangements, for example. They subcontract them to a travel company who can then take advantage of scale economies and the experience curve to provide a better and cheaper service then the company could, if it were to carry out the activity itself. It is also doubtful if it is wise to carry out activities in which the company shows little expertise or skill.

Thus, if the activity is of little strategic significance to the company, it should be bought in, even if the company would be very proficient at carrying it out itself. It is not the best use of its scarce resources. If, however, the activity is fairly-to-very strategically significant, and the company carries it out very well, this activity should be performed internally. If the activity is very strategically significant, and the company performs only fairly well, it should invest to improve its performance in the activity. If, however, the activity is fairly-to-very strategically significant, and the company performs it moderately to poorly, an alliance may be needed to enable the company to learn the necessary skills to improve its performance in the activity.

Of course, if there are doubts regarding the company's core business and some claim within the firm that activities in which it is acknowledged to be excellent might actually be of high rather than low strategic significance with a change in business focus, then the matrix cannot help much. A strategic debate needs to take place and be resolved on the issue 'What is our core business and hence our strategic core competences?'

The operational value of the above schema depends on how accurately it is possible to measure strategic significance and efficiency of performance and on an agreed corporate view of the company's mission and scope.

The horizontal axis is relatively easy to measure. Benchmarking activities against those of competitors should give a reasonable measure of a firm's relative competence in a particular activity. Measuring strategic significance is, however, much more difficult. Perhaps the key measure is whether the activity is important to the achievement of competitive advantage. Hence, when Apricot, a computer hardware company, subcontracted all its manufacture to Mitsubishi in 1988, it was taking a large strategic risk, as it was consigning the production of items upon which its reputation depended to a company it did not control. The outcome was that Mitsubishi ultimately bought the whole of Apricot's hardware business in 1989, leaving the company to operate independently only in software.

Tonka Toys is an illustration of a company that subcontracts all its production. It might be thought therefore that, like Apricot, it is putting out a strategically significant activity and thereby making itself vulnerable. However, the company is basically a product selection and marketing company, so the risk is less, since Tonka's competitive advantage lies in the selection of particular toys and their brand marketing.

In selecting a strategic alliance partner, both firms need to complete the matrix noting which activities fall into the ALLY 'L' shape on the matrix. If their prospective partner's ALLY 'L' activities are counterbalanced by an appropriate one in their own 'MAKE' inverted 'L' then synergy exists between them. Thus in Rover's MBA matrix manufacturing quality was in its top-left-hand box but in Honda's top-right-hand box; thus Honda could help Rover improve its quality significantly. This is not yet enough for an alliance. However, Honda's top-left-hand box contained the styling skills necessary for European entry and this corresponded with Rover's styling skills being in their top-right-hand box. This configuration of MBA matrices provided the basis for an alliance which came to involve mutual learning at its core.

PARTNER SELECTION

The two basic qualities sought in a partner are contained in the simple terms:

1. Strategic fit,
2. Cultural fit.

This can be illustrated on the matrix shown in Fig. 5.2. The optimal alliance partners will be in Box 2. In contrast, partners in Box 4 have little chance of being successful. They have no obvious way of achieving competitive advantage in the markets in which they operate, and their cultures are likely to clash. Partners in Box 3 are unlikely to do much better, since, although they may get

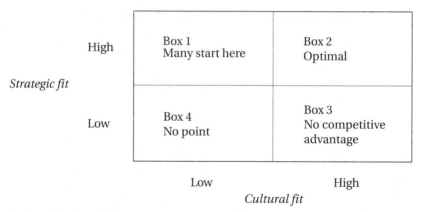

Fig. 5.2. The strategic fit–cultural fit matrix

on well together, their lack of strategic fit will limit their market effectiveness. Box 1 represents a good strategic fit, through which partners have the incentive to work on their cultural differences and reduce the potential conflict in this area. In highlighting the main issues of appropriate partner selection, however, the above matrix also raises the question of how the factors comprising strategic and cultural fit are to be identified.

Strategic fit

The fundamental issue in assessing strategic fit is whether the joint value chain of the partners seems likely to achieve sustainable competitive advantage for the partners. This can be assessed by means of the MBA matrix described above, and in addition by use of Porter's (1985) value-chain tool for company internal analysis. If the answer is that the companies are indeed complementary in asset and capability terms, then the problem of how to set up the alliance should not prove too intractable. If competitive advantage from the joint value chain seems unlikely, then the success of an alliance would be doubtful regardless of its nature and form. The two aspects of the individual value chains to be sought are complementary assets, and potential synergies (Porter and Fuller 1986; Lynch 1990; Bleakley 1991; Lorange and Roos 1992). Both are necessary for success but each insufficient by themselves. Two partners may have complementary assets; for example, one may have good products and the other an efficient sales force. But unless these strengths are sufficiently synergistic to beat the competition, success cannot be expected. Similarly two management teams may display synergistic working methods, but without complementary assets the alliance is likely to have problems settling the issue of who does what, and how the joint organization is to function.

Given synergies between the companies and complementary assets, the potential for achieving competitive advantage will be strong. This will not, however, necessarily guarantee a successful and enduring alliance. For this, the balance of need between the partners must be similar in strength, although it will probably differ in nature (Bleeke and Ernst 1991). Otherwise the alliance will tend towards one-sided dependency (Bertodo 1990). As noted in Chapter 4, resource dependence of one form or another is often a significant factor in bringing the partners together. One partner may have only moderate need of some of the other's resources or skills, but be quite capable alternatively of buying them in the market, if the alliance runs into difficulties. However, the other partner may have urgent need of partner one's resources. In this case, partner two will become excessively dependent on partner one, and this will adversely affect the power balance within the alliance. In the Rover–Honda alliance, the partnership's architect Roland Bertodo (1990) was always afraid that the relationship would, as he put it, fly off into a centrifugal orbit in that Honda would become independent and no longer need Rover in Europe, or a centripetal one in that Rover would become too dependent on Honda and lose its autonomy. In fact Rover was ultimately sold to BMW and so lost its autonomy anyway.

Such a power imbalance may arise if partners are of a significantly different size or, as Bleeke and Ernst (1991) suggest, if one is strong and the other weak. Cooperation between a very large and a very small partner is unlikely to be successful in the long term as an alliance, although of course it may lead to competitive advantage and eventually to the more powerful partner buying the less powerful one on terms acceptable to both, as happened when Mitsubishi Electric bought Apricot Computers, its UK partner, in 1989.

A further criterion of strategic fit is that both partners must supply a deficiency in the other's resources, skills, or other qualities. There is no strategic fit, for example, where one partner has good products but is resource dependent for marketing skills, and the other partner is cash rich, product deficient, but also lacks marketing strength. In this set of circumstances the first mentioned company should probably seek a different partner with strong marketing ability, which also values access to its products, or it should seek to strengthen its marketing by external recruitment. The second mentioned company might consider an acquisition to deploy its financial strength most effectively.

An important condition for continuing success in an alliance is that the long-term objectives of the partners do not conflict (Spekman and Sawhney 1991). This does not mean that they need to be identical, an unlikely scenario where two or more companies are determined to retain their separate identities. Thus in an alliance one company may be concerned to develop its technology worldwide, while the other wishes to economize on R&D expenditure by employing the partner's technology on developing its local market. There is no conflict in this. However, if both wish to develop globally, yet the one importing the technology has limited itself at the outset to being a local partner, future conflict will be difficult to avoid. This was the case when Courtaulds Coatings, a worldwide player and indeed market leader in marine paints, set up an alliance in Japan with Nippon Paint, at the time number four in market share in the Japanese domestic market. The agreement was limited to Japan, with the contractual clause inserted by Courtaulds that Nippon agree not to compete with Courtaulds in the rest of the world. The alliance was very successful in Japan, and Nippon rose to number two in Japanese market share; whereupon its global ambitions increased and the partners' corporate objectives ceased to be congruent. This caused severe problems to the future of the alliance, and led both companies into an extended phase of renegotiation.

The above example illustrates the fact that a strategic fit present when an alliance is set up may not endure several years on. When Henri Wintermans, the Dutch cigar company, concluded an alliance with the cigar division of the Imperial Group in 1989, the two companies had strategic fit. Wintermans wanted market share in cigar sales in the UK, and the Imperial sales force was able to achieve it for them. Imperial's cigar division needed to update its cigar manufacturing technology, and Wintermans was able to help it do this. Four years into the alliance, however, Imperial's technology was 'state of the art', and Wintermans had its coveted UK market share. However, technology only has to be transferred once, but market share has to be won every year. Thus the strategic fit that had brought the alliance into being was no longer there four years later. Imperial would have been excused for being pleased if Wintermans had withdrawn from the UK market, as it could then fill the gap with its own brands. The nature and durability of the strategic fit are therefore as important as its initial existence.

To summarize, a good strategic fit is likely to involve partners of similar size and/or strength, with a similar degree of mutual resource or skill need, and with congruent or at least not overtly conflicting objectives, possessing such complementary assets and potential mutual synergies as are likely to enable them to achieve and retain competitive advantage through optimal use of their joint value chains over at least the medium term.

Culture fit

It is possible that an alliance will show tangible results, justifying itself unconditionally on the grounds of meeting its declared objectives, but will still be in danger of foundering, owing to friction between the partners. This demonstrates the importance of cultural factors in the smooth running of an alliance (Kanter 1989; Lorange and Roos 1992). It is not necessarily important, as we emphasize in Chapter 11, for the cultures of the partners to be similar. If it were, few alliances would succeed, since cultural similarity between companies is extremely rare, especially between partners from different nationalities. Also, since organizational learning is a key to successful alliances, companies that are too similar are unlikely to have much to learn from each other. However, an attitude of understanding of cultural differences, and a willingness to compromise in the face of cultural problems, may well be vital to alliance effectiveness.

The culture of a company inheres in more than just its systems and structures (Hampden-Turner and Trompenaars 1993). Waterman, Peters, and Phillips (1980) with their 7 S model of a firm, which describes the seven aspects of an organization they believe are key, demonstrate that there is more to a firm than the 'hard' factors of strategy, structure, and systems. Its style, the nature of its staff, its skills and perhaps above all its superordinate goals are equally important in contributing to the evolution of its culture. A culture web of the type depicted by Johnson and Scholes (1993) in which a central corporate paradigm is encased in a set of dimensions including symbols, power structures, organization structure, controls, rituals and routines, and stories may be a valuable device for revealing the cultural characteristics that lie behind the way a company operates. If prepared for both partners, it can reveal possible sources of future cultural conflict in the absence of mutual adaptation. Fig. 5.3 illustrates the cultural web of a UK clearing bank in the eyes of some of its managers, as described at a training course run by Faulkner.

Bronder and Pritzl (1992) suggest a further way of assessing cultural fit, which is illustrated in Fig. 5.4. This spider diagram develops a profile of both companies that is overlaid the one on the other to show clear areas of potential cultural conflict. The areas of culture selected by Bronder and Pritzl are employee orientation, environmental orientation, international orientation, customer orientation, technology orientation, innovation orientation, cost orientation, and quality orientation. Clearly the importance of these factors will vary by industry and other contingent circumstances, but a clear difference between the profiles of two prospective partners on any of these dimensions would raise an issue.

Buono and Bowditch (1989) suggest a number of alternative reactions on identifying areas of potentially conflicting cultural orientation:

1. *Cultural pluralism.* The two distinct cultures may be allowed to exist next to each other.
2. *Cultural assimilation.* The positive aspects from both cultures can be combined to form a new culture over a period of time.
3. *Cultural transfer.* One partner may attempt to transfer its culture, as both partners regard it as the stronger culture and the more likely to be successful in the competitive market.
4. *Culture resistance.* The cultural differences may be ignored and a strong 'us and them' attitude will develop to the detriment of the smooth working of the alliance.

When ICI Pharamaceuticals set up a joint venture with Sumitomo Chemicals to manufacture and market some ICI drug products in Japan, strategic fit clearly existed between the companies, but the cultural fit and cultural sensitivities were not present and the venture was only a limited success. Similarly the Dowty Group created a joint venture with the Sema group to tender for Ministry of Defence command and control projects. A considerable amount of work was won, but little profit was made as the cultural incompati-

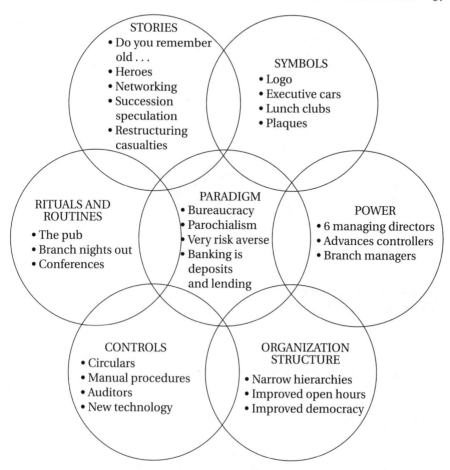

Fig. 5.3. The culture web of a UK clearing bank
Source: adapted from Johnson and Scholes (1993).

bilities of the Dowty 'harbourmasters' and the Sema software 'techies' limited the company's ability to produce to time and at cost and hence achieve budgeted profit.

Of course, if no more than a short-term relationship is expected, dealing with a transitory situation, and it is envisaged that the alliance will eventually be resolved by merger, or dissolution, then cultural fit is less necessary, and a regime of mutual caution, and detailed adherence to closely negotiated contractual arrangements, may well be the most appropriate policy. However, if the alliance is intended to be long term, compatible cultural attitudes assume greater significance, especially in respect of flexibility towards cultural

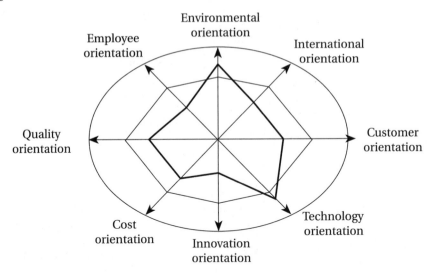

Fig. 5.4. The cultural profile
Source: adapted from Buono and Pritzl (1992).

differences, an eagerness to learn from a partner different from oneself, and strong commitment and mutual trust between the partners.

The ideal partner

The motivations for setting up alliances appear to stem principally from feelings of resource and skill inadequacy in the face of the challenges presented by an increasingly global market affording scale and scope economies, but requiring ever higher investment. Clearly globalization is a key factor at this point in business and economic history. It is of course in an overall sense only a special case for determining alliances. The general motivating case can be stated in the form: if the skill and resources are perceptibly less than those required to meet a challenge or opportunity most effectively, and the prospective partners appear to be able to supply each others' deficiencies, then there is a motivation to form an alliance to supplement those skills and resources.

Thus firms tend to seek a partner whom they perceive to have complementary assets from which synergies can be realized. They prefer firms of similar size and stature, in order to minimize the risk of domination, avoid excessive dependence, and to achieve an equitable balance of benefits. They do not so frequently consider compatible cultures as key criteria in partner selection (Faulkner 1995), but, to the degree that this aspect of a potential partner is ignored, the probability of future inter-organizational problems is increased. This chapter has thus far discussed some criteria for choosing partners, concentrating on those which have strategic fit, and those whose cultural sensitivities are such that they can reasonably be expected to develop cultural fit. Once a partner has been found, however, there is a need to agree on the best form for the alliance to take.

FORMS OF COOPERATION

Although, as illustrated below, many writers have addressed the question of how to classify the different types of cooperative agreements, the classifications that have emerged from their deliberations have varied widely and few have successfully met the accepted taxonomic principles of mutual exclusivity and parsimony. Furthermore, little empirical work has been done relating circumstance to choice of appropriate alliance form and ultimately to performance. This part of the chapter outlines the nature of a number of cooperative arrangements, suggests a robust taxonomic approach to alliances, and proposes situations in which the major alliance forms may most appropriately be adopted.

Inter-organizational forms are defined in a wide variety of ways in the literature. Porter and Fuller (1986) talk of 'international coalitions', while Oliver (1990) dubs such arrangements IORs (inter-organizational relationships), a term also used by Ring and Van de Ven (1994). Jarillo (1988) uses the term 'strategic networks', whilst Miles and Snow (1986) choose 'dynamic networks' as their descriptive term. Borys and Jemison (1989) talk of 'hybrid organizational arrangements', while Kanter (1989) coins PALS (P–pools resources, A–ally, L–link systems). Perlmutter and Heenan (1986) talk of 'industrial systems constellations' and Ulrich (1983) has MOEs (multi-organizational enterprises). There are also the ubiquitous 'strategic alliances' and 'joint ventures', frequently used interchangeably, and of course the Japanese have their 'keiretsu', and the Koreans their 'chaebols', hub and spoke subcontracting systems developed around the major manufacturing and other corporate giants.

Cooperative arrangements are characterized neither by fully market-dominated relationships, nor by the organizational hierarchy characteristics of fully merged companies. In relation to Williamson's (1975) dichotomy of markets and hierarchies, Powell (1990: 296) explains:

Transactions that involve uncertainty about their outcome, that recur frequently and require substantial transaction specific investments of money, time or energy, that cannot be easily transferred, are more likely to take place within hierarchically organized firms. Exchanges that are straightforward, non-repetitive and require no transaction specific investments will take place across a market inter-face. Hence, transactions are moved out of markets into hierarchies as knowledge specific to the transaction (asset specificity) builds up. When this occurs the inefficiencies of bureaucratic organizations will be preferred to the relatively greater costs of market transactions.

However, there are many intermediate points between markets and hierarchies, as Thorelli (1986) points out. He suggests that, for networks or alliances to come about, there needs to be at least a partial overlap between some of the dimensions of the partners' corporate domain—that is, product, function, clientele, territory, or time: 'The network can be viewed as an alternative to vertical integration and to diversification, and as an instrument for reaching new clientele and additional countries' (Thorelli 1986: 46).

As we discuss in more detail in Chapter 6, such cooperative forms can be categorized in ascending levels of integration or interdependence between the two extreme pure forms of markets and hierarchies, with the market end of the spectrum dominated by the price mechanism, and the hierarchy end by organizational fiat. The intermediate forms may be assumed to exist, due to what Masten (1984) calls their 'differentiated efficiency' as organizational forms.

When an enterprise starts up in business, it initially purchases its supplies in the market. In this sense a market is defined as a transaction in which there is no future obligation between buyer and seller, and no relationship beyond the spot transaction. However, arm's-length market relationships frequently develop into established suppliers and distributors as the entrepreneur continues in business. In such circumstances relationships do develop, and future expectations come about between the transactors. If the relationship is satisfactory, each builds the other into their plans for the future, and they begin to discuss how they can do more business together. This may be as far as matters go.

In some relationships an even closer relationship develops both between the two operators and others at different points in the value chain and value system in which they are located. This takes on the nature of an equal-partner network which can be operationalized by any member wanting to embark upon a project needing the skills of network members. The relationship is normally informal and does not actively extend beyond the project in hand. However, members are always there, available for future projects. Many small management consultancy networks operate in this fashion. In a network each member has immediate access to specialized skills and competencies to meet special situations, without the need to meet the overheads involved in developing the competencies internally.

As Powell (1990: 303) comments,

The basic assumption of network relationships is that one party is dependent on resources controlled by another, and that there are gains to be had by pooling resources. [On the other hand] all the parties to network forms of exchange have lost some of their ability to dictate their own future and are increasingly dependent on the activities of others.

Further up the ladder of integration are the closely knit subcontractor networks like the Japanese keiretsu, or, nearer home, the close relationships Marks & Spencer has with its suppliers. In the latter, annual prices are determined so as to give the supplier an acceptable margin, product is scheduled over a long period and delivered as required, and very demanding inspectors are introduced by Marks & Spencer into the supplier firm to ensure product quality. Such systems are described as dominated networks in Chapter 6, as they are normally dominated from the centre by the brand-name company.

Licensing agreements come next in degree of integration. In such agreements the relationship between the licensor and the licensee is integrated from the viewpoint of activities in a defined area, but both retain their separate identities and ownership. Licensing arrangements vary in nature considerably. A franchise is a form of licence in which the licensee takes over the personality and brand of a brand name normally for a specified geographical area. The licensor provides such support as marketing and training. The licensee agrees to present the licensor's product in a way specified by the licensor and pays royalties on all sales. Other licences may be less onerous than franchises and will include varying degrees of exclusivity with regard to competition in an area.

In terms of levels of interdependence a new form of network is currently manifesting itself, that of the virtual corporation also described in Chapter 6. This form has come about as a result of the information revolution, and is composed of activity performers linked by various types of information software. Each activity is normally separately owned, but the configuration of the virtual value chain enables the virtual corporation to present itself to customers as an enterprise able to deliver packages of goods and services competitively with those of more traditional corporations.

Between virtual corporations and traditional hierarchies, where rule by price (markets) is replaced by rule by fiat (hierarchies), comes the most integrated form of rule by 'adaptive coordination' (Johanson and Mattsson 1991)— namely, that found in strategic alliances. This form differs from all other forms of cooperative agreements in that its fundamental purpose is that of organizational learning. All other forms of cooperation have as their base the fact that each partner is regarded as competent to carry out a specific function, and owes its place in the network to this perceived competence. There is no assumption that one partner will attempt to become competent in the skills provided by another. In the strategic alliance there is just such an assumption. Indeed the least successful alliances are those where skill substitution is the limit of the relationship. In the most effective alliances both or all partners grow in competences as they learn from each other.

Fig. 5.5 illustrates the two basic motivational drives that lead to different cooperative forms: those that seek organizational learning, and those that aim at skill substitution, as described in Chapter 4. This chapter deals with the learning forms—that is, alliances—whilst Chapter 6 deals with skill-substitution cooperative forms.

Alliance forms

After the decision has been taken to form an alliance, and a partner chosen, the selection of an appropriate form is an important element in the design of

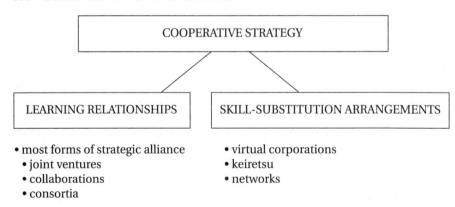

Fig. 5.5. The two fundamental motives for cooperative strategy

the alliance. The forms of alliance may take a variety of different configurations, and are defined in different ways by different researchers. There are technology-development coalitions, marketing and distribution agreements, operations and logistics coalitions, single-country and multi-country alliances, joint ventures creating a daughter company from two or more parent partners, minority share exchange agreements, licensing agreements, and no doubt others.

Ghemawat *et al.* (1986) attempt to classify all alliances as either *x*—that is, vertical coalitions, alliances between partners carrying out different activities in the value chain—or *y*—that is, horizontal coalitions, partners carrying out the same activity in the value chain. Garrette and Dussauge (1995) also talk of horizontal strategic alliances, joining competing firms operating in the same industry (scale alliances), and vertical strategic alliances linking buyers and suppliers in separate industries, or positioned at different stages in the value chain (link alliances), but capable of being integrated in the same business system. They consider these two types of alliance as quite distinct in nature. The horizontal alliance (scale) brought about by cooperative behaviour between competitors blurs the distinction between rivalry and cooperation at least within a defined domain. Vertical alliances (link), however, do not, and are therefore potentially more stable.

Thus, instead of buying in components in a single arm's-length market-priced deal, the vertical alliance between manufacturer and supplier removes much of the price and availability uncertainty from the relationship, at the potential cost of sacrificing the efficiency regulating power of the price mechanism. Many alliances, however (for example, Rover–Honda), do not fit this taxonomy, as they cover both scale and link activities. In cases where the taxonomy does apply, however, there is no doubt that more tension between the partners is likely to exist in scale than link alliances. Scale alliances are between potential competitors come together to achieve economies of scale. In such circumstances each partner must always have the thought in the back of his mind that his partner might just break away and become his competitor again. In link alliances there is no such risk, as the partners specialize in different value-chain activities and therefore mutual suspicion is far less likely, and the alliance is thus more likely to be a stable one.

In addition there is a third variety of alliance within this basic concept—that is, 'the diagonal alliance' (Bronder and Pritzl 1992), which applies to cooperative activity between companies in different industries. However, the concept of industry is a difficult one here. In the Dowty–Sema joint venture, for example, the Dowty Group is in the engineering industry, and Sema in the software industry, yet from a different viewpoint both are in the defence industry. Allocation of an industry to a company or an alliance may be more perceptual than objective.

Ghemawat, Porter, and Rawlinson (1986) classify strategic alliances according to their legal nature (joint ventures; licences; supply agreements) and also according to their functional areas of concern (technological; operations and logistics; marketing, sales, and service). However, an alliance may typically be a technological one from the viewpoint of one partner, yet a market-access one from the viewpoint of the other.

Garrette and Dussauge (1995) classify alliances additionally into three further principal types:

1. shared upstream and downstream integration;
2. additive alliances in which each partner contributes assets to each other—e.g. R&D manufacturing and distribution functions as appropriate;
3. those involving complementary assets.

Within this somewhat complex taxonomy, they arrive, through their research, at three clusters of alliances in which shared integration (1) is seen as the most common in R&D and manufacturing alliances. The relationships are frequently self-contained limited partnerships, and often found in the semi-conductor and automotive industries, spanning continents and with multiple partners. Additive alliances (2), they claim, are complex large-scale ventures typically found for example in the aerospace industry, and covering whole value chains. The motivation behind these alliances is frequently to achieve an entry strategy on a major scale. Complementary alliances (3) are frequently found in manufacturing and in marketing and are normally two-partner alliances. Telecommunications is a typical industry for this configuration. These taxonomic categories are arrived at by cluster analysis of empirical research data, and by implication may only apply to a limited range of high-technology industries.

Pucik (1988) notes that in the past alliances were mainly concerned with reducing capital investment needs, and lowering the risk of entry to new markets. Whilst these motivations are often still present, the dominant emphasis has shifted currently to taking advantage of the increased speed of technological change, and adjusting to the rapidly growing competitiveness of global markets. However, the one motivation will no doubt relate to one partner, but the other partner may have quite a different one.

The types of alliance in Pucik's classification are:

1. alliances for technological change reasons—e.g. cross-licensing;
2. co-production and OEM agreements;
3. sales and distribution ties;
4. joint product-development programmes;
5. the creation of joint ventures.

All have the aim, he states, of 'attaining the position of global market leadership through internalization of key added value competencies' (Pucik 1988: 78).

Kanter (1989) identifies three fundamental types of alliance:

1. multi-company service consortia—e.g for R&D;
2. opportunistic alliances set up to take advantage of specific situations— i.e. most joint ventures;
3. stakeholder alliances: these are what other researchers refer to as vertical alliances, or alliances between companies at different parts of the value chain—e.g. supply/producer complementary coalitions.

Consortia, she notes, try to achieve the benefit of large-scale activity by pooling resources. For example, Micro-electronics and Computer Technology Corporation (MCC) was set up to compete with the Japanese in R&D. These alliances are very popular in new technology areas, between companies that are normally competitors. They often founder though, she states, as a result of a low level of commitment by their members, and from having mediocre seconded staff. Opportunistic joint ventures are, she believes, the most unstable of alliance forms. Each partner supplies the competencies that the other lacks. The principal driving forces are technological transfer and market access. However, due to their opportunistic nature, these alliances find difficulty in achieving the necessary robustness when circumstances change, especially if they change asymmetrically for the parties. Stakeholder alliances institutionalize previous interdependence, and are often quality or innovation driven. That is, a firm treats a supplier as a partner in order to increase quality and cement the alliance. These alliances should be stable, as they have high commitment and little competition. Kanter's taxonomy does not necessarily involve mutually exclusive categories of alliance, since, for example, any one alliance might be an opportunistic vertical consortium. Airbus Industrie, and other combinations, are cases in point.

Collins and Doorley (1991) identify six forms of alliance:

1. strategic partnerships between large companies—e.g. GM and Toyota, or ICL and Fujitsu;
2. collaborative R&D alliances;
3. relationships with suppliers especially for just-in-time (JIT) purposes;
4. venture-capital-backed joint ventures normally in new technology areas;
5. value-added distribution alliances, customizing for local markets;

6. partial mergers, often in mature markets to organize phased withdrawal from a market by one partner.

This categorization, whilst ingenious, might also involve alliances that fall into several categories at the same time, a cardinal sin for taxonomists.

Cravens, Piercy, and Shipp (1996) have developed a classification of wider cooperative forms which they present as a matrix with volatility of environment as one axis and degree of collaboration as the other. This is shown in Fig. 5.6. The four types of networks, as they call them, are *hollow* networks, *flexible* networks, *value-added* networks, and *virtual* networks.

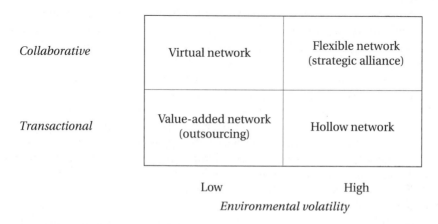

Fig. 5.6. Classification of network organizations
Source: adapted from Cravens *et al.* (1996: 209).

Volatility of environmental change implies characteristics such as speed, degree, unpredictability, and uncertainty of radical change in the markets addressed. The *hollow* network is a largely transaction-based network of the kind that is addressed in Chapter 4 of this book. It is largely transaction based and therefore not a true alliance, and relies heavily on other organizations and individuals to carry out many of the functions necessary to present its offering to the customer. It represents a buffering mechanism against the vagaries of the environment by providing the flexibility to shift rapidly to new opportunities and sources of contribution.

A *flexible* network is Craven *et al.*'s name for what we call a strategic alliance or alternatively a 'keiretsu'. It comes about in environmentally volatile conditions but involves real collaboration. It has intra-organizational links that tend to be long term in duration, and requires the development of considerable depth of knowledge, technological competence, and response capability.

The *value-added* network is much more transactional in nature and develops in environments that are fairly stable. It is the product of the subcontracting, outsourcing movement. The core organization typically may retain responsibility for R&D and product design but then outsource many of the other functions such as production and sales to low-cost suppliers. It is largely transactional in nature because the subcontracting companies do not need to make large product-specific investments and can be relatively easily replaced by other subcontractors if quality is unsatisfactory.

Craven *et al.*'s fourth category in the *virtual* network, which is similar to the virtual corporation we describe in Chapter 6. It is collaborative in that the members of the virtual corporation conceive of themselves as forming a long-term enterprise not merely subcontracting on an arm's-length basis. It is most likely to arise in high-technology industries where electronic communication is the norm.

Despite the interesting variety of taxonomies in cooperative forms there is little unanimity amongst researchers into one set of classifications. Some classify according to legal form: joint ventures, minority equity exchange, distribution agreements, and so forth. Others classify according to the position in the value chain of the partners: for example, vertical alliances, horizontal alliances; or by the functions performed, such as sales and distribution, manufacturing, or R&D alliances. Yet others, like Kanter (1994), use a more eclectic taxonomy, including opportunistic alliances, service consortia, and stakeholder alliances.

However, if alliance form is analysed on three distinct dimensions—namely, scope, legal nature, and size of membership (Faulkner 1995), the major form-selection options can be categorized mutually exclusively. Thus such a taxonomy can be represented on three axes (Fig. 5.7), with scope represented on a focused/complex continuum, the corporate legal entity shown on a joint-venture/collaboration dimension, and the number of partners shown on a two-partner/consortium axis.

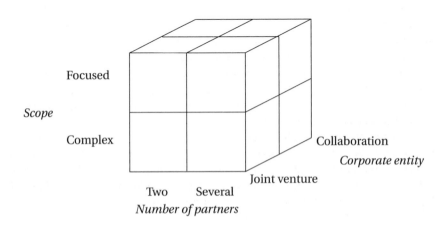

Fig. 5.7. A taxonomy of alliance forms

The scope of the alliance

The focused alliance is a collaborative arrangement between two or more companies, set up to meet a clearly defined set of circumstances in a particular way. For example, a US company seeking to enter the EU market with a given set of products may form a focused alliance with a European distribution company as its means of market entry. The US company will provide the product and the market and sales literature, while the European company provides the sales force and local know-how. The precise form of the arrangement may vary, but the nature of the alliance is a focused one with clear remits, and understanding of respective contributions and rewards. Thus, in November 1989 Cincinnati Bell Information Systems (CBIS) of the USA set up an alliance with Kingston Communications of Kingston upon Hull to market CBIS's automated telecommunications equipment throughout the European Community. CBIS provides the equipment and Kingston the sales effort.

The complex alliance may involve large parts of, or even the complete value chains of, each partner. The companies recognize that together potentially they form a far more powerful competitive enterprise than they do apart. Yet they wish to retain their separate identities, and overall aspirations, whilst being willing to cooperate with each other over a wide range of activities. Rover–Honda is a good example of a complex alliance. It includes joint R&D, joint manufacturing, joint development, and joint sourcing of parts. The companies remain separate, however, in the critical marketing and sales areas, and both companies retain clearly distinct images. Until BMW's purchase of Rover from BAE in 1994, the alliance involved a 20 per cent share exchange between Rover and Honda UK Manufacturing Company, but this is not a necessary condition for this type of alliance.

The legal form of the alliance

A joint venture involves the creation of a legally separate company of which the alliance partners are normally founding shareholders. A US company, for example, may set up a joint venture with a UK company to market in the EC. The partners normally provide finance, and other support resources including some personnel, until the venture is able to develop its own. The aim of the joint venture is typically that the new company should ultimately become a self-standing entity with its own aims, employees, and resources quite distinct from its parent shareholders. Unilever is a good example of a successful joint venture set up in the 1920s by Dutch and English companies and now a major multinational enterprise.

A collaboration is an alliance form that has no joint-venture company to give it boundaries. It is therefore both the most flexible form, and potentially the least committed form, at least at the outset. Companies can set up a collaboration on a very minimal basis to see how matters develop, and then allow it to deepen and broaden by feeding new projects into it over a period of time.

Just as the collaboration requires no major initial commitment, it also has no limitations. It is probably the most appropriate form where the extent of the possible relationship is impossible to foresee at the outset, when the alliance is not bounded by a specific business or set of assets, and when joint external commitment at a certain level is not specifically sought. It may be that the collaborative form is most appropriate if the activity concerned is a core activity of the partners. If it is non-core, a joint venture may be more appropriate. Such guidelines, however, are often not crucial in choice of alliance form. The alliance of the Royal Bank of Scotland and Banco Santander is a good example of a successful collaboration. The partners collaborate over a wide range of activities, but have no single joint-venture company to provide boundaries to the alliance.

The number of alliance partners

A two-partner alliance may be taken as the most common form. However, the consortium is a distinct form of strategic alliance that has more than two partners, and is normally a large-scale activity set up for a very specific purpose, and managed in a hands-off fashion by the contributing shareholders. Consortia are particularly common for large-scale projects in the defence industry, where massive funds and a wide range of specialist skills are required for specific purposes. Airbus Industrie is a consortium where a number of European shareholders have set up an aircraft manufacturing enterprise to compete on world markets with Boeing–McDonnell Douglas (they have now merged). The European shareholders, although large themselves, felt the need to create a large enough pool of funds and skills to ensure that they reached critical mass in terms of resources for aircraft development, and chose to form an international consortium to do this.

Strategic alliances, therefore, can be categorized by reference to:

1. whether they have a focused objective, or the relationship is a complex one involving many parts of the partners' value chains;
2. whether they involve a legally separate joint-venture company or not;
3. whether they have two or more than two partners.

Choice of form

An evolutionary perspective on organizational form (Hannan and Freeman 1989) might suggest that the particular alliance form will be chosen that fits the relationship between the set of activities involved in the agreement and the environment, and that the pressures of natural selection will bring about alliance failure if an inappropriate organizational form is chosen: 'Ecologically, intergroup relations that persist over time must be effective. Otherwise the groups would decouple or be integrated in one unit' (Williamson 1975).

Economists frequently fail to note that many existing forms may in fact ultimately be bound to 'decouple' owing to their lack of fit with the environment, but at the time the research is carried out are still in existence. Indeed, little definitive work has been done relating alliance form to appropriate internal and external conditions. Lorange and Roos (1992) take a contingency approach and claim that: 'No particular type of strategic alliance is better or universally more correct than others; what matters is to make the appropriate choice of strategic alliance form given the particular conditions at hand.'

Gupta and Singh (1991) are more precise, and recommend the selection of the joint venture if the assets are specific and separable, and if there is a need to manage them separately. Johnson and Scholes (1993) adopt a similar view but add the comment that the joint-venture form with each partner holding shares in the alliance vehicle reduces the risk of asset appropriability, and is therefore more appropriate as a vehicle when partners fear this. If the joint venture grows away from the partners, and becomes ultimately a self-standing entity, and ripe for divestment, and capitalization of the investment, then this may be more a sign of success than of failure of the alliance. Such potential is always inherent in the joint-venture form, and is often seen by the partners, even at the outset, as a possible and acceptable outcome.

The conditions appropriate to joint-venture formation are ones which enable the partners to regard the alliance as something distinct from their overall relationship, like the son or daughter of a marriage. Faulkner's (1995) research suggests that a strategic alliance should be set up as a separate joint-venture company if:

1. the scope of the alliance constitutes a distinct business;
2. the alliance assets are specific, easily separable from the parents, and need to be jointly managed;
3. the alliance objectives can be clearly measured in relation to the use of the assets;
4. there is a perceived need to tie in the partners;
5. it is legally necessary—for instance, to enter a national market;
6. the partners wish to allocate a predetermined level of resources to the venture;
7. the scope of the venture is not central to the partners' core business, or is at least geographically distinct.

Frequently, when potential partners identify each other, they cannot, at the outset, determine the extent or the nature of their possible collaboration, as it may develop over time. Also they may not wish to announce, internally or to the world, the nature of their cooperative strategy, and may prefer to allow the relationship to develop in a flexible and incremental way. In these circumstances the collaboration, with its inherently flexible nature, may be the preferred alliance form. The collaborative form is appropriate for an alliance if:

1. there is high uncertainty as to what tasks will be involved in the cooperative enterprise;

2. there is a great need for flexibility between the partners;
3. visible commitment by the partners is not sought;
4. the boundaries of the alliance do not circumscribe a distinct business area.

Consortia are difficult to manage, as they involve a number of simultaneous relationships, and as a result almost always require a joint-venture form to prescribe and set limits for their boundaries. Even in these circumstances the varied agendas of the partners, the different cultures, and the frequent dilution of management control inherent in working with a number of partners, makes the consortium a difficult form to manage. They seem, therefore, to be resorted to principally if the scope and scale of the challenge make this the only solution. However, most defence and aerospace enterprises and other industries requiring very high levels of R&D have these characteristics, and the consortium form is most frequently met in these sectors (Kanter 1989; Collins and Doorley 1991; Lei and Slocum 1991). A consortium is the appropriate alliance form if:

1. two partners alone cannot realistically provide sufficient resources to meet the identified challenge or opportunity;
2. large size is necessary for the enterprise to be credible to potential customers, such as governments;
3. the specialist skills required are so wide and varied that two companies could not provide them adequately;
4. extensive geographical coverage is needed to achieve strong market presence;
5. there is the need to spread and limit the financial risk to each partner.

SUMMARY

This chapter has identified some criteria for partner selection, constructed a taxonomy of alliance forms, and suggested conditions in which each of the taxonomic alliance forms is likely to be the most appropriate form. Important criteria for partner selection are the need for the partners' assets to be complementary, and for the identification of potential synergies between the prospective partners. It has been stressed that, whilst strategic fit is normally carefully assessed prior to concluding an alliance, the extent of cultural compatibility is frequently neglected. Yet culture clashes are the most commonly cited reason for alliance failure.

There are several basic forms of alliance—joint ventures, collaborations, and consortia being the most common forms. The conditions under which each of these forms can most appropriately be adopted can be identified. Joint ventures are most appropriate for distinct businesses, collaborations where flexibility is the key requirement, and consortia where two partners are not enough to ensure competitive advantage. These forms refer only to strategic alliances, however, and also ignore the other way of looking at form—namely, the scale alliance (cooperation between competitors to realize scale economies) and the link alliance (cooperation between firms at different stages of the value chain). Chapter 6 looks at some other forms of cooperative activity—namely, the various forms of network and the so-called virtual corporation, and identifies some of their distinct characteristics.

REFERENCES

Bertodo, R. (1990), 'The Collaboration Vortex: Anatomy of a Euro-Japanese Alliance', *EIU Japanese Motor Business* (Summer), 29–43.

Bleackley, M. (1991), 'Strategic Alliances—Guidelines for Success', *Institute of Management Consultants Report* (London: IMC), 47–50.

Bleeke, J., and Ernst, D. (1991), 'The Way to Win in Cross-Border Alliances', *Harvard Business Review* (Nov./Dec.), 129–35.

Borys, B., and Jemison, D. B. (1989), 'Hybrid Arrangements as Strategic Alliances: Theoretical Issues in Organizational Combinations', *Academy of Management Review*, 14/2: 234–49.

Bronder, C., and Pritzl, R. (1992), 'Developing Strategic Alliances: A Conceptual Framework for Successful Co-operation', *European Management Journal*, 10/4: 412–20.

Buono, A. F., and Bowditch, J. L. (1989), *The Human Side of Mergers and Acquisitions: Managing Collisions between People, Cultures, and Organizations* (San Francisco: Jossey-Bass).

Collins, T., and Doorley, T. (1991), *Teaming Up for the 90's* (Homewood, Ill.: Irwin).

Cravens, D. W., Piercy, N. F., and Shipp, S. H. (1996), 'New Organizational Forms for Competing in Highly Dynamic Environments: The Network Paradigm', *British Journal of Management*, 1: 203–18.

Faulkner, D. O. (1992), 'Cooperating for Competition: A Taxonomy of Strategic Alliances', paper presented at British Academy of Management Conference, September.

—— (1995), *International Strategic Alliances: Cooperating to Compete* (Maidenhead: McGraw-Hill).

Garrette, B., and Dussauge, P. (1995), 'Patterns of Strategic Alliances between Rival Firms', *Group Decision and Negotiation*, 4: 429–52.

Geringer, J. M. (1991), 'Strategic Determinants of Partner Selection Criteria in International Joint Ventures', *Journal of International Business Studies*, 22: 41–62.

Ghemawat, P., Porter, M. E., and Rawlinson, R. A. (1986), 'Patterns of International Coalition Activity,' in M. E. Porter (ed.), *Competition in Global Industries* (Boston, Mass.: Harvard Business School Press), 345–67.

Gupta, A. K., and Singh, H. (1991), 'The Governance of Synergy: Inter-SBU Coordination vs External Strategic Alliances', paper presented at Academy of Management Conference, Miami.

Hampden-Turner, C., and Trompenaars, F. (1994), *The Seven Cultures of Capitalism* (New York: Doubleday).

Hannan, M. T., and Freeman, J. (1989), *Organizational Ecology* (Cambridge, Mass.: Harvard University Press).

Jarillo, J. C. (1988), 'On Strategic Networks', *Strategic Management Journal*, 9: 31–41.

Johanson, J., and Mattsson, L.-G. (1991), 'Interorganizational Relations in Industrial Systems: A Network Approach Compared with the Transaction-Cost Approach', in G. Thompson, J. Frances, R. Levacic, and J. Mitchell (eds.), *Markets, Hierarchies and Networks* (London: Sage), 256–64.

Johnson, G., and Scholes, K. (1993), *Exploring Corporate Strategy* (3rd edn., Hemel Hempstead: Prentice Hall).

Kanter, R. M. (1989), *When Giants Learn to Dance* (London: Simon & Schuster).

—— (1994), 'Collaborative Advantage: The Art of Alliances', *Harvard Business Review*, (July/Aug.), 96–108.

Killing, J. P. (1983), *Strategies for Joint Venture Success* (New York: Praeger).

Lei, D., and Slocum, J. W., Jr. (1991), 'Global Strategic Alliances; Payoffs and Pitfalls', *Organizational Dynamics*, 44–62.

Lorange, P., and Roos, J. (1992), *Strategic Alliances: Formation, Implementation, and Evolution* (Oxford: Blackwell).

Lynch, R. P. (1990), 'Building Alliances to Penetrate European Markets', *Journal of Business Strategy* (Mar./Apr.), 4–8.

Masten, S. E. (1984), 'The Organization of Production: Evidence from the Aerospace Industry', *Journal of Law and Economics*, 27: 413–18.

Miles, R. E., and Snow, C. C. (1986), 'Organizations: New Concepts for New Forms', *California Management Review*, 28: 62–73.

Oliver, C. (1990), 'Determinants of International Relationships: Integration and Future Directions', *Academy of Management Review*, 15/2: 241–65.

Perlmutter, H. V., and Heenan, D. A. (1986), 'Cooperate to Compete Globally', *Harvard Business Review* (Mar./Apr.), 136–42.

Porter, M. E. (1985), *Competitive Advantage* (New York: Free Press).

—— and Fuller, M. B. (1986), 'Coalitions and Global Strategy', in M. E. Porter (ed.), *Competition in Global Industries* (Boston, Mass.: Harvard Business School Press), 315–44.

Powell, W. W. (1990), 'Neither Market nor Hierarchy: Network Forms of Organization', *Research in Organizational Behaviour*, 12: 295–336.

Pucik, V. (1988), 'Strategic Alliances, Organizational Learning, and Competitive Advantage: The HRM Agenda', *Human Resource Management*, 27/1: 77–93.

Richardson, G. B. (1972), 'The Organisation of Industry', *Economic Journal*, 82: 883–96.

Ring, P. S., and Van de Ven, A. H. (1994), 'Developmental Processes of Cooperative Interorganizational Relationships', *Academy of Management Review*, 19/1: 90–118.

Ryle, G. (1949), *The Concept of Mind* (London: Penguin).

Spekman, R. E., and Sawhney, K. (1991), 'Towards a Conceptual Understanding of the Antecedents of Strategic Alliances', *Management Science Institute*, Report No. 90/114.

Thorelli, H. B. (1986), 'Networks: Between Markets and Hierarchies', *Strategic Management Journal*, 7: 37–51.

Ulrich, D. (1983), 'Governing Transactions: A Framework for Cooperative Strategy', *Human Resource Management*, 22/1–2 (Spring/Summer), 23–39.

Waterman, R. H., Peters, T. J., and Phillips, J. R. (1980), 'Structure is not Organization', *Business Horizons*, (June), 14–26.

Williamson, O. E. (1975), *Markets and Hierarchies* (New York: Free Press).

6

Networks and Virtuality

NETWORK RATIONALES

The terms 'strategic network' and 'strategic alliance' are often used inter-changeably, and indeed there are situations in which they do overlap—as, for example, in the Japanese keiretsu form. However, there is a clear distinction between the idea of a network with its implication of close but non-exclusive relationships, and that of an alliance which, however loosely, implies the creation of a joint enterprise at least over a limited domain. A virtual corporation generally carries some of the impression of both.

The term 'network' is in fact often very loosely used to describe any relationship, from an executive's 'black book' of useful contacts, to an integrated company organized on internal market lines (see Snow *et al.* 1992). Powell (1990), however, attempts to distinguish between a network and Williamson's (1975) famous dichotomy of markets and hierarchies by means of the framework set out in Table 6.1, adapted by the authors to include the virtual corporation.

As the last row in Table 6.1 concedes, however, many markets have some of the aspects of networks, and indeed networks have some of those of hierarchies. The terms, it would seem, are destined to remain more indicative than precise.

Johanson and Mattsson (1991) make a useful additional distinction between network theory and the form of strategic-alliance theory that is based upon transaction-cost analysis. Alliances may be concluded for transaction-cost reasons, but networks never are. Networks generally exist for reasons stemming from resource-dependency theory—that is, one network member provides one function which is complementary to and synergistic with the differing contribution of other members of the network. Although costs enter into the calculus of who to admit and persevere with as network members, the existence of the network, and the loose bonding implied by it, emphasize autonomy and choice, in contrast to the more deterministic governance structure and stable static equilibrium applied to alliance theory by transaction-cost theorists.

Table 6.1. *From hierarchies to markets*

Key features	Hierarchy	Virtual corporation	Network	Market
Normative basis	Employment relationship	Complementary strengths	Complementary strengths	Contract property rights
Means of communication	Routines	Electronic	Relational	Prices
Conflict resolution	Fiat; supervision	Leadership of brand	Reciprocity and reputation	Haggling and resort to law
Flexibility	Low	High	Medium	High
Commitment	High	Medium	Medium	Nil
Tone	Formal Bureaucratic	High-tech Modern	Open-ended Mutual benefit	Precision Suspicion
Actor preference	Dependent	Independent	Interdependent	Independent
Mixing of forms	Informal organization	Equality Subjugation	Status Hierarchy	Repeat transactions
	Profit centres Transfer pricing	Market relations	Multiple partners Formal rules	Contracts

Source: adapted from Powell (1990).

We think the relationships among firms in networks are stable and can basically play the same coordinating and development function as intra-organizational relations. Through relations with customers, distributors, and suppliers a firm can reach out to quite an extensive network. Such indirect relationships may be very important. They are not handled within the transaction cost approach. (Johanson and Mattsson 1991: 264)

Networks of whatever type arise for a number of distinct reasons:

1. *To reduce uncertainty.* Indeed this motive has been suggested as the prime reason for the development of all institutions (North 1996). Impersonal relationships in markets are fraught with uncertainty, in that a transaction once made can never be assumed to be repeatable, since it implies no more in relationship terms than is contained in the exchange. Networks imply developing relationships and thus promise more in terms of mutual solidarity against the cruel wind of economic dynamics.

2. *To provide flexibility.* This quality is offered not in contrast to markets but to hierarchies. Vertically integrated companies establish overheads and production capacity, and in doing so forsake the flexibility of immediate resource reallocation that networks provide.

3. *To provide capacity.* A firm has certain performance capacities as a result of its configuration. If it is part of a customary network, however, such capacity

can be considerably extended by involving other network members in the capacity-constrained activity.

4. *To provide speed.* Speed may be needed to take advantage of opportunities that might not exist for long, and may require a fast response—the classical 'window of opportunity' which is open for a short period and then shut for ever. An existing network can put together a package of resources and capacities to meet such challenges in a customized response which, in its flexibility and scope, lies beyond the capacity of an unnetworked vertically integrated firm.

5. *To provide access to resources and skills not owned by the company itself.* In a network such as those found in the clothing industry of northern Italy (Lorenzoni 1982) the strength of one company is a reflection of the strength of its position in its network, and the facility with which it can call on abilities and skills it does not possess itself to carry out tasks necessary to complete a project.

6. *To provide information.* Network members gain access to industrial intelligence, and information of a diverse nature with far greater facility than executives imprisoned in a vertically integrated company. In such firms the 'need-to-know' principle is far more likely to operate than in networks where all members regard information-gathering as one of the principal reasons for establishing themselves in networks. Even in companies that recognize the importance of making their knowledge and experience available to all their members often by appointing Chief Knowledge Officers, as does Coopers & Lybrand, the breadth of knowledge may still be more limited than that embedded in a wide network. Networks are vital to the newly recognized increasing-returns knowledge-based industries (Arthur 1996) described in Chapter 2. They tend to operate in dense networks which provide advantages under all six factors listed above. Microsoft could not have achieved its dominance of the word-processing software market without its intense involvement in networks including Intel and others. It has become powerful, not because it has the best system, but because it has the largest installed base of customers. To survive in such industries involves a mindset that emphasizes strategic flexibility and cooperation simultaneously with competition. Networks provide the appropriate ecology for companies operating in such fast-changing markets.

POWER AND TRUST

If price is the key regulator and dominant factor in markets, then, in Thorelli's view (1986), power and trust are the factors that dominate network relationships. They are the dominant factors in any political economy, and networks have many of the qualities of such institutional forms. 'The interorganizational network may be conceived as a political economy concerned with the distribution of two scarce resources, money and authority' (Benson 1975: 229, cited in Thorelli 1986: 39).

To create a network, firms whose domains (that is, their products, markets, mode of operation, and territories) overlap need to contact each other and perceive the benefit of working together. Until a certain critical mass has been achieved in the level of cooperation and exchange transactions, the network does not merit the name.

Thorelli (1986) identifies five sources of network power for a member: its economic base, technologies, and range of expertise, coupled with the level of trust and legitimacy that it evokes from its fellow members. It needs to be differentially advantaged in at least one of these areas. All network members, although formally regarded as equals by virtue of their membership, will not have the same degree of power, and it is the linkages between the members and their respective power over each other in causing outcomes that determine the culture of the network.

Although networks accord membership to firms, they are not static closed bodies. Entry, exit, and repositioning are constantly going on in networks occasioned by a particular firm member's success, or failure, and the strength of demand or otherwise for the contribution other member firms believe it can make to their proposed projects. The ultimate justification for the cost to a firm of maintaining its position in a network is the belief that such network activity strengthens its competitive position in comparison to operating on a purely market-based philosophy.

Even networks themselves, however, wax and wane in power. As Thorelli (1986: 43) puts it, 'In the absence of conscious coordinative management—i.e. network management—networks would tend to disintegrate under the impact of entropy.' Networks depend on the establishment, maintenance, and perhaps strengthening of relationships in the hope of profits in the future. In this sense they are different from markets, which exist to establish profit today. It is, therefore, the perceived quality of relationships in networks that matters, since quantitative measures cannot easily be applied to them.

As has been discussed in Chapter 3, trust may be classified in three forms. *Trust based on calculation* is trust which exists at the outset of a relationship because the partners perceive that it is in their self-interest to set up the relationship, and to do so they must accord their partner some measure of trust. *Trust based on understanding* develops as the partners discover by working together that each is as good as his word, and one partner's actions may therefore be accurately predicted to be as it commits them to be. *Trust based on bonding* or personal identification through a warm human relationship may then develop over time, but does not necessarily do so in all business relationships. If it does, however, it is the best guarantor of a successful relationship.

Parts of networks are often appropriable by individuals in a way that technologies and production capacities are not, partly because only the calculative trust stage has been achieved. To that extent, although a firm may join a network to reduce its vulnerability, it may end up replacing one form of vulnerability for another. The successful corporate finance directors of merchant banks in the City depend almost entirely on their networks, and are eternally at risk of being bid away to other institutions through a large enough offer.

The network, as opposed to other intra-organizational forms, brings with it its own strengths and vulnerabilities. In a turbulent and global economic world, however, few players can risk being entirely without networks, or conversely being entirely dependent upon them.

Richardson (1972) sees firms as 'islands of planned coordination in a sea of market relations'. But, as Powell (1990) stresses, the sea is by no means clear, and this description of the alternative methods of exchange in economies is of doubtful use. Strong relationships and dense commercial networks have always existed wherever economic exchange occurs, sufficient to make the metaphorical antithesis of solid land and fluid sea an unrealistic one. It would be extreme, however, to blur the distinctions between markets, networks, and hierarchies such that they are rejected as useful categories. At the very least their underlying philosophies differ in essence. In markets the rule is to drive a hard bargain, in networks to create indebtedness for future benefit, and in hierarchies to cooperate for career advancement. As Powell (1990: 302) notes:

Prosperous market traders would be viewed as petty and untrustworthy shysters in networks, while successful participants in networks who carried those practices into competitive markets would be viewed as naïve and foolish. Within hierarchies, communication, and exchange is shaped by concerns with career mobility—in this sense, exchange is bound up with considerations of personal advancement.

Powell believes that networks score over other governance forms, particularly where flexibility and fast response times are needed, 'thick' information is needed, and varied resources are required owing to an uncertain environment. He also points out that the social cement of networks is strengthened by obligations which are frequently left unbalanced, thus looking to the future for further exchanges. This differs from other governance forms, where the pursuit of exchange equivalence in reciprocity is the norm.

Although trust and its general antecedent 'reputation' are necessary in all exchange relationships, they are at their most vital in network forms. It is true that you need to trust your colleagues in a hierarchy, and you need to trust the trader who sells you a product in a market, at least to the extent of believing that the good is of the declared quality. But in these circumstances tacit behavioural caution and legal remedies can to some degree compensate for doubtful trust in hierarchies and markets respectively. However, without trust, and a member's reputation on admission to a network, such a mode of cooperation would soon wither, probably into a market form.

Jarillo (1993) looks at a network as more than a rather randomly determined set of business relationships created because its members felt uncertain of the future, and believed that knowing particular differentiated trading partners well provided a stronger capability than the flexibility that comes with having only market relationships or the costs involved in vertical integration. In Jarillo's view what he calls strategic networks are merely another, and often better way of running the 'business system' necessary for the production and sale of a chosen set of products. By business system he means the stages and activities necessary for designing, sourcing, producing, marketing, distributing, and servicing a product; a form of analysis similar to Porter's (1985) value chain.

From this perspective Jarillo's strategic network requires a hub company to provide scope definition and leadership. It decides if it will carry out a particular activity internally or through network subcontractors. His exemplars of such a network system are thus Toyota and Bennetton. Conditions that make such a system the preferred solution to vertical integration are in Jarillo's view:

1. widely varying optimal scale for different activities in the business system; some activities benefiting from small-scale providers;
2. varying optimal cultures for the most efficient production of particular activities;
3. business systems in which innovation most commonly comes from small entrepreneurial companies;
4. widely varying expected rates of profitability from different business-system activities, as a consequence of their positioning in different industry structures as analysed by a five-forces method (Porter 1980).

Jarillo bases his theory of the growth of strategic networks largely on the observation of the current trend towards company 'downsizing', a major component of which is the replacement of internal non-core functions by subcontracted providers, thereby contracting the size of the core salaried workforce. Frequently the company contracted to carry out the outsourced activities is a newly formed management buyout from the previously vertically integrated company. Greater motivation is instilled in the subcontractor at a stroke, better services are provided, greater flexibility is achieved by the hub company, and the size of the company's required capital base is accordingly reduced. There are in theory gains all round, although the motivation of those removed from the parent company may often be damaged, and the feeling of security of those remaining may be compromised.

Davis et al. (1994: 565) confirm this movement in their description of the decline and fall of the conglomerate firm in the USA in the 1980s. The authors talk of the firm as an institution being increasingly replaced by a reductionist view of the firm as a network without boundaries. They cite Zukin and DiMaggio's (1990: 7) description of firms of the future as no more than: 'dense patches in networks of relations among economic free agents'. This modern construct is developed further by Snow et al. (1992: 5), who also claim that the modern firm is becoming 'a new form of organization—delayered, downsized, and operating through a network of market sensitive business units—[which] is changing the global business terrain'.

This is clearly Jarillo's strategic network in another guise, although Snow et al. go further. They identify three distinct types of network:

1. *The internal network.* This is a curious identification as a network, since it is described as the introduction of the market into the internal organization of the firm. Thus activities are carried out within the firm and then 'sold' to the next stage of the value chain at market prices, with the purchaser having the right to buy externally, if he can get a better deal. The activity may also in turn develop third-party clients external to the firm.

2. *The stable network.* This is the firm employing partial outsourcing to increase flexibility and improve performance, with a smaller base of permanent employees. It is similar to the Japanese keiretsu in Western form.

3. *Dynamic networks.* These are composed of lead firms who identify new opportunities and then assemble a network of complementary firms with the assets and capabilities to provide the business system to meet the identified market need. Dynamic networks are sometimes otherwise described as Hollow Corporations (*Business Week*, 3 March 1986), since the entrepreneur lacks the capacity to carry out the range of necessary activities from its own resources.

Snow *et al.* take the network concept further by observing that the change in organizational form leads inevitably to a change in the required qualities of executives. In markets traders need above all to be quick witted, streetwise, and able to negotiate effectively. In hierarchies executives need a range of personal attributes including leadership qualities, administrative abilities, and diplomatic capacity. An autocratic style although not fashionable is not necessarily an inhibitor to success in many company cultures. In setting up and running networks, however, such a style would almost inevitably lead to the failure of the network or at least to the executive's replacement.

Snow *et al.* identify the broker as the ideal network executive, and they specify three distinct broker roles:

1. *The architect.* He is the creator of the network or at least of the project in which appropriate firms in an existing network are to be asked to play a part. The architect is the entrepreneur, and, dependent upon his creativity and motivational abilities, he may be instrumental in providing the inspirational vision that brings a network into being, in introducing new members to it, or merely in resourcing a project from existing network members.

2. *The lead operator.* This broker role is often carried out by a member of a downstream firm in the network according to Snow *et al.* He is the manager rather than the entrepreneur, and provides the brain and central nervous system that the network needs if it is to function effectively on a defined mission. As the name suggests, he needs to provide leadership, but in a more democratic style than would be necessary in a hierarchy, as the members of the team in which he needs to operate are not his employees.

3. *The caretaker.* This role prevents Thorelli's (1986) famous 'entropy' risk being realized. The caretaker will need to monitor a large number of

relationships. He will need to nurture, to enhance, and even to discipline network members if they fail to deliver their required contribution. In Axelrod's (1984) 'tit-for-tat' strategy it will probably be the caretaker who applies the network discipline if one member defects or threatens to defect.

Snow and Thomas (1993) conducted some qualitative research into the validity of these broker roles in networks and found them to be broadly valid. Whilst this contribution to network theory is valuable, it may be questioned whether the threefold taxonomy of Snow *et al.* is a valid one, since the internal network is in reality not a network at all, but merely a method of running an integrated hierarchy. There is no doubt, however, that the network with a strong hub firm at the centre is very different in nature and character to that which is set up amongst firms with greater claims to mutual equality. Even equal-partner firms will inevitably be differentiated in terms of their actual power though, and such power relationships will themselves almost inevitably change over the lifetime of the network's operation.

NETWORK RELATIONSHIPS

It is difficult to position networks on the cooperative strategy spectrum of ascending interdependence, since some networks exhibit firm-like qualities like the Japanese keiretsu, whilst others are little more than media for the fast transmission of informal industry information. However, the problem becomes easier to solve, if networks are classified into two distinct categories as suggested above—that is, the *dominated network*, where one firm maintains bilateral relations with a number of normally smaller companies, and the *equal-partner network*, in which a number of firms develop close relationships with each other, and work together in variable configurations on a variety of projects. These forms approximate to Snow *et al.*'s (1992) stable and dynamic networks. Their third category, the internal network, is regarded as outside the brief of cooperative strategy.

The spectrum of ascending interdependence, as shown in Fig. 6.1, runs, therefore, as follows. Markets exhibit the lowest degree of interdependence, indeed no interdependence at all in their pure form, with each transaction implying no specific probability of a repeat transaction.

The first level of interdependence is probably the *equal-partner network*. In such networks, firms, in Powell's (1987: 82) words, engage in 'reciprocal, preferential, mutually supportive actions. Reputation, trust, tacit collusion, and a relative absence of calculative quid pro quo behaviour guide this system of exchange. In network forms of organisations, individual units exist not by themselves, but in relation to other units'. Yet they do not submerge their personalities in each other or engage in wide exclusive arrangements with each other. In Pfeffer and Salancik's view (1978), such networks are formed to

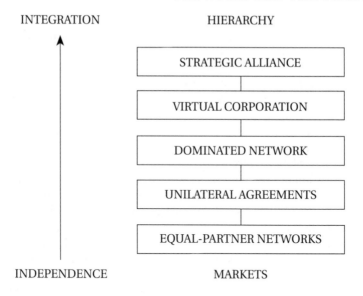

INTEGRATION   HIERARCHY

STRATEGIC ALLIANCE

VIRTUAL CORPORATION

DOMINATED NETWORK

UNILATERAL AGREEMENTS

EQUAL-PARTNER NETWORKS

INDEPENDENCE   MARKETS

Fig. 6.1. Level of ascending integration of cooperative forms

reduce the level of uncertainty in a firm's perceived environment. It is these networks that will form the major focus of this chapter.

Continuing up the chain of interdependence, we reach the *unilateral cooperative agreements* (DeFillippi and Reed 1991). In such arrangements one firm provides another with a service on a fairly intimate basis in exchange for money. Consultancy projects, training programmes provided by an outside training company, technology-transfer agreements, and relational subcontracting are all illustrations of such unilateral agreements. A minority investment by a large company in a smaller one can also be classified as a unilateral cooperative agreement. Thus, where one firm has a product and another market access, a unilateral agreement may be set up on an exclusive geographically limited basis, including royalties, minimum sales levels, and special distributor prices. This form falls short, however, of a mutually dependent strategic alliance. Such arrangements are purely financial, in the sense that a defined service is carried out in exchange for payment, and therefore represent very limited firm interdependence. In general the ending of a relation as a supplier or distributor with one firm is followed by the development of a similar relationship with a replacement firm.

The next level of interdependence beyond the unilateral cooperative agreement is the *dominated network*. This is most frequently exemplified by the Japanese keiretsu (Gerlach 1992), in which a major corporation—e.g. Mitsubishi—exists with a wide and varied network of subcontractors and associated companies, which provide it with services on a regular basis. The network is regarded by all the institutions concerned as a kind of family, with the hub company as the *pater familias* and the periphery companies as its children. Hub companies often have seats on the boards of the keiretsu companies and may hold a small percentage of their equity. The network structure is used to ensure reliability and quality of supply components, and to make production tools like just-in-time logistics easier to administer.

The next level of interdependence is to be found in the *virtual corporation*, which is a loosely coupled enterprise in which the parts are held together through the medium of sophisticated information-technology packages. Virtual corporations may be a transitional stage of company development on the path to complete hierarchy, or they may be loosely packaged specialist functions coordinated by one firm to meet a market opportunity that may be short term. As with networks, the virtual corporation may be an equal-partner one or a dominated one, little different from a keiretsu mediated by IT. The virtual corporation will be described in more detail later in the chapter.

The highest level of interdependence short of hierarchy is the *strategic alliance*, which may cover a wide variety of functions but is normally one of three basic structures—the equity joint venture, the collaboration (little or no equity exchange and no created boundary company), and the consortium. In the strategic alliance, companies merge a limited part of their domain (Thorelli 1986) with each other, and attempt to achieve with their joint value chains the competitive advantage that might individually have eluded them.

A *hierarchy* (Williamson 1975) is, of course, a fully integrated corporation in the traditional mould, which has been created normally to take advantage of economies of scale and scope, and of risk reduction, and to facilitate administrative coordination (Chandler 1962, 1990). They flourish best in only incrementally changing product–market environments, and display weaknesses of structural inertia when required to respond rapidly in turbulent economic conditions.

The focus of this chapter, then, is on three inter-organizational forms: the equal-partner network, the dominated network, and the virtual corporation. Because of its greater stability and simplicity as an organizational form, we will begin with the dominated network.

The dominated network

This network form owes its recent growth in the West to two major unconnected factors: the international success in certain high-profile markets of industrial Japan, and the fall from grace of the large vertically integrated multi-divisional industrial corporation, and its replacement as a favoured paradigm by the downsized, delayered, core-competence-based 'lean and mean' organization, relying on outsourcing for its production in all functions except those deemed to be strategically vital and close to its core competences.

The Japanese industrial keiretsu represents the archetype of the dominated network. In Gerlach's words (1992: 68):

the vertical keiretsu are tight hierarchical associations centred on a single large parent and containing multiple smaller satellite companies within related industries. While focused in their business activities, they span the status breadth of the business community, with the parent firm part of Japan's large-firm economic core and its satellites, particularly at lower levels, small operations that are often family-run. . . . The vertical keiretsu can be divided into three main categories. The first are the sangyo keiretsu or production keiretsu, which are elaborate hierarchies of primary, secondary, and tertiary-level subcontractors that supply, through a series of stages, to parent firms. The second are the ryutsu keiretsu or distribution keiretsu. These are linear systems of distributors that operate under the name of a large-scale manufacturer, or sometimes a wholesaler. They have much in common with the vertical marketing systems that some large US manufacturers have introduced to organize their interfirm distribution channels. A third—the shihon keiretsu or capital keiretsu—are groupings based not on the flow of production materials and goods but on the flow of capital from a parent firm.

Whilst Gerlach's description of the different types of keiretsu in Japanese industry is clear and categorical, in the complex world of reality the webs of the keiretsu do in fact frequently overlap, and it is possible to have keiretsu with dual centres, the one a manufacturing or trading centre and the other a bank. It is also not unusual for the outer members of keiretsu to deal preferentially with each other as well as with the core company.

Such dominated networks are not unique to Japan, although they are a strong feature of the Japanese industrial system of production and distribution. In the UK Marks & Spencer's relationship with its suppliers has many of the characteristic features of the dominated network, including control over quality and supply in exchange for large annual order commitments.

Relationships within dominated networks typically take the form illustrated in Fig. 6.2. There is often only limited networking between satellite companies, except in relation to the business of the dominant company. The dominant company may establish formal links with the satellite through a minority

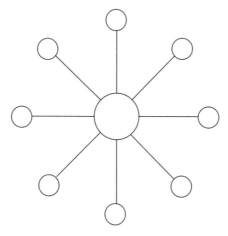

Fig. 6.2. The typical pattern of communication in a keiretsu

shareholding and/or board membership. But this is not always or even generally the case. The advantage of such networks from the viewpoint of the dominant company is that it can rely on regular quality supplies at a pre-agreed price without the need to put up the capital and management resources to create them directly. From the satellite's viewpoint, it can economize on sales and marketing expenditure and have the security of reliable orders and cash flow for its planning purposes, which removes many of the risks from its business. Of course at the same time it also removes some of the autonomy, and if the satellite allows too great a percentage of its business to be with the dominant company it is at risk of ceding all independent bargaining power over such matters as price changes or product development.

The equal-partner network

Equal-partner networks are so named because, unlike in a dominated network, there is no single partner which sets up and controls the network's activities. However, this does not necessarily imply that all partners do in fact have equal power. In all equal-partner networks power relationships are varied and constantly shifting with the fortunes of members. The equal-partner network differs from the dominated network also in that it is not a substitute organizational form to the integrated firm. Rather it is the expression of a set of developed relationships between firms that form a substructure from which competitive organizational entities may emerge.

Fig. 6.3 illustrates in a stylized fashion the nature of relationship and contacts between members in equal-partner networks in contrast to those in dominated networks illustrated in Fig. 6.2. Equal-partner networks can be configured and reconfigured to meet changing market opportunities, and often with a different lead partner in the ascendant. This is both their strength

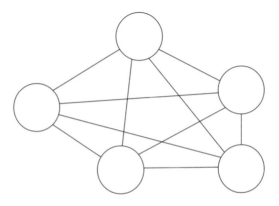

Fig. 6.3. The typical pattern of communication in an equal-partner network

and their weakness. Whilst it implies great flexibility, and an ability to respond to changing often turbulent environments, an equal-partner network lacks the permanent brain and central nervous system that will ensure it combative ability against an organization that is so endowed. Any organization hoping to compete with vertically integrated companies, which possess production and sales capacity and strong identifying brand names, needs to convince the public of its enduring existence. It also requires a leadership capacity to plan and execute strategy, and information systems sensitive enough to convey what needs to be done and to ensure that it is done. This cannot easily be achieved via the loose linkages of an equal partner network, despite its other already identified advantageous qualities. For this reason an equal-partner network is more of the nature of a dense set of mutually aware capabilities than an actual organization form. Such networks may therefore often be in transitory forms which will develop into dominated networks, virtual corporations, or even integrated companies in due course. In economies where networks traditionally flourish like Silicon Valley, California, the emergence of new firms out of a deeply embedded network substructure does not disturb the basic network characteristics of the economy.

A network overview

Network theory has become prominent in the 1990s as the basis for new organizational forms (Nohria and Eccles 1992; Cassells 1996) and for the growth of cooperative strategy as a counterbalance to the self-sufficient philosophy underlying competitive strategy theories. At one level, however, networks have always been with us. Shortly after any individual starts up a business, or engages in any repeated endeavour, he begins to build up a network out of the associates with whom he interacts. In the business world they will be suppliers, distributors, and perhaps to a lesser extent competitors and customers. He will always consider the degree to which he should outsource some of his potential activities, and the level to which he should deal directly with the customer or develop his sales through a network. In some areas—for example, northern Italy—this has traditionally led to strong specialization of activity amongst family firms, and therefore the network as the fundamental underpinning of business activity. In other areas, notably much of the USA, vertical integration has been more the norm until the 1990s, with cooperative networked activity therefore treated with some suspicion.

The degree of prominence networks have received has significantly increased in recent years. This is due largely to the globalization of markets and technologies, leading to the widespread growth of cooperative activity as a necessary strategy, if firms with limited financial strength, focused competences, and limited 'global reach' are to be able to compete in global markets.

An attractive characteristic of many networks, then, is that they help members to achieve increased global reach at low cost and with minimum time delay. They are flexible within their membership, and able to respond rapidly to changing environmental situations. In an increasingly turbulent world, they reduce uncertainty for their members. They enable synergies between members to be captured, and provide the conditions for the achievement of scale-and-scope economies through specialization. They are also good vehicles for the spreading of information and for all forms of market intelligence. Under conditions of trust between members, they may also reduce transaction costs, in contrast to vertically integrated companies with internally competitive cultures. But such costs are very difficult to assess in any situation, particularly *ex ante.*

However, networks, if they are to be contrasted with vertically integrated companies and with the arm's-length nature of the pure-markets form, do not score well on all counts. In dominated networks, the risks for the dominant partner are of unlicensed technology leakage, of poor quality assurance, and of a possible diffusion of internal feelings of identity and motivation in the outlying companies. There is also the difficulty of communicating tacit knowledge, and of achieving a sufficient level of coordination between members in different companies to compete successfully with the systems of integrated companies—the 'singing-from-several-hymn-sheets' problem. For the smaller companies in the dominated network, there are the problems of feeling too dominated, and thus of loss of autonomy and motivation, of lack of promotion opportunities, of insecurity, and of the difficulty in recruiting high-quality personnel to small companies with limited prospects.

In equal-partner networks the primary problems relate to the lack of a brain and a central nervous system. By their nature they are loosely organized coalitions without a permanent acknowledged leader. Major investment in such networks is difficult to organize, and there is the perpetual tension between trust and the risk of prisoner's-dilemma defection by partners—that is, the potential creation of competitors as a result of too much misplaced trust. There is also the difficulty for a network of driving consistently towards a vision of the future, in the way a successful vertically integrated company can and does.

The global economy of the future will undoubtedly see a growth of networks in the search for reduced uncertainty in the face of the increasing turbulence of world economic activity resulting from the globalization of technologies and markets. Cooperative strategy will become more prominent. But it can never replace competitive behaviour in the ultimate market place, if pressures for efficiencies are to be maintained.

THE VIRTUAL CORPORATION

Just as network theory and the strategic alliance have become the popular phrases to describe the growing intra-organizational forms of the 1990s, it seems likely that the 'virtual corporation' will fill that role in the first decade of the new millennium. The virtual corporation differs from the strategic alliance in that it places its emphasis, not primarily on how two or more firms can work together to their mutual advantage, but on how one firm can be created with flexible boundaries and ownership aided by the facilities provided by electronic data exchange and communication. As Nagel and Dove (1991) put it: 'A virtual company is created by selecting organizational resources from different companies and synthesizing them into a single electronic business entity.'

However, as with many new concepts, differing understandings develop of what the concepts actually entail, and the distinction between the heavily outsourced company, the strategic alliance, and the virtual corporation is sometimes difficult to discover from the literature. *Business Week* (February 1993), for example, defined the virtual-corporation organizational form as follows: 'The Virtual Corporation is a temporary network of companies that come together quickly to exploit fast changing opportunities. In a Virtual Corporation companies can share skills and access to global markets with each firm contributing what it is best at.' In this definition no mention is made of the electronic aspect of the corporation, and the outsourced company and the strategic alliance could easily be incorporated within the *Business Week* definition. It might also be claimed by advocates of the 'nothing-changes' school that such networked enterprises have always existed.

Similarly we have the Doughnut Corporation (Handy 1989) with its small solid core of full-timer staff exhibiting core competences, organizing and managing resources, and a large open space with an often fuzzy boundary, full of just-in-time subcontracted resources, consultants, alliance partners, and suppliers. All we need is the panoply of electronic communications and surely we have the virtual corporation.

There is, however, one crucial difference between the strategic alliances and the virtual corporation beyond the electronic aspect of the latter. The strategic alliance is generally created to bring about organizational learning. Many commentators highlight the point that successful alliances are not composed of partners involved in skill substitution—that is, one partner produces and leaves the selling to the other. They are concerned to learn from each other, and thus strengthen the areas in which they are weak. This does not apply to the virtual corporation. In this intra-organizational form, companies each provide different functions, and are linked electronically. Organizational learning is not a basic objective of the exercise, but rather the creation of a flexible organization of companies, each carrying out one or more functions excellently to deliver a competitive product to the customer.

Mowshowitz (1994), however, attempts a deeper and more conceptual view of the way in which the virtual corporation differs essentially from earlier organizational forms. Mowshowitz points to the non-incremental changes in society in history (echoes of punctuated equilibrium!). Thus the factory system developed rapidly in the nineteenth century when, owing to the advantages of the steam engine as a source of power, great productivity could be achieved, thereby separating the means of production from other social interaction, in a way that the earlier handicraft workshop did not.

He believes the virtual organization will have similar dramatic results, bringing equally great social transformation in its wake. Mowshowitz (1994: 270) states: 'The essence of the virtual organization is the management of goal-orientated activity in a way that is independent of the means for its realization. This implies a logical separation between the conception and planning of an activity, on the one hand, and its implementation on the other.' There is, therefore, no problem, as there is in the traditional organization, with allowing extraneous matters such as company loyalty or human relationships to enter the equation of how best to realize abstract goals in concrete terms. The concept of infinite switching capacity, which is central to Mowshowitz's virtual-corporation concept, allows such realization to be achieved from the best combination of inputs, despite their spatial separation. Electronic communication overcomes the problem of the spatial separation of inputs.

Mowshowitz adopts the concept of metamanagement as central to operating the virtual corporation effectively. Metamanagement involves the following steps:

1. an analysis of the inputs needed from outside sources, independent of the examination of particular suppliers;
2. tracking and analysis of potential suppliers;
3. revising and improving the allocation procedure;
4. updating the requirement-supplier table.

He then identifies the three pillars of virtual organization as:

1. *Standardization of interaction.* Thus suppliers can be coupled and decoupled with ease to meet changing objectives, and the perceived optimal means of achieving them.
2. *Commoditization of information.* This is necessary to facilitate switching and thus realize the flexibility necessary for the new form of organization:

   by reducing dependency on the human being as the bearer of knowledge and skill, it is possible to increase the flexibility of decision-making and control to unprecedented levels. Knowledge is a basic factor of production, and if it can be supplied by computer-based artifacts, it can be manipulated and combined with other factors of production in ways that are not possible with human labourers. (Mowshowitz 1994: 281)

3. *Abstractification of property.* Thus a house is made abstract in the form of its title deeds. Abstract property rights, as Mowshowitz observes, simplify the preservation of wealth over time, and its movement over space. Since switching means functions may be carried out anywhere in the world, the problems of currency and interest-rate risk need to be controlled through such abstract instruments as currency hedging, and the use of currency futures and option contracts.

Moving back into the traditional mainstream of organization theory, Mowshowitz (1994) claims that the virtual organization is consistent with the contingency-theory approach of Lawrence and Lorsch (1967). The contingencies are, however, not wholly environmental, but are more concerned with the elements that managers can use to craft organizational solutions to meet specific objectives.

Perceived in this way, the virtual corporation has such dehumanizing aspects that it invites rejoinders, notably from Walsham (1994), who notes the absence in the concept of any reference to the contribution of the culture of organizations, or to the need for meaning and a sense of identity in a person's working life. He claims that 'it can be suggested that a human being acting as a "whole person" is likely to be more economically productive than one enfeebled by the adoption of an amoral role subservient to powerful interests'(1994: 291).

This is reminiscent of the debates between the Fordists or Taylorists, who would, in the interests of efficiency, break a task down to its component parts, deskill it, and dehumanize the operative. This is in contrast to the more modern ideas of those like Wickham Skinner (1978), who would organize a task to meet the needs of the whole man. This may be the key constraining factor in the growth of the virtual corporation—that is, efficiency may be reduced, rather than increased, if the human interest and motivating factors are removed from the day's work. If so, the Mowshowitz vision will require considerable modification before it can hope to become a dominant organizational paradigm.

Harrington (1991) draws attention to a distinction between perceptual organization and physical organization which may attenuate the harshness of Mowshowitz's vision to some degree. Using this distinction, Harrington claims that an organization needs only to be logically perceived as one to become one. The organization thus has virtual (logical) qualities, and physical existence in its traditional form. The virtual and physical aspects of a firm coexist, and interact with each other. Power, culture communication, knowledge perception, and self are seen by Harrington as virtual characteristics, whilst resources, management, personnel, organization structure, information systems, and production are seen as epitomes of the physical organization. The virtual characteristics are less clearly bounded, and are more dominant in some types of business than in others. An advertising agency may perceive itself to be a single entity, even though most of its contributors may be self-employed. The organization itself is shaped by the interaction of its virtual and physical parts. Information technology unbalances the firm towards virtuality, which can limit or increase effectiveness, according to how its introduction is handled.

The Harrington concept is more human than the Mowshowitz idea. However, if we are concerned with efficiency and effectiveness of organizational forms, it may be helpful, in assessing the validity of the Mowshowitz twenty-first century vision, to measure it against the identification by Child

(1987) of the three key characteristics an organizational form needs if it is to flourish. The three great strategic challenges faced by a corporation in the turbulent, global economy of the current and immediate future are, according to Child, *demand risk, innovation risk,* and *efficiency risk.*

By 'demand risk' he means the risk that capacity will have been created to produce and sell in a market that then fluctuates widely, either booming or rapidly melting away. In such circumstances a virtual corporation, or at least one with a relatively limited fixed central core, and a large and flexible periphery, is in a better position to survive, and adjust to changed market conditions than a wholly integrated corporation. Mowshowitz's virtual corporation is then well suited to cope effectively with demand risk. The switching function ensures this.

By 'innovation risk' Child refers to the risk of falling behind rivals in the race for the new generation of products. There are mixed arguments for the virtual corporation here. Child advances the view that a specialized core, buying in parts outside that specialism, helps innovation by concentrating the specialists on developing new products and technologies related to their area of core competence. Chesbrough and Teece (1992), however, champion the integrated firm in areas of systemic technological innovation, since they argue that only such a corporation will have the will and the funds to risk such major R&D programmes. They relegate the virtual corporation to a position of being able to deal effectively only with what they term autonomous innovations—that is, those that involve far less than a whole system. Chesbrough and Teece would question the ability of the Mowshowitz virtual organization to cope with systemic innovation as effectively as the more traditional integrated corporation. However, we are in the domain of theory, as there is currently little more than anecdotal evidence to support either argument.

By 'efficiency risk' Child alludes to the ever-changing nature of costs as technologies change. Here the virtual corporation would seem to have an advantage over the vertically integrated hierarchy, as virtual companies, coupled on the basis of specialization, are likely to be well equipped to achieve optimal scale economies and consequently to contribute low-cost parts to aid the production of an aggregatively low-cost product.

Child (1987) also stresses that coordination within such virtual corporations can be achieved only through attention to what Boisot (1986) calls the increased codification and diffusion of information, by means of the increasingly sophisticated channels of modern information technology. 'IT has, in short, changed the economic cost–benefit balance in favour of greatly enlarging the information processing capabilities of organizations. Additionally it has expanded the options for the codification and diffusion of information. The availability of these options makes a significant contribution towards the viability of externalizing transactions' (Child 1987: 43).

The Walsham rejoinder to Mowshowitz does, however, give pause to the conclusion that efficiency without motivation necessarily leads to greater productivity than that achieved through a lower level of efficiency coupled with the high motivation achieved from working in a committed dedicated team. So the dominance of the dehumanized virtual corporation is by no means assured.

It is interesting to note the tension that is ever present in a discussion of cooperative strategy between, on the one hand, the identification of the human qualities of compromise, forbearance, consensus development, and trust as keys to success, with, on the other, the dehumanized virtual corporation with its elimination of loyalty, human eccentricities, or even culture as extraneous to efficiency needs. Yet they are two sides of the same coin of cooperation between independent companies in the pursuit of the satisfaction of an economic need.

Characteristics of the virtual corporation

Using a less purist vision than that of Mowshowitz, we might develop a concept of the virtual corporation based on three premises:

1. Few companies are excellent at all functions. Greater value can, therefore, be created if each company concentrates on performing only the functions which it does best, and relies on cooperating partners to carry out the other functions, rather than by attempting to do all things internally within a fully integrated company.
2. The globalized trading world is increasingly volatile and turbulent. In order to survive, companies need to link together flexibly, and be immediately ready to effect IT-based architectural transformations to meet changing conditions.
3. Cooperative attitudes even between competitors, and the existence of increasingly sophisticated electronic software, make points 1 and 2 possible.

Such a model includes those humanistic cooperative aspects of a potential virtual corporation which are so dramatically absent from that of Mowshowitz. *Fortune Magazine* (1994) endorses this characterization, seeing the virtual corporation as dependent upon six prime characteristics:

1. A repertoire of variably connectable modules built around an electronic information network.
2. Flexible workforces able to be expanded or contracted to meet changing needs. The 'shamrock' (Handy 1989) pattern may well be an appropriate one here, with a small central core and several groups of self-employed workers selling their time as required.
3. Outsourcing but to cooperating firms with strong and regular relationships as in the Japanese keiretsu.
4. A web of strategic partnerships.
5. A clear understanding amongst all participating units of the current central objectives of the virtual corporation. In the absence of such an

understanding there is a high risk that the corporation will lack the will and purpose to compete successfully with more integrated corporations.

6. An enabling environment in which employees are expected to work out for themselves the best way of operating, and then to get things done. This is in contrast to the traditional system of working according to orders conveyed with the aid of operations manuals, organigrams, and job descriptions.

Such a corporation would be unlikely to work effectively in the pre-electronic age, as failures of communication and computation would lead to unacceptable inefficiencies and misunderstandings within the virtual network. However as *Datamation* (July 1994) shows, there are nowadays a wide range of software packages and systems in existence able to provide the electronic systems for the virtual corporation, as illustrated in Table 6.2.

Table 6.2. *Illustrative software packages*

Software packages	Purpose
SCM	Supply Chain Management
ERP	Enterprise Resource Planning
MRP2	Manufacturing Resource Planning
EPOS	Electronic Point of Sale for market research
DRP	Database Resource Planning to replenish stock
MPS	Master Production Scheduling
EDI	Electronic Data Interchange
CAD	Computer Aided Design

The virtual corporation is not so much a new concept, as one that has become more fully developed as the electronic age exerts an ever-increasing influence upon how business is managed. For example, the concepts of subcontracting and multi-firm projects have existed as long as business itself. Entrepreneurial start-ups have always had to rely on subcontracted activities, generally due to lack of adequate capital resources or capabilities to carry out all functions internally. Indeed this has led to their descriptions as 'hollow corporations' in somewhat derogatory fashion. Major construction projects have also been organized in a virtual fashion for decades—for example, hospital projects in the Middle East are traditionally carried out with a lead contractor and an appropriate number of subcontractors to carry out specialist functions.

Some companies such as Sinclair Research or Tonka Toys have always adopted a philosophy of carrying out directly only the functions in which they claim special expertise and subcontracting the others. Even a major corporation like Apple began as a 'hollow corporation', carrying out only a limited number of activities directly, but doing them extraordinarily well. Furthermore, many large management consultancies operate with a relatively small number of salaried employees, and a large network of self-employed fee workers.

However, the fashion in the 1970s for vertical integration has generally been reversed, and the resource-based view of the firm (Wernerfelt 1984) has taken over much of management thinking, with a consequent increased emphasis even amongst large firms of concentrating on the core business, and particularly on exercising the core competences, whilst 'downsizing' its overall employee numbers by subcontracting other functions considered to be less 'core'. The virtual corporation is, however, more 'virtual' than this model, and this is made possible above all mainly through electronics that even non-technically minded executives can handle competently.

Many companies now have some virtual characteristics, although few have all those enumerated above. An illustration of the trend towards the virtual corporation even amongst existing large international companies is Roche in the pharmaceutical industry, which carries out R&D through virtual research teams working in different parts of the world by means of e-mail, video conferencing, and other IT systems, although all are, of course, employed by Roche. In the USA the insurance industry is becoming increasingly specialized, with risk-taking, back-room processing, and sales all carried out in separate companies linked in a virtual fashion. Virtual companies are common in the computer industry with Dell, Compaq, and Sun Microsystems all configured in a virtual fashion. The Agit Manufacturing Enterprise Forum (AMEF) is a collaboration of eleven companies plus twenty-four other organizations formed to develop a fifteen-year plan to create a high-tech infrastructure. It has many of the characteristics of a virtual corporation.

A comparison

To appreciate the difference between the integrated hierarchical company and the virtual corporation, it may be useful to look at both organizational forms and contrast them on a number of criteria. Table 6.3 attempts such a comparison on six basic dimensions.

The basic differences are of an autocracy and a democracy, if one takes an analogy from the political sphere. In the autocratic hierarchically organized company, employees are paid salaries, and therefore are implicitly bound to accept the orders of those in authority over them, even if they disagree with them. Considerable resources are expended in constructing a governance framework based on motivating devices, sanctions, communications systems, job descriptions, organigrams, and layers of middle management that are neither the board of directors nor 'front-line troops'. A culture is established that encourages all employees to 'sing to the same hymn sheet' and identify with the corporations in all possible ways.

Table 6.3. *A comparison of integrated and virtual corporations*

Organizational dimensions	Integrated corporation	Virtual corporation
Organization structure	Formal and flexible	Flexible network, flat
Decisions	Ultimately by fiat	By discussion and consensus
Culture	Recognizable, encouraging employees to identify	Pluralist, linked by overlapping agendas
Boundaries	Clear 'us and them'	Variable
Management	High overheads	Minimal overheads
Power	From the board ex officio	Through possession of competences in demand
		Being the brand company

Virtual corporations are quite different. Their culture is pluralist and task orientated. Decisions are necessarily consensual, and overheads are minimal. Furthermore the boundaries of the corporation are as narrow or as wide as the personal networks of each member. Core competences are similarly flexible, as new members can always be brought on board without difficulty. It is the flexible boundary issue in fact that provides perhaps the most attractive feature of the virtual corporation. However, it is important to emphasize that the difference between cooperation and competition is not, as is sometimes suggested, necessarily highly correlated with ownership and the boundaries of the firm. As Jarillo (1993) suggests, there may be competition inside a firm and cooperation outside it, as illustrated in Fig. 6.4. Thus, under common ownership (the firm), there may be cooperation (e.g. the vertically integrated company united by a common vision and culture), or competition (e.g. many functionally hostile bureaucracies). Similarly, in conditions without common ownership there may be cooperation (e.g. the virtual corporation), or competition (e.g. the market).

There are, of course, limitations and disadvantages too with the virtual corporation: difficulties in achieving scale-or-scope economies, absence of tacit knowledge, problems with proprietary information leakage, and difficulty in financing critical mass level R&D, difficulties in maintaining commitment, and so forth.

When then should activities be treated through the virtual-corporation format, and when in hierarchies? This question is partly subject to analysis by the familiar transaction-cost analysis method (Williamson 1975) described in Chapter 3 above. However, such an analytic technique will only address cost-efficiency issues, and says nothing on matters of strategic vulnerability or competitive advantage.

The above quest for an optimal governance form in a given set of circumstances is not of course always the way in which virtual corporations are formed. Industries are populated by firms that have existing networks of relationships. These undergo frequent change in response to changing strategic imperatives—market power, success and failure, and variable levels of ambition. Virtual corporations may, therefore, be realized in a largely incremental way.

Thus a firm may start out by performing some activities itself and subcontracting others. As it grows and establishes trust and commitment relationships with its subcontractors, it may establish single-source relationships not unlike those of the Japanese keiretsu, where a high degree of operational interdependence is developed between firms at different stages of the value chain of activities, but with little if any common ownership.

The next stage in this electronic age may be the development of a strategic network between the operators, and then ultimately probably the establishment of a corporate identity through some form of joint ownership of profit streams. The virtual corporation has arrived, and may be followed as required by lesser or greater levels of integration, and by the development of a variable repertoire of configurations to meet changing market needs.

Rayport and Sviokla (1996) extend the concept of virtuality from the corporation to the value chain that depicts graphically the activities carried out by

	Cooperative approach	Non-cooperative approach
Common ownership	Vertically integrated company Shared goals	Bureaucracy Frequently adversarial relationships
No common ownership	Virtual corporation Belief that 'we are stronger together'	Market Arm's length relationships

Fig. 6.4. Competition and cooperation do not depend on ownership patterns
Source: adapted from Jarillo (1993).

the corporation (Porter 1985). The physical value chain (PVC), as they differentiate it, has typical primary activities of inbound logistics, operations, outbound logistics, marketing and sales, and after-sales service. These activities are supported by activities such as technology development, human-resource functions, the firm's infrastructure, and procurement. The PVC incurs costs, sometimes very high costs, as activities move from one linkage in the chain to another, and the most efficiently configured PVC takes advantage of what economies of scale and scope exist in the technologies and process of the firm. Rayport and Sviokla depict a virtual value chain (VVC) that exists in the age of the microchip alongside the PVC. It needs to be managed separately from the PVC, but in concert with it. It does not require the realization of scale-and-scope economies to achieve cost efficiency. Often an activity may be moved from the PVC to the VVC with advantage; thus Ford used to conduct product design by gathering an engineering team in a specific location and charging it with the job of designing a car. This can now be done by a virtual team in different parts of the world operating through cad/cam, e-mail, and teleconferencing.

Creating value in the VVC involves five sequential activities: gathering, organizing, selecting, synthesizing, and distributing information. If these five activities are applied to each activity in the PVC, then a value matrix is created that can transform the operations of the company, and thus even the 'rules of the game' of the industry.

Boeing, for example, has been able to develop a peardrop-shaped aero engine in virtual form, tested it virtually in a wind tunnel, and determined the best design at almost zero cost. Rayport and Sviokla talk of shifting activities from the market place to the 'market space'. As they say: 'Managers must therefore consciously focus on the principles that guide value creation and extraction across two value chains (PVC and VVC) separately and in combination' (1996: 34).

The benefit of virtuality as a result of the arrival of the information age has then enabled information to be transformed from a support activity in IT departments into a value-creating activity capable of totally changing the way companies compete in an industry.

The Box describes Benetton, a frequently cited virtual corporation. In Japan, Toyota is often cited as little different from a virtual corporation, with the following comparison cited as justification. General Motors of the USA, the archetypal integrated corporation, produced around 8 million cars a year in the 1980s with a wholly employed workforce of 750,000. Toyota produced 4.5 million with less than one-tenth as many employees (65,000), as most of its activities were heavily subcontracted. Indeed the Toyota involvement in the manufacturing process does not start before the assembly stage, as the components are subcontracted very widely. Of course Toyota again is not a real virtual corporation, as the electronic links are not key, and there is no equality between the eponymous company and the component manufacturers. However, it, like Benetton, illustrates an early and very successful form of

Benetton: A Virtual Corporation?

Benetton is sometimes described as the original virtual corporation, set up in the 1970s when the term had not even been coined. It lacks an essential part of the modern concept—namely, the dependence upon electronic linking, and is also not a virtual integration of equals each contributing what they are good at. However, it uses electronic communication extensively, and has many of the other key features of the modern virtual corporation, particularly the diffusion of value-chain activities amongst many different contributors and the emphasis on linking entrepreneurs carrying out those activities rather than employing a salariat. The company carries out very few activities directly: choice of designs, technical advice to manufacturers, the dyeing function (strategically critical and needing very specific and expensive assets), and overall management of the sales team, who are individually all self-employed both sales agents and retailers. Thus the salaried part of the Benetton team is the visible part of the iceberg, with seven-eighths of the virtual corporation residing below the surface, using the Benetton brand name but running and owning their own businesses.

organization in which many companies join together under a common banner but retain separate ownership and independence.

Appraisal

To be a successful virtual corporation it is not sufficient to be able to put together a competent set of value-chain activity performers, able to deliver the required output on time to specification. More than this is required for an opportunistic linking to be converted into a virtual corporation.

First, it is necessary to have a brand name under which to trade, that comes to be accepted as a mark of quality. Speed and flexibility are the next essential elements that the virtual corporation needs to pitch against the integrated corporation's established physical presence and proven competences. It also needs a brain and a central nervous system. By this is meant a centre from which direction emanates, and which is able to make difficult choices according to a consistent vision. Such a 'nervous system' must also provide a communication system able to convey information and requirements rapidly and accurately, and through which key aspects of quality control systems can be performed. It is, therefore, difficult to conceive of a successful competitive virtual corporation that is not dominated by one brand-name company at its centre. As in networks, the dominated network is likely to succeed when in competition with the less directed equal-partner network.

This information architecture, as it has come to be called, normally includes a data highway to link partners, private access for partners to access key data and applications software, the ability to monitor integrity and security, and an appropriate set of communication tools. Given these characteristics, the virtual corporation should be in a position to compete successfully against integrated corporations in many industry segments.

Why then has the movement to virtuality proved so slow in coming? The technology necessary for virtuality has been in existence for at least a decade. The strongest factor inhibiting the movement has probably been the secretive and over-competitive psychology of companies. Rigid mindsets wedded to the integrated form have dominated, coupled with a reluctance to single source in the belief that this gives away bargaining power. There has been a similar reluctance to share information with suppliers and distributors, regarding them more as arm's-length relationships than as business partners, part of the same team.

Until recently the global telecommunications network was insufficiently flexible and probably lacked sufficient capacity to cope with a fast-growing number of virtual corporations. However, the growth of the strategic-alliance movement in response to the globalization of markets and other factors, coupled with major user-friendly improvements in software availability for multiple uses, is now causing the virtual corporation to flourish as an organizational form in many areas.

Such a development is not, however, without its risks for major corporations. When IBM, although far from a virtual corporation itself, decided to make its PC in a virtual fashion, coupling IBM hardware with Microsoft software and an Intel microprocessor, it provided the necessary impetus for Microsoft and Intel to grow from small beginnings to a size larger than that of IBM itself. The company must regret the missed opportunity to make the microprocesssor itself, and develop the software in-house, which it clearly had the resources to do. It made the fatal mistake of not doing in-house the things that it was both good at and which had high strategic significance.

The virtual solution is not a solution to all situations. It has certain inherent weaknesses that are more important in some situations than in others. For example, if an industry is dominated by virtual corporations, it is unlikely to achieve major systemic innovation. This probably requires an integrated firm to take a risk and commit large R&D funds to developing a new technology. It then needs to exercise its market power to change the 'rules of the game' in its industry, as IBM did back in the 1960s with its 360 modular computer. This is very difficult for a virtual corporation to do, as it lacks sufficient legitimacy or reputation.

Chesbrough and Teece (1994) develop a matrix shown in Fig. 6.5 in which they differentiate between autonomous innovations and the more major systemic ones. They suggest that for systemic innovations (e.g. compact discs as opposed to vinyl records) integrated companies are generally the more appropriate forms. However, they suggest that, with autonomous innovations

	Autonomous	Systemic
Capabilities exist in-house	Multi-divisional	Integrated
Capabilities exist outside	Virtual corporation	Alliance
Capabilities must be created	Alliance, integrated	Integrated

Autonomous   Systemic
Types of innovation

Fig. 6.5. Autonomous and systemic innovations require different handling
Source: adapted from Chesbrough and Teece (1994).

within a technological paradigm, virtual corporations are much more appropriate. Systemic change costs more in resources up-front, and needs the driving force of an existing major player to see it through. A loosely knit coalition with resources belonging to the different partners would find this major activity difficult to achieve, though not, of course, impossible, as Apple Corporation showed with its major innovations in Windows and icon-based software. It has been notable, however, that they have been unable to appropriate major long-term benefits from these systemic innovations.

If the communication of 'tacit' (Polanyi 1966) knowledge, or the existence of very effective and efficient internal systems, is the key to success, a virtual corporation is unlikely to compete successfully against an integrated company with similar competences in every other way. Similarly, if there is a need for a high level of high-tech interdependence, an integrated company is more likely to be able to achieve this than a virtual corporation.

Thus, integrated corporations are likely to remain the dominant form of organization where internal coordination is key, where innovation is systemic, where there is a need to establish an industry standard, where tacit knowledge needs to be communicated, and where the major growth opportunities are the extension of existing activities into neighbouring markets.

In certain circumstances, however, virtual corporations are likely to outperform integrated corporations. These are in markets that do not exhibit the characteristics described in the previous section, where considerable turbulence leads to the need for speed of response, robustness, and flexibility, and of course where the onset of globalization demands resources not available to a single firm. In these circumstances the virtual corporation is likely to exist alongside the integrated corporations over the coming decades as the naturally selected winner in certain markets, and not in others. For many of the reasons outlined above, it may never come to replace the integrated form, and indeed may often exist on the interface between a number of integrated corporations involving parts of them in variable configurations.

SUMMARY

It has been argued that the network form of governance is most appropriate in conditions where partners provide specific assets, where demand is uncertain, where there are expected to be frequent exchanges between the parties, and where complex tasks have to be undertaken under conditions of considerable time pressure. An example of such conditions is found in the film industry, where 'film studios, producers, directors, cinematographers, and a host of other contractors join, disband and rejoin in varying combinations to make films' (Jones *et al.* 1997: 916). Other examples are frequently found in the bio-technology industry. As Jones and her colleagues state, 'When all of these conditions are in place, the network governance form has advantages over both hierarchy and market solutions in simultaneously adapting, co-ordinating and safeguarding exchanges' (p. 911).

The virtual corporation is often thought of as outsourcing, with electronic information controls and communication. In this sense the growth of the fashion for configurations around key competences with outsourcing has led to the corresponding growth of virtual-corporation theory. This differs from strategic-alliance theory in that the virtual corporation does not have inter-company organizational learning as its prime objective, as does strategic-alliance theory. Virtual corporations are indeed all about putting together a variable configuration company from existing companies with excellent specific skills. No inter-company learning is necessarily involved.

However, outsourcing has reached such a level that the pendulum threatens to swing back in the other direction. A senior bank economist at Morgan Stanley, after years of advocating downsizing and outsourcing changed his views in a 1996 news interview and now states that cutting back and back eventually ends up with no corporation at all. Even the core competences may be inadvertently outsourced—for example, R&D or design. It cannot be a source of sustainable advantage. Furthermore, as more functions are taken over by what are termed 'contingent workforces', loyalty to the firm and commitment tend to disappear. Indeed a study of several hundred UK companies by PA Consulting in 1996 revealed that they outsource over a quarter of their total budgets for what they regard as their key business processes. There were only three activities that more than 35 per cent of the companies in the survey regarded as 'core'— business strategy, information-technology strategy, and new-product development. This meant that everything else, including R&D, customer service, finance and accounting, and manufacturing were regarded as non-core by two-thirds of the companies surveyed.

This leads to one further thought on the subject. It may be very possible to set up a virtual corporation by identifying a strategically vital centre, outsourcing everything else, and linking the whole by IT packages, with the central core representing the brain, owning the brand name, and maintaining the motivation even amongst the outlier partners by sophisticated relationship development. It is quite another matter, however, to slim down an existing integrated corporation and transform it into a virtual corporation. The demotivation resulting from being cast into the outer periphery, or from fear that one will be the next to go, makes such a transformation fraught with human difficulty and unlikely to lead to a happy and thus competitively successful company.

REFERENCES

Arthur, W. B. (1996), 'Increasing Returns and the New World of Business', *Harvard Business Review* (July–Aug.), 100–9.

Axelrod, R. (1984), *The Evolution of Cooperation* (New York: HarperCollins).

Boisot, M. H. (1986), 'Markets and Hierarchies in a Cultural Perspective', *Organization Studies*, 7: 135–58.

Cassells, M. (1996), *The Rise of the Network Society* (Oxford: Blackwell).

Chandler, A. D. (1962), *Strategy and Structure* (Cambridge Mass.: MIT Press).

—— (1990), *Scale and Scope: The Dynamics of Industrial Capitalism* (Cambridge, Mass.: Harvard University Press).

Chesbrough, H., and Teece, D. J. (1994), 'When is Virtual Virtuous: Integrated Enterprises and Competitive Advantage', paper presented at the Strategic Management Society Conference, Paris, September.

Child, J. (1987), 'Information Technology, Organization and the Response to Strategic Challenges', *California Management Review*, 30: 33–50.

Davis, G. F., Diekmann, K. A., and Tinsley, C. H. (1994), 'The Decline and Fall of the Conglomerate Firm in the 1980s: The Deinstitutionalization of an Organizational Form', *American Sociological Review*, 59: 547–70.

Defillippi, R., and Reed, R. (1991), 'Three Perspectives on Appropriation Hazards in Cooperative Agreements', paper presented at the Strategic Management Society Conference, Toronto, October.

Gerlach, M. L. (1992), *Alliance Capitalism* (Berkeley and Los Angeles: University of California Press).

Handy, C. (1989), *The Age of Unreason* (London: Hutchinson).

Harrington, J. (1991), 'Virtual Organization', in *Organization Structure and Information Technology* (Hemel Hempstead: Prentice Hall), 207–38.

Jarillo, J. C. (1988), 'On Strategic Networks', *Strategic Management Journal*, 9: 31–41.

—— (1993), *Strategic Networks: Creating the Borderless Organization* (Oxford: Butterworth Heinemann).

Johanson, J., and Mattsson, L.-G. (1991), 'Interorganisational Relations in Industrial Systems: A Network Approach Compared with the Transaction-Cost Approach', in G. Thompson, J. Frances, R. Levacic, and J. Mitchell (eds.), *Markets, Hierarchies and Networks* (London: Sage), 256–64.

Jones, C., Hesterly, W. S., and Borgatti, S. P. (1997), 'A General Theory of Network

Governance: Exchange Conditions and Social Mechanisms', *Academy of Managerial Review*, 22: 911–45.

Lawrence, P. R., and Lorsch, J. W. (1967), *Organization and Environment* (Boston, Mass.: Harvard Business School Press.

Lorenzoni, G. (1982), 'From Vertical Integration to Vertical Disintegration', paper presented at the Strategic Management Society Conference, Montreal, September.

Mowshowitz, A. (1994), 'Virtual Organization: A Vision of Management in the Information Age', *The Information Society*, 10: 267–94.

Nagel, P., and Dove, M. (1991), 'The Virtual Corporation', working paper (Le High University, Illinois).

Nohria, N., and Eccles, R. G. (1992) (eds.), *Networks and Organizations* (Boston, Mass.: Harvard Business School Press).

North, D. C. (1996), 'Reflections on Economics and Cognitive Science', public lecture, Judge Institute of Management Studies, University of Cambridge, May.

Pfeffer, J., and Salancik, G. (1978), *The External Control of Organizations: A Resource Dependence Perspective* (New York: Harper & Row).

Polanyi, K. (1966), *The Tacit Dimension* (London: Routledge & Kegan Paul).

Porter, M. E. (1980), *Competitive Strategies: Techniques for Analyzing Industries and Competitors* (New York: Free Press).

——(1985), *Competitive Advantage: Creating and Sustaining Superior Performance* (New York: Free Press).

Powell, W. W. (1987), 'Hybrid Organizational Arrangements: New Form or Transitional Development', *California Management Review*, 30: 67–87.

——(1990), 'Neither Market nor Hierarchy: Network Forms of Organization', *Research in Organizational Behavior*, 12: 295–336.

Rayport, J., and Sviokla, J. (1996), 'Exploiting the Virtual Value Chain', *McKinsey Quarterly*, 1996/1: 20–38.

Richardson, G. B. (1972), 'The Organisation of Industry', *Economic Journal*, 82: 883–96.

Skinner, W. (1978), *Manufacturing in the Corporate Strategy* (London: Wiley).

Snow, C. S., Miles, R. E., and Coleman, H. J. (1992) 'Managing 21st Century Network Organizations', *Organizational Dynamics*, 20: 5–20.

——and Thomas, J. B. (1993), 'Building Networks: Broker Roles and Behaviours', in P. Lorange (ed.), *Implementing Strategic Processes* (Oxford: Blackwell).

Thorelli, H. B. (1986), 'Networks: Between Markets and Hierarchies', *Strategic Management Journal*, 7: 37–51.

Walsham, G. (1994), 'Virtual Organization: An Alternative View', *The Information Society*, 10: 289–92.

Wernerfelt, B. (1984), 'A Resource-Based View of the Firm', *Strategic Management Journal*, 5: 171-80.

Williamson, O. E. (1975), *Markets and Hierarchies* (New York: Free Press).

Zukin, S., and DiMaggio, P. (1990) (eds.), 'Introduction', in *Structures of Capital: The Social Organization of the Economy* (Cambridge: Cambridge University Press), 1–36.

7

....

Negotiation and Valuation

ALLIANCE NEGOTIATION

If strategic alliances are to continue to grow in number and importance, as is the trend in the 1990s, it is important to be clear on some ground rules for negotiating them, and in particular for valuing the contribution each partner is able to make to the joint enterprise, in a way acceptable to both or indeed all the partners. In this regard a number of issues arise:

1. In negotiations, should an alliance be treated in a similar fashion to an acquisition, and if not how should it be different?
2. What are the key outcomes desired from the negotiation of a strategic alliance?
3. How is it possible to value a partner's contribution in the varying types of alliance forms adopted?

This chapter will address these issues by suggesting a number of ideas, which it will then relate to a number of existing case studies of international strategic alliances with which the authors are familiar, in order to examine whether the evidence in these case studies appears to support the ideas.

Strategic alliances differ from acquisitions in a number of ways. In particular, acquisitions involve the transfer of ownership and hence authority to make decisions from the acquired to the acquiring company. The acquiror has thus the right to make any changes in the operation of its new subsidiary that it thinks fit, constrained only by law and the specific conditions of sale involved in the deal. Certain characteristics are normally found in acquisition deals. First, the acquiror may have had to pay a premium of up to 30 per cent for the company, if it is a company whose shares are quoted on the stock exchange. If the bid has been a strongly contested one, the premium may be even higher. At all events, it is certain that the sellers will have been determined, if they were to sell their company, to get the highest possible price for it. Other frequent side-effects of acquisitions are the demotivation of executives made rich by the deal, and the disappearance of key executives unhappy about the change of ownership. A further characteristic of acquisitions is that the purchasers are often only able to gain access to limited information about the operation of the target company prior to the conclusion of the deal, and they may therefore encounter some unpleasant surprises when they actually take over control.

None of these factors is likely to obtain in a strategic alliance. Therefore strategic alliance negotiations should be and are likely to be conducted in a different fashion from acquisitions. Far more attention will be given to the fact that the negotiators need to work closely together once the alliance is successfully concluded. Thus a 'successful' negotiator who has driven a hard bargain may come to regret his 'success' when he encounters resentment in working with his new partners.

Both acquisitions and alliances seek synergies through the putting-together of potentially complementary assets and skills. However, strategic alliances do not seek, as a price for the realization of these synergies, the incorporation of the partner into one enterprise and the subjugation of its identity, as is often the case in acquisitions. Alliances normally concede the separate identity of its partner or partners, and seek to maximize the benefit that can be obtained from putting together parts of two value chains (Porter and Fuller 1986) in order to achieve competitive advantage in chosen markets together, when this could not be achieved alone. Thus the negotiation of an alliance seeks to achieve a relationship between partners that can enable them together to achieve business success, without either partner needing to accept loss of identity or ultimate independence.

In negotiating a strategic alliance, or collaborative agreement of any sort, two frequently conflicting aims must be simultaneously held in the mind of each body of negotiators. First, how do we configure the collaboration so as to achieve the greatest possible level of competitive advantage for the joint enterprise, and secondly how do we get the best deal for our company?

The agenda for dealing with the first issue will include the following items:

1. *An analysis of the strategic fit between the companies.* Unless there is a clear complementarity of assets and competences, so that a joint value chain can be constructed with a high probability of giving competitive advantage, the alliance will not succeed in economic terms.
2. *An analysis of the cultural fit between the companies.* It is unreasonable to expect the prospective partners to be culturally similar, since corporate cultures are as varied as fingerprints. However, it is valuable to attempt to identify possible cultural barriers to smooth working, and to reassure oneself that both partners are sensitive to the need to adjust culturally. Chapter 11 will deal with this issue more fully.
3. *Identification of goal congruence.* Goals and objectives need not be the same. However, they must not be in conflict if the alliance is to succeed. It is valuable to identify clearly one's own and one's partner's objectives both generally and from the alliance at this early stage.
4. *Identification of a primary joint project and of its scope.* Until a clear pro-

ject has been identified, the alliance is little more than a declaration of intent. The first project should often be a relatively limited one embarked upon with a primary objective of developing methods of working together.

5. *Identification of the level and nature of the contribution expected from each partner.* Issue 4 will require resources, and the initial negotiations can usefully move forward to discussing broadly what each partner would expect to contribute to the joint project.

6. *Agreement on the structure of the alliance and its decision-making machinery.* This is often left for later, and then becomes a problem. If addressed at the outset it will give confidence to both parties that the alliance is being professionally and competently approached.

7. *Agreement on a termination formula in the event of one or both partners wishing to exit the alliance.* This may seem an odd item to discuss at the start of a relationship. However, both partners will know that a significant percentage of alliances are dissolved within five years. To agree at the outset on a formula for such a termination therefore is a sensible move to avoid possible later acrimony.

Issue 2—namely, the question of how to do the best deal for one's company—inevitably involves striking a bargain of some sort. All alliances involve compromises of some sort, even if only voluntarily to limit a partner's autonomy in certain areas. For a bargain to be possible, there needs to be an overlap between the strength of the perceived needs of both partners. Thus, in a bazaar negotiation where your highest buying price for the souvenir is £20, and the trader's lowest selling price is £10, a deal is possible with the final price dependent upon the respective negotiating skills of the players, which will include their respective abilities to imply at each move that they will go no further; this is their last offer. If, however, your highest buying price is £10 and the trader's lowest selling price is £20, then no deal is possible, and any time spent negotiating is time wasted. The basic situation is the same in alliances, but the attitudes of the negotiators need to be subtly different.

Since the negotiation is the prelude to working together on a project, it is vital that both parties leave the negotiation feeling that they have not just a workable deal, but a positively good one for them. Thus, paradoxically, if both partners negotiate generously and take it as a primary objective to ensure that their partner has a good deal, thereby sub-optimizing on their immediate deal from a selfish viewpoint, they lay the groundwork for optimizing the long-term probability of success of the proposed alliance. Fig. 7.1 illustrates graphically the best approach to the negotiation with a potential alliance partner. An attempt must be made to end up in the top right-hand box of the matrix. This contrasts starkly with the attitudes typically adopted in acquisition negotiations, when both parties attempt to arrive at a deal that will put them in either the top left-hand box or the bottom right-hand box respectively.

A's interests	*A* wins *B* loses	*A* wins *B* wins
	A loses *B* loses	*A* loses *B* wins

B's interests

Fig. 7.1. Possible negotiation outcomes

The very fact that negotiation is taking place implies a willingness on the part of both parties to make some compromises with regard to their interests in relation to those of the other party, and such a cooperative activity is seen to be in the best interests of both parties. Otherwise the imposition of force would be the method chosen to achieve one's ends. This fact was recognized in the management literature as far back as 1968, where Nierenberg stated: 'Negotiation is a cooperative enterprise; common interests must be sought; negotiation is a behavioural process, not a game; in good negotiation, everybody wins something . . . there are other advantages to the cooperative approach. Results can be greater, solutions more lasting' (Nierenberg 1968).

However, as Lewicki and Litterer (1985) point out, negotiation may take place in two quite different situations: that involving a zero-sum game and that involving a non-zero-sum game. In a zero-sum game, a fixed-size pie is divided up between the parties and where one gains the other loses. In such situations compromises mean pain and loss. In non-zero-sum games, this is not the case. A potentially expanding pie is conceived so that, if the right deal is struck, both parties may hope to benefit without sacrifice. Often such negotiations require imaginative proposals, and an understanding of the differing strength of individual needs that make gain possible without perceived loss. A hypothetical Arab company in a desert may be very willing almost to give away petrol but would pay dearly for water. A Western company may be willing to pay dearly for petrol but will give away water. In such an imaginary situation a deal can be struck that will make both parties happy, as they are each able to trade commodities that have close to zero marginal utility to them, for a commodity with a relatively high marginal utility. Similarly, as in the theory of comparative costs in international trade where countries have different ratios of costs for their factors of production, there is an opportunity for trade to their mutual advantage. The theory of mutual advantage can be extended dynamically where companies have complementary assets able to achieve synergies when combined. However, as in prisoner's-dilemma games, the competitive solution and the cooperative solution may both exist in the same situation, and the achievement of the mutually beneficial cooperative solution depends upon one player's belief in the trustworthiness and perceptive imagination of the other.

Lewicki and Litterer call the win–win approach *integrative bargaining*. This is contrasted with *distributive bargaining*, where the objective is to achieve a mutually acceptable distribution of the resources available. Integrative bargaining depends upon firstly identifying a common shared goal and then developing a process to achieve it. They stress that this approach is by no means the only one or even the most obvious one available to the parties.

Five possible avenues are open to the negotiator. He or she may:

1. compete and attempt to force the other party to back down;
2. accommodate, i.e. back down himself;
3. compromise, i.e. agree to split the difference;
4. take avoidance action by refusing to consider the issue;
5. collaborate by inventing and considering problem-solving approaches.

Blake and Moulton (1964) integrated these five possible approaches into a matrix that they called the Managerial Grid, illustrated in Fig. 7.2. This shows clearly that a collaboration approach, as shown in the top right-hand corner of the grid maximizes the result from a strong concern by both parties for each other's outcome as well as for their own.

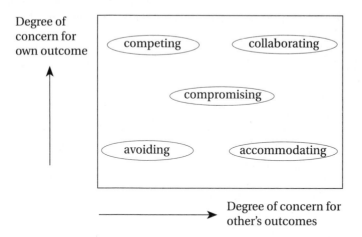

Fig. 7.2. The managerial grid of negotiating possibilities
Source: adapted from Blake and Moulton (1964).

Lewicki and Litterer identify a number of preconditions for achieving success in the collaborative integrative-bargaining approach. It is necessary genuinely to understand the nature and strength of each other's needs. There must be a free flow of accurate and honestly presented information between the partners. The negotiators must have the ability to focus on what they have in common rather than their differences, and they must be willing energetically to search for solutions that meet both sides' primary goals. Such negotiations will be characterized by a high degree of trust, strong motivation and commitment, the development or identification of a binding common objective, and a willingness by both sides to accept that the other's needs are valid.

Should such a negotiation start to move into conditions of conflict, Osgood (1962) suggests a procedure he entitles GRIT (graduated reciprocation and tension reduction). This involves role reversal, keeping the number of issues debated under strict control, searching anew for superordinate goals to reunite the parties, and repackaging proposed solutions to make them more attractive.

Pruitt (1981) identifies similar possible behaviour options to Lewicki and Litterer but stresses that they are psychologically extremely difficult to combine. You cannot easily start off competitively and then move into collaborative mode with any credibility, as the other party will suspect your motives. Pruitt sees two types of coordinative behaviour:

1. concession exchange;
2. problem-solving discussions.

Clearly concession exchange is intellectually less taxing. So long as the respective concessions are tracked and realistically evaluated, a fair deal can be struck. The problem-solving approach involves far more imagination but can also be far more rewarding as it is more likely to establish the real non-zero-sum nature of the situation which concession exchange will not. Pruitt identifies three levels of risk in coordinative behaviour—high risk, medium risk, and low risk. *High-risk behaviour* may be exemplified by the late Anwar Sadat's trip to Jerusalem in an attempt to break the Arab–Israeli deadlock. Such an act involves a lot of trust as it risks loss of face and is difficult to reverse. *Moderate-risk coordinative behaviour* occurs when less trust exists. It may involve signalling a willingness to exchange concessions in such a way that, if the gesture is not reciprocated, it can be cancelled with no loss of face. *Low-risk coordinative behaviour* may involve indicating a willingness to deal in minor and unimportant areas, but with the underlying motive of getting negotiations underway, in order subsequently to move to more substantive matters. Pruitt confirms the view that, the greater the level of trust and bonding, the greater the likelihood of coordinative behaviour.

Another aspect of the art of negotiating is to understand the culture of your partner. This is particularly relevant in the setting-up of cross-border alliances, as the other party will be from a different nationality, possibly will speak a different language, and will certainly have a different culture with all the attendant opportunities for misunderstanding that follow from this. This is illustrated by Hendon and Hendon (1989) in their citation of two quotations respectively from a Japanese describing the Americans, and from an American describing the Japanese.

Most Americans are very very individualistic—you could almost say egotistical.

Executive of Kyocera Corporation of Japan

We're the father and you're the children. We'll tell you what's good for you, and you do everything you can to make us successful. That doesn't wash here.

Executive of the AFL-CIO of America talking about the Japanese.

At least it can be said that these two executives had at least a caricatured view of the cultures of their respective potential partners, and were not totally ethnocentric in their assumptions. It is vital in Hendon and Hendon's view to make a list of cultural assumptions regarding your negotiating partner if you are to avoid misinterpreting signals. However, one should also note that individuals do, of course, differ from their national caricatures.

Tung (1984) brings this issue to life with her characterization of the qualities to be expected in the Japanese when engaged in negotiations, as compared with the Americans:

1. The Japanese generally operate through consensus-making with frequent reference back to head office, whereas US companies take more individual decisions at a lower level and consult less.
2. The Japanese have a much longer time perspective in regard to expected corporate results, and also conduct negotiations at a deliberately leisurely pace. The Americans want fast results and expect to fly in Friday and have an agreement by Monday.
3. The Japanese are much more thorough in their preparation and their scrutiny of documents than the Americans.
4. The Japanese are much more concerned than the Americans if an agreement has to be changed after it has been agreed.

Tung follows with some pertinent advice for Westerners negotiating with the Japanese.

1. Be patient; things take longer and a longer time-frame is adopted.
2. Maintain the continuity of negotiating teams as trust is the key to success and this is personally allocated, and takes time to build up.
3. Do not adopt ethnocentric attitudes, respect cultural differences.
4. Study the foreign market and work within the system, noting that some Japanese industries are open to foreign goods and some are not.
5. Ensure compatibility of objectives and complementarity of needs. Western companies generally seek profit while Japanese companies usually seek growth and market share.
6. Equity levels are always a sensitive issue. You will only get a majority in a joint venture in Japan if you have a unique and exceptionally valued product.
7. Maintain a constant and continuous dialogue to avoid misunderstandings.

Advice such as this emphasizes the importance of not just getting to know the other party personally, but also developing an understanding of the culture that has brought about his value system if the alliance negotiation is to be successful and the subsequent relationship to be lasting.

THE PROCESS

Fisher and Ury (1981) suggest that there are seven important steps to the successful negotiation of a strategic alliance:

1. Gather all possible information.
2. Identify and evaluate the strength of your own and your partner's needs.
3. Identify the major issues for negotiation and assign minimum values to your position.
4. Make proposals and listen to the responses.
5. Show flexibility by suggesting alternative approaches.
6. Exchange concessions and compare notes honestly about their value.
7. Close the deal and tie up the details carefully.

1. *Information-gathering*. Find out all you can about your prospective partner's current position—e.g. financial strength, capabilities and vulnerabilities, aims and objectives, personnel, technologies, and market position in the main markets in which it operates. Draw up a similar catalogue of your own qualities, and satisfy yourself that there is probably an acceptably broad zone of possible agreement.

2. *Needs assessment*. This step is frequently a difficult one, since it involves seeing behind both your own and your partner's confident public posture to the world, and trying to discover how it sees the inevitably uncertain future, and its own ability to survive and prosper in it. This step involves not only estimating these factors from the viewpoint of the prospective partner firm, but also from the viewpoint of the negotiating team. Is the chief negotiator close to retirement, or an up and coming executive, intent upon making his mark? The success of this step may be vital to knowing how far to go later in the process when trading concessions.

3. *Issue identification*. This step attempts to set the agenda for the negotiation. The issues will emerge from the work done in steps 1 and 2. Once you have agreed on what they are, it is important to role play a practice negotiation within the company and agree worst positions that may be conceded for each issue. This will involve discovering whether you have a credible BATNA and how strong it is. A BATNA is the 'Best Alternative to a Negotiated Position' option, and it clarifies the strength of one's negotiating position, when compared with the partner's BATNA. Thus if you determine that your BATNA is either to go it alone, or to form an alliance with another well-positioned company then you are in a strong position. If you have great difficulty in seeing any realistic BATNA, then your negotiating position is not strong, and it is likely that the other party will know this. Recognition of such a situation should influence you in your attitude to the making of concessions.

4. *The proposals stage*. The time has now been reached to negotiate in earnest face to face. Fisher and Ury recommend that the other side should be encour-

aged to make the first set of proposals, and that these should not then be met by a counter-proposal but by a set of questions designed to raise issues in a constructive manner. The attitude should always emphasize the win–win nature of the negotiations, and that both partners are looking at a situation objectively rather than 'negotiating a deal' that is in their individual self-interest. Open questions (how?) rather than closed ones (yes or no?) are recommended at this stage to tease out issues and attitudes. Signalling positively through choice of words and body language helps build momentum and develop consensus.

5. *Show and encourage flexibility.* Take opportunities to repackage proposals that seem to be meeting resistance. Flexibility can also be demonstrated by increasing the number of variables under discussion. It may be valuable to have a list ready of items that might be introduced if the negotiations start to lose momentum or to meet road blocks.

6. *Exchange concessions.* There is always a risk in negotiations that, when one party makes a concession to help the negotiations along, the other party pockets it and continues on its way. A concession by one side should generally be met by one on the other side so that the perception of equity is retained.

Negotiation with the Chinese

Negotiating alliances or trade deals with the Chinese usually generates considerable uncertainty among the representatives of foreign organizations, which can easily turn into anxiety if the foreign negotiators do not appreciate what is going on. The Chinese have a long tradition of putting the other side at a psychological disadvantage, which goes back to classic writings such as Sun Tzu's *The Art of War*. Child arrived at the following guidelines for negotiating with Chinese partners, based on his own experience and on conclusions drawn from research studies:

- be prepared for erratic progress, with prolonged periods of no movement;
- practise patience;
- discount Chinese rhetoric about future prospects and the value of friendship, control against exaggerated expectations;
- steel yourself against Chinese attempts to influence proceedings through shaming and extreme language;
- try to understand the Chinese culture of negotiation and resist the conclusion that difficulties are necessarily brought about by your own mistakes;
- always keep in mind your negotiating objectives and the limits beyond which you are not prepared to go.

Source: Child (1994: 234–9).

It is best, of course, not to use the term concessions but rather to describe the movement in position as an alternative way of dealing with a problem or issue.

7. *Close the deal.* This stage, of course, is the crucial one, in the absence of which the alliance will not come about. It involves accurately summarizing the position reached, getting both sides to agree to the summary, and following up with a written record of the agreement composed in plain English rather than legal jargon. Frequently in the euphoria of a successfully concluded alliance, the details are not dealt with and consequently a time bomb is planted for future meetings.

These recommendations are offered for a negotiation between Western parties. They require modification to take account of cases where there are more marked cultural differences between the negotiators. As Child (1994), Pye (1982), and others have pointed out, for example, the process of negotiation in an East Asian environment such as China can be rather more complex and fraught (see Box).

PARTNER-CONTRIBUTION VALUATION

The second part of this chapter deals with the difficult issue of how to place a value on the partner's initial contribution to the alliance. It is far more difficult to calculate the value of a partner in a strategic alliance than in an acquisition. In an acquisition, after all, the market will decide the ultimate price in most cases, and opportunities will be afforded for other bidders to enter the process. This is far less the case in an alliance, as most alliances are concluded largely outside the view of the market, as a result of confidential negotiations carried out over a period of time. The form that the alliance is to take also affects the valuation. If no joint venture company is formed, it is, for example, very difficult to determine where the boundaries of the alliance start and stop. Thus the assessment of a partner's value to the alliance will depend on an estimation of its present and future likely contribution, and will vary in its measurability on the choice of alliance form and the nature of the assets involved.

Once the partners have decided to form an alliance and more specifically to adopt a particular alliance form, they have to face the issue of how to value each other's contribution. This is a very uncertain art rather than a precise science as the following case studies will show.

Rover–Honda

This alliance takes the form of a complex two-partner collaboration. Rover's principal objectives from the alliance were to improve its production processes, and to develop new car models faster and more economically than it could alone. Honda's objectives were to establish themselves as a significant European, as well as Japanese and US car-production company.

Since a collaboration has no legal entity distinct from the partners, the question of valuation is frequently not expressly addressed, since there is no requirement for either partner to put capital or specific assets into a new enterprise. This was the case with Rover–Honda. The collaboration took the form of a series of projects each of which needed to be separately resourced and provided with an action plan. For example, the first project was for Rover to buy a knock-down Honda kit from Japan, assemble it in England, badge it as a Triumph Acclaim, and sell it on the UK market. The only valuation for this initial project involved agreeing a price for the kits, which was done by Honda costing them, applying a mark-up, and adjusting the price to take note of the price points existing on the UK mid-range car market.

Subsequent projects involved joint design, joint manufacture, joint component sourcing, and ultimately share exchange. These valuations were more complex. However, John Bacchus, Director of Honda collaboration, assured the authors that no precise or complicated calculations took place. Design input by Honda or Rover was dealt with by applying the car industry conventional level of royalties. Components involved a negotiated transfer price.

The valuation of the transfer of Honda's technology and manufacturing process expertise might be thought to have generated the greatest amount of debate, as these factors represented the highest amount of value-added to Rover, and stood between the company and its aspirant reputation as a high-quality car producer. However, it would appear that Honda attempted no form of value billing, but transferred its engineers' time at a day rate that they conventionally applied in Japan.

The share exchange was also done with little attempt to maximize profit by either party. Honda exchanged 20 per cent of Honda Manufacturing Company (UK) for 20 per cent of Rover, with a balancing figure paid in cash. As neither company was quoted on the stock exchange, there was no independent value upon which to base the calculations. An attempt was, therefore, made to value the assets of both companies on basic accountancy conventions. It was claimed that the share exchange was anyway merely a symbolic gesture of commitment by both parties to the alliance, and not an investment as such.

Thus although some attempt was made to value cost in relation to the collaboration, no real attempt was made to value benefit, and thus discuss how it should be appropriated. Given the state of Rover's perceived technological and operational competence at the commencement of the alliance, and its perceived subsequent dramatic improvement, it might be argued that, by neglecting to value potential future benefit, Honda considerably suboptimized the profit it might have gained from the alliance.

Royal Bank of Scotland–Banco Santander

These two banks formed a complex collaboration alliance that also involved a number of joint ventures and a funds transfer consortium involving a number of additional banks. The rationale behind the alliance in this case was that two somewhat insular European banks (Scottish and Spanish) were concerned both that the development of the EU would lead to a regional rather than a national banking structure and that their relatively small size in European terms when compared with giants like Deutsche Bank or Crédit Agricole would be a disadvantage. There was therefore an attempt to develop a whole laundry list of activities in which the two banks might operate together, to the overall improvement of both their reputations and their effectiveness.

The philosophy behind the alliance was at all times one of equality, although in fact Santander were somewhat the richer bank. A decision was therefore taken to exchange a small percentage of shares, which, since both banks were publicly quoted, represented no problem of valuation. Subsequently Santander bought a further tranche of RBS shares from the Kuwait Investment Office, with RBS's active agreement, since RBS had come to regard these shares as a potentially volatile holding in its porfolio of equity holders. This further purchase by Santander was not, however, allowed to disturb the underlying philosophy of the two banks of an alliance of equals.

This philosophy dictated their 50 per cent each shareholdings in the Gibraltar, German, and Belgium financial-services acquisitions that they made. There were, therefore, no valuation negotiations in this alliance that might have involved specific difficulties in valuing the two banks' respective contributions to the partnership. Issues of which bank's needs were the greater were, given the equality philosophy, not allowed to arise, and thus did not become a factor in contribution valuations.

The Cable & Wireless Consortium

This alliance is an international telecommunications consortium instigated by C&W to tender (successfully) for the second Japanese international carrier licence. In order to do so C&W developed a focused consortium joint venture with seventeen Japanese and one US partners. The consortium has been very successful during its short life, and has certainly enabled C&W to achieve its main aim of being accepted in Japan as a good corporate citizen, welcome to do business in that country.

In a new joint venture, whether a consortium or otherwise, basic ownership of the company is determined by the distribution of the equity. Either this is allocated at par in proportion to the capital contributed or a more complicated formula is adopted of which there are many variants. If specific tangible or intangible assets are contributed by a particular partner, they may reasonably make claims that this be reflected in an appropriate increase in its shareholding. C&W brought all the telecommunications expertise. However, this was not reflected in its shareholding.

C&W was allocated 17 per cent of the equity and paid for it with cash when the consortium was set up. There were three major shareholders: C Itoh, Toyota, and C&W, each with 17 per cent, totalling 51 per cent, a bare majority. The remaining shareholdings were thus widely distributed and generally small in percentage terms. The presence of C&W in the top three equity holders was a largely symbolic recognition of its telecommunications expertise, and of the fact that it was the initial entrepreneurial instigator of IDC.

No consideration was given to what each partner differentially brought to the consortium, or to recognizing this by means of valuations of expertise, royalties, or any other rewarding device. For C&W, the investment was a 'strategic' one to help establish the company in Japan, and to enable corporate learning about the Far East theatre of operations to take place. In such circumstances it was not motivated to risk damaging partner relations by developing sophisticated valuation formulae that might more fairly have reflected its expertise contribution. Indeed, so concerned was it to maintain good relations that it did not object when it was decided that only the Japanese would have cheque-signing power in the company.

ICI Pharma

This joint venture between Sumitomo Chemicals and ICI Pharmaceuticals in Japan is a focused two-partner joint venture. Although it was set up in 1972 and is still in existence, it is generally regarded as an example of a cross-border alliance that has not really flourished. ICI's objectives were to develop its business in Japan. Sumitomo's were to develop its pharmaceutical business, which at that time was not very strong. ICI provided the product specifications for a number of pharmaceutical products, some capital, and the use of the brand names. Sumitomo agreed to manufacture the products, provided licensing credibility in Japan, and provided the marketing and sales network. A 50:50 joint venture named ICI Pharma was set up in Japan, at the time of going to press owned 60 per cent by ICI and 40 per cent by Sumitomo. It is ICI's belief that in the initial negotiations Sumitomo got the best of the bargain, and has reaped most of the profit. The deal has not, however, been renegotiated, and ICI has developed subsequent business in Japan through other vehicles. If ICI had taken the C&W view and regarded the investment as the price of learning how to do business in Japan, all might have been well. However, it took a more carefully calculated view, and perhaps owing to lack of knowledge of Japanese circumstances arguably miscalculated.

When interviewed, an ICI senior executive said that in valuing its own and its partners' contribution to a joint venture, it takes the following factors into account:

1. *The actual expenditure the partner has made on the asset to be put into the joint venture, not the current market value, however calculable, of that asset.* Thus, if an entrepreneurial company had developed a very specific technological asset giving competitive advantage, the partner might find difficulty in getting ICI to value it at more than its cost.
2. *The overall strength, however defined, of the potential partner company.* Thus if a small company stretched for capital were to approach ICI with a proposal for a joint venture, ICI would it seems be likely to take advantage of its greater industrial strength in the negotiations.
3. *The perceived urgency of the partner's need.* Negotiations taking advantage of this factor would be very likely to cause resentment once that need lessened in the future.
4. *A comparison of prices put on similar deals in the market.* This is, of course, a valuable benchmark for acquisition deals. However, for alliances such prices are more difficult to unravel, are rarely published, and may well militate against the win–win philosophy that must be applied in alliances if they are to survive and prosper over the longer period.
5. *The value to be put on control.* Thus ICI would expect to pay more for 51 per cent of a joint venture, thereby failing to give much credence to the understanding that alliances only really prosper if the partners are genuinely equals at least in the relationship, and need to act in a consensual rather than a hierarchical mode.

Given these somewhat power-based attitudes to joint-venture partner-contribution valuation, it is very difficult to make the mental transition to that required for a successful alliance. If the negotiations have been power-based, and implicitly centred on each potential partner driving the hardest possible bargain supposedly for its shareholders, the subsequent management of the venture is likely to reflect similar attitudes. It is not perhaps surprising, therefore, that ICI has felt less than enthusiastic about the management and evolution of ICI Pharma in Japan.

Dowty-Sema

This joint venture, stimulated by the Ministry of Defence, was set up to provide the MOD with an alternative tenderer to Ferranti in naval command and control systems. Dowty provided the hardware expertise and Sema the software, and a 50 : 50 joint venture provided the vehicle for the MOD contracts. However, the vehicle remained, in the words of its managing director, more a shop window than a substantial company, as 90 per cent of the work was subcontracted from the official contract holder to the partner companies.

Valuation then became an easy task as all the major assets remained in the partner companies. A certain amount of capital was needed to set up the joint venture, and establish a small staff, and that was all. Political control remained with the partner companies. Profits were taken in the partner companies, and no patents or other intangible assets were ceded to the joint venture. Staff joined the payroll of the partner companies and were seconded where necessary to the venture. It may be questioned whether this is the best way to run a joint venture, but it does make the valuation process easy, as there is no need to do any, and the sometimes difficult negotiations to get agreement on 'who brings what to the party' are obviated.

Eurovinyl Chloride

This is a joint venture between ICI and Enichem of Italy, set up for the purpose of achieving the management of the oversupplied PVC market in Europe through the rational withdrawal of the most inefficient supply—generally that owned by the two partners.

The joint venture is owned 50:50 by the two partners, but involved some complicated valuation negotiations at set-up. Estimates were made and agreed of the value of the assets and their potential earnings over their remaining life given expected market conditions.

In order to capitalize the venture appropriately, EVC was allowed to take on loans at an agreed rate of interest, repayment to be made from joint venture profits. The 50:50 share of the partners was achieved by agreeing the assets to go into the venture and then the partner with the smaller amount of assets introduced providing cash to make up the difference and ensure equality of contribution.

Most of the production assets remained in the partner companies, as that is where they were physically, and the joint venture agreed to buy the assets in stages over a period of years. Materials were bought at the same price from both partners. This soon became onerous, since the agreed prices were on average 10 per cent higher than the market prices, and therefore reduced EVC's competitiveness.

The case of China

Finally, the case of China illustrates the problems which can attend valuation in an environment where some local assets are priced according to administrative fiat rather than market forces, and where it may be politically necessary to value the local partner's assets so as to afford to give it a share of joint venture equity (see Box).

A valuation overview

The cases examined reveal very clearly that the valuation of partner contributions to alliances is a very inexact process, and depends very much on the

Valuation of Contributions to Joint Venture Equity in China

While the majority of foreign investors in China contribute to joint venture equity wholly in the form of cash, this is the exception rather than the rule among Chinese partners. It is often difficult for cash-starved Chinese state-owned enterprises to subscribe to joint venture equity through cash payments and the question arises how they can compensate through having other inputs valued as equity. Chinese partners are, therefore, likely to insist that non-cash resources be valued as joint venture equity in order to preserve some rights as part-owners. Many have had their land, buildings, plant, and equipment valued as equity. A few manage to get agreement that brand names, distribution channels, and production technology should also be valued as part of their contribution to equity.

In the absence of a non-administered market for land, it can be difficult for the Chinese and foreign sides to agree a 'fair' price. The Chinese party will seek to have land it supplies classified by the local government as being zoned for commercial use, in which case its valuation as a component of equity is raised according to administrative rules made by the very authority which has a sponsoring interest in the Chinese enterprise. Similarly, the Chinese side tends to value plant and equipment by reference to original cost and subsequent depreciation, the annual rate of which is very low compared with international norms. The foreign side will value the same plant and equipment in terms of its income-generating capability compared to equivalent assets which are of world-class standards. If the plant and equipment supplied by the Chinese partner can produce outputs which are technically acceptable and cost effective when combined with relatively low local labour costs, that partner has a basis on which it can insist on a higher valuation being accorded to those resources than would be warranted in a high-labour-cost developed country. In practice, Chinese facilities and equipment are often antiquated and in poor shape. Quite often the valuation which is given to Chinese assets represents what is acceptable in order to get a partnership agreed rather than an economic calculation.

partners' attitudes to alliances, and the way in which they expect them to be managed and to evolve over time. It becomes an even less exact process in countries like China where a market price for some assets does not exist. From the limited number of cases examined, it would seem that, the more sophisticated the valuation process, the greater the risk of the development of a subsequent 'them-and-us' attitude amongst alliance members, to the detriment of good cooperative strategy. However, there are some principles that can be applied to partner contribution valuation.

First, different types of alliance have different valuation needs. Joint ventures, whether two partner or consortium, have corporate forms, and therefore some of the assets that may need to be valued if they are introduced into the joint-venture company are capital, a partner's expertise, specific assets, a network of contacts including those involving market access, and any technology transfer. The sum total of the valuation of these factors accounts for the value of the partner's equity share.

Collaborations do not have a corporate form. Therefore there is no equity to crystallize contribution valuations. Similar factors need to be considered as in joint ventures, although, since there is no company, assets are not introduced, nor is capital. The more intangible factors like technology transfer, access to markets and other contacts, use of brand names, and expertise also need to be considered. Valuation in collaborations is generally carried out when projects are costed, but frequently the intangibles are not expressly valued, as can be seen from the case studies described above.

The following factors should be taken into account in valuing the respective types of asset introduced to the alliance:

1. *Fixed assets.* Here a number of considerations will influence valuation, notably the cost of the asset, the specificity or uniqueness of the asset, its replacement value, and whether it is possible to assess its net present value calculated on the basis of the income stream it is expected to generate and the appropriate discount rate.
2. *Working capital.* Usually valued at face value, unless there are reasons for discounting it to some degree, as with possible bad debts that are taken over.
3. *Expertise.* This is normally ignored in calculations, on the basis that the partner's expertise is the basic reason it was approached for partnership. If a return is demanded on it, this can be based on a time approach—e.g. so many man-years at so much per day. Strength of need may also be a factor, and here we may note Rover's comment that 'We would have paid five times as much!'
4. *Contact network.* This is also often vital in partner selection, but then not given a valuation. It might be valued on the basis of a royalty or possibly an introductory commission for successful sales in collaborations. In joint ventures it will have a notional valuation in determining the equity shares. The same considerations apply to the ability by one partner to provide access to the market that the other partner wants.
5. *Brand names.* These intangible assets can be crucial to the success of a product in a market. Accountants have great difficulty in valuing them. However, acquiring companies are often willing to pay large sums for them—e.g. Nestlé's purchase of Rowntree. Although based on somewhat uncertain numbers, the DCF (discounted cash flow) or NPV (net present value) methods of valuation seem most appropriate here.
6. *Technology transfer.* There are several possibilities here, including time-based valuation as for other forms of expertise, royalties on subsequent sales using the new technology, and a capital value based on forecast

future benefits. It may even be possible to develop an acceptable formula including all of the above.

If a joint venture is the chosen alliance form, the sum total of the valuation of the above six factors will account for the equity share, balanced by a cash item if a 50 : 50 deal is politically determined. If royalties are included in the valuation or time-based fees, these will, of course, not feature in the capital valuation.

In a collaboration the means of paying for the assets in the broadest sense brought by each partner to the alliance is more difficult to manage. In many cases the most intangible of the assets are just ignored, and those subject to royalties or fees dealt with in that way. The remaining assets are usually picked up in the project by project costing as the alliance gets under way.

SUMMARY

This chapter has emphasized that negotiations in alliances must be win–win, since the partners will be working together subsequently, which is not necessarily the case in acquisition negotiations. It stresses the importance of trying to make the negotiations a positive rather than a zero-sum game, so that both parties may feel they have gained from the process.

On the question of partner-contribution valuation, it is clear that this is a very inexact science and depends heavily on corporate politics and the respective attitudes of each partner to their future work together. Some strike a very hard bargain, and others a very easy one in the interests of future goodwill and cooperation. Some principles, however, apply universally:

1. The creation of a perceived win–win situation leads to a more effective alliance, even if it means negotiating in a less hard-nosed way than is customary in company negotiations.
2. The benefits and not just the costs should be considered in valuing assets to be put into or used in the alliance.
3. The strength of need of the partners will influence the value negotiations to some extent.
4. The uniqueness of a particular asset, such as brand name or technology, creates a premium value determinable only by negotiation.
5. The valuation range of an asset will be somewhere between its existing value and the assessed NPV of the future benefits to the alliance accruing from its use.
6. The position in that range will depend upon the relative strength of the partners, their possible alternative courses of action to the alliance, the uniqueness of the assets, and the negotiating ability and forbearing or hard attitude of the partners.

REFERENCES

Blake, R. R., and Moulton, J. S. (1964), *The Managerial Grid* (Houston, Tex.: Gulf Publications).

Child, J. (1994), *Management in China during the Age of Reform* (Cambridge: Cambridge University Press).

Fisher, R., and Ury, W. (1981), *Getting to Yes* (London: Hutchinson).

Hendon, D. W., and Hendon, R. A. (1989), *How to Negotiate Worldwide* (London: Gower Press).

Lewicki, R. J., and Litterer, J. A. (1985), *Negotiation* (New York: Irwin).

Nierenberg, G. I. (1968), *The Art of Negotiating* (New York: Hawthorn Books).

Osgood, R. (1962), *An Alternative to War or Surrender* (Urbana, Ill.: University of Illinois Press).

Porter, M. E. (1985), *Competitive Advantage: Creating and Sustaining Superior Performance* (New York: Free Press).

——and Fuller, M. B. (1986), 'Coalitions and Global Strategy', in M. E. Porter (ed.), *Competition in Global Industries* (Boston, Mass.: Harvard Business School Press), 315–44.

Pruitt, D. G. (1981), *Negotiation Behavior* (New York: Academic Press).

——(1983), 'Strategic Choice in Negotiation', *American Behavioural Scientist*, 27/2: 167–94.

Pye, L. W. (1982), *Chinese Commercial Negotiating Style* (Cambridge, Mass.: Oelge-schlager, Gunn & Hain).

Tung, R. L. (1984), *Business Negotiation with the Japanese* (New York: Lexington Books).

III

MANAGING COOPERATION

Part III deals with what happens when the dust has settled and the alliance partners start to work together. Managing an alliance presents more of a challenge than is generally the case with a unitary organization. It has to accomplish the creation and development of a viable new enterprise, usually with a heterogeneous mix of staff provided by the partners, plus others newly recruited. It involves maintaining good relations with several principals, and fostering their cooperation. It also has to take account of a wide range of external groups, some of which, like a host government, may be partial to the interests of one partner rather than another.

Chapter 8 considers the critical and difficult role of general management in contributing to the success of cooperation, and how the form of the alliance bears on the appropriate approach to that role.

Chapter 9 reviews the different forms of control partners can exercise in alliances, noting that tight control is by definition impossible in cooperative activity, but this should not lead to the total abnegation of all control, especially over strategic decisions.

Chapter 10 looks at alliances from a human-resources viewpoint. It shows how much more difficult it is to establish a coherent human-resources management policy when there are at least two companies involved with different cultures and missions. The chapter also considers the contribution that a well-thought-out HRM policy can make to achieving the strategic and knowledge-acquisition intentions that partners may have towards cooperation.

Chapter 11 turns to the question of culture and highlights how difficult and critically important are company and national cultural issues in enabling an alliance to work effectively. It explores the difficulties that can arise because new partners have given inadequate attention in the pre-alliance phase to attempting to understand the other partner's culture and ways of behaving.

Chapter 12 discusses how the whole area of cooperative management can be addressed in one increasingly important area—namely, alliances between companies based in developed parts of the world and those from emerging economies. In a sense this provides a synthesis in a particular area for the lessons outlined in Chapters 8 to 11.

8

General Management

Despite the increasing popularity of strategic alliances as an inter-organizational form, developed in large measure to meet the needs of global-izing markets and technologies, the record of running successful alliances is somewhat mixed. The dissolution rate for joint ventures is reported to be about 50 per cent, which is almost as high as that for mergers and acquisitions in new industries (Park and Ungson 1997). Porter (1987) found that no more than half the alliances he identified were successful by any reasonable criteria. Management consultants Coopers & Lybrand, and McKinsey, in separate studies came to similar conclusions (Bleeke and Ernst 1993).

One reason for failure lies in the disparity between the concern top manage-ment shows in the formation of alliances and the attention it pays to manag-ing them once they are established. As Rosabeth Moss Kanter (1994: 96) has commented from her research into a variety of international alliances: 'too often, top executives devote more time to screening potential partners in financial terms than to managing the partnership in human terms. They tout the future benefits of the alliance to their shareholders but don't help their managers create those benefits. They worry more about controlling the rela-tionship than about nurturing it.'

This disparity is also evident among writers on the subject. They have gen-erally given more attention to the reasons for the creation of alliances than to their management. Most, if they deal with the question of alliance manage-ment at all, content themselves with laying out a few basic ground rules (Killing 1983; Kanter 1989; Lynch 1990; Collins and Doorley 1991; Spekman and Sawnhey 1991; Bronder and Pritzl 1992; Lorange and Roos 1992; Urban and Vendemini 1992).

The quality of alliance management is a vital requirement for their success. Some, like Harrigan (1986), have argued that 'alliances fail because operating managers do not make them work, not because contracts are poorly written'. Inkpen and Crossan (1995) conclude that, when strategic alliances fail to capitalize on their opportunities for mutual learning, the fault lies primarily in the attitudes of their senior managers. Niederkofler (1991: 238) has argued that: 'a major cause for cooperative failure is managerial behaviour. In nature, cooperation differs fundamentally from competition. Whereas competitive processes are well understood and practised daily, the key success factors in cooperative processes are widely ignored.'

The following chapters in this part of the book focus on different aspects of alliance management—namely, control, human-resource management, culture, and cooperation in transitional economies. This chapter concentrates on general management. It begins with the job of the general manager in alliances and how this compares with that of general managers in unitary companies. This comparison points up the particular conditions for alliance success which general managers have to foster. The tasks and conditions that alliance general managers face naturally leads on to the qualities they require, and the chapter closes by reviewing these.

The significance of a delineated general-management function is pointed up by Yoshino and Rangan's case studies of global strategic alliances. They comment: 'Our research suggests that firms which make the most effective use of alliances tend to assign responsibility for their management to a specific manager or group' (1995: 123).

GENERAL MANAGEMENT ROLES

General management is a rather amorphous term, which can be identified more precisely by referring to the roles it covers than to the various positions which may carry the name. General management has responsibility for a whole organizational unit, covering the range of functional, product, or geographical activities the unit carries out. There are long, medium, and short-run aspects to this responsibility. For the long run, general managers are expected to establish goals, set the direction of their companies, decide which business to be in, and ensure adequate resource provision including investment. For the medium term, they have to determine the effective allocation of resources. In the short run, they have to ensure that human, financial, and material resources are used efficiently (Kotter 1982).

In a large, multi-divisional, and multi-functional company, several positions can come into the category of general management. These include the chief executive officer (who may be called executive chairperson, president, or managing director), divisional general managers (who may be termed divisional or regional vice-presidents), and multi-functional heads. In some cases, the scope of a business development manager's job may be that of general management *vis-à-vis* a range of new ventures for which he or she is responsible. The managers placed in charge of cooperative ventures also occupy a general-management position in respect of those ventures, even though they may report to regional or product divisional managers. Alliance general managers also face some special challenges to which we return shortly.

Within this domain of responsibility, a general manager normally has to carry out several key and overlapping roles. As a *decision-maker*, he or she is responsible to the board of directors or corporate head office for seeing that the decisions necessary for policy implementation have been carried out. The decisions which a general manager is likely to take encompass the initiation of change, the allocation of resources, negotiation with groups within and outside the organization, and handling disturbances. Secondly, the general manager also needs to be an *internal integrator*, aiming to ensure that the collective effort is coherent. In this role, he or she manages both vertical and horizontal relationships. The former are relations with subordinates, with a view to motivating and supervising them. The latter are interpersonal and inter-group relationships across the organization, in which the general manager forms teams and ensures activities are appropriately linked across the organization. A third role is one of *external integrator*, between the organization and its context. This requires the general manager to act as a networker overseeing the boundary conditions of the organization, and it includes fostering key connections, negotiating opportunities, managing the expectations of stakeholders, and preserving the organization's freedom of action. In performing these three roles, general managers also have a special responsibility for a fourth role, that of *information manager*. He or she plays a particularly important part in receiving and disseminating information of a strategic nature, and is expected to inform others on behalf of the organization as a whole.

These roles have to be performed by the general managers of any organization for it to enjoy success, and that includes the strategic alliance as well as a unitary and purely national firm. In the case of alliances, additional requirements arise because their general managers are beholden to two or more partners and because they will normally have to create the conditions for effective cooperation between staff who are likely to hail from different organizational and (in the case of an international alliance) societal cultures. The extra requirements placed upon alliance general management are, therefore, particularly taxing and crucial for organizational success.

The additional difficulties likely to face alliance general managers, especially international ones, are summarized in Table 8.1. This contrasts the four general-management roles as they are found within a single, national firm with the additional difficulties likely to attend the performance of the same roles within an international joint venture.

It is evident from Table 8.1 that there are two features of alliance general management which add significantly to its difficulty. The first, and most salient, stems from the presence of multiple principals in the form of the two or more parent/partner companies. If there are just two partners, their demands are likely to be direct and forceful, and potentially conflicting, unless one clearly dominates. When there are more partners, each with a smaller stake, the pressure that each can exercise over the alliance general manager will be reduced, but the demands they place on the alliance will tend to be more diverse.

Table 8.1. *General management roles in unitary companies and international joint ventures (IJVs)*

	General manager of unitary company	General manager of an IJV
Decision-maker		
Innovator	Initiates change	This role takes on the added complication that it is necessary to convince the parent companies as well as the IJV's own board
Resource allocator	Decides where efforts and energies will be directed	Very difficult, owing to multiple sets of resources and expectations. Becomes easier to perform if the IJV has some autonomy
Negotiator	Deals with situations involving negotiations on behalf of the company	Perhaps the primary skill required of the IJV general manager. Can be more difficult if the GM is an expatriate
Disturbance handler	Takes charge when crises arise and the firm is threatened	Influences and pressures from parent companies and the IJV board of directors can complicate the decision
Internal integrator		
Leader	Manages relationships with subordinates, motivating and supervising them	The general manager may find it more difficult to motivate and supervise staff of another nationality and/or coming from another partner's organization, owing to different values, ethics, and acquired practices
Teambuilder	Forms teams and ensures that activities are appropriately linked across the organization	Has to overcome potential barrriers to teamwork between staff arising from different organizational or national cultures
External integrator		
Figurehead	Represents the firm on ceremonial and other official occasions	In some host countries, protocol and legal requirements may necessitate a greater emphasis on this role
Networker	Interacts with managers, officials, and members of other groups outside the firm	This is likely to be a very prominent role. The presence of several partners complicates the network with which the IJV general manager has to interact.

	General manager of unitary company	General manager of an IJV
		In many contexts, it is particularly important to interact with government officials. There may be problems if the GM is an expatriate and does not have good external connections
Information manager		
Monitoring	Receives and collects key information, usually of an informal nature, both inside and outside the firm	It may be more difficult for an IJV general manager to pick up information from internal staff and external sources who do not share the same language or identity
Disseminator	Ensures information is transmitted to members of the firm	Again, communication breakdown may arise because of language and cultural (interpretative) differences. More effort will be required to explain what is communicated, clarify misunderstandings and teach members of the IJV about the partners' protocols
Spokesman	Informs external persons about, and on behalf of, the firm	Similar factors can add to the difficulties of this general management role

Source: adapted and extended from Beamish (1988), Schaan and Beamish (1988).

In addition to the partners, the general managers of alliances may find themselves having to take account of the expectations of multiple groups, such as governmental agencies and community organizations, in the context where the venture is located. The expectations of these local groups do not necessarily coincide with those of either or all partners, and this sets up further potentially conflicting pressures on an alliance general manager. In the case of an international alliance, these conflicting pressures will typically be contained within a net of relationships (as illustrated by Fig. 8.1).

The second source of difficulty arises from the cultural heterogeneity that has to be managed within the alliance. This heterogeneity is a product of the parents' different corporate cultures, and it increases in the case of international alliances, when a mix of national cultures is also present. The more that the alliance partners have different structures, modes of operation, and cultural attitudes, the more challenging is the situation facing the general manager.

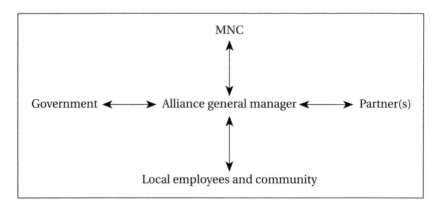

Fig. 8.1. Typical net of relationships of an alliance manager

These aspects of the alliance general manager's role have been analysed with reference to two concepts: role conflict and role ambiguity (Shenkar and Zeira 1992). Role conflict arises when the priorities of one alliance partner conflict with those of another, which means that the alliance general manager faces conflicting simultaneous demands from those partners. Cultural heterogeneity within the alliance adds to role conflict because it presents the general manager with conflicting expectations about the values which should inform the alliance and the manner in which it should be managed. Role ambiguity arises when the general management of an alliance is unclear about the expectations which various key groups have of it—the partners, the various employee groups in the alliance, and institutions of the country where the alliance's operations are located. Role ambiguity for alliance general management therefore arises from the lack of clarity about what is expected of it, whereas role conflict arises from differences in the expectations that are placed upon it.

This analysis implies that the general managers of an alliance will experience higher levels of role conflict when there are a few but active alliance partners, who differ markedly in the objectives they have for the alliance and in their defining corporate characteristics such as size and ownership. One would similarly expect that having a larger number of partners, especially if they are culturally diverse, would increase the role ambiguity experienced by alliance general managers. In the main study of the subject conducted so far, Shenkar and Zeira (1992) found among international joint ventures in Israel that having fewer parent companies was associated with greater role conflict, while divergence between the parent companies' national cultures gave rise to role ambiguity.

The factors we have identified as predictors of role conflict and ambiguity are all aspects of the situation in which alliance general managers find themselves working. This leaves open the important possibility that managers with more experience of handling such situations will not perceive the conflict and ambiguity inherent in them to be so much of a problem. They may, indeed, even be able to turn situations of this kind to their advantage by negotiating between the parents to secure greater autonomy for the venture under their charge, and perhaps to encourage competition among the parents in their provision of resources to it. Shenkar and Zeira in fact found that joint-venture general managers with longer tenure in their jobs suffered less from role conflict and ambiguity, while better-educated general managers also tended to report less ambiguity in their roles. Those who were permitted, or had negotiated, greater autonomy for themselves also experienced less ambiguity about their roles.

Nevertheless, the conditions which create role conflict and ambiguity are ones which, if not handled deftly, could threaten the breakdown of an alliance. Role conflict often reflects the presence of a competitive undertone to a partnership, and this clearly contributes to the high failure rate of alliances. Both role conflict and role ambiguity can generate stress, dissatisfaction, and difficulties in decision-making for alliance general managers. Severe role conflict, due to incompatible demands from the partners, could make the role an impossible one to fulfil. Role ambiguity is more likely to present opportunities for general managers to formulate their own policies for the alliance, especially if the ambiguity arises from the partners' lack of clear policy or disinterest, and if the general manager has the requisite skills, experience, and standing to chart his or her own course.

There are in effect two main aspects to managing an alliance successfully. The first requires that the expectations of the partners are reconciled and incorporated into the strategy for the alliance. The more that their expectations are met, the less onerous is likely to be the control that the partners place upon alliance management. Meeting the expectations of alliance partners therefore involves a combination of securing their consensus on the alliance's strategic objectives as well as maintaining the partners' continuing support in achieving them.

In a joint venture, the board of directors should, in principle, establish its strategic objectives, leaving the general manager free to achieve them so long as he or she is supported with adequate capital and other resources. By contrast, in an alliance without its own legal form such as a consortium, parent resourcing mainly takes the form of non-contractual resourcing. This may lead to a more direct form of parental intervention in the alliance. The management of relationships between the alliance and its partners will always form an important part of alliance general management, as will attention to its strategic direction and viability, but the autonomy that general managers are granted to lead the alliance is likely to vary according to how that alliance is constituted.

In collaborations without a joint-venture form to focus managerial attention, the running of the alliance is carried out through high-level decisions to embark upon joint projects. The principles of project management then hold, but with the additional difficulty that the designated project manager has the problem of managing personnel from different home companies over whom he does not have ultimate responsibility. The management of such projects has then to be carried out with extra sensitivity.

The circumstances which generate role conflict and other special difficulties for alliance general management are ones which lend a certain delicacy, even fragility, to the process of cooperation between organizations. This means that alliance general managers need to have a special concern for the conditions required to nurture and develop the cooperative relationship in which they play a pivotal part.

The other aspect to managing alliances successfully is located within the framework of cooperation between partners. While the ease with which it can be performed adequately is conditional on the quality of that cooperation, it is in principle akin to the general management of all companies. It concerns measures to promote the alliance's internal effectiveness as an ongoing operation. These include establishing appropriate organizational arrangements, providing leadership to achieve cooperation and motivation among employees, and ensuring appropriate information flows within the alliance.

These two aspects are now considered in more detail.

GENERATING AND MAINTAINING COOPERATION

There is wide agreement that, for an alliance to be effective, the long-term goals and objectives of the partners should not conflict (Spekman and Sawhney 1991). It is not necessary that the objectives dovetail exactly; clearly those of Rover and Honda did not. Their objectives must not, however, actually conflict and they must possess an attractive degree of complementarity otherwise the alliance will have difficulty in developing consensus for a particular course of action. Even if some partner goals diverge in the short term, they must be able to perceive considerable mutual benefit from cooperation over the long term.

For the greatest hope of successful evolution, a philosophy of constant learning should be adopted by the partners. Alliances that are set up with the prime purpose of substituting for skills or products in which a partner is deficient tend to have limited scope for development. Where both or all partners have the prime objective of learning from each other, the prognosis for the future is much brighter. It is interesting to observe how, in the early days of the Rover–Honda alliance, Rover merely sought a model to market as a mid-range saloon. It was not until much later, when learning became Rover's primary objective, that the company experienced dramatic benefit from the alliance. At that stage, Rover adopted the Honda philosophy of continuous learning and even set up a company, the Rover Learning Business Limited, to ensure that the philosophy became embedded within its organization. For an alliance to succeed long term it needs to evolve through the partners constantly seeking new things to do together (Lorange and Roos 1992). Their willingness and enthusiasm to do this depends largely on the quality of cooperation which has been established. Alliance general managers are in a pivotal position to put forward new projects on which the partners' cooperation and desire to learn together can feed.

The attitude of partners towards the cooperation between them is critical to its success. A positive attitude is demonstrated by:

1. a sensitive attitude to national and corporate cultural differences (i.e. the willingness to undertake mutual sense-making);
2. strong commitment by top- and lower-level management in the partner companies;
3. mutual trust.

Kanter (1989) identifies the critical nature of corporate and national cultural sensitivity between the partners; Anderson and Narus (1990) point to strong top- and middle-management commitment as a key factor for alliance success, and Lynch (1990) emphasizes the need for mutual trust. Inkpen and Crossan (1995) found that, when top managers in partner companies did not understand or commit themselves to their alliances, their companies failed to realize the potential learning benefits that cooperation offered.

It is easier to state the requirement for cooperation between alliance partners and their members than it is to achieve it, which is a prime concern of alliance general managers. In this respect, Ring's (1996) studies of six international alliances throw valuable light on the formal and informal processes through which cooperative strategies develop and can be sustained. He identifies three formal processes: negotiational, transactional, and administrative. Negotiational processes tend to be particularly significant during the formation of an alliance, but they can persist during the life of an alliance when the cooperation between partners has advanced to an operational stage. Transactional processes involve the partners in making commitments to action and in settling the terms on which the alliance will operate. Administrative processes are concerned with managing the execution of partners' commitments in order to maintain the alliance as a operating organization.

The successful accomplishment of these three formal processes depends on achieving a series of informal processes: sense-making, understanding, and committing. Sense-making processes help individuals view and align their own preferences in relation to the others involved in a cooperative relationship. Understanding is a process whereby the parties to a cooperative relationship reach a shared understanding of the context in which their alliance operates. Committing is an informal process that produces psychological contracts between the cooperating individuals, in which they come to accept unwritten and largely non-verbalized expectations and assumptions about each other's prerogatives and obligations.

Ring found that the intensity of these processes, and the time needed to take them to an outcome which could support effective cooperation, varies considerably between different cases. For example, where cooperative strategies are based on kinship or other close social ties (that is, on an already established network), there is less need to rely heavily on sense-making and understanding processes; in larger, more complex alliances, such as research consortia or international joint ventures, sense-making, understanding, and committing processes will generally be more intensive for everyone involved and are likely to take much more time to conclude (Ring 1996: 12). In other words, the more 'embedded' the prospective partners are in a shared social context, the less intense informal processes required for them to advance through the negotiational, transactional, and administrative phases are likely to be, and the cooperation will be established on a viable basis in shorter time.

By contrast, where the proposed alliance is between organizations coming from two cultures with different assumptions about how to conduct business relations, each phase (and especially negotiation) is likely to require intense effort and considerable patience to achieve the necessary sense-making, understanding, and commitment. This kind of challenge arises in the formation and operation of alliances between companies from cultures with explicit procedures for conducting business, such as the USA, and those from cultures where the rules of business transacting are much more implicit and grounded in the quality of interpersonal relationships—such as China and Japan. It is also likely to arise in the case of alliances between organizations within the same country, but coming from sectors which have very different values and traditions, such as private and public sector organizations.

Ring's analysis draws attention to the formal and informal processes which the creators and managers of cooperative ventures have to bring to a positive conclusion if the cooperation is to succeed. It indicates that the foundations for effective collaboration have to be laid down at the formation stage, including an understanding and personal acceptance of the cooperation by those who will work within it. As we note in Chapter 10, the human-resource preparation for alliances is often left until a so-called 'implementation' stage, which is too late. In other words, it is vital to regard the formation and operation of an alliance as interdependent stages in one and the same continuing process. It is the task of alliance general management to ensure that there is continuity between these stages so that the conditions for cooperation develop without unnecessary setbacks. It is for this reason very helpful for the first general manager of an alliance to be chosen from one of the leading players in the formation process, who will be aware of the sense-making and understanding reached during the negotiation process and can carry this forward enjoying the respect of both partners.

Mohr and Spekman (1994) found from a study of 140 personal-computer manufacturers and dealers that the successful management of alliances depends on processes which are comparable to those Ring has identified. In regard to negotiation between partners, Mohr and Spekman draw attention to the benefits of constructive conflict-resolution processes such as joint problem-solving rather than attempts either to dominate or to smooth over problems. They also recommend the creation of commitment, interdependence, and trust, which is promoted by participation, information-sharing, and a high quality of communications. They conclude that all these processes serve better to align partners' expectations, goals, and objectives. The processes emphasized by Mohr and Spekman have a clear affinity with the sense-making, understanding, and committing processes identified by Ring as necessary conditions for cooperation to develop and thrive.

Faulkner (1993) was able to assess the extent to which features of alliance general management were associated with long-term success in sixty-seven international strategic alliances. Success was assessed by reference to five criteria:

1. the achievement of agreed alliance objectives in quantifiable terms;
2. the achievement of spin-off benefits;
3. high morale amongst alliance members;
4. a good alliance reputation in the partner companies;
5. a good alliance reputation in the industry at large.

The commitment of partners to the alliance, their positive attitudes towards it, and congruent partner goals all discriminated strongly between successful and less successful alliances as Table 8.2 shows.

Table 8.2. *Significance of partner commitment and cooperation to the success of alliances* (%)

Feature	Level of significance[a] (%)
Commitment by partner top management	99.9
Mutual trust between partners	99.9
Sensitivity to partner's culture	99.9
Congruent partner goals	93.0

[a] Level of significance indicates the likelihood, based on a Chi square test, that the association between the named feature and alliance success did not arise by chance.

Yoshino and Rangan (1995) were able from their case studies of global strategic alliances to identify a number of 'critical tasks' for alliance management, several of which amplify the considerations of cooperation between partners which have already been raised. One task they call 'establishing the right tone'. This is largely concerned with building trust between the partners through encouraging personal relationships between their staff, who have to work together for the alliance to succeed: senior managers, functional managers, engineers, and technical staff. A second key activity which a general manager can perform is to monitor the contributions that the partners are making to the alliance and to initiate appropriate corrective action if these are found to be insufficient or unsatisfactory. These contributions can range from the tangible and relatively easy to monitor, such as supplies of components, to more difficult cases, such as the quality of staff and information offered by a partner. A third task is to be aware of strategic reassessments by the partners and their implication for the alliance. They may offer opportunities for alliance general management to propose new activities for the alliance which will contribute to its long-term development.

ORGANIZATION AND ALLIANCE SUCCESS

Faulkner (1993) found that clear well-thought-out organizational arrangements, and the dissemination of information within the alliance, were associated with alliance success.

Others have proposed that certain principles should underpin organizational arrangements if frictions and other problems are to be avoided, and that their explicit adoption is important to a smoothly functioning alliance. Collins and Doorley (1991) emphasize the establishment of a clear dispute resolution mechanism. Lorange and Probst (1987) stress the importance of giving a joint-venture managing director clear authority. Faulkner (1992) suggests the importance of choosing the most appropriate organizational form. Taucher (1988) argues that partners will feel much more comfortable with each other if they have an agreed exit formula if things go wrong; and Kanter (1989) mentions the importance of a good information dissemination system with the partner companies and the alliance itself.

This suggests that clear organizational arrangements need to be set up in an alliance if it is to be managed effectively notably:

1. the establishment of clear dispute-resolution mechanisms;
2. in a joint-venture alliance, clear authority vested in the chief executive;
3. a divorce mechanism agreed at the outset;
4. processes for wide dissemination of information within the alliance.

Ten case studies which Faulkner (1993) also conducted illustrate these features in more detail. The cases comprised four joint ventures (ICI Pharma set up by ICI Pharmaceuticals and Sumitomo, EVC set up by ICI and Enichem of Italy, Dowty–Sema, and 'Eurobrek' which is a fictitious name to disguise the identity of a joint venture set up by a European and an American breakfast-food company); five collaborations (Imperial–Wintermans, Courtaulds–Nippon, Rover–Honda, Royal Bank of Scotland–Banco Santander, and ICL–Fujitsu); and one consortium organized by Cable & Wireless. These cases are described in more detail in the Appendix.

When initially surveyed by means of a questionnaire, most alliances claimed to have a good dispute-resolution mechanism, yet the case studies provide evidence that puts this into question. In general, the alliances claiming good dispute-resolution mechanisms are those with joint ventures. Only Rover–Honda and RBS–Banco Santander among the collaborations studied made such claims. Of course dispute systems are easier to set up in joint ventures, since they have clear hierarchies with a chief executive at the apex reporting to a Board of Directors. In those circumstances day-to-day disputes can be resolved in the normal way as within other companies. Where disputes arise between joint-venture personnel and partner-company personnel, they can be resolved ultimately at joint-venture board level, which almost always contains representatives of the partner companies, as well as of the joint-venture management.

The collaborations, ICL–Fujitsu, Imperial–Wintermans, and Courtaulds–Nippon Paint admit to less than adequate dispute-resolution mechanisms, and the collaborative form is inevitably the one with the greatest ambiguity in the area of resolving disputes. Yet Imperial–Wintermans and Courtaulds–Nippon Paint collaborations have adopted a form of the 'gateway' system, which gives a degree of focus to the contacts between the companies, and Fujitsu has seconded a small number of senior personnel to ICL headquarters in Putney to take care of such relationships. The mission of the gateway executives is boundary-spanning (Killing 1988; Niederkofler 1991). The gateway is normally personified in a senior executive in each company who directly manages the interfaces between the companies, and hence by implication the disputes, or is at least kept informed of all such contacts. As the senior gatekeeper executive for Banco Santander points out, the gateway system is a good one, but the ultimate aim must be for it to wither away, as relationships between the partner companies become closer.

Niederkofler (1991: 251) has argued that: 'By limiting the actual amount of cooperation, by a careful selection of appropriate boundary spanners, and by stepping up the involvement with the partner as the firms get to know each other, the effects of organizational incompatibilities may be moderated.' Thus, boundary-spanning is a critical aspect of alliances, particularly collaborations, and the skill with which it is carried out seems to have considerable impact on the success of the alliance.

On the question of the clarity of authority in the hands of the managing directors of the joint ventures, there is again mixed experience. Managers in the Dowty–Sema alliance admit that such authority was not granted; consequently an inordinate amount of time was spent in meetings in which both partners argued for action clearly in the interest of their respective companies but not necessarily in the interests of the joint venture, or the efficient pursuance of the project. The result was that projects, although successful in their outcome from a physical performance viewpoint, were frequently unprofitable.

The other joint ventures claim that their Managing Directors have such authority. However, such claimed authority was of no avail to the Managing Director of EVC in his quest for greater independence to choose where to buy raw material, or the Managing Director of Eurobrek, should he have wished to run his own sales force. Of the other alliances with separate joint-venture companies, the C&W consortium is run as a Japanese company, so consensus rather than clear authority is the dominant culture, and the same is the case in ICI Pharma.

Interestingly, this factor did not appear as a significant variable in the statistical tests, which means not that it is not important, but that it is not overall seen to be so.

It is suggested by Taucher (1988) that the most comfortable alliances are those who have agreed at formation upon a formula for their dissolution, should it be felt by either partner to be no longer of value. This seems logical, since it should reduce anxiety that a failing alliance might destroy the partners in its wake, as the ill-fated Dunlop–Pirelli alliance so nearly did. However, only Dowty–Sema, Eurobrek, and EVC claimed to have dealt with such matters on their negotiating agenda. Since all the alliances investigated are in being at the time of writing (except for Rover–Honda), and therefore successful at least by minimal criteria, the implications of having no pre-agreed formula have not been tested. This factor did not appear as significant in the wider survey either.

A further condition which requires an appropriate organizational system is that of managing the information flows between the partner companies and ensuring that information on the alliance is adequately disseminated to them. The purpose is to stimulate interest in the alliance, to encourage support for it, and to encourage the diffusion of the knowledge that can always be gained through close exposure to another company, and the absorption of know-how, embedded knowledge, and routines from the partner.

The management of information, however, has a double edge to it. A degree of information-sharing is essential for the viability of an alliance and its capacity to realize both the economies and learning potentials of cooperation. On the other hand, alliances can become conduits for the flow of commercially valuable information from one partner to another. This is, paradoxically, more likely to happen when managers and staff from one partner come to trust and feel comfortable with their counterparts from another company. Alliance general managers have to handle this paradox in a balanced and constructive manner.

Of the alliances investigated, all except ICI Pharma claimed that information on the alliance was either acceptably or well disseminated in the partner companies. The importance of this would of course vary with the degree to which the alliance involved core activities of the partner companies or only peripheral activities (Lorange and Roos 1992). In most of the alliances, core activities were involved. However, in certain cases this was not so. Eurobrek involves only a very small part of both its partner owners. EVC involves a relatively small part of ICI, but a core part of Enichem. The Imperial–Wintermans alliance is only for cigars, which are central to Wintermans, but peripheral to Imperial, and the RBS–Banco Santander collaboration affects only a small part of the staff of both basically national banks.

Where a non-core activity is involved for a partner, unless there is a greater onus on that partner to ensure wide information dissemination, there is a risk that the alliance will become of decreasing interest to the rest of his company. It is noteworthy that Rover managers claimed that much of the benefit they received from the Honda alliance has been through information dissemination within Rover, and the consequent organizational learning that has taken place (Faulkner 1992).

Clear and appropriate organizational arrangements are intended to ease the process of managing both internal and external alliance relationships. The two are highly interdependent and equally important. Yoshino and Rangan (1995), for instance, point out that middle managers and technical specialists often view alliances either as peripheral to their core activities or even detrimental to their firm's interests when the alliance is with a competitor. They recommend on the basis of their case studies that alliance general managers should approach internal relationships as enthusiastic champions for the alliance, rather than as representatives for one of the partner firms, maintain open communications and links at all levels, and seek in this way to promote mutual understanding and realistic expectations of what the other partner(s) can do for the alliance.

ALLIANCE MANAGEMENT QUALITIES

A great deal is expected of an alliance general manager under conditions which could become quite frustrating if full support is not forthcoming from one or more of the partners. Yet, although various surveys and writings identify the abilities and skills required of 'international' or 'global' managers (e.g. Barham and Oates 1991; Lane and Distefano 1994), less attention has been given to the desirable profile of alliance managers. In the case of international cooperative ventures, the two roles overlap and the skills of international management will be relevant. The two roles also share a need to effect cooperation between diverse, and potentially antipathetical, groups. Other desirable abilities and skills can be inferred from our review of the general-management role.

It is widely agreed that a fundamental attribute for effective international managers is to possess the broader strategic awareness which is necessary for operating on a global scale, or within an international network. The parallel for alliance managers, even those with responsibility for purely domestic alliances, is that they have to understand and accept the strategic rationale for the alliance and the business objectives the partners place upon it. Yoshino and Rangan (1995: 143) comment that:

If the mission of an alliance is to be closely aligned with a firm's business strategy, the manager must be in a position not only to understand the firm's strategy but also to have a voice in its formulation and implementation. To manage effectively an alliance that involves multiple projects and therefore competing priorities, the manager must be intimately acquainted with company strategy.

International and alliance managers must also be willing to work towards a set of objectives which is both defined and realized through meaningful relationships with others. Hence further requirements for success in both roles are the ability to communicate effectively and to be flexible in relating with others. These requirements point to relevant personal skills and sensitivities. They imply that, whatever training is offered, certain kinds of people are better suited to the demands of the job than are others. In the case of international managers, the relevant personal skills which have been identified include adaptability, the ability to function in fluid conditions and to cope with ambiguity and personal stress, the capacity to work in and manage teams with diverse memberships, personal self-reliance, relationship and negotiating skills, and the capacity to communicate in more than one language. All of these, except in some circumstances the last, are also necessary for an alliance general manager. Several sensitivities have been identified as requisities for international managers: sensitivity to different cultures, awareness of their own cultural background, and openness to learning from new situations and diverse points of view. Again, these requirements also apply to alliance general managers, although the cultural diversity may be organizational rather than national.

Alliance managers have to work with large numbers of people over whom they have no direct authority, especially when the alliance takes the form of a collaboration or consortium. They have to possess a capacity to build trust among people, many of whom may be on secondment and will therefore tend to retain their identification with their own parent organizations and career paths (Child and Rodrigues 1996). This clearly places a premium on personal flexibility and finely tuned interpersonal skills.

This chapter has emphasized that the success of alliances requires the development of sound relationships between partners and their staff, coupled with a strategic sense of how the alliance can meet partner objectives. The skills needed for alliance management are quite similar to those for international management, especially when the two spheres overlap; namely (1) to cope with the exigencies of working with diverse social groups (in this case the partners) and (2) to promote constructive cross-cultural relations. The main characteristic which the management of an alliance requires in greater measure is an understanding of the organizational arrangements required to avoid frictions and other problems in a situation which is not merely one of trading (as can be the case in international business) but one in which a hybrid organization has to be managed in its own right and on a continuing basis. An ability to manage the relationship between alliance partners in ways that permit their cooperation to flourish requires particular skills and self-confidence which generally develop with experience.

The pressures bearing on alliance managers can be severe, as we have seen, especially when they are working in unfamiliar environments. Quite a number are unable to stand the pressure and the cost is high both to the individual who has failed in a highly exposed position and to the alliance itself, which may be placed under severe strain as a result. In the case of international alliances, the purely financial cost of extricating a failed general manager can run to $1 million. It is therefore vital to select people who are acceptable to all the alliance partners, and who have characteristics suited to the demands of the role.

It is equally important to prepare people to undertake the position of an alliance general manager. Several pertinent questions need to be asked. Do they already have experience of working with staff from the other partner(s)? Have they been adequately briefed about the cultural and socio-political background of the location to which they are being sent? Has attention been paid to how well their family circumstances fit with their appointment, and have the views of their family been solicited? Has there been a discussion of what they are expected to achieve as general manager and how success in these terms will advance their career? Has this discussion included the question of how they will be reintegrated into the parent organization from which they have come?

SUMMARY

The general management of alliances is more challenging than that of unitary firms, because it involves maintaining active cooperation between two or more partner companies. In addition, many alliances are today international in scope and this means that their general managers may find themselves having to take account of the expectations of various groups, such as governmental regulators and community organizations, in an unfamiliar national environment. It is particularly difficult where the cooperation does not have a joint-venture company on which to focus managerial attention, and where more informal boundary-spanning gatekeepers therefore need to be appointed to monitor relationships.

The importance of managing external relationships concerning the partners and internal relationships within the alliance itself is indicated by the factors that are associated with alliance success. Positive partner attitudes, especially trust and commitment, are the major external factors, while clear organizational arrangements and the management of information flows are important internal factors. To be more specific:

1. The most important factors necessary for the development of a successful alliance would seem to be contained in the concept of a close relationship between the partners—that is to say, flexibility, trust, and committed attitudes towards each other. An alliance general manager can do much to facilitate the development of this relationship through helping the partners to make sense of the alliance in terms of their own

expectations, and to reach a shared understanding of the context in which it operates.

2. Good organizational arrangements, especially in relation to information dissemination, and dispute resolution—for example, the establishment of gateways—enable the inevitable and difficult problem of managing an enterprise by consensus to be carried out with a good chance of success.

3. The essence of a successful alliance must be to learn from one's partner, and not just to use the partner's skills to substitute for one's own deficiencies. Adoption by both partners of a learning philosophy, but within a situation in which personal and inter-company bonding has taken place, is a likely sign of an enduring alliance.

Of the factors identified above, by far and away the most important seem to be the commitment, mutual trust, and flexibility in the relationship between the partners. Given positive attitudes, frictional problems can normally be resolved. However, in the absence of flexible and trusting relationships any problem encountered places the relationship in jeopardy. Managing the relationship between the partners, to foster both their strategic and their personal motives for cooperation, seems to be the key to a successful alliance, and a top priority for its general management.

The next four chapters of the book will deal with specific aspects of cooperative management in more detail.

REFERENCES

Anderson, J., and Narus, J. (1990), 'A Model of Distribution Firm and Manufacturing Firm Working Partnership', *Journal of Marketing*, 54: 42–58.

Barham, K., and Oates, D. (1991), *The International Manager* (London: The Economist Books).

Beamish, P. W. (1988), *Multinational Joint Ventures in Developing Countries* (London: Routledge).

Bleeke, J., and Ernst, D. (1993) (eds.), *Collaborating to Compete: Using Strategic Alliances and Acquisitions in the Global Marketplace* (New York: Wiley).

Bronder, C., and Pritzl, R. (1992), 'Developing Strategic Alliances: A Conceptual Framework for Successful Co-operation', *European Management Journal*, 10/4: 412–20.

Child, J., and Rodrigues, S. (1996), 'The Role of Social Identity in the International Transfer of Knowledge through Joint Ventures', in S. Clegg and G. Palmer (eds.), *The Politics of Management Knowledge* (London: Sage), 46–68.

Collins, T., and Doorley, T. (1991), *Teaming Up for the 90's* (Homewood, Ill.: Irwin).

Faulkner, D. O. (1992), 'Cooperating for Competition: A Taxonomy of Strategic Alliances', paper presented at British Academy of Management Conference, September.

—— (1993), 'International Strategic Alliances Need not be Temporary', paper presented at British Academy of Management Conference, Milton Keynes.

Harrigan, K. R. (1986), *Managing for Joint Venture Success* (New York: Lexington Books).

Inkpen, A. C., and Crossan, M. M. (1995), 'Believing is Seeing: Joint Ventures and Organizational Learning', *Journal of Management Studies*, 32: 595–618.

Kanter, R. M. (1989), *When Giants Learn to Dance* (London: Simon & Schuster).

—— (1994), 'Collaborative Advantage: The Art of Alliances', *Harvard Business Review* (July–Aug.), 96–108.

Killing, J. P. (1983), *Strategies for Joint Venture Success* (New York: Praeger).

—— (1988), 'Understanding Alliances: The Role of Task and Organisational Complexity', in F. J. Contractor (ed.), *Comparative Strategies in International Business* (Boston, Mass.: Lexington Books), 55–67.

Kotter, J. P. (1982), *The General Managers* (New York: Free Press).

Lane, H. W., and Di Stefano, J. L. (1994), 'The Global Manager', in P. W. Beamish, J. P. Killing, D. J. Lecraw, and A. J. Morrison (eds.), *International Management: Text and Cases* (Burr Ridge, Ill.: Irwin), 165–82.

Lorange, P., and Probst, G. J. B. (1987), 'Joint Ventures as Self-Organizing Systems: A Key to Successful Joint Venture Design and Implementation', *Columbia Journal of World Business* (Summer), 71–7.

—— and Roos, J. (1992), *Strategic Alliances: Formation, Implementation, and Evolution* (Oxford: Blackwell).

Lynch, R. P. (1990), 'Building Alliances to Penetrate European Markets', *Journal of Business Strategy* (Mar.–Apr.).

Mohr, J., and Spekman, R. (1994), 'Characteristics of Partnership Success: Partnership Attributes, Communication Behavior, and Conflict Resolution Techniques', *Strategic Management Journal*, 15: 135–52

Niederkofler, M. (1991), 'The Evolution of Strategic Alliances: Opportunities for Managerial Influence', *Journal of Business Venturing*, 6: 237–57.

Park, S. H., and Ungson, G. R. (1997), 'The Effect of National Culture, Organizational Complementarity, and Economic Motivation on Joint Venture Dissolution', *Academy of Management Journal*, 40: 279–307.

Porter, M. E. (1987), 'From Competitive Advantage to Corporate Strategy', *Harvard Business Review* (May/June), 43–59.

Ring, P. S. (1996), 'Patterns of Process in Cooperative Interorganizational Relationships', unpublished paper (Department of Management, College of Business Administration, Loyola Marymount University, Los Angeles, March).

Schaan, J.-L., and Beamish, P. W. (1988), 'Joint Venture General Managers in LDCs', in F. J. Contractor and P. Lorange (eds.), *Cooperative Strategies in International Business* (New York: Lexington Books), 279–99.

Shenkar, O., and Zeira, Y. (1992), 'Role Conflict and Role Ambiguity of Chief Executive Officers in International Joint Ventures', *Journal of International Business Studies*, 23: 55–75.

Spekman, R. E., and Sawhney, K. (1991), 'Towards a Conceptual Understanding of the Antecedents of Strategic Alliances', Management Science Institute, Report No. 90/114.

Taucher, G. (1988), 'Beyond Alliances', IMD Perspectives for Managers No. 1.

Urban, S., and Vendemini, S. (1992), *European Strategic Alliances* (Oxford: Blackwell).

Yoshino, M. Y., and Rangan, U. S. (1995), *Strategic Alliances: An Entrepreneurial Approach to Globalization* (Boston, Mass.: Harvard Business School Press).

9

Control

CONTROL AS AN ISSUE

Control is widely regarded as a critical issue for the successful management and performance of strategic alliances. It might appear strange that it generates so much concern in the case of organizations founded on collaboration. This is because the formation of an alliance requires each partner to share some control, which introduces an additional dimension of uncertainty. As Geringer and Hébert (1989: 236) have put it rather graphically with reference to international joint ventures, 'although each partner must, by definition, relinquish some control over an IJV's activities, such a move is often accompanied by great consternation'.

In a strategic alliance, the collaboration between partners is balanced against the potentially competitive aspects of their relationship, and each partner seeks to reconcile the alliance's activities with its own strategy and pattern of operations. Insufficient control over an alliance can limit a partner's ability to protect as well as efficiently utilize the resources it provides to the alliance, and to achieve the goals it has set for the alliance. It is particularly critical for a partner to control the core technology and know-how that it provides, which is proprietary, unique, and hard to duplicate under normal competitive conditions.

The general problem of how corporate owners can exercise sufficient control over the direction of their companies has become widely recognized, following the seminal study by Berle and Means (1932). It is one of the key challenges of corporate governance. It raises questions concerning the rights of smaller versus dominant stockholders and how managers can be held accountable, as the agents of business owners. Although these questions have been addressed mainly to unitary enterprises, comparable issues arise in strategic alliances, albeit in a rather different form.

The partners in strategic alliances are also in the position of owners. In the case of equity joint ventures, their ownership is legally vested in the equity they have contributed. However, partners resource some kinds of alliance on a non-equity basis, and even in equity joint ventures, equity alone would constitute a narrow definition of the contributions which partners provide in an essentially ownership role. Because partners normally establish strategic alliances to exploit complementarities between themselves, they will supply those alliances with a range of resources, skills, and knowledge. These are assets with an intrinsic value which are in the possession of partner firms, and they amount to ownership inputs with implied property rights. They may be provided on the basis of contracts, but they need not be. The partners face the problem of protecting the integrity and use of the resources they supply in these ways, and they therefore have a motive for seeking a certain level of control over their alliance.

Alliance partners may face several threats to the integrity of the resources they provide. An alliance can give another partner privileged access to its core competences, bringing with it various risks such as strengthening a future potential competitor, facilitating a partner's intervention in critical decisions, and possibly diluting the company's distinctive image as a technology leader. There is the danger that proprietary technology and know-how will 'leak' to another partner and its wider affiliates, and hence undermine the competitive advantage which the supplying partner enjoys through possession of that technology. This is a particularly acute problem in countries which have not yet established an effective system for the protection of intellectual and commercial property rights.

Hamel (1991) has illustrated how a shift in technological advantage took place in alliances between Japanese and Western partners because of the superior ability of the Japanese to learn from their partners within the process of collaboration. He points out that the formation of an alliance may be viewed as an alternative to other modes of skill acquisition such as acquisition, licensing from a partner, or developing the needed skills through internal efforts. This clearly sounds a warning for alliance partners either to match the learning abilities of their partners and/or to ensure that they retain sufficient control over their core competences.

The need for control over an alliance in order to safeguard integrity can take other forms as well. In some countries financial probity can be a problem, which is a major reason why many multinational companies insist on appointing the chief financial officer when they establish joint ventures with local partners. Another difficulty concerns the counterfeiting or illicit marketing of high-reputation international brands, sometimes aided or even undertaken by an alliance partner. A French wine-maker in China, for example, discovered that its joint-venture partner was secretly bottling wine from inferior grapes and selling it under the joint venture's brand label, the quality of which was guaranteed by the French partner.

A partner will also be concerned with how the resources it provides to a strategic alliance are used. It seeks to obtain a rate of return from those resources which compares with their alternative applications elsewhere. A poor use of the resources could also threaten the good name of its products in other market places, if as a result their quality suffers and they are provided with inferior after-sales support. Alliances between partners from developed and developing countries are often not marriages of equals so far as skills and competences are concerned, and this can provide a strong incentive for the more advanced partner to seek control over the alliance's operations (Meier *et al.* 1995).

A further reason why a partner may seek to secure control over the management of a strategic alliance stems from the fear that a shared system of management may lead to a lack of cohesion and unity which would threaten the alliance's performance. The sharing of ownership and contributions to an alliance between its partners always carries the risk of segmenting control in a way that could lead to problems of integration. If this arises, it threatens not only the operating efficiency of an alliance but also, as we note in Chapter 13, the achievement of mutual learning between the partners as well. Killing (1983) argued that the risk of confusion and fragmented efforts would be reduced the more that one parent company assumed a dominant managerial role. On the other hand, when partners can provide truly complementary inputs to an alliance, dominance by one partner may work against the value of the other partners' inputs being recognized and so inhibit the full sharing of their benefits within the alliance. The empirical evidence on the impact of dominance versus shared control on alliance performance is at present very mixed. The argument in favour of dominant control is, nevertheless, widely held among business people and managers who are engaged in alliances.

The reasons why control is an issue in strategic alliances stem from problems which may arise in relations both between the partners and between the partners and their agents who are actually managing the alliances. We noted in Chapter 5 that the appropriateness of alliance partners can be defined by reference to the fit between their strategic objectives and the fit between their organizational and national cultures. It is extremely difficult to achieve these fits. This means that, while alliances depend very importantly on trust between the partners, that trust is not likely to be absolute. Partners' objectives are not likely completely to coincide and their working relationship can be disturbed by cultural misunderstandings. For these reasons, control will be an issue between alliance partners concerned with the extent to which each of them can influence the alliance so that it meets their objectives and cultural preferences. They have to work out an acceptable solution to this problem, which ideally should reflect the levels of involvement they seek to have in the alliance and the distinctive competences they bring to it.

Another aspect of control is concerned with ensuring that the managers of an alliance are held accountable for its performance to its owners. This is present in any organization and is not unique to alliances. It can, however, be complicated in a strategic alliance by the presence of multiple partners, who may seek to introduce different performance priorities into the alliance and to reflect these in different control and information-reporting systems. In China, for example, until the mid-1990s, the higher authorities of state-owned alliance partners insisted that alliances continue to produce accounts according to standards inherited from the days of a socialist economy, which had to coexist with accounts produced to the international standards required by the foreign partner.

THE NATURE OF ALLIANCE CONTROL

Control in strategic alliances refers to the process by which the partners influence, to varying degrees, the behaviour and output of the other partners and the managers of the alliance itself. Their influence may be exercised on the basis of a number of attributes including:

- *power*, such as the command of resources that are key for the alliance's success;
- *authority*, such as the rights deriving from majority equity share;
- *expertise*, such as the possession of specialized expertise relevant to the alliance's operations;
- *rewards*, such as the ability to deliver good returns to other, less active, partners and to offer favourable compensation to alliance staff (cf. French and Raven 1960).

Geringer and Hébert (1989) identify three dimensions of control in international joint ventures which in principle apply to all alliances. These are the *extent* of control exercised over a joint venture, the *focus* of that control, and the *mechanisms* by which control is exercised.

Extent of control

Most of the studies which have examined its extent have thought of control as being dependent upon the centralization or location of the decision-making process. One of the important contributions of this perspective is that it regards control as a continuous variable. In other words, parents can exercise different degrees of control over their alliance rather than it being a question of having either total control or no control. One of the pioneering studies adopting this perspective was that undertaken by Killing (1983) in thirty-seven joint ventures. He argued that joint ventures are intrinsically more difficult to manage because of the way they are constituted, with a small number of powerful parents who are liable to disagree on many issues. He observed that some joint ventures were easier to manage than others, and this was when one parent, or set of parents, was willing to adopt a passive role, leaving the other dominant parent to run the venture. Killing concluded that, the more a joint venture can be run as if it has only one parent, the simpler will be its management task and the better its performance.

Killing assessed the extent of parent-company control over a joint venture by examining its degree of influence on nine areas of decision-making. He enquired whether each decision was made by (1) the joint-venture manager alone, (2) by one parent alone, (3) by the other parent alone, (4) by the joint-venture general manager with input from the first parent, or (5) with input from the second parent, or (6) with input from both parents. This enabled Killing to classify the thirty-seven joint ventures into three categories:

- *dominant-partner joint ventures*, where only one of the parent companies plays a dominant role in decision-making;
- *shared-management joint ventures*, where each parent plays an active role;
- *independent joint ventures*, where neither parent plays a dominant role and the joint-venture general manager enjoys extensive decision-making autonomy.

Child and his colleagues (1997) assessed the relative extent of parent companies' control over the management of Sino-foreign joint ventures by reference to the influence each was perceived to exercise in thirteen areas of joint-venture management, including decisions of both a strategic and an operational nature. They found that this method distinguished between the extent of control exercised by the partners. It also emerged that the distribution of each partner's level of control generally varied across different areas of management.

Research of this kind on the extent of alliance control recognizes several features which are of practical significance. One is that control applies to a range of activities and decisions. The implication is that it is possible for partners to achieve comparable levels of control over a strategic alliance on the basis of different dominance profiles. A dominance profile represents the set of alliance activities over which the partner has predominant influence. In one case it may suit an alliance partner to exercise dominance over activities related to technology, but in another case a partner may seek to exercise dominance over market-related activities. Depending on factors such as the partner's key competences and the criticality of such activities for the sector in which the alliance is operating, each profile may furnish the basis for a similar extent of overall control.

Another implication is that the extent of each partner's control over an alliance has to be assessed in its own right. The relationship between them with respect to control is not likely to be either simply zero sum or wholly convergent. The balance between these two extremes will alter if an alliance matures on the basis of growing mutual confidence and trust between the partners. In the event that this happens, and a shared management based on a heightened sense of common purpose emerges, then the ability of one partner to extend its control over an alliance should be experienced as an improvement, or at least not as a threat, by the other partner.

Consideration of the extent of control also draws attention to the danger of over-control. The attempt to exercise more control than is necessary will not only incur additional direct costs; it could have negative consequences. If one parent tries to exert too much control within an alliance, this may threaten the quality of its relations with its partners. As Schaan (1988: 5) put it, 'in order to ensure the success of a joint venture, managers seek to strike a subtle balance between the desire and need to control the venture on the one hand, and the need to maintain harmonious relations with the partner(s) on the other hand'. Moreover, if parents either singly or together try to control their alliances too much, this may inhibit the flexibility which the latter need in order to develop within their own competitive environments (Bleeke and Ernst 1993). So, as Ohmae (1993: 42) argues, 'Managers must overcome the popular conception that total control increases chances of success.'

Focus of control

The realization that control in alliances does not have to be an all-or-nothing phenomenon has drawn attention to the possibility that parents may seek to focus their control on specific activities, decisions, or processes which they perceive to be crucial for the alliance's performance or for the achievement of their own strategic objectives (Geringer and Hébert 1989). Schaan (1983) explored this possibility in a study of ten international joint ventures located in Mexico. He explicitly defined control as 'the process through which a parent company ensures that the way a JV is managed conforms to its own interest' (1983: 57), and he demonstrated that parent companies tended to seek control over 'strategically important activities' rather than over the whole joint venture. Geringer's (1988) study of ninety developed-country joint ventures supported Schaan's finding that control had a focus dimension, in that parents may choose to exercise control over a relatively wide or narrow range of the joint venture's activities. Geringer and Hébert (1989: 240) conclude that 'these findings support the notion of parent firms' parsimonious and contingent usage of resources for controlling international joint ventures'.

The research conducted on Sino-foreign equity joint ventures by Child *et al.* (1997) also found that foreign- and local-partner control was focused to some extent on those areas of joint-venture activity in which they enjoyed competence advantages. The areas in which foreign partners had the greatest competence advantage and exercised the greatest control—technology, quality maintenance, and marketing—are particularly critical for bringing the performance of Chinese joint ventures up to internationally competitive standards and for extending the joint ventures' market penetration within China. Areas in which the Chinese partners had relative competence advantages, such as personnel and welfare, were ones in which their influence was higher than average. However, in a developing country situation like China it is the foreign partners who normally bring most of the technology and expertise to alliances, and this leads to an overall imbalance between levels of foreign and Chinese control.

The implication of the focus dimension to control is that it is effective for alliance parents to exercise control selectively over those activities and decisions the parent regards as critical. The criticality of some alliance activities is likely to be greater than that of others. The resource deficiency of many developing countries in technology and marketing systems should lead a foreign parent to consider these among the key items for it to supply and control in order to achieve viability for an alliance. In view of the problem of corruption, the foreign partner may also feel it necessary to control the alliance's financial management. This selective approach becomes more sensible in view of the transaction costs of exercising control. The costs of managing some areas of alliance activity may be less for one partner, because of its acquired competence and familiarity in so doing, than for another partner.

Control mechanisms

In order to achieve effective managerial control, the parent companies of equity joint ventures frequently rely upon a *majority equity shareholding*. There is evidence to indicate that equity share does in practice convey considerable control leverage (e.g. Tomlinson 1970; Stopford and Wells 1972; Lecraw 1984; Child *et al.* 1997), and that the senior managers of parent companies also believe this. Schaan (1988: 4), for example, quotes the vice-president of a large electronics firm as saying with reference to joint ventures that 'We like to have full control over our operations. We always have majority ownership.' The Dowty–Sema joint venture illustrates how problems can arise when neither partner has a majority of equity (see Box).

There can, however, be three limitations relying on equity holding as a control mechanism. The first, and most obvious, is that it may not be available. Several forms of cooperation do not involve the creation of equity and the legal rights which accompany it, and even in an equity arrangement, majority equity share is not always an available option. The second is that the decisions of a joint venture's board of directors cannot be expected to reflect a majority equity position without any qualification. The third is that majority equity share may not be an effective means of control at the operational level where the protection of core knowledge and its effective use come into play.

The option of implementing wholly-owned or dominant ownership ventures is often constrained by the increasing scale and risk which accompanies many projects. External constraints may be placed on control by host-government policies which, as in China, promote local-partner equity participation in order to encourage technology transfer, the development of expertise, or market access (Pearson 1991). Moreover, in China and some other developing countries, most local joint-venture partners are state enterprises which report to higher governmental authorities. This means, as Nolan (1995: 9) comments with reference to one of Coca-Cola's joint ventures, that the state is 'an important shadow figure' on its board of directors. There is also the fact that some

Control in the Dowty–Sema Joint Venture

Dowty–Sema was a joint venture set up by the two eponymous companies in 1982 to provide command and control systems for the British navy. The Ministry of Defence (MOD) was the client. Dowty provided the hardware and Sema provided the software. The venture was 50:50 in terms of equity, and the venture company was largely a 'shop window' for tendering, in that the 100-odd staff were all assigned to the payrolls of one parent or the other, dependent on their function. Software engineers were assigned to Sema and hardware engineers to Dowty.

Control was exercised in the following way. A project was divided up between the two companies and 90 per cent of it was carried out in the parent companies, leaving only 10 per cent, principally project management, for the venture company to do. Dowty controlled contract negotiation and administration and Sema controlled finance. Each parent appointed its own project teams, and an element of competition and tension developed between them. The board membership was 50 per cent from each partner. At first there were joint Managing Directors, but later one single Managing Director was appointed. Difficult decisions led to very lengthy meetings by a committee of the board. The venture grew to £50 million sales but unclear control meant that deadlines were missed and the venture made no profit.

Source: Faulkner (1995).

forms of alliance are not founded upon equity participation in the first place, or they take the form of consortia in which equity is too dispersed among a larger number of shareholders for any one of them to exercise much control through that route.

If the alliance is a joint venture, meetings of its *Board of Directors* will normally decide on policy issues such as the venture's business plans, overall performance, and key appointments. As Schaan (1988) points out, in the absence of safeguards built into the joint-venture contract to protect minority interests, majority equity holding ultimately confers control over the issues which a board covers. The frequency with which the board meets and the scope of its agenda therefore bear upon its effectiveness as a control mechanism for the majority partner. However, control through the board is necessarily qualified. If exercised too frequently and in a domineering manner, it is likely to lead to significant ill will and the eventual breakdown of the alliance. Board meetings also provide a channel for keeping minority partners adequately informed and for allowing their views on policy to be expressed. They have the opportunity to discuss and negotiate issues which are placed before the board. The ability of minority partners to influence the management of the alliance will be enhanced if they appoint as their board representatives people who have a good understanding of the alliance's operational and strategic situation, good negotiating skills, and an empathy for the partner's culture. Indeed, minority parents may be able to negotiate the inclusion in a joint-venture contract of the right to veto board decisions that are important to their interests.

Where it is available as an option, majority equity ownership can provide for control over alliance policy, but it cannot guarantee operational control. This is because considerable reliance often has to be placed upon another partner's managers and staff for the implementation of policy. This is especially true of alliances whose operations are located in the other partner's country. A lack of operational control, as we have noted, can have serious consequences for the integrity and use of resources provided to the alliance.

These considerations have led to an interest in mechanisms for control over alliances other than equity share. The *appointment of key alliance managers* to run the operation or manage critical functions such as marketing or R&D can be an important means for a partner to maintain operational control. This is particularly true in cases where the partner is geographically remote or is a minority equity-holder. *Formal contractual agreements* can be made which set out certain rights to the partner relating to technology (e.g. licensing) or management (e.g. key appointments, management systems, and services). Managers in partner companies can enhance their control over an alliance by *structuring the relationships* the alliance has with the partner company. These include the reporting relationships upwards from the alliance to a parent company, formalizing its planning and approval processes for capital budgeting and resource allocation, and laying down procedures and routines for the alliance to follow. The *provision of HRM programmes and systems* for the alliance, for selection, training and development, career advancement, and compensation, can both help to control the quality of the alliance's staff and help to lay down an organizational culture which is consistent with the partner's own (Frayne and Geringer 1990). Generally, multinational companies are interested in promoting corporate culture to improve the control, as well as the integration, of their foreign affiliates (Edstrom and Galbraith 1977, Milliman *et al.* 1991).

In addition to these relatively formal methods to improve operational control over an alliance, a number of important informal mechanisms are also available. One is the maintenance of regular personal relations with the alliance's senior managers. The partner company can assign an executive with sufficient time and resources both to monitor the alliance's progress and to support this with the necessary personal contact. Personal relations between partner and alliance functional and technical staff are also important, especially if a partner is relying on its superiority in technical and other competences as a means of guaranteeing participation in the management of the alliance's day-to-day operations. Technical, advisory, and managerial inputs offered to an alliance on a continuing non-contractual basis, and accompanied by the maintenance of close relations between the parent and its alliance, can have a considerable potential for enhancing operational control.

Schaan (1983) distinguished negative from positive control mechanisms. Negative mechanisms are used by a parent company to stop an alliance from implementing certain activities or decisions. These include laying down a requirement for approval of specific decisions by the parent or the alliance board, particularly of items such as capital expenditure plans and budgets, and nominations of senior appointees. A parent may also insist on its approval before projects are discussed with another parent. The other mechanisms we have listed are generally positive in nature because they are used to encourage and promote certain behaviours. Schaan found that negative control depended principally on formal agreements approved by parents and the use of an alliance's board of directors or management committee. Contracts, for example, can lay down restrictions on an alliance's use of technology and brand names, as well as its suppliers and market access. Positive control was most often exercised through staffing, participation in the planning process, reporting relationships, and informal mechanisms.

Bjørn (1997), in a study of the interfaces in Danish companies between headquarters and foreign subsidiaries, advances a typology of control and coordination mechanisms which helps to categorize the different mechanisms we have discussed. Table 9.1 adapts and selects the most relevant examples from Bjørn's typology.

The use of different mechanisms for controlling alliances is in practice likely to reflect a number of considerations. One is the extent to which the performance achieved in an area of activity carried out by the alliance can be assessed though direct measures. If an activity has a measurable output, such as cases of beverage shipped per week or the percentages of rejects, then control can be exercised through formal monitoring systems. This control could be quite tightly administered, if so desired, in the sense of frequent and precise reporting. If, on the other hand, the outputs or consequences of an alliance's activities are not amenable to such precise definition, as is the case with much HRM and marketing work, then it is appropriate to employ a mode of control which is primarily based on behavioural assessments of how the activity is being carried out (Ouchi 1978). Control in this case is likely to be more personal, less formal, and less frequently conducted.

A second consideration is whether the way in which an alliance performs a certain activity has a direct bearing upon a parent company's overall international operations and standing. Interfaces with other parts of the parent's global operations are likely to be carefully planned, particularly when they constitute an integral part of a global sourcing, production, or marketing network. Similarly, an alliance's activities relating to core technical competences and core products, such as the quality it achieves for those products, are likely to be very closely controlled by the parent company.

Thirdly, a parent company's cultural preferences may well be expressed in the modes of control it prefers to install for an alliance in which it is involved. Contrasts of American and Japanese approaches to management would, for example, suggest that the former prefers to rely upon formal mechanisms of

Table 9.1. *A typology of control mechanisms*

Control mechanism	What the mechanism does	Examples
Input control	Facilitates action on grounds of controlled conditions	Transfer prices, distribution of resources, information management, training and personnel development
Behavioural control	Specifies the correct way to do the work	Policies, plans, specification of methods, rules, direct supervision
Output control	Specifies intended results, monitors and rewards their achievement	Targets, budgets, reporting of results, performance-related pay
Value socialization	Defines and creates common values	Organizational cultures expressed through belief systems, rituals, traditions
Adaptation socialization	Makes people familiar with each other's values and practices	Skills standardization, peer pressure, culture sensitivity progammes
Personal involvement	Signals what partner managers think is important	Visits and participation by managers, spoken communication
Hierarchical structure	Emphasizes and supports partner and alliance goals	Boards of directors, appointment of managers, reporting lines
Lateral structure	Influences people to interact across formal boundaries	'Gatekeepers' between partners, cross-partner teams

control including performance-contingent employment contracts, whereas the latter relies rather more on developing motivation and identity with the parent through the promotion of cultural symbols and practices (Hickson and Pugh 1995). It has indeed been found in previous studies of international joint ventures in China and Hungary that American, German, and Japanese foreign owners prefer to introduce different management philosophies, of which control is an important element (Child *et al.* 1994).

CONTROL IN COLLABORATIONS

The discussion so far has confined itself to the issue of how to exercise control without stifling performance in joint ventures, as it is in this area that the research has largely been conducted. However, it must be remembered that typically of any sample about a quarter of alliances will be collaborations—that is, alliances in which a separate company is not created. Rover–Honda and the RBS–Banco Santander are the alliances to which we keep returning in this book as examples of this genre. There was no Rover–Honda company and there is no RSB–Banco Santander company. Control of collaborations has therefore two major focal dimensions:

1. The 'gatekeeper' role established on both sides to ensure accurate communication between the two companies. For this to be successful, a friendly and forbearing attitude between the two gatekeepers is vital. They must grow to enjoy each other's company, and be able to take a viewpoint which extends beyond the narrow short-term self-interest of their employer, if they are to carry out their role successfully. Gatekeepers play a vital role in controlling an alliance in the sense of monitoring its implementation, guiding it towards fruitful areas of joint activity and keeping partner top managers informed of progress (see Box).
2. The leaders of the joint company project teams upon which the economic success of the alliance depends have a role of equal importance to that of the gatekeeper.

The dimensions of control which Geringer and Hébert (1989) have identified for joint ventures apply *mutatis mutandis* to collaborations as well. However, some of the differences should be noted. The philosophy behind the *extent* of control should be that of flexibility and a resolution not to seek to over-control. In a collaboration, the *focus* of control must be on not unintentionally transferring proprietary information beyond that agreed. The major *mechanisms* of control are the project plans, their Gantt charts, appointments to the project teams, and the monitoring of progress on the projects, and the provision of finance and other key resources to the alliance. The agendas of the gatekeepers also provide a mechanism for control of the development of the alliance, as do the members of the supervisory committee that should be set up to oversee the overall maturing of the alliance.

It should be noted, however, that the collaboration form of alliance does not allow access to certain mechanisms that are available to joint-venture alliances. There is no joint-venture company and therefore no formal permanent management structure, board of directors, or equity holdings by the partner companies. These provide important control mechanisms to the joint venture as described earlier. Despite these control limitations, if similar philosophies are adopted, the collaboration may be controlled just as successfully as the joint venture, although the risk of over-control is perhaps rather less in this inherently more flexible alliance form.

The Gatekeeper Role in the Collaboration between the Royal Bank of Scotland and the Banco Santander

The two gatekeepers for this collaboration are both senior and experienced executives. One is an Assistant Director of the RBS formally reporting to its Managing Director of Corporate Banking. The other is the Banco Santander's Director for the Alliance with the Royal Bank, and he reports formally to the Santander Managing Director. In practice, however, both men have the freedom to cross any organizational lines within their banks. They have a special responsibility for facilitating the collaboration between the two banks. They do this through two main activities. One is representing the alliance to the partners' top management. The other is facilitating the implementation of the collaboration within the two banks' ongoing activities. They meet in person about every two months.

They prepare reports for, and informally brief, the top-level group which oversees the collaboration, aptly named the Surveillance Committee. The two banks' chief executives are members of this committee, as are at least two other executive directors. It meets at least every six weeks. The Surveillance Committee tends to concentrate on broad policy issues and initiatives concerning the two banks. The two gatekeepers have the job of working together to implement the collaboration on a continuing basis within the policy guidelines. Their coordinated reports to the Committee keep the top managers of both banks well informed about the progress, and therefore the value, of the collaboration.

José Saavedra, the Banco Santander's Alliance Director described the operational side of the gatekeeper role:

This job is partly a banker's job and partly a diplomat's job. Because we don't have any authority over anyone, on either side, but we've got to make things happen through persuasion . . . What we try to do, we take the head of, say, Advances, Santander, and the head of Advances, Royal Bank, we put them together, we shake them, and we hope something happens. But it's difficult. Because, on both sides, the perception is 'well, we've got things to do, we are very busy'. But we make sure they talk at least once a year.

The persuasion has to appeal to bottom-line results that can arise from active collaboration. He instanced the successful programme to second Royal Bank staff to Santander branches in Spain, where there is a customer base of British tourists and expatriates:

On the secondee programme, for instance, clearly I present myself to the branch network management as an ally. I say, I can give you someone, a human resource, who will help build up your profits cost-effectively. You will pay so much and you will earn a multiple of that. And they love it. . . . And that's my job, effectively—to find areas where I can say that to as many people as possible.

Source: John Child, personal interview.

THE BASES FOR CONTROL

Rather more attention has been given in literature and research to the reasons for the formation of strategic alliances than to how they are managed once they have been established. As a result, there is relatively little evidence on control in strategic alliances, or on the factors which provide for control, despite its importance for partner companies. Indeed, among the available research studies, there is also the complication that some have examined control in alliances between partners from developed countries, while others have investigated control in alliances between developed and developing country partners. The distinction between these two situations has to be borne in mind because they may produce contrasting findings with different practical implications (Beamish 1988).

The main theories on the subject of control identify three main factors which provide bases for control in strategic alliances. These factors are often related to one another. The first is *majority equity shareholding*, which obviously applies to those alliances which can have an equity basis—namely, joint ventures and consortia. A majority equity shareholding provides the legal voting rights to determine the venture's policies through its board of directors unless specific restrictions are placed on those powers.

The second factor has been identified as an alliance partner's *bargaining power*. This is assumed to derive from the availability of alternative partners, the importance of the alliance for the partner's own strategy, and the partner's commitment of resources to the alliance. A partner possessing bargaining power may be able to negotiate to have a larger equity share when a joint venture is being formed.

A partner's *ability or willingness to commit key resources* to an alliance links to the third factor which, it is argued, can provide a lever for control. This is the advantage a partner has over others in being able to provide resources which are critical to the alliance's success. The provision of such resources may bring with it the justification for installing the partner's managerial and technical systems, and for the nomination of staff to run these, which are themselves further levers for exercising control. Resource provision also relates to formal ownership in two respects. First, equity ownership is itself constituted through the provision of resources which are valued as equity, such as cash, land, plant and technology. Secondly, equity shareholding has a legal status with formal rights and in this respect it parallels the contractual provisions under which resources may be provided to an alliance, whether it be equity based or not. These contracts often include legally defined rights accruing to the resource-providing partners, as in technology-transfer agreements. These rights may include fees and royalties as well as the imposition of restrictions on the use of the resources.

Equity share has been a focus of attention in most studies of alliance control. A number of studies have found that, while many multinational corporations, especially those of US parentage, seek to acquire a majority equity holding in their overseas ventures, this may be dependent upon prior factors which contribute to their bargaining power. Lecraw (1984), for example, found among 153 ASEAN region affiliates of 'transnational' corporations (TNCs), that as the bargaining power of the TNCs increased relative to the bargaining power of the host country, and as their desire for a high level of equity ownership increased, so the per cent equity ownership they held in their affiliates increased. TNC bargaining power was assessed in terms of their technology advantage, their size and capital intensity, their advertising intensity, and the dependence on their subsidiaries for accessing export markets. The bargaining power of the host country was assessed with reference to the attractiveness of its local market, the degree to which it controlled access to that market, and the availability to the host country of proprietary assets from sources other than the TNC. Blodgett (1991) analysed data on 279 two-party equity joint ventures between US and a variety of developed- and developing-country foreign partners. She concluded that the possession of valued technology appears to give considerable bargaining power to a joint-venture partner leading to its acquisition of more equity share, particularly once that partner gains familiarity with the local market and environment and so relies less on its local associate for such knowledge. On the other hand, host-government persuasion could reverse the process, enabling the local partner to increase its equity ownership.

A pioneering study into the control effects of equity ownership was conducted by Killing (1983), who examined thirty-seven equity joint ventures, of which thirty-five were alliances between developed-country partners. He distinguished between joint ventures with dominant parents, those with shared management, and independent ventures, using the criteria mentioned earlier in this chapter. He concluded that ownership and dominance are not necessarily related. He found four cases where a dominant joint-venture parent had only a shared equity stake. As explanation, Killing offered the interpretation given by an experienced and successful joint-venture general manager— namely, that in any alliance which depends on the goodwill and cooperation of both partners for its success, the majority owner cannot force issues by taking them to a vote. ' "You can only do something like that once," he stated, "the second time you try and force it you'll lose your joint venture" ' (Killing 1983: 21). Nevertheless, all of the parent companies which had a more than 50 per cent equity share were classified by Killing as dominant parents. A reasonable conclusion from this pioneering study would be that a majority equity share goes a long way towards providing the partner with a basis for dominant control over a joint venture, but that it is also possible for a non-majority shareholder to develop a strong position through the other mechanisms of control we have identified.

Glaister (1995) examined the same issues in a study of control in ninety-four UK joint ventures with partners from Western Europe, the USA, and Japan. Of these, sixty-five were equity joint ventures and twenty-nine were non-equity joint ventures involving formal long-term cooperation agreements between the partners. In other words, they were what we have called collaboration. Glaister found that most of the non-equity cooperative alliances operated on a basis of shared control. Their management teams tended to be drawn equally from both partners, both partners tended to have the right to veto decisions made by the joint-venture management, and management-control systems tended to be derived from both partners.

In the case of the equity joint ventures, those UK partners which owned at least a half share of them not only possessed the control advantages associated with being the majority equity-holder, but had also in most cases been able to build upon this advantage by deriving several other mechanisms of control. These included appointing the joint venture's general manager, sourcing the joint venture's management team, providing its accounting, planning, and control systems, and being the more active partner in its general management and in all the main management functions except R&D and marketing. When the foreign partner held a majority equity share, it was similarly able in many cases to introduce much the same pattern of additional control mechanisms.

Schaan's (1988) conclusion that a joint-venture partner can secure control even while owning a minority equity share therefore appeared difficult to realize in this sample. This may well be due to the contrast between ventures between developed-country partners and those between developed- and developing-country partners. Whereas Glaister investigated joint ventures between developed-country partners, Schaan's conclusions were drawn from joint ventures between companies from developed and developing countries. In this second case, alliances depend quite highly on the developed-country partner for technical and managerial skills, thus providing it with a substantial alternative basis for exercising control, even if it has a minority equity holding. By contrast, alliance partners from highly developed countries will tend to be more balanced in their managerial, and even technological, competences and they are therefore less likely to be able to use these to derive further control advantages unless they enjoy the right to do so which flows from a majority equity share.

Further light is shed on the developing country alliance by recent studies of joint ventures formed between Chinese enterprises and foreign partners from developed countries. Yan and Gray (1994a, 1994b, 1996) conducted a qualitative study of partner bargaining power and control in four Sino-US equity manufacturing joint ventures and a complementary qualitative study in ninety such ventures. They assessed parent-company bargaining power during negotiations to form the joint ventures in terms of two dimensions: the alternatives each partner possessed when negotiating the venture and the strategic importance of the joint venture to each partner. Equity share and the relative provision by parent companies of non-capital resources were taken as measures of bargaining power during the operational life of the joint venture. Parent-company control over the joint ventures was assessed indirectly with reference to the composition of their boards of directors (as a measure of strategic control), the nomination of the general and deputy general managers and the decision-power distance between them (as a measure of control over operational issues), and similarities between joint-venture and parent-company organizational structures and operational procedures (as a measure of structural control).

Yan and Gray found that their four case studies supported the predicted relationship between the level of a parent company's bargaining power and its control over the management of a joint venture. Their survey did not, however, provide any support for a link between bargaining power during joint-venture negotiation and the subsequent level of control exercised by the parent companies. Equity share strongly predicted the amount of control a parent company exercised over the joint venture's strategy and, to a lesser extent, its level of operational control. The more that one parent company provided non-capital resources relative to the other(s), the greater tended to be the operational control it exercised.

An investigation into sixty-seven Sino-foreign equity joint ventures located in the electronics and fast-moving consumer goods sectors, throws further light on the bases for control over such alliances (Child *et al.* 1997). The investigators examined three categories of ownership input to the joint venture: capital resources (equity) and two forms of non-capital resources—namely, those provided on the basis of contracts and those provided on a non-contractual basis. They also examined the role of joint-venture board composition and the staffing of senior positions in the joint ventures. They assessed control primarily in terms of the level of influence which the Chinese and the foreign-parent companies (and their representatives) were reported to exercise over thirteen joint-venture activities and decisions.

The investigation identified four significant bases for control in the joint ventures. *Majority equity share* provided for dominant control over key policy decisions, including a joint venture's strategic priorities, reinvestment policy, and profit distribution. As expected, the right to a majority on the joint-venture board secures this general policy control. Majority equity share also bolsters a parent company's influence over key managerial appointments in a joint venture—namely, its general manager and the heads of major functions.

The nomination of the *general manager* and the *heads of certain functions* increases a foreign parent's control over a wide range of joint-venture decisions. These appointments are by no means wholly determined by equity share, and can therefore be negotiated separately. The right to appoint to given management posts can be specified in the joint-venture contract. As well as having a foreign general manager, heading up *finance* enhances foreign influence in the large majority of joint ventures. Many foreign parent companies saw it as essential to have their own financial manager in the joint ventures in order to ensure accurate reporting according to their own accounting conventions. In the electronics and fast-moving consumer-goods sectors, *technology* and *marketing* are respectively key competences.

Managing these functions therefore contributed importantly to the overall direction of the joint ventures.

Legal *contracts* are intended primarily to provide security for foreign technology, to guard against leakage, to guarantee standards, and to secure an income stream from royalties. They are also used to protect brands. Providing resources under contract can therefore assist foreign control over certain key parameters, though the enforcement of contracts remains a problem in China. It did not, however, appear to affect the balance of influence within management, except in the area of technology development.

Non-contractual support is provided without any contract or fee, and includes product know-how, production technology, marketing assistance, management systems, and training. The provision of non-contractual support by Chinese joint-venture parent companies on an ongoing basis adds appreciably to the influence they possess in many areas of joint-venture management. Whereas equity share impacts most on the *strategic* influence available to a joint-venture parent company, the provision of non-contractual support impacts most on the influence it has over *operational* activities—purchasing, production, quality, and sales/distribution. An exception was that when Chinese parents assisted with the management of external governmental relationships, this tended to enhance their influence over the joint venture's strategic decision-making as well. The level of non-contractual support provided by parent companies was to a large extent independent of their equity shares, and it is therefore an important lever for control in its own right.

A number of practical implications can be drawn from this research, which, although it was located in China, is likely to apply to foreign cooperative ventures in many other emerging economies as well (see Box).

These conclusions are broadly comparable with those of Yan and Gray (1996) for US–China joint ventures, regarding the impact of resource provision by parent companies upon their levels of joint-venture control. Yan and Gray found that the equity share held by a parent is a stronger predictor of what they called strategic control than is non-capital resource provision, while they found that non-capital resourcing is more predictive of operational control. However, Yan and Gray assessed strategic and operational control in terms of respectively the parent companies' ratio of joint-venture board members and the nomination of the joint venture's general and deputy general managers. This tends to obscure the very germane question of whether such appointments themselves provide important bases for joint-venture control in addition to the provision of financial and material resources.

A majority equity share was in most cases reflected in an equivalent majority on the joint venture board, but not necessarily so. Some joint ventures, for example, have a foreign majority share but a board with equally divided membership. Moreover, equity share was a stronger predictor of the level of control than was the ratio of board members, suggesting that its leverage on control works through other channels in addition to the board. One such channel is provided by senior managerial appointments.

Policies to Enhance Control in the Management of Chinese Ventures

1. Acquire a majority equity share, and preferably a substantial majority such as 75 per cent. This establishes the clear right to control the joint venture's policy as a whole (strategic control).
2. However, do not rely so highly on the legal rights embodied in equity and contracts as might be done in a Western context. Legal contracts tend to have a negative connotation in China. It is unwise to insist too often on the assertion of these rights, since this is readily interpreted as offensive and damaging of mutual respect by Chinese partners.
3. Involve foreign staff both in heading key functions and in the provision of continuing non-contractual support. This is, of course, costly, but it significantly increases the ability to determine the quality of the joint-venture management process. It also creates active personal links within the parent company which enable its senior management to learn from the experience of operating in a relatively unfamiliar and difficult environment.
4. Focus control on areas that are both key for the business and where foreign expertise and experience are paramount. In China these are generally finance, technology, and marketing, though the development of human resources also needs considerable attention and support.
5. Above all, use the rights and powers of ownership to manage relationships. It is essential to approach these in a non-confrontational manner. In China this is a condition for accepting the contribution and authority of foreign management. Also to recognize the importance of sending high-profile corporate personnel to China. This is interpreted as a positive gesture, and it can do a great deal to remove constraints on joint-venture management.

Source: adapted from Child (1995).

The great majority (79 per cent) of the sixty-seven Sino-foreign joint ventures investigated by Child *et al.* (1997) had a foreign general manager, and, of the five major functions, on average almost two (1.8) were headed by foreign managers. The roles which were mostly occupied by Chinese nationals—deputy general manager and head of personnel/HRM—are ones for which foreign joint-venture partners do not necessarily possess superior competences. Nevertheless, it is surprising to find so many joint ventures in which several functional areas, in addition to general management, were headed by non-PRC appointees in view of the high costs of expatriate managers in China. It emerged that the greater the equity share and the provision of non-contractual resources by a foreign parent company, the more key appointments were likely to be held by managers from that parent. Joint ventures still at an early stage of development were also more likely to have foreign managers or foreign parent nominees in charge of production, finance, and marketing.

These connections imply that parent companies appoint managers to enhance their control in areas of importance to them. The occupancy of senior joint-venture positions did, in fact, add to the relevant parent company's control over the joint venture, over and above the impact of equity share. In other words, there is support for Schaan's argument that the determination of a joint venture's management structure can provide alliance partners with a lever for control in addition to its ownership commitment. Because senior appointments are not entirely dependent on equity and other resource commitment, the implication is that they can to some extent be negotiated in their own right.

Another lesson to be drawn from the research just reviewed lies in the distinction between a partner's strategic control over an alliance and its control in operational areas of the alliance. The two levels of control are clearly not the same, and this offers the prospect of a reconciliation between the desire to promote harmonious relationships between partners and the need to control an alliance's operations to achieve the necessary level of competitive performance and return on resource investments. If there is broad compatibility between the partners' objectives, then it should be possible for control, in the sense of influence, to be shared at the strategic level, even if one partner clearly enjoys greater operational competences and should therefore exercise the greater control at that level. The proposition, in other words, is that cooperation between firms will usually work best if they each perceive that they have a sufficient voice over the strategic direction it will take. Within an agreed set of long-terms goals and priorities, it may then be quite acceptable to all concerned for one partner to take the lead in controlling certain operational areas in which it clearly enjoys superior expertise, experience, or knowledge.

CONTROL AND PERFORMANCE

Investigations into the implications of partner control for alliance performance have produced mixed results (Geringer and Hébert 1989). There are a number of likely reasons for this. The first arises from the fact that the assessment of alliance performance is far from straightforward and has not been consistent across different investigations. Some have assessed performance in terms of a 'goal' model—namely, how far partners think the alliance has met their objectives. One problem with this is that the partners' objectives can differ. Thus, in an alliance between developing- and developed-country partners, the former may evaluate the alliance's performance in terms of how far it has provided access to technology and foreign capital, whereas the latter may evaluate success in terms of its profitability and competitiveness. Other studies have assessed alliance performance in 'system' terms, with reference to how far the alliance is able to sustain and strengthen itself as an ongoing system by producing a return on the resources invested in it and by resourcing its growth (see Seashore and Yuchtman 1967).

A second problem stems from the difficulty of obtaining 'hard' performance data for alliances and the fact that assessments of profitability in particular can be distorted by factors such as transfer pricing between the alliance and its partner companies. An alternative approach has been to request the subjective assessments of partner or alliance managers, but these are likely to be qualified by the expectations which such managers hold and possibly by their desire to put a favourable interpretation on the alliance's performance (Geringer and Hébert 1991).

The practical consequence of these difficulties in assessing alliance performance is illustrated in the research that Child and Yan (1997) carried out on Sino-foreign joint ventures. They assessed joint-venture performance with reference both to the goal model (joint-venture managers' perceptions of how far Chinese and foreign-partner objectives had been attained) and to the systems model (subjective and hard data on joint-venture profitability and growth). A mix of subjective (perceptual) and hard data were gathered for the assessment. However, while the perceptual indices were positively intercorrelated, there was only a limited correspondence between the subjective and 'objective' indicators: the indicators of profitability correlated, but those for growth did not.

Discrepant findings on whether and how alliance control has an impact on performance have also almost certainly arisen because different investigations have not focused on alliances of the same type, operating in comparable situations. In some circumstances greater control may afford benefits which outweigh the costs that are incurred, but in other situations the cost–benefit equation for control may be different. Contractor (1990) has argued that in industries where there is an additional return from global standardization of products and/or processes, multinational companies are likely to seek strict control over their cooperative ventures in order to achieve this standardization. This means that wholly owned subsidiaries will be their preferred mode of entry to new markets. By contrast, in industries with strong local-consumer preferences or a high level of economic nationalism, shared control through partnership with a local firm is preferable. Similarly, Anderson and Gatignon (1986) suggested that entry modes offering greater control would be more effective for highly proprietary products or processes.

Franko (1971), who studied the control–performance relationship in MNCs with international joint ventures, concluded that it depended upon the parent company's strategy. Their joint ventures were more stable (measured by the absence of liquidation or significant ownership change) when the MNC parents followed a diversification strategy and demanded less control over the venture than when the MNC's strategy emphasized product concentration (e.g. globalization) which usually relied on strong control. The implications of control for joint-venture performance therefore appeared to be contingent upon the parent company's chosen strategy and structure.

Bleeke and Ernst (1993) argue that acquisitions in which one side in theory assumes total control over the other work well for core businesses and existing geographic areas where the acquiring company already possess relevant knowledge and experience. On the other hand, alliances with a degree of shared control are, they claim, more effective for edging into related businesses or new geographic areas. Much of this boils down to the adage that there is no point for a partner to try to control what it does not understand until it has had the opportunity to acquire the necessary knowledge, and there is no point either in trying to exert control if this will generate strong counter-productive reactions.

These considerations lay down the basis for a contingency approach to partner control and alliance performance, which is illustrated in Fig. 9.1 (adapted from Bartlett 1986). Although this approach needs to be clarified through further research, it points the way to the kind of judgement which companies need to make when establishing alliances.

High	Dominant control *Consumer electronics*	Initially shared control, but attempt to move towards dominant control as partner learns *Branded foods*
	Shared or dominant control depending on partner's management culture and attitude towards risk	Shared or limited control
Low	*Cement*	*Construction*

Returns to partner from global standardization of products (vertical axis label, High at top, Low at bottom)

Low ———————————— High

Significance of specific local factors

Fig. 9.1. A partner's choice of alliance control policy in the light of contingencies
Notes: Illustrative sectors are shown in italics. Local factors include strong local consumer preferences, economic nationalism, or partner's unfamiliarity with context.
Source: adapted from Bartlett (1986).

This contingency analysis extends considerations of transaction costs in alliance management to take account of strategic factors, particularly global product strategy, as well. In the light of this more complex analysis, it is not surprising that the simple proposition advanced by Killing (1983)—alliances having dominant control by one partner will be more successful because they are easier to manage—has not been consistently supported. Killing found that ventures with 'dominant' parents 'significantly outperformed' those with shared management. This finding was based on two quite limited measures of joint-venture performance which, nevertheless, provided a similar interpretation. These were the manager's own perception of his venture's performance and whether the venture had either failed through demise or undergone a major reorganization because of poor performance. Killing did, however, qualify his conclusions by arguing that a critical requirement for joint-venture success is that partners which have required skills and knowledge should be able to exercise an appropriate level of control in those areas of competence. This means that in situtations where, for example, one parent company has a special knowledge of technology, and the other a knowledge of the market, a shared management venture is the appropriate solution despite the likelihood that it will be more difficult to manage.

Killing's thesis on the performance advantages of dominant parents has received some further support, largely from studies of multinationals having alliances in developing countries. For example, a study was undertaken by A. T. Kearney International of fifty-five large American and European multinational corporations operating in East Asia. This indicated that wholly owned subsidiaries accounted for almost 50 per cent of the cases achieving a return on investment greater than their cost of capital, while 50–50 and minority joint ventures and agent–partner arrangements made up more than 60 per cent of the operations with a return below their cost of capital (*Business Asia* 1992). Hu and Chen (1994) found from a survey of 382 Hong Kong subsidiaries and ventures operating in China by 1986 that wholly owned subsidiaries were more likely to be successful than equity joint ventures or those based on contractual agreements. This again suggests that sole management control has performance advantages. The results must, however, be treated with caution, since there were only twenty-seven wholly owned subsidiaries in the sample, and very indirect measures of performance were employed: duration of the alliance and total partner investment in it. Yan and Gray (1996), in their study of Sino-US joint ventures, assessed performance in terms of the extent to which joint-venture general managers or deputy general managers perceived each parent company's strategic objectives to have been achieved. Path analysis suggested that, the higher the level of operational control a parent company exercises in the joint venture relative to its partner, the greater the extent to which that parent was perceived to be achieving its objectives. This finding appears to lend support to Killing's thesis that dominant control by one joint-venture partner is associated with higher performance, but one should bear in mind that Yan and Gray's assessment was based on a goal model of performance rather than a direct measure of joint-venture performance *per se*.

Other studies have failed to confirm Killing's findings. For instance, Janger (1980) used a classification scheme similar to Killing's in a study of 168 international joint ventures in both developed and developing countries. He did not, however, find that one type of joint venture tended to be more successful than another. Awadzi *et al.* (1986) failed to find any relationship between the extent of parent control and the performance of joint ventures. Bleeke and

Ernst (1993) found among a sample of forty-nine cross-border alliances, chiefly, it appears, between partners from developed countries, that those with 50–50 ownership turned in a superior performance. Bleeke and Ernst considered that an alliance was successful if it passed two tests: both partners achieved their ingoing strategic objectives and both recovered their financial costs of capital. The reasoning they advance to account for their finding is particularly interesting because it stresses the benefits of strong management *within* an alliance rather than Killing's argument in favour of strong management *over* an alliance, as well as the virtues of developing trust between the partners: 'when ownership is even, it is more likely that the joint venture will be set up as a separate entity with its own strong management. But 50–50 ownership is important for another reason: It builds trust by ensuring that each partner is concerned about the other's success' (Bleeke and Ernst 1993: 28).

Beamish (1988) reviewed studies, including his own, on the control–performance link in developed- and developing-country alliances. Several of these investigations conclude that, when alliances are formed between developed- and less-developed-country partners, there tends to be an association between satisfactory performance and less dominant control by the foreign partner. The argument is that a sharing of control with local partners will lead to a greater contribution from them which can assist in coping with circumstances that are unfamiliar to the foreign partner, and therefore result in a higher return on investment. Beamish (1988: 21) concluded that 'What the literature seems to indicate is a different emphasis—in fact a weakening of the link—between dominant management control and good performance when study focus shifts from the developed countries to the less developed countries.'

Osland and Cavusgil (1996) conducted interviews with forty-three managers and government officials representing eight Sino-US joint ventures. Noting that previous investigations provide conflicting results about the relative effects on performance of dominant, shared, and split control, they reported that a third variable—size of the joint venture measured in annual sales, equity, and expatriate personnel—affects the relationship between control and performance. They assessed performance in terms of partner satisfaction with goal attainment and with joint-venture profitability. In each of the three small joint ventures, split control was satisfactory to both sides. When the American partners had committed more money and personnel to the joint ventures, it became desirable in their eyes to control more of their management functions. They were not satisfied with their joint ventures' performance unless they had dominant control in them.

Child and Yan (1997), drawing from the investigation of sixty-seven Sino-foreign joint ventures mentioned earlier, looked at both the possibility of a direct relationship between control and performance as well as the association which the degree of 'fit' between owner resourcing and control might have with performance. There was no consistent link between the relative level of control over the joint ventures held by the parent companies and assessments of their performance. However, the joint ventures for which their senior managers rated profitability and growth highly tended to have a close match between levels of control and partners' equity and resource provision than did the lower performing joint ventures. A similar trend, though not so sharply defined, distinguished between more and less successful joint ventures when performance was assessed in terms of hard profitability and growth data. This suggests that achieving a balance between the level of a partner's resourcing commitment to an alliance and its management control of the alliance can impact upon the performance that is achieved. In the absence of such a balance, a parent company may well not have sufficient control to ensure an effective use of the resources it has provided

SUMMARY

Control is a critical issue for the successful management and performance of cooperative ventures. It can also become an extremely sensitive matter. If partners compete for control and do not arrive at a mutually acceptable solution, this can jeopardize their relationship and inhibit its potential for realizing complementarities and achieving learning. A subtle balance may have to be struck between the need for control and the equal need in an alliance to maintain harmonious and constructive relationships between the partners.

Control is a complex multidimensional feature of management, and the complexity is increased when the activity to be managed comes under the purview of two or more separate organizations. This chapter has concentrated on three of these dimensions as they apply to alliances. These are the extent of control exercised by partners over their alliance, the activities and decisions which they control (focus), and the mechanisms by which control is exercised. The extent of control available to a partner does not necessarily rest upon its formal rights through ownership and contractual agreement. It may depend quite considerably on informal practices such as a partner company maintaining close personal links with managers and staff working directly in the alliance. It may also be enhanced by a partner's initiatives, such as offering to provide new techniques and training for members of the alliance which lay down a set of practices and a culture that is consistent with the partner's own. In these ways, the extent of control can be conditioned by the mechanisms that are adopted and the activities to which these are applied. Control of a collaboration, which may be based on little or no contractual foundation, will depend very largely upon the relationship between the partners' respective gatekeepers, and the accord they can work out.

Control is also a subtle phenomenon. In some circumstances it is accepted and regarded as legitimate, in others not. The paradox is that resistance by one partner to the exercise of control by another may diminish the overall control that the former can exercise. Genuine cooperation in a non-zero-sum relationship enables the partners together to exercise greater control, through the fact that they each have greater influence than is the case if the alliance is beset with conflict and low trust.

Although it is a basic tenet of managerial wisdom that adequate and appropriate control is a requirement for satisfactory performance, the evidence on this issue for alliances does not offer clear guidelines on the key issue of whether it is advantageous to share control or to have one leading partner. This chapter has suggested that a partner's control policy should be worked out with a consideration of its goals in forming an alliance and the nature of its dependence on the partner for realizing these. In this respect, it is important for the partners to distinguish between strategic and operational levels of control. Cooperation between firms will usually work best if they each perceive that they have a sufficient voice over the strategic direction it will take. Within an agreed set of long-term goals and priorities, it may then be quite acceptable for one partner to take the lead in controlling certain operational areas in which it clearly enjoys superior expertise, experience, or knowledge.

REFERENCES

Anderson, E., and Gatignon, H. (1986), 'Modes of Foreign Entry: A Transaction Cost Analysis and Propositions', *Journal of International Business Studies*, 17: 1–26.

Awadzi, W., Kedia, B. L., and Chinta, R. (1986), 'Performance Implications of Locus of Control and Complementary Resources in International Joint Ventures—An Empirical Study', paper presented at the Academy of International Business Conference, London.

Bartlett, C. A. (1986), 'Building and Managing the Transnational: The New Organizational Challenge', in M. E. Porter (ed.), *Competition in Global Industries* (Boston, Mass.: Harvard Business School Press), 367–401.

Beamish, P. W. (1988), *Multinational Joint Ventures in Developing Countries* (London: Routledge).

Berle, A. A., Jr., and Means, G. C. (1932), *The Modern Corporation and Private Property* (New York: Macmillan).

Bjørn, L. B. (1997), 'Managing Uncertainty in Transnational Headquarters–Subsidiary Interfaces: Danish Companies in Japan and Germany', unpublished Ph.D. dissertation (University of Aarhus, Denmark, Mar.).

Bleeke, J., and Ernst, D. (1993) (eds.), *Collaborating to Compete: Using Strategic Alliances and Acquisitions in the Global Marketplace* (New York: Wiley).

Blodgett, L. L. (1991), 'Partner Contributions as Predictors of Equity Share in International Joint Ventures', *Journal of International Business Studies*, 22: 63–78.

Business Asia (1992), 'Corporate Structure: Stay Single, Stay Wealthy', 7 December: 9.

Child, J. (1995), 'Exercising Strong Direction', *Financial Times*, 6 Nov.

——and Yan, Y. (1997), 'Predictors of Performance in Sino-Foreign Joint Ventures', unpublished paper, Judge Institute of Management Studies, University of Cambridge, October.

Child, J., Markóczy, L., and Cheung, T. (1994), 'Managerial Adaptation in Chinese and Hungarian Strategic Alliances with Culturally Distinct Foreign Partners', *Advances in Chinese Industrial Studies*, 4: 211–31.

—— Yan, Y., and Lu, Y. (1997), 'Ownership and Control in Sino-Foreign Joint Ventures', in P. W. Beamish and J. P. Killing (eds.), *Cooperative Strategies: Asian Pacific Perspectives* (San Francisco: New Lexington Press), 181–225.

Contractor, F. J. (1990), 'Ownership Patterns of US Joint Ventures Abroad and the Liberalization of Foreign Government Regulations in the 1980s: Evidence from the Benchmark Surveys', *Journal of International Business Studies*, 21: 55–73.

—— and Lorange, P. (1988) (eds.), *Cooperative Strategies in International Business* (New York: Lexington Books).

Edstrom, A., and Galbraith, J. R. (1977), 'Transfer of Managers as a Co-ordination and Control Strategy in Multinational Organizations', *Administrative Science Quarterly*, 22: 248–63.

Faulkner, D. O. (1995), *International Strategic Alliances: Cooperating to Compete* (Maidenhead: McGraw-Hill).

Franko, L. G. (1971), *Joint Venture Survival in Multinational Corporations* (New York: Praeger).

—— (1976), *The European Multinationals* (London: Harper & Row).

Frayne, C. A., and Geringer, J. M. (1990), 'The Strategic Use of Human Resource Management Practices as Control Mechanisms in International Joint Ventures', *Research in Personnel and Human Resources Management*, suppl. 2: 53–69.

French, J. R. P., Jr., and Raven, B. (1960), 'The Bases of Social Power', in D. Cartwright and A. Zander (eds.), *Group Dynamics: Research and Theory* (2nd edn., New York: Harper & Row), 607–23.

Geringer, J. M. (1988), *Joint Venture Partner Selection: Strategies for Developed Countries* (Westport, Conn.: Quorum Books).

—— and Hébert, L. (1989), 'Control and Performance of International Joint Ventures', *Journal of International Business Studies*, 20: 235–54.

Glaister, K. W. (1995), 'Dimensions of Control in UK International Joint Ventures', *British Journal of Management*, 6: 77–96.

Hamel, G. (1991), 'Competition for Competence and Inter-Partner Learning within International Strategic Alliances', *Strategic Management Journal*, 12: 83–103.

Hickson, D. J., and Pugh, D. S. (1995), *Management Worldwide: The Impact of Societal Culture on Organizations around the Globe* (London: Penguin).

Hu, M. Y., and Chen, H. (1994), 'The Performance of Hong Kong Foreign Subsidiaries in China', *Advances in Chinese Industrial Studies*, 4: 185–98.

Janger, A. R. (1980), *Organization of International Joint Ventures* (New York: The Conference Board).

Killing, J. P. (1983), *Strategies for Joint Venture Success* (New York: Praeger).

Lecraw, D. J. (1984), 'Bargaining Power, Ownership, and Profitability of Transnational Corporations in Developing Countries', *Journal of International Business Studies*, 15: 27–43.

Meier, J., Perez, J., and Woetzel, J. R. (1995), 'Solving the Puzzle: MNCs in China', *McKinsey Quarterly*, 1995/2: 20–33.

Milliman, J., Von Glinow, M. A., and Nathan, M. (1991), 'Organizational Life Cycles and Strategic International Human Resource Management in Multinational Companies: Implications for Congruence Theory', *Academy of Management Review*, 16: 318–39.

Nolan, P. (1995), 'Joint Ventures and Economic Reform in China: A Case Study of the

Coca-Cola Business System, with Particular Reference to the Tianjin Coca-Cola Plant', Cambridge ESRC Centre for Business Research Working Paper, WP24, Dec.

Ohmae, K. (1993), 'The Global Logic of Strategic Alliances', in J. Bleeke and D. Ernst (eds.), *Collaborating to Compete* (New York: Wiley), 35–54.

Osland, G. E., and Tamer Cavusgil, S. (1996), 'Performance Issues in US–China Joint Ventures', *California Management Review*, 38: 106–30.

Ouchi, W. G. (1978), 'The Transmission of Control through Organizational Hierarchy', *Academy of Management Journal*, 21: 173–92.

Pearson, M. M. (1991), *Joint Ventures in the People's Republic of China: The Control of Foreign Direct Investment under Socialism* (Princeton: Princeton University Press).

Schaan, J.-L. (1983), 'Parent Control and Joint Venture Success: The Case of Mexico', unpublished doctoral dissertation (University of Western Ontario).

—— (1988), 'How to Control a Joint Venture even as a Minority Shareholder', *Journal of General Management*, 14: 4–16.

Seashore, S., and Yuchtman, E. (1967), 'Factorial Analysis of Organizational Performance', *Administrative Science Quarterly*, 12: 377–95.

Stopford, J. M., and Wells, L. T., Jr. (1972), *Managing the Multinational Enterprise* (New York: Basic Books).

Tomlinson, J. W. C. (1970), *The Joint Venture Process in International Business: India and Pakistan* (Cambridge, Mass.: MIT Press).

Yan, A., and Gray, B. (1994a), 'Bargaining Power, Management Control, and Performance in United States–China Joint Ventures: A Comparative Case Study', *Academy of Management Journal*, 37: 1478–517.

—— —— (1994b), 'An Empirical Investigation of a Negotiations Model in American–Chinese Joint Ventures', paper given to the Conference on Management Issues for China in the 1990s, St John's College, Cambridge, England, Mar.

—— —— (1996), 'Linking Management Control and Interpartner Relationships with Performance in US–Chinese Joint Ventures', in J. Child and Y. Lu (eds.), *Management Issues in China: International Enterprises* (London: Routledge), 106–27.

10

Human-Resource Management

Until recently, the human-resource issues arising in strategic alliances have received rather little attention. This is despite evidence that many performance problems in alliances stem from poorly designed and executed human-resource-management (HRM) policies (Frayne and Geringer 1990). When alliances are established, the feasibility studies which are undertaken and negotiations between partners typically focus on matters of technology, markets, ownership, and management structures. They often neglect HRM issues, in the belief that these either are less consequential or can be sorted out once the alliance is up and running (Drouin 1996). It was, for example, estimated that only about 4 per cent of the time spent in creating collaborative ventures is spent resolving human-resource-related issues (Coopers & Lybrand/Yankelovich, Skelly & White 1986). Failures of international cooperation between firms can result from the poor adjustment of managers and staff to working with their partner's nationals. American firms have in particular been noted for a neglect of rigorous selection and training for international assignments, and this has been associated with a high failure rate among their expatriates (Adler and Ghadar 1990).

Many HRM issues have to be resolved for strategic alliances to realize their full potential. These tend to be more complex than in a unitary, domestic company, because alliances typically contain two or more cultural systems which can set the stage for conflict and which may promote personnel processes unique to that type of enterprise. As Shenkar and Zeira (1987) point out, the human resources of an international joint venture can comprise as many as eight different employee groups, each with its own distinct characteristics—parent-company expatriates, host-parent transferees, host-country nationals, third-country expatriates of foreign parents, third-country expatriates of host-country parents, third-country nationals recruited directly by the venture, foreign-headquarters executives, and host-parent headquarters executives.

The partners to an alliance bring to their cooperation their own corporate cultures and associated HRM practices. In the case of an international alliance, the situation is further complicated by the presence of different national cultures and practices conditioned by different home-country institutions, such as legal regulations and professional standards. HRM policies have to be tailored to social environments like China which are relatively unfamiliar to Western multinational enterprises.

A carefully considered set of HRM policies and practices can make a significant contribution to the success of alliances. It can assist the adjustment of corporate cultures and practices to the partnership, offer mechanisms of control, promote organizational learning, and foster the selection and development of staff who are capable of working effectively in a milieu of inter-organizational collaboration. In these and other ways, HRM can help to enhance the productivity of alliances, as well as the ability of partners to benefit from them. The HRM activities through which these contributions can be made are recruitment and staffing, training and development, performance appraisal, and compensation and reward policies.

The purpose of this chapter is to examine how HRM can contribute to the successful implementation of a cooperative strategy in the ways just mentioned. It also examines the national specificity of HRM practices, illustrating this with reference to the experience of foreign joint ventures in China.

HRM AND ALLIANCE CULTURES

For an alliance to realize its full potential, there has to be not only a match between the partners' strategic objectives and the resources they contribute, but also a fit between their respective cultures and practices. International joint ventures (IJVs) are the form of alliance in which achievement of this cultural fit is likely to present the greatest difficulties. Communication blockages and conflicts of loyalty are among the personnel problems most often highlighted by research into IJVs (Shenkar and Zeira 1987). Barriers to communication between IJVs and parent companies, and between the parents themselves, can easily arise not only due to geographical dispersion but also because differences of culture and organizational identity are obstacles (Child and Rodrigues 1996). Similarly, loyalty problems arise if there is not a reconciliation of the values and goals expressed by the different groups involved in the set of relationships in and around IJVs.

Appropriate HRM policies can play an important role in fostering a shared corporate culture which articulates goals and standards for the alliance, and a willingness to adopt common practices in the pursuit of those objectives. Thought needs to be given to the selection criteria applied to managers and staff who are recruited to work in and with the alliance, both from within the parent companies and externally. These criteria should refer not just to required technical competencies, but also to the openness and flexibility of candidates' attitudes towards working in ways that are compatible with those of the partner companies. The attitudes and behaviours helpful to the success of an alliance can be further developed through training and reinforced by the systems adopted for performance appraisal, reward, and promotion. Depending on the nationalities involved in the alliance, training in partners' national cultures and languages can be a most important step towards breaking down internal cultural barriers and blocks to mutual understanding. This rather obvious point appears to be widely accepted in principle but less often carried out in practice, judging by recent evidence from Eastern Europe (Villinger 1996).

It is particularly important that the partners' staff who have to work together do receive language instruction (where relevant) and training designed to promote their understanding of the partner's culture, national institutions, mindsets, and codes of behaviour. This preparation will not compensate for errors in selection which result in people who are intolerant, inflexible, or otherwise ill-suited to working with other organizational or national cultures. It will, however, enable those who are well chosen to avoid some of the pitfalls which can otherwise jeopardize the effectiveness of cross-partner teams and meetings. The facility and willingness to converse, at least to some degree, in the partner's language expresses goodwill and in so doing opens the psychological door to further communication. An appreciation of the likely cultural or political sensitivities of a partner's staff can avoid unnecessary conflict and mistrust. For example, in collective meetings with East Asian staff, it is vital not to place individuals into a position where they are shamed before their colleagues—this is an extreme cultural sensitivity. This does not mean, however, that opinions and evidence should not be challenged in the management meetings held by, say, a Sino-Western joint venture. It means, rather, that care and time have to be taken over the course of several meetings to move towards a shared understanding that everyone present, especially the senior foreign manager, can be questioned in a courteous way without any face being lost, and that this amounts to a 'testing of reality' which is of benefit to everyone in carrying out their work. The aim, in this case, is to blend the personal courtesy of the East with the open enquiry of the West. It is much more difficult to achieve this if the partners' HRM routines do not include suitable briefings and role plays to prepare staff for these situations.

The approach to communications and information flow pursued within the alliance can also support the objective of achieving a positive cultural adjustment. Communication policies can be adopted to create an awareness among employees of the reasons for changes which are under way within the alliance and how these relate to its *raison d'être*. A company newsletter can be an important source of information about the vision and philosophy of the alliance, and efforts can also be made for information on policy and other developments to be displayed regularly in areas where employees have access. Regular meetings between partners' managers and staff may also be another means of enhancing communication. An emphasis on communication, of course, requires that there is a good strategic fit between the partners and that the joint message they give out is therefore positive and sincere; otherwise the exercise is likely to be counter-productive.

Cyr and Schneider (1994*a*) cite the case of a joint venture between a Swedish multinational and a Hungarian company in the field of telecommunications, where a conscious attempt was made to create a new organizational culture (see Box). This culture emphasizes people as well as excellence in products and services, and the results for the venture were claimed to be impressive. There was a sound base for the development of a shared culture because the joint venture was considered beneficial to both partners. The Swedish company wished to establish a presence in East European markets and was also attracted by the lower costs of operating in Hungary. The Hungarian partner welcomed the opportunity to learn new technologies and the creation of more employment. The development of the new joint-venture culture was promoted by a number of HRM policies, summarized in the box display, which appeared to have achieved this aim. A survey of employees indicated that they generally perceived foreign and local managers to have the same goals, that cultural differences were respected, and that the joint venture had a good long-term future. There was less satisfaction with other matters, such as the persistence of a language barrier and the lack of a bonus system, but the efforts devoted to HRM had resulted in a high level of cultural compatibility.

HRM Policies Promoting the Development of a New Culture for a Swedish–Hungarian Joint Venture

1. A sharing of responsibility through the appointment of Hungarians to key positions within the joint venture, including general manager, financial controller, and HRM manager.
2. Promoting awareness of the other partner's culture, including the organization of visits by Hungarians to the Swedish company.
3. The use of various mechanisms for information exchange, including electronic mail (with linkages to all other companies in the Swedish group), a newsletter published in Hungarian and English, regular senior management meetings (usually weekly), departmental meetings, and occasional 'brainstorming' sessions for managers.
4. A high priority given to training. For example, US$1.36 million was spent on the training of Hungarian engineers in the first year of the joint venture. Some of the training content covered the behavioural norms of the Swedish partner company.
5. Payment levels which are somewhat higher than those for similar jobs in the area, with salary increases partly determined by performance appraisal.

Source: Cyr and Schneider (1994*a*).

CONTROL THROUGH HRM

Frayne and Geringer (1990) consider the role of HRM practices as control mechanisms. They refer particularly to IJVs in which the control exercised by partners may be an issue of acute concern because many such alliances are between competitors. We noted in Chapter 9 that control is a general requirement in alliances partly to ensure that the contributions made by partners are implemented satisfactorily. Controls to ensure the quality standards associated with respected brand names provide a familiar example of this need.

The recruitment and staffing of a joint venture, especially for its senior positions, can be a crucial control mechanism. It not only adds to the formal control rights provided by equity share; it may provide an important basis for the exercise of control even for a parent company which has a minority ownership (Schaan 1988). Even when the alliance does not involve the establishment of a new joint organization, the assignment of capable members of its staff to joint teams, meetings, and other activities is likely to be a necessary condition for a partner to exercise influence as well as to learn from the other partners. Research by Child and his colleagues in Sino-foreign joint ventures has also indicated that the holding of senior management positions, especially the posts of general manager and financial manager, is a basis for partner influence. The staffing of senior positions adds to the control leverage offered by equity share and the provision of key non-capital resources.

The staffing of an alliance is an issue which needs to be considered at a very early stage in its formation, for decisions taken then have major consequences. A key decision concerns who is to participate in the formation process. Selection of people who have the required technical competence, authority within their companies, and interpersonal skills can assist the successful formation and management of an alliance. They are likely to promote confidence and trust among the partner(s), and be able to champion the alliance within their own company. These qualities improve their chances of securing their company's negotiating priorities. If they retain a connection with alliances once they are formed—serving, for instance, as the first general manager—they should both be able to capitalize on the trust they have established for the benefit of the alliance and, at the same time, enjoy the authority to exercise considerable control over it. Future expansion of the cooperation will usually require both additional investment from the partners and support from authorities and influence groups in its particular location. Key appointees of the kind we have mentioned are in a good position to develop the necessary internal networks within their own parent company and the external ones to the partners and the local environment.

Frayne and Geringer argue that the training and development of alliance employees can also be a control mechanism. They see this aspect of HRM offering three specific control benefits (1990: 59–60):

1. By removing performance deficiencies, training and development can improve the employee's ability to perform better and so allow the organization to become more effective.
2. Training can be used to encourage people to think and behave in ways consistent with the parent companies' cultures, objectives, and interests.
3. Training can also be used as a mechanism to establish and maintain a unique culture for the alliance which is appropriate to its specific circumstances.

The Swedish–Hungarian joint venture previously mentioned, provides an example of how training was used in these ways.

Performance appraisals are a further HRM practice which partners can employ in their efforts to exercise control in their alliances. They help to identify training and development needs, provide a point of reference for the provision of incentives, and permit partner companies to monitor progress towards the attainment of critical objectives for their cooperation. It is also important that the performance evaluation criteria and methods used are suited to the specific circumstances of the alliance. Many alliances are formed in order to develop a field of technology, or a geographical market, which is novel to one or all the partners. Their established systems of performance evaluation may well not be entirely relevant to the new circumstances. There is evidence that, even when this point is appreciated, parent companies tend to employ the same performance evaluation methods for their alliances as they use for other of their operations which are located in more conventional, stable, and low-risk settings (Anderson 1990).

The need to pay attention to local circumstances also applies to the use of compensation and reward practices as a control mechanism. At the local level, compensation systems are intended to control the quality and contribution of employees by attracting good recruits, motivating them to perform, and retaining them within the alliance. The retention of good managers and employees within the alliance organization can be facilitated by tying bonuses and possibly career paths to the attainment of the alliance's long-term strategic objectives. However, this may encourage the staff in question to identify exclusively with the alliance rather than with the partner company. Problems may also arise if the compensation benefits a company offers diverge substantially across the various partnerships in which it is involved, and between such partnerships and its own core units. Multinational enterprises are for this reason now tending to reduce the additional payments and allowances they often used to offer to expatriate staff.

The use of HRM practices as control mechanisms within a cooperative strategy evokes the cooperation–competition dilemma identified by game theory (see Chapter 2). On the one hand, in order to promote effective collaboration, partners should seek agreement on the matter of how their alliance's human resources are to be managed. On the other hand, the strategic management of human resources can be a valuable mechanism for securing influence over an alliance to protect an organization's interests when these do not wholly coincide with those of its partner. If authority over human resources and HRM policy is shared with a partner in these circumstances, the abdication of control and of opportunities to make appointments which are critical for learning from other partners may place the organization at a severe disadvantage. This dilemma is examined further in the two following chapters.

HRM AND ORGANIZATIONAL LEARNING

Pucik (1988*a*, *b*) draws attention to the key role of HRM policies in the context of strategic alliances which involve competitive collaboration. Such alliances are between competitors, for whom 'the change from competitive to collaborative strategies is often merely a tactical adjustment aimed at specific market conditions. . . . The objective is similar: attaining the position of global market leadership through internalization of key value-added competencies' (1988*a*: 78). Unlike the physical resources which may be contributed to alliances, competencies are fundamentally information-based invisible assets, that cannot be purchased, whose market value cannot easily be established, and which are difficult to control. They include management and organizational skills, knowledge of the market, and technological know-how.

Invisible assets are embodied in the people within organizations. Pucik argues that, in situations of competitive collaboration, a company can preserve its competitive advantage only through being better at accumulating competencies than its partners. This means basically that it has to achieve a superior organizational learning capacity. Since the object of this learning is knowledge embodied in people, 'the object of . . . HRM activities is to complement line management in providing a supporting climate and appropriate systems to guide the process of learning' (1988*a*: 81).

The significance of this point has been illustrated by the experience of many Western joint ventures with Japanese partners (Pucik 1988*b*; Hamel 1991). Pucik studied twenty-three existing or dissolved joint ventures which US and European manufacturing firms had established in Japan. The results, for the Western partners, were mostly disappointing and to the advantage of the Japanese partners. He concluded that many of the reasons for this poor performance had to do with poorly designed and executed human-resource strategies (see Box).

Pucik (1988*a*) identifies failures to support competitive learning in five main areas of HRM. First, a partner company may lack adequate human-resource planning for its alliances, so that its strategic intention in the alliance is not communicated to its staff, learning is given a low priority, and there is a lack of involvement by the human-resources function in matters such as staffing the venture. Staffing is the second area that may be neglected. For instance, low-quality staff may be assigned to the venture, or staffing may be left to the other

Human resources practice and competitive learning: the case of Western joint ventures in Japan

Evidence collected by Vladimir Pucik from interviews with Western and Japanese managers of twenty-three US and European manufacturing firms having joint ventures in Japan showed clearly that the execution of a successful competitive strategy in the Japanese market was often severely handicapped by deficiencies in the human-resource system. So many times, the Western firms underestimated the critical role of human resource management strategies for the long-term viability of the cooperative venture. This was in contrast to the behaviour of the Japanese partner, where human-resource concerns were often close to the top of the managerial agenda.

The strategic intent of most Japanese partners in the joint ventures studied was often to learn as much as possible about technology contributed to the joint venture by the Western firms. A carefully implemented human resource strategy secured a rapid diffusion and assimilation of the newly available know-how to the Japanese parent, while, at the same time, very little of the local knowledge filtered back to the Western parent. Without such a reservoir of local knowledge, the Western firm's freedom of action in the Japanese market was greatly reduced.

From the typical Japanese perspective, control over human resource strategies should over time push the joint venture firmly into the orbit of the Japanese parent firm. This was happening irrespectively of the actual distribution of the equity in the joint venture or the initial input or know-how. As confided by the Japanese president of a fifteen-year-old joint venture where the Western partner was the majority owner: 'We have constant problems dealing with our guests from overseas. They believe that because they own 65 percent of us, they are entitled to exercise control. But obviously, that can't be the case.'

In this particular venture, the main office was in a building next to the headquarters of the Japanese partner. More than half the top managers were seconded from the Japanese parent; all others, except for a single expatriate without language skills, also came from the Japanese parent firm when the venture was originally formed. New employees were recruited through the personnel office of the parent. Recruiting materials did not even mention the fact that the majority owner of the company is a foreign firm. Training programs at all levels were contracted out to the Japanese partner. The level of bonuses paid to all employees paralleled closely bonuses paid at the parent firm. Under these conditions, the president's statement is rather natural.

Source: Pucik (1988*b*: quotation from 496).

partner. Thirdly, the training of both the partner's staff and that of the alliance may be neglected, particularly in matters such as language and cross-cultural competencies which can be vital in opening doors to the other partner's know-how. Fourthly, the company's performance appraisal and reward systems may not encourage learning and the transfer of know-how. Fifthly, the company's organizational design and control systems may not allocate clear responsibilities for learning, or provide the means for bringing together the people who have access to the other partner's know-how. Control over the HRM function within the alliance may also be given away.

In recognition of these problems, Pucik advocates the adoption of a ten-point plan for the HRM function in firms engaged in alliances (particularly international ones) which seek to incorporate a continuous organizational learning capacity into their strategy. The ten points are (1988a: 89–91):

1. get the human-resource function involved early, at the stage of forming an alliance;
2. build learning into the partnership agreement—for instance, by agreement on the exchange of personnel;
3. communicate the company's strategic intent *vis-à-vis* the cooperation;
4. maintain HRM input into the alliance;
5. staff up the alliance with the purpose of learning;
6. set up learning-driven career plans, including repeat assignments to the alliance;
7. use training to stimulate the learning process—for instance, in team-building and cross-cultural communication;
8. responsibility for learning should be specified; for instance, include learning objectives in the business plans for managers transferred to the alliance;
9. learning activities should be rewarded, so that, for instance, expatriate transfers into critical locations are made sufficiently attractive;
10. monitor the HRM practices of the other partner, and the pattern of staff assignments to and from the alliance made by the partner.

HRM AND ALLIANCE MANAGER QUALITIES

As Chapter 8 emphasized, cooperative strategies cannot be implemented without managers who have the appropriate competencies to make them work. This truism has two main implications for HRM practice. The first is to select people with the required abilities and then to develop these further. The second is to ensure that the corporate career system recognizes the importance and responsibility of roles which are directly concerned with making alliances work.

A symposium organized by the American Society for Training and Development listed the 'traits' of the future executive (Galagan 1990). Since the future for many corporations has already become one of operating in the global market, making increasing use of cooperative strategies, this list of traits provides quite a good basis for identifying the kind of skills required by alliance managers. The list, somewhat adapted, specifies that the future executive:

1. has a global vision and understanding;
2. facilitates the vision of others;
3. intuits the future rather than predicting it from the past;
4. recognizes need for continuous learning;
5. facilitates the initiative of others in addition to using authority;
6. specifies processes;
7. operates as part of an executive team;
8. accepts the paradox of order amid chaos;
9. is multicultural;
10. inspires the trust of a wide range of stakeholders, including alliance partners.

The personal characteristics from which these traits can most readily be developed are open-mindedness, flexibility, self-confidence, sensitivity to others, and a multicultural experience, together with the basic requirements of ability, drive to achieve, and necessary technical knowledge. In selecting managers and employees to work with alliance partners, HRM departments should assess the extent to which candidates possess these characteristics.

Lane and DiStefano (1994) identify seven abilities which constitute 'a profile of effective global executives'. These abilities are equally necessary for managers involved in purely domestic alliances, except that the first would require amendment to 'strategic skills in the domestic market':

1. ability to develop and use global strategic skills;
2. ability to manage change and transition;
3. ability to manage cultural diversity;
4. ability to design and function in flexible organization structures;
5. ability to work with others and in teams;
6. ability to communicate;
7. ability to learn and transfer knowledge in an organization.

This list provides a useful point of reference against which the adequacy of a company's HRM activities to develop alliance managerial skills can be assessed. It encompasses a wide range of abilities which, taken together, demand a great deal from any single manager. They certainly require time and experience to develop. Quite often a team of people from one partner share in the management of an alliance with staff from the other partner, and this should allow some spread of the necessary qualities between them. None the less, as is emphasized in other sections of this book, the abilities to communicate, work with others, and manage cultural diversity are particularly fundamental ones for managers to be effective in a cooperative context.

Several of the abilities in the list are considered in more detail in other chapters. Designing and functioning in the flexible organization structures of alliances were addressed in Chapters 8 and 9. Managing cultural diversity is discussed in Chapter 11. The ability to learn and transfer knowledge is central to Chapter 13. The management of change and transition runs through several chapters, particularly 12, 13, and 14. The question of strategic awareness also enters into policy on learning within alliances. The motives behind cooperative strategy were the subject of Chapter 4. The two remaining abilities are, however, absolutely central to the management of cooperative relationships themselves, and HRM can do a great deal to develop them. They are the ability to work in teams and the ability to communicate.

The ability to work in teams is becoming ever more essential along with the increasing number of specific competencies companies have to bring together, whether through alliances or on their own. The range of necessary competencies widens as product portfolios become more comprehensive, as more geographical markets are entered, and as a growing number of external groups become relevant, including governments, environmental, and community bodies. In some cases, alliance partners are expected to offer certain of these competencies; this in turn adds to the work that has to be accomplished jointly with partner staff in meetings and in teams. The competitive advantage that can result from working closely together with suppliers and customers also places a requirement on effective teamwork that crosses the boundaries of organizational, if not national, cultures.

The development of managers to work effectively in teams can build on both the task and maintenance functions which have been identified as necessary for successful group dynamics (Cartwright and Zander 1960). The task side requires an understanding of the necessity for objectives, targets, timetables, and procedures to be agreed by members of the team. The way this is accomplished may require some working through cultural differences about, for example, the value of explicit as opposed to implicit group norms. The maintenance side is concerned with sustaining the emotional tone of the team so that its members remain willing to work constructively with each other and committed to the achievement of the team's purpose. Recognition of the need for this function can be generated through reflection on the experience of group processes. Exposure to these processes can be provided through role-playing and incorporated into a training programme intended to enhance whatever learning has previously taken place through a person's team-working experience. Teams can generate a high level of internal emotion, particularly those bringing together diverse views while under pressure to achieve results. It is, therefore, particularly important to develop people's sensitivities to the interpersonal and group processes which are involved, so that they can better cope with them constructively.

The ability to communicate is an even more basic requirement. The particular communication abilities that alliances require, especially international ones, are multilingual skills and high levels of cross-cultural awareness and sensitivity. Sensitive communication is an aid to the building of trust and the promotion of an awareness of the common goals which an alliance has been established to pursue. The manner of communication must not be ethnocentric if it is to be acceptable to the recipients. The technologies for communication that are available today, such as e-mail and video-conferencing and shortly video-phoning, can do much to promote its reach within an alliance or even network of alliances. These technologies can also be adapted to the forms of presenting and disclosing information which are mutually acceptable to partner organizations.

As a company enters into cooperative alliances, especially those with partners in other countries, it needs to adjust its policies on career development in order to ensure that appropriate staff will be willing to take up positions of alliance management. The managers and other employees it appoints to, or hires for, its alliances should not suffer career disadvantages compared with those who advance through purely 'in-house' positions. Otherwise, it will be difficult to attract people with the required abilities to undertake roles in the alliance, and the significance of the company's cooperative arrangements will be devalued. This can be a particularly serious problem for a firm that has begun the process of internationalization through alliances, but has not reached the point where its global business is significant in relation to its domestic business. In these circumstances, managers who are assigned to overseas alliances tend to find re-entry into the company's mainstream activity and career lines very difficult. They may well have grown used to a level of decision-making autonomy and breadth of responsibilities which it is difficult to match within the domestic structure, even with promotion. Perhaps more significantly, they may well become marginalized in terms of the informal corporate power system. Such managers rarely make it to the top of the corporate hierarchy, and there is a danger of losing them to competitors (Adler and Ghadar 1990).

An increasing number of companies have, however, already developed global lines of business and are proceeding to build complex networks of joint ventures, subsidiaries, and project alliances which are intended to align the advantages of local responsiveness, global integration, and learning (Malnight 1996). This places a premium on those companies recognizing the importance of the managers who are implementing these networks of cooperative arrangements and adjusting their career opportunities and compensation packages accordingly. The development of corporate networks coordinated by regional units will eventually blur the distinction between 'in-house' and alliance management roles sufficiently for the problem to recede. The intensification of communication between all a company's units, using electronic media, should also promote the same effect. As these developments proceed, corporate cultures and career structures are likely to become increasingly transnational.

In many of the emerging markets, other HRM problems arise because of specific local conditions. These may, for example, be widely regarded as hardship posts, with many staff, and their families, reluctant to take up positions of alliance management there. Good experienced local managers may be in very short supply, with the result that market forces jeopardize orderly compensation policies. China, which is the most significant emerging market in the world, exemplifies many of these special HRM problems.

HRM ISSUES IN SINO-FOREIGN JOINT VENTURES

By the end of 1995, there were approximately 120,000 operational foreign affili-ates in China, mostly joint ventures. These organizations accounted for 13 per cent of China's industrial output. They employed around 16 million people. This is not a huge proportion of China's 625 million labour force, but enough to pre-sent its own significant challenge in each of the key areas of HRM—recruitment, training and development, performance assessment, and compensation.

HRM is considered to be one of the major problems facing companies with joint ventures in China. There are several aspects to the HRM problem. At the level of overall policy, Chinese and foreign conceptions of the human aspects of management differ so substantially that it is a major innovation to intro-duce Western or Japanese HRM procedures into alliances which are over-whelmingly Chinese in their staffing (Warner 1993; Easterby-Smith *et al.* 1995). In China, the linking of rewards to performance, the use of appraisal as a sup-port for personal development, and employer discretion in hiring and firing have not been part of normal practice (Von Glinow and Teagarden 1988). It may, therefore, be difficult to implement an HRM policy which is agreed between the Chinese and foreign partners not just because of incomplete con-gruence between their goals, which can arise in any alliance, but also because of the different cultural understandings which underlie approaches to person-nel management (Shore *et al.* 1993). This creates a dilemma over the most appropriate appointment to head the HRM area—should this be a nomination of the Chinese or the foreign partner? In the short run, a Chinese nominee will have the advantage of understanding local conditions and norms. In the longer term, however, a foreign nominee may be instrumental in introducing greater innovation based on a wider knowledge of good international practice. This issue is not unique to China. It will arise in any alliance between compa-nies from developed and developing countries, or between a partner with international experience and one with purely local background.

At an operational level, the most vexing problem is the recruitment and retention of good local Chinese managers. Björkman and Lu (1997) mention that as many as 59 per cent of the participants at a round-table discussion with the Chinese government concluded that recruiting and retaining man-agers was the number one problem facing firms with foreign investment. This was twice the percentage who considered the Chinese bureaucracy to be the major issue. There are particularly acute shortages of qualified and experi-enced Chinese people in the areas of financial management and HRM.

It is often not possible to find suitable recruits for joint-venture managerial positions from among the Chinese partner's staff. Applicants often lack the competencies expected by the foreign partner, and they may well have deeply embedded work practices of the kind that the foreign partner is seeking to avoid. Recourse, therefore, has to be made to the very tight managerial labour market. The activities of head-hunting companies reflect the keen competition between foreign-funded companies for the best managerial recruits, and encourage a high level of managerial mobility between firms. As a result, there has been a steady rise in the costs of compensating local managers. A senior Chinese executive working for a major joint venture could in early 1996 be earning up to US$3,600 per month, and a middle manager up to US$1,200 per month. Many foreign companies also provide their Chinese managers with expensive fringe benefits in order to retain them; benefits such as housing, pensions, insurance, company cars, and overseas training (including generous allowances while abroad).

The process of recruitment can also be problematic. The most common method is to use personal contacts to find new members of staff, in a society where this may engender an additional degree of loyalty to the organization among those selected. It is used much more often than newspaper advertisements. However, nepotism can be a serious problem and when a foreign manager takes formal responsibility for the selection process, this assists Chinese staff to resist external pressures to recruit non-optimum candidates. It has also in the past been difficult to get the agreement of the previous employer to release the personal file (*dang'an*) of the applicant (Tsang 1994). In some cases, companies are still obliged to pay a 'transfer fee' which is negotiable and which during the first half of 1996 varied between US$240 and US$2,400. However, it appears to be increasingly common nowadays for the applicant to arrange the release of his or her personal file rather than for the joint venture or foreign subsidiary to pay for this (Björkman and Lu 1997).

The obverse to employing local Chinese managers is to rely on the use of more expatriates. In fact, it appears that most international companies in China are increasing their numbers of expatriate managers. While, as Chapter 9 noted, this has certain advantages for maintaining control over joint ventures, it is extremely expensive, with overall annual costs of up to US$500,000 per expatriate and family. There is, then, a heavy economic incentive to replace expatriates with local managers, and one of the activities required to support this is management training.

Most of the sixty-seven joint ventures studied by Child and his colleagues have been increasing their expenditures on training over time, and this was also the case among the thirty foreign-invested enterprises surveyed by Björkman and Lu (1997). In the early period of joint-venture operation, the greater part of training efforts is concentrated on technical training, but there then tends to be a shift in emphasis towards the training of Chinese managers.

Many companies send their managers and staff with managerial potential to local universities and business schools on short courses, especially to develop functional specialists in areas such as finance and HRM where a knowledge of local conditions is essential. They may then use international management training companies to provide focused higher-level training subsequently. Key staff are often sent abroad for formal training. Although this is expensive, it offers several advantages. Training abroad can improve the quality of cooperation by demonstrating the effectiveness of the foreign partner's practices in other parts of the world, including other Asian countries which can provide role models for Chinese employees. It can reduce resistance to changes which the foreign partner seeks to introduce. It is also an important reward for such employees. There is a considerable risk of people who have undergone foreign training being poached, and one measure that can help to counteract this is to break up the training period into a number of shorter visits spread out over several years (Björkman and Lu 1997).

Foreign managers in China often complain that their Chinese colleagues are reluctant to accept responsibility (Child 1991; Lu *et al.* 1997). One antidote to this would be the introduction into joint ventures of assessment systems. These would also help to identify opportunities to develop local middle managers for promotion to senior positions in the future. Regular assessment and a systematic approach to promotion have not, however, always been installed or fully used. One of the reasons for this points up a dilemma in the partner relationship. The foreign partner can be reluctant to promote middle managers who have been recruited from the Chinese partner, because they have doubts about their attitude, competence, and loyalty. The Chinese partner can be unwilling to accept the promotion of externally recruited local people into senior positions and they may be in a position to deny approval for such promotions in the joint venture's board (Björkman 1995). The assessment and promotion process can therefore easily become transformed into a battle for loyalty between the partners and their respective criteria. In order to avoid problems of this kind, joint-venture contracts increasingly specify that the general manager has complete authority to make managerial appointments.

Other developments in China present new challenges for HRM policy and practice. With encouragement from the central authorities, trade-union organization is spreading within foreign firms there, so that it is estimated that about 45,000 such firms now have trade-union branches. Bargaining and contracts may become increasingly collective. As the larger multinational companies multiply their joint ventures within China, in some cases establishing holding companies for them, so it becomes necessary to have an integrated HRM policy and the appointment of an all-China HRM manager may be appropriate.

SUMMARY

This chapter has argued that a carefully considered set of HRM policies and practices can make a significant contribution to the success of alliances. They can assist the adjustment of corporate cultures and practices to the needs of the partnership, offer mechanisms of control, promote organizational learning, and foster the selection and development of staff who are capable of working effectively in a milieu of inter-organizational collaboration. In these and other ways, HRM can help to enhance the productivity of alliances, as well as the ability of partners to benefit from them.

HRM should have a central role in an organization's cooperative strategy. It needs to be brought into the planning and negotiation of alliances, when many of the relevant parameters, such as staffing and the allocation of managerial rights, are being decided. The quality of cooperation will be enhanced by selection, training, and staffing policies which focus on communication competencies (including relevant language skills) and which promote cultural understanding. Consideration also needs to be given to organizational procedures which facilitate adjustment and bonding between partners, such as the wide reporting of progress made through the cooperation.

Central HRM procedures for selection, training, appraisal, and compensation need to be aligned with a partner's policies on control and learning within his alliances. The chapter has identified how HRM procedures can contribute to the realization of these policies as they are applied to the particular circumstances of the partnership.

The potential benefits which can be realized from closely aligning HRM activities to a company's cooperative strategy point to the desirability of having this function represented at the highest level in the meetings and other discussions which formulate the strategy. If HRM is confined to the periphery of cooperative strategy formulation, as is quite often the case in practice, then its ability to facilitate the successful implementation of the strategy will be correspondingly limited.

REFERENCES

Adler, N. J., and Ghadar, F. (1990), 'International Strategy from the Perspective of People and Culture: The North American Context', *Research in Global Business Management*, 1 (Greenwich, Conn.: JAI Press), 179–205.

Anderson, E. (1990), 'Two Forms, One Frontier: On Assessing Joint Venture Performance', *Sloan Management Review*, 31: 19–30.

Björkman, I. (1995), 'The Board of Directors in Sino-Western Joint Ventures', *Corporate Governance*, 3: 156–66.

——and Lu, Y. (1997), 'Human Resource Management Practices in Foreign Investment Enterprises in China: What Has been Learnt?', *Advances in Chinese Industrial Studies*, 5: 155–72.

Cartwright, D., and Zander, A. (1960) (eds.), *Group Dynamics: Research and Theory* (2nd edn., New York: Harper & Row).

Child, J. (1991), 'A Foreign Perspective on the Management of People in China', *International Journal of Human Resource Management*, 2: 93–107.

——and Rodrigues, S. (1996), 'The Role of Social Identity in the International Transfer of Knowledge through Joint Ventures', in S. Clegg and G. Palmer (eds.), *Producing Management Knowledge* (London: Sage), 46–68.

Coopers & Lybrand/Yankelovich, Skelly & White (1986), *Collaborative Ventures: A Pragmatic Approach to Business Expansion in the Eighties* (New York: Coopers & Lybrand).

Cyr, D. J., and Schneider, S. C. (1994a), *Creating Cultural Change in a Swedish-Hungarian Joint Venture* (Case Study; Fontainebleau: INSEAD, ref. 01/95-4473).

—— —— (1994b), *Creating a Learning Organization through HRM: A German–Czech Joint Venture* (Case Study; Fontainebleau: INSEAD. ref. 01/95-4476).

—— —— (1996), 'Implications for Learning: Human Resource Management in East–West Joint Ventures', *Organization Studies*, 17: 207–26.

Drouin, N. (1996), 'Strategic Management of Human Resources in International Joint Ventures', unpublished first year report, doctoral programme (Judge Institute of Management Studies, University of Cambridge, June).

Easterby-Smith, M., Malina D., and Lu, Y. (1995), 'How Culture-Sensitive is HRM? A Comparative Analysis of Practice in Chinese and UK Companies', *International Journal of Human Resource Management*, 6: 31–59.

Frayne, C. A., and Geringer, J. M. (1990), 'The Strategic Use of Human Resource Management Practices as Control Mechanisms in International Joint Ventures', *Research in Personnel and Human Resources Management*, suppl. 2: 53–69.

Galagan, P. A. (1990), 'Executive Development in a Changing World', *Training and Development Journal*, June: 23–41.

Hamel, G. (1991), 'Competition for Competence and Inter-Partner Learning within International Strategic Alliances', *Strategic Management Journal*, 12: 83–103.

Lane, H. W., and DiStephano, J. J. (1994), 'The Global Manager', in P. W. Beamish, J. P. Killing, D. J. LeCraw, and A. J. Morrison (eds.), *International Management: Text and Cases* (Burr Ridge, Ill.: Irwin), 165–82.

Lu, Y., Child, J., and Yan, Y. (1997), 'Adventuring in New Terrain: Managing International Joint Ventures in China', *Advances in Chinese Industrial Studies*, 5: 103–23.

Malnight, T. W. (1996), 'The Transition from Decentralized to Networked-Based MNC Structures: An Evolutionary Perspective', *Journal of International Business Studies*, 27: 43–65.

Pucik, V. (1988a), 'Strategic Alliances, Organizational Learning, and Competitive Advantage: The HRM Agenda', *Human Resource Management*, 27: 77–93.

—— (1988b), 'Strategic Alliances with the Japanese: Implications for Human Resource Management', in F. J. Contractor and P. Lorange (eds.), *Cooperative Strategies in International Business* (New York: Lexington Books), 487–98.

Schaan, J.-L. (1988), 'How to Control a Joint Venture even as a Minority Shareholder', *Journal of General Management*, 14: 4–16.

Shenkar, O., and Zeira, Y. (1987), 'Human Resources Management in International Joint Ventures: Directions for Research', *Academy of Management Review*, 12: 546–57.

Shore, L. M., Eagle, B. W., and Jedel, M. J. (1993), 'China–United States Joint Ventures: A Typological Model of Goal Congruence and Cultural Understanding and their Importance for Effective Human Resource Management', *International Journal of Human Resource Management*, 4: 67–83.

Tsang, E. W. K. (1994), 'Human Resource Management Problems in Sino-Foreign Joint Ventures', *International Journal of Manpower*, 15: 4–21.

Villinger, R. (1996), 'Post-Acquisition Managerial Learning in Central East Europe', *Organization Studies*, 17: 181–206.

Von Glinow, M. A., and Teagarden, M. B. (1988), 'The Transfer of Human Resource Management Technology in Sino-US Cooperative Ventures: Problems and Solutions', *Human Resource Management*, 27: 201–29.

Warner, M. (1993), 'Human Resource Management "with Chinese characteristics"', *International Journal of Human Resource Management*, 4: 45–65.

11

Culture

This chapter examines the ways in which culture can impact upon the implementation of cooperative strategies. It shows how culture can create barriers to collaboration between organizations, and yet how, at the same time, the knowledge embodied in cultures can provide a valuable resource for an alliance. We ask what culture is, why it is relevant for cooperative strategy, what specific consequences culture can have, what policy options there are for managing cultural diversity within alliances, and how cultural fit can be achieved.

THE NATURE OF CULTURE

Culture is a heavily used but elusive concept. Although it refers to a supposedly universal phenomenon, political and social scientists continue to debate how much culture really matters in the broad sweep of history (cf. *The Economist* 1996). The problem is that, while culture may be pervasive and widely manifest in social behaviour, artefacts, and the humanly created environment, it is in itself intangible and elusive. Indeed, some writers regard culture more as a metaphor than as a 'real' phenomenon.

This elusiveness has encouraged a great deal of 'conceptual chaos' so far as the definition of culture is concerned (Martin 1992: p. iii). Kroeber and Kluckhohn back in 1952 isolated no less than 164 different definitions of culture, drawn primarily from the study of anthropology. Taken together, these definitions identify the features which express a culture: knowledge, values, preferences, habits and customs, established practices and behaviour, and artefacts. They range between an emphasis on culture as a set of ideas and culture as a series of tangible expressions in art, architecture, and even technology (Keesing 1974).

Nevertheless, the past two decades have witnessed a growing interest by practising managers, consultants, and management researchers in the implications of culture. Hofstede's work (1980, 1991; Hofstede and Bond 1988), originating with a large-scale investigation across different national branches of IBM, has been one of the most influential contributions. Hofstede defines culture as 'the collective programming of the mind which distinguishes the members of one group or category of people from another' (1991: 5). He therefore focuses on the aspect of culture that is in the mind rather than its physical manifestations, and stresses that culture is learned and shared within social collectivities. The two collectivities of present interest as the sources of mental programming are the organizations in which people work and the societies in which they live. These have given rise to the concepts of 'organizational culture' and 'national culture'.

Brown (1995: 6–7) cites fifteen different definitions of *organizational* culture. Those writers who treat culture not as a metaphor but as an actual phenomenon generally agree that culture comprises shared values, beliefs, and ways of behaving and thinking that are unique to a particular organization. From his review of research and case studies, Brown concludes that 'an organisation's culture has a direct and significant impact on performance. . . . Organisational strategies and structures and their implementation are shaped by the assumptions, beliefs and values which we have defined as a culture' (1995: 198).

One of the more influential theories of organizational culture is that developed by Edgar Schein (1985). He distinguishes between assumptions, values, and artefacts. Assumptions lie at the core of an organization's culture. They are what the members of an organization take for granted and what they believe to be reality. They therefore influence what they think and how they behave. At a somewhat more conscious level, organization members hold values, which are the standards and goals to which they attribute intrinsic worth. Artefacts are the tangible and surface manifestations of a culture, such as an organization's physical decor and dress code, its ceremonies, its stories and myths, its traditions, rewards, and punishments.

Martin identifies and illustrates three main perspectives on organizational culture. These respectively draw attention to (i) the culture which may be shared by all the members of an organization and which therefore acts as a unifying force; (ii) the subcultures of different groups within an organization—such as specialist groups or managers compared with workers, or the staff drawn from different strategic alliance partners—which tend to act as a differentiating and divisive force; and (iii) cultures as a fragmented mix of cross-cutting personal identities, full of paradoxes and ambiguities which are promoted, *inter alia*, by the constant flux of change in modern organizations and societies. In the light of these possibilities, culture may respectively be (i) a means to integrate people around a common task or operation, like a strategic alliance; (ii) a divisive factor which threatens to fragment the alliance; or (iii) a source of confusion for employees which may be alienating and distressing for some of them.

Organizational cultures are associated with places of work which may be relatively short-term employment locations for many people. Also such cultures may change substantially and suddenly with circumstances—the experience of downsizing has been a case in point. The economic threat and psychological shock accompanying compulsory redundancy can rapidly destroy any sense of sharing a common culture with management. The practices which people have learned within the framework of a particular organizational culture may be more deeply embedded and therefore persist beyond a cultural change.

National cultures, by contrast, are acquired with upbringing and are deeply embedded as a result. The mental programming which takes place during childhood, and is reinforced during a lifetime of living in a particular society, is therefore likely to be resistant to change. For this reason, culture becomes a particularly significant phenomenon in alliances which are international rather than purely domestic. As well as having their roots in the traditions of a country, national cultures are also tied up with the specific institutions of that country and its prevailing political ideologies. These institutions and ideologies can within a generation or two have a significant impact upon national cultures, as comparisons between the PRC and Taiwan or Hong Kong, or between the East and West Germanies, have made abundantly clear.

The fact that national economic and political ideologies can generate their own mental programming serves to remind us that national culture, though historically embedded, does not necessarily rule out the capacity for some mental adaptation on the part of the individual. As Ralston and his colleagues (1995) have found in the case of China, the younger generation which has grown up and entered employment during the age of reform displays more individualistic and materialistic (and therefore in some respects more Western) attitudes than does the older generation. Earlier research by industrial sociologists into 'central life interests' suggests that people can draw a distinction between work-related values and behaviour and those they adopt within their families and communities (Dubin 1956; Dubin *et al.* 1975). In other words, under conditions which motivate them to do so, many people may be able and willing to adapt their national cultural dispositions in clearly delineated situations such as working in an international cooperative venture.

Another complication is that there is only partial agreement over which are the key dimensions of national culture for people's behaviour in organizations. Trompenaars (1993) proposes a model of seven fundamental dimensions of national culture relevant, he claims, to understanding diversity in business (see also Hampden-Turner and Trompenaars 1993). These are summarized in the Box.

It is evident that there is a substantial overlap between these dimensions, especially in regard to individualism (dimensions 2, 5, 6, and 7), relationships (dimensions 4, 5, and 7), and universalism (dimensions 1, 3, and 4). Hofstede, the source of the other widely applied approach to measuring national cultural differences, criticizes Trompenaars on this score. He concludes from a reanalysis of Trompenaars's data that only two dimensions can be confirmed statistically—individualism/achievement and universalism/diffuse—and that both are correlated with Hofstede's individualism dimension (Hofstede 1996).

Trompenaars's Seven Dimensions of National Culture

1. *Universalism versus particularism*—always applying the best way or a standard rule vs. deciding on the basis of the specific case, especially when friendship is involved;
2. *Individualism versus collectivism*—people regarding themselves primarily as individuals vs. as part of a group or community;
3. *Neutral versus emotional*—attaching importance to being objective and detached as opposed to permitting emotions to become involved;
4. *Specific versus diffuse*—confining business to the contractual versus involving personal contacts as well;
5. *Achievement versus ascription*—evaluating people on achievement versus evaluating them according to background and connections;
6. *Attitudes towards time*—future versus past orientation and how past, present, and future are seen to be related;
7. *Attitudes towards the environment*—the view that individuals can shape the environment and other people ('inner-direction') versus one that we have to live in harmony with the environment and with other people and hence take our cues from them ('outer-direction').

Hofstede's own dimensions of national culture relevant to organizational behaviour are fivefold, as shown in the Box.

CULTURE'S RELEVANCE TO COOPERATION

Cooperative strategies bring together people from different organizations into a working relationship. The organizations from which they come will each have developed their own distinctive 'cultures'. These cultures embody shared attitudes and norms of behaviour. They encourage people to regard their organization as different from, and often as superior to, other organizations, and therefore to hold onto their ways of doing things, particularly when confronted with those of a new and unfamiliar partner. If the collaborating organizations originate from different countries, their members will have a sense of belonging to distinct 'national' cultures as well, and the sense of difference between partners' managers and staff will be exaggerated as a result. When different cultures are brought together through a strategic alliance, they can generate barriers to cooperation while at the same time offering the potential for each partner to learn from the positive aspects of the other's ways of thinking and acting. However, the mutual learning cannot take place until the barriers are removed.

Hofstede's Five Dimensions of National Culture

1. *Individualism versus collectivism*—the extent to which the ties between individuals are loose, with everyone expected to look after himself or herself and his or her immediate family rather than belonging to strong, cohesive wider ingroups.

2. *Power distance*—the extent to which the less powerful members of institutions and organizations within a country expect and accept that power is distributed unequally.

3. *Uncertainty avoidance*—the extent to which the members of a culture feel threatened by uncertain or unknown situations.

4. *Masculinity versus femininity*—the distinction between a set of values and attitudes usually associated with men (e.g., assertiveness, competitiveness) in contrast to those usually associated with women (e.g., concern for people, attaching value to cooperative relationships).

5. *Time-orientation*—long-term versus short-term gratification of needs, where the former is more oriented towards the future emphasizing the value of perseverance and thrift, combined with valuing ordered relationships and having a sense of shame or honour. [This fifth dimension emerged from research among Chinese populations and has sometimes been called 'Confucian Dynamism'.]

Source: Hofstede (1980, 1991); Hofstede and Bond (1988).

Culture as a barrier

One barrier to effective cooperation can arise when culture becomes an expression of social identity (Tajfel 1982), symbolizing the group with which people identify and which distances itself from other groups. If the bringing-together of two or more groups through a cooperative strategy is interpreted as threatening the interests of any one of them, this sense of distance between them will be heightened. People in groups and organizations often resist changes to structures and practices of the kind which can result from an alliance because they regard the changes as threatening their real interests. The culture they share will serve to express and also rationalize their concerns (Sathe 1985). Finding ways of bridging and reconciling the strong and distinctive organizational and national cultures which partners may bring to an alliance is, therefore, a major challenge which they cannot avoid if their cooperation is to succeed.

National cultural differences can present barriers to cooperation both at the level of simple misunderstanding and at the more fundamental level of conflicts in values. Misunderstanding can arise from culturally associated differences in language and the interpretation of behaviour. For example, the same words or phrases can convey inconsistent meanings to people from different cultures. The brand name 'Nova' denotes a star in English, but is likely to be understood as 'No va' (i.e. doesn't work, doesn't go) in Spanish. The English idiom 'out of sight, out of mind' will be understood as referring to someone who is blind and incompetent when translated into Arabic. What is understood as humorous or ironic in one language may well be taken literally in another. There are also cultural differences in the approved mode of discourse between people which, if not appreciated, can readily lead to misunderstanding and antagonism. In Anglo-Saxon culture it is polite to wait until another person has finished speaking before speaking oneself. In East Asian societies, it is a mark of respect to pause before replying, thus indicating that what the other person has said is deserving of careful thought. In Latin cultures, by contrast, to interrupt another before he or she has finished speaking is to show acceptable enthusiasm for what they are saying. The same interpersonal behaviour is likely to be interpreted in quite contrasting ways by people from different national cultures. Shouting can convey importance or a lack of credibility. Eye contact can signify respect in one culture but a lack of it in another. Touching may denote warmth or an invasion of personal privacy.

These types of linguistic and behavioural cultural differences can have serious consequences for cooperation if they are not addressed with sensitivity. They are, however, relatively superficial and it should not be too difficult for the members of cooperating organizations to cope with them so long as they are well briefed and willing to accept the differences in others' behaviour with humour and respect. It is the deeper level of culture, where the socially embedded values held by partners and their employees may clash, that more serious problems concerning the priorities for the alliance and how it is to be run have to be resolved. The impact of deeper cultural values can be illustrated with reference to the two dimensions of universalism versus particularism and individualism versus collectivism.

In a country where universalistic values predominate, what is good and right can be defined and always applies. In a country where particularistic values predominate it is valid to take specific circumstances into account and to make exceptions, particularly if personal relationships and obligations come into play. To point up this difference Trompenaars (1993: 34) cites a story created by two American social scientists Stouffer and Toby (1951):

You are riding in a car driven by a close friend. He hits a pedestrian. You know that he was going at least 35 miles per hour in an area of the city where the maximum allowed speed is 20 miles per hour. There are no witnesses. His lawyer says that if you testify under oath that he was only driving at 20 miles an hour, it may save him from serious consequences. What right has your friend to expect you to protect him?

In a universalistic culture, people will tend to adopt the view that the friend has no right to expect protection because he broke the law and because further disregard for the law through false testimony would only compound the harm. The more serious the offence against the law, the less right the friend has to expect protection. In a particularistic culture, people will tend to adopt the view that the friend deserves support, the more so when he is in serious trouble. Trompenaars has applied this question, and others bearing on the same cultural dimension, to around 15,000 employees in many different countries, 75 per cent of whom are managers, the rest working in administration. His results suggest the 'Anglo-Saxon' and 'northern' countries to be high on universalism: Australia, Canada, Denmark, Finland, West Germany, Ireland, Japan, Norway, Sweden, Switzerland, the UK, the USA. At the other end of the scale, the most particularistic countries tend to be China, South Korea, Indonesia, Russia, Venezuela, and the former Yugoslavia.

The implication of this analysis is that where there is a partnership between organizations from countries that contrast greatly along the universalism/particularism dimension, it will be more difficult to establish the mutual trust on which a good relationship has to be based. The two parties are likely to be suspicious of each other, with the universalists thinking of their partners that 'they cannot be trusted because they will always help their friends' and the particularists thinking of the other group that 'you cannot trust them; they would not even help a friend'.

The differences in selection criteria applied by Chinese and foreign joint-venture partners, noted in Chapter 10, reflect a clash between universalistic and particularistic norms. Most foreign companies adhere to the principle of selecting the best available recruits according to the requirements of the job, regardless of any personal connections they may have with existing managers or staff. Indeed, personal connections may be frowned upon as opening the door to subsequent favouritism which would distort the procedures for assessment and advancement, and in so doing probably demoralize other employees. By contrast, Chinese companies tend to favour the recruitment of family members. It is a Chinese social norm that members of an extended family should help each other, and managers also believe that recruitment on the basis of personal connections will encourage the employees concerned to be loyal members of the organization. The clash here between two cultural norms poses a problem the resolution of which demands special care and attention on the part of joint-venture management.

In a country where individualistic values predominate, people tend to have a prime orientation towards the self rather than towards common goals and objectives. Judging by the Hofstede and Trompenaars research, countries in which individualism is relatively pronounced include most highly industrial ones, including the Anglo-Saxon nations, the Netherlands, and some East European countries. Austria and Germany are an exception, with less individualistic attitudes than most other West European countries. Countries in which collectivism is relatively pronounced include most of the poorer nations and those sharing a Chinese cultural heritage. Japan emerges somewhat in the middle overall, but is the most collectivist, or communitarian, among the highly industrialized countries (Hampden-Turner and Trompenaars 1993).

Considerable difficulties can arise in cooperation between companies which manage and organize according to individualistic and collectivistic principles. In the former, for example, high value will tend to be placed in quick decisions, individual responsibility, expression of individual views and goals, competition between people for recognition and advancement, and individual incentives. In the latter, high value will tend to be placed on taking time to consult and secure consent before decisions are made, group or team responsibility, sharing common superordinate goals, a high level of interpersonal and interdepartmental cooperation, and systems of rewards that do not single out individuals. It is far from easy to reconcile these contrasting principles when managing a strategic alliance, though the attempt could pay off handsomely through realizing the benefits of their complementary strengths.

The countries in which individualism prevails tend to be creative but rather poor at managing the collective effort required to convert invention into products which can be produced efficiently through organized effort and so made attractive to the market. By contrast, the countries in which a collectivist culture prevails tend to be less a source of invention but extremely good at developing ideas and putting them into practice. A revealing example is the way that Japan took up and developed management techniques such as total quality management (TQM), originally invented in the USA, so effectively that they became part of what we now call the 'Japanese system of management'. There is an evident potential synergy between partners bearing these respective strengths of individualistic and collectivistic cultures, if only ways can be found for them to cooperate together to draw out and meld the complementary strengths of their two approaches. It was, indeed, the expectation of many US–Japanese joint ventures that they would achieve synergy between the technical inventiveness which is fostered by American individualism and the ability to carry this through to efficient production which is fostered by Japanese collectivism in the form of good teamwork. In the event, as we shall see in Chapter 13, some of these joint ventures came under strain because the Japanese learnt more from them than did their American partners. Although some commentators are inclined to the view that, in being smarter joint-venture partners, the Japanese are also rather underhand, Casson (1995) offers a rather different interpretation. He argues that the disparity in benefit from these joint ventures is due, at least in part, to cultural differences. The Americans' individualism and competitiveness breed a sense of mistrust which prevents them from learning from the cooperation, while the high-trust Japanese are more open and engage with their alliance partners to learn as much as possible.

National differences in management

Contrasts in the value priorities which the members of different societies tend to hold are expected to give rise to consistent differences in their behaviour, as the previous section has illustrated. This has led writers on management to explore whether certain management practices have become characteristic of different countries as a result of their cultural differences and, in addition, of their particular political and economic systems. From what has been said already in this chapter, one might expect there to be a large difference in the management practices adopted by American and Japanese companies. If there is a gap of this kind, it may well present difficulties for cooperation if and when companies from those two countries form an alliance. This is an important aspect of the 'cultural fit' between partners which was discussed in Chapter 5.

The authors have highlighted the management practices which previous research suggests is characteristic of the main industrialized nations (Child *et al.* 1997). These are listed below and the contrasts between them are evident. Their research into the impact of foreign companies on management practice in recently acquired UK subsidiaries largely bears out the characterizations which have been made of US and Japanese practice. By contrast, there is not much support for the characterizations of French and German management practice which are, in any case, based on relatively sparse evidence. The East–West contrast between Japanese and US practice, which has caused problems for some alliances between firms from those countries, is today being extended (though not in exactly the same form) as firms from other East Asian companies enter into alliances with partners from the USA (Whitley 1992*a*, 1992*b*).

1. *Japanese management practice*

   The policies and practices particularly associated with Japanese companies are:

   - Long-term orientation:
     - strategic rather than financial,
     - emphasis on growth,
     - long-term employment commitment;
   - Rewards based primarily on seniority and superior's evaluation;
   - Internal training and seniority system; heavy investment in training;
   - Collective orientation
     - decision-making and knowledge creation via collective participation and responsibility
   - flexible tasks:
     - low specialization,
     - synthetical orientation;
   - emphasis on lean production and continuous improvement.

2. *Management practice in the USA*

   The management policies and practices particularly associated with US companies are:

   - short-term financial orientation;
   - rewards related to specific performance indicators;
   - high rate of job change and inter-company mobility;

- rationalistic approach: emphasis on analysis and planning;
- reliance on formalization and systems;
- delegation down extended hierarchies.

3. *German management practice*

There is some disagreement between investigators over the key charac-teristics of (West) German management—these may reflect differences in sampling (for example, large versus *Mittelstand* firms) and methodology (Ebster-Grosz and Pugh 1996). However, while the picture which emerges of German management policies and practices is not so clear cut as that portrayed for US and Japanese management, its main contours are the following:

- long-term business orientation:
  - towards production improvement rather than short-term profit distribution,
  - but orientation towards employment is not necessarily long term;
- strong technical and production emphasis, including a substantial investment in training;
- managers and staff tend to remain within one functional area during their career;
- emphasis on planning, procedures, and rules;
- preference for participation and collective action.

4. *French management practice*

France is also a particularly difficult country to categorize, and the same applies to its management practice. Hampden-Turner and Trompenaars (1993: 333) comment that 'France defies easy categorization. It requires a sense of irony, for which the French are famous, to make sense of seem-ingly contradictory results.' Bearing this caution in mind, the manage-ment policies and practices which have been described of French companies are:

- strategic rather than financial orientation;
- tall organizational hierarchies, with a large proportion of managerial personnel;
- high degree of specialization;
- widespread use of written media;
- individual rather than collective working and decision-making, though the latter tends to be centralized.

5. *British management practice*

The management policies and practices particularly associated with British companies have some similarity with those associated with US companies, but with considerably less emphasis on formal systems and records:

- short-term financial orientation;
- large general management superstructures;

- low level of functional specialization;
- high mobility of managers between functions;
- use of formal meetings, especially committees;
- interactive informality—limited formal and paper-based reporting;
- limited importance attached to systems and standard operating procedures.

The previous section has already indicated that culture is important for cooperative strategy. There are, however, a number of more specific ways in which organizational and national cultures can be consequential for the formation and operation of an alliance. These illustrate the two faces of culture for cooperative strategy: as a challenge and as a resource.

Culture as a challenge

First, the degree of distance between the cultures of prospective partner organizations may have an effect on the type of cooperation they are willing to form. Shane (1994) presents evidence that when US-based manufacturing multinational corporations entered low-trust countries, direct foreign investment rather than licensing was the preferred mode for reasons both of cultural distance (these were low-trust countries relative to the USA) and the low trust levels of local entrepreneurs. He interprets his findings as showing that cultural distance is associated with a preference for modes of market entry offering higher control. These results suggest, through extrapolation, that the presence of greater cultural distance between prospective alliance partners will encourage them to seek managerial as well as legal safeguards for their crucial interests. The main investor, and/or provider of key resources such as advanced technology, is in cases of high cultural distance likely to seek to form an equity joint venture in which it has the majority equity share rather than an alternative form which does not offer the right to managerial control.

Secondly, a large cultural distance between prospective partners is likely to protract the process of forming an agreement to cooperate. While it can be assumed that each partner recognizes that there is an advantage to be gained from cooperation with the other, cultural distance between them will add to the difficulties of finding a mutually acceptable basis for that cooperation. Because cultural differences increase the chances of mutual misunderstanding and even personal offence, they have to be transcended before a basis for trust can be established. And without mutual acceptance and trust, the risk of cheating and non-compliance with contacts is greater (Williamson 1979). Particularly if the representatives and negotiators on behalf of the prospective partners are not familiar with each other's organizational and national cultures, the transcending of their cultural differences can come about only through a time-consuming process of recognizing the other cultures, demonstrating mutual tolerance, and then finding ways of reconciling the differences as they impinge upon practical aspects of the proposed cooperation. Additionally, the partner who is not familiar with the country context in which the alliance is to operate has to invest further time and effort in finding out how the cultural norms and institutional practices of the host country are likely to effect its calculations and plans for making the alliance into a profitable operation. Can it, for example, market and promote its products through the alliance in its normal tried-and-tested ways?

Thirdly, cultural differences can lead to a good many operational problems. At worst, they can lead to a breakdown in the working relations between partners' managers and staff. If the partner's cultures convey conflicting priorities and norms of behaviour, they will heighten the sense of separateness between staff seconded or recruited by the partners to work together. This sense of being different is bound to be present anyway in the early stages of cooperation. Sharp cultural differences will reinforce and perpetuate this unless considerable effort is made to overcome them. This is illustrated by one such case where cultural insensitivity and inflexibility almost led to the breakdown of a

---

The Need for Cultural Sensitivity and Flexibility

A joint venture between a European and a Chinese partner almost collapsed because its first general manager, a European with only limited international business experience, insisted on the introduction of practices and procedures from his parent company in an aggressive and culturally insensitive manner. Not only did he fail to consult his Chinese colleagues, but he engaged in brow-beating and shaming behaviour in meetings with them, conduct that is particularly offensive to Chinese cultural norms. In this case, the Chinese partners held 60 per cent of the joint-venture equity and were, through their majority on the board, able to insist that a replacement be made before relations broke down completely. The replacement, a Canadian with wide international business experience, was able to mend the relationship through adopting a much softer style more acceptable culturally to the Chinese. Important aspects of this softer style were regular consultation with the Chinese deputy general manager, especially before all senior management meetings, care not to cause public loss of face in those meetings, and a greater involvement of Chinese managers in the downward communication of information.

Source: John Child, personal research.

---

joint venture (see Box).

Alliances are communication intensive and relationship dependent, and they therefore cannot function well if they are internally divided by substantial cultural barriers. If cultural distance is not reduced, or at least channelled into a form that avoids conflict, it is likely to give rise to serious breakdowns in communication of information and integration within the alliance. Chapter 13 will indicate, for example, how such breakdown would seriously inhibit the learning capability of the alliance. The achievement of accommodation between partner cultures is also a condition for a strategic alliance or other form of cooperation to develop its own culture.

Cultural accommodation in alliances may also require the acceptance of what appear to be some inefficiencies according to the norms of one partner. Take the case of a Western company in partnership with one from East Asia—say China or Japan. The Western company probably operates according to rather individualistic, universalistic, specific, and short-term performance norms. The East Asian company probably operates according to relatively collectivistic, particularistic, diffuse, and longer-term performance norms. From the Western perspective, the other partner's decision-making processes will appear to be protracted because of the time taken to achieve prior consensus according to collective norms. The way of organizing work preferred by that partner will seem to submerge individual accountability within the group or department as a whole. The Western company will probably regard its partner's approach to personal-performance assessment as insufficiently focused on achievement in the job as measured by standard criteria, and unduly particularistic. This is because the East Asian partner is likely to take into account considerations such as the employee's commitment and loyalty to the company, as evaluated by the person's supervisor or manager, rather than apparently more objective information. East Asian partners will probably pay considerable attention to particular personal circumstances which have affected performance, as well. The Western preference would be to evaluate at regular intervals in terms of task-specific criteria, and to link reward directly to such evaluation.

In this reasonably representative example, the Western approach emphasizes criteria which relate to a limited, defined set of responsibilities over an equally limited time period, whereas the East Asian approach emphasizes criteria which are more holistic and more relevant to the longer-term contribution of people to the whole organization. Managerial effort clearly has to be devoted within the alliance to reconciling, or building upon, these different approaches which for the other partner will be seen to suffer from significant limitations.

Differences over operational issues can arise even within the ambit of so-called Western culture. Trompenaars (1993: 32–3) provides an example of this from the experience of an American computer manufacturer with operations in various European countries. Differences arose between a strong Anglo-Saxon belief, held by managers from the USA and UK that a substantial part of remuneration should depend on an individual's achieved performance and the greater allowance that managers from Mediterranean countries wished to make for personal circumstances which affected people's levels of performance in a particular year.

Culture as a resource

The marked differences between, say, US and Japanese management practice can, from one perspective, create difficulties for mutual understanding and cooperation. From another perspective, they denote potential complementarities between US and Japanese cultural strengths. Each partner has something distinctive and valuable to offer. In other words, under the right conditions, a mix of cultures does not just create problems; it can also bring positive benefits to cooperating organizations. Cultural diversity creates an opportunity to use the competences and knowledge contained in each partner's culture for the benefit of the alliance.

Take the example of a Western company which forms a joint venture to enter an emerging economy market. Its culture will probably emphasize universalism, specificity, achievement, future time orientation, and inner-directedness, all values which help to create a well-organized yet dynamic approach to organizational management. At the strategic level, this culture will encourage a focus on key objectives, long-term planning, and a determination to succeed. In operational terms, it should provide a good basis for efficient production, high-quality standards, and attractive products. In many emerging economies, however, the local partner's culture is likely to attach relatively greater value to particularism, collectivism, and diffuseness. These values can contribute to the alliance's success in a number of ways. Particularism can inform the alliance management's ways of relating to significant government authorities and members of key business networks, some of which may open up significant market opportunities. Recognition of the value attached to collectivism in the host society can contribute to a modification of HRM policies in ways that encourage the commitment and loyalty of local employees, such as orienting assessment to group rather than individual performance. An appreciation of how the norm of diffuseness applies to business relations can improve the chances of achieving useful transactions in the host society. For example, in a cultural milieu such as China's, it is of great value for the executives of international companies to recognize that the way into local business and governmental networks lies in understanding and respecting the highly diffuse mode of transacting that prevails in that country (Boisot and Child 1996).

At the same time, the alliance should benefit if it develops its own corporate culture. So long as it is not undermined by unfulfilled expectations or internal conflict, which in an alliance would most obviously concern the relation between the partners, a corporate culture can be an important resource available to the leaders of organizations (cf. Deal and Kennedy 1982; Hampden-Turner 1990; Brown 1995). It can promote social cohesion and act as a 'cement' that bonds an organization together. Because a shared culture encourages people to accept a common goal and to identify with each other, it can also facilitate the processes of coordination and control within an organization. By giving the members of an organization common reference points and ways of interpreting reality, a shared culture can reduce uncertainty and promote consistency of effort. In providing meaning to their work and to their membership of an organization, an appropriate and cohesive culture can also be an important source of motivation for employees. For these reasons, an alliance between partner companies should benefit if they permit, and indeed encourage, it to develop its own culture.

In seeking to develop a common culture for their alliance, the partners should attempt to analyse the relative strengths of their own organizational and national cultures, and build these into the norms and behaviours adopted by their cooperative venture. Two considerations inform this recommendation: first, the opportunity for the alliance to benefit from its parents' accumulated cultural capitals, and, secondly, the need for the partners to retain sufficient control over their alliance and to maintain an identity by alliance managers with their goals. Unless a partner is content to regard the alliance as merely an investment opportunity and to adopt the role of a sleeping partner, it needs to maintain an active link with the venture, which the maintenance of a shared identity, as well as regular reporting procedures, can both symbolize and underwrite. These links are a necessary complement to the development of the alliance's own culture. They enable the strengths of partner cultures to feed into the alliance culture while, at the same time, reducing the risk of the alliance forming an identity and pursuing objectives which become at odds with those of its parents. The collaboration between the Royal Bank of Scotland in Britain and the Banco Santander in Spain illustrates how two partners came to realize the cultural strengths and limitation of the other, and learned from the comparison (see Box).

The ideal for cultural management in alliances, then, is to harvest from the diversity of partners' cultures while at the same time building effective bridges between them. It is beneficial to have a diversity of cultures among organizational members because this offers a stimulus to learning, and sensitivity to local environments, but at the same time there is a need to manage the cultures so that they become forces for integration rather than division. There is a parallel here with the path to effective organizational learning within alliances, to be discussed in Chapter 13. The parallel lies in the necessity of combining a variety of contrasting and even conflicting perspectives (differentiation) with ways of drawing together the advocates of these perspectives into a shared commitment to implementation (integration). The management of culture and of learning within alliances each requires a reconciliation of the paradox of organizational differentiation and integration. The two are, of course, closely related because cultures embody knowledge which may be highly relevant to the success of the alliance in its specific context.

The Alliance between the Royal Bank of Scotland and the Banco Santander of Spain

In 1988 the Royal Bank of Scotland and the Banco Santander, two banks small in European terms but large in Scotland and Spain respectively, formed an alliance in order to develop the critical mass to compete successfully on the European banking stage. Although they were too similar in functional terms to have high complementarity of assets and resultant synergy, the alliance has been successful because of the partners' cultural affinity, and the consequent development of commitment and trust. The respective cultures, however, provided some surprises for the partners in the early days of the alliance. Santander operated more by word of mouth, whereas RBS committed everything to paper. Santander took much longer to answer letters than RBS. The Spaniards were much more comfortable with personal physical contact than the Scots. However, perhaps surprisingly, they were more concerned with protocol at meetings and dinners, and were apt to take offence if what they deemed an inappropriate seating plan was drawn up by RBS. However, the two banks grew to realize that they could benefit from exposure to other ways of doing things, and what could have been cultural clashes became opportunities for mutual learning in many cases. Both sides learnt not to be so ethnocentric in their attitudes, a necessary precursor to success in the new polyglot European market.

Source: Faulkner (1995).

MANAGING CULTURAL DIVERSITY

When organizations decide to cooperate, they often bring diverse cultures to their alliance. Cultural diversity is becoming more common with the rapid increase in alliances between organizations from different countries, which is one of the key features of contemporary globalization. A diversity of organizational cultures is also becoming more frequent with the growing cooperation between large and small companies in newer industries such as biotechnology and electronics in which research-based companies link with those having broad market access, and specialist component-makers link with assemblers. Nationality is the main source of distinction between social cultures, while differences in company size and types of primary competence are sources of corporate cultural variation.

  The more that the cultures of cooperative partners diverge, the more of a challenge it becomes to achieve a 'fit' between them. Fit refers to the extent to which different cultures are brought into a workable relationship that permits the alliance to operate without undue misunderstanding and tension between the partners or between the staff they attach to the alliance. Cultures that do not match, in the sense that they are different, may or may not be fitted together depending on the intentions, goodwill, and skills of the members of the different cultures.

As Chapter 5 noted, the active management of cultural diversity aimed at the achievement of a 'cultural fit' between partners is essential if their cooperation is to achieve its full potential. Cultural fit refers to a condition in which the partners' cultures (and that of a third host country, if that applies) are either combined or accommodated in a mutually acceptable manner. 'Fit' does not necessarily mean integration of the cultures and their associated practices; there may be other ways in which they can be acceptably accommodated. For an alliance to work well there has to be trust between the partners and their staffs. Trust and cultural fit are interdependent. A poor cultural fit is likely to breed suspicion and act as a barrier to the building of mutual trust. If actions or events damage trust between the partners, this will rekindle their sense of cultural difference and of having a separate rather than a common identity. There are a number of broad policy options on the management of cultural diversity, some of which, however, provide a better cultural fit than others.

The two fundamental policy choices in the management of cultural diversity are:

1. whether one partner's culture should *dominate* the operation of the alliance versus striving for a balance of contributions from the partners' cultures;
2. whether to attempt an *integration* of the partners' cultures (with the aim of deriving synergy from them) versus a preference for segregating their application within the alliance (with the aim of avoiding possible conflict and reducing the effort devoted towards cultural management).

These two dimensions of choice give rise to the four broad possibilities shown in Fig. 11.1. The first three are all options offering a basis for cultural fit, though not realizing the same level of benefit from the different cultures; the fourth possibility is one of failure, likely to lead to the early demise of the cooperation:

1. *synergy*, which is a policy aiming at cultural integration on the basis of a melding of both or all partners' cultures;
2. *domination*, which is a policy aiming at cultural integration on the basis of dominance by one partner's culture;
3. *segregation*, which is a policy aiming at an acceptable balance between the influence in the alliance of each partner's culture, but not striving for integration between them;
4. *breakdown*, which is a policy adopted by one partner seeking domination, which fails to secure integration on the basis of the other partner's acceptance.

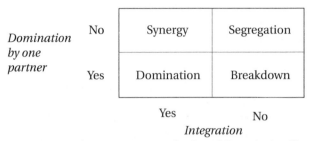

Fig. 11.1. Four options on the management of cultural diversity in alliances
Source: adapted from Tung (1993: fig. 1).

Synergy aims at achieving the fullest possible fit between cultures. It is the policy best suited to optimizing bonding between alliance partners as well as to promoting learning between them. With synergy, the better elements from each partner's culture are combined to bring about an effective management system and deployment of resources. We have already cited the example of combining US inventiveness with Japanese production efficiency and quality, which was potentially very attractive for both partners, though difficult to achieve in practice. Another example, from John Child's experience in running a Sino-European educational joint venture, concerns methods of communicating information. In the days before e-mail and local area networks, he found it beneficial to combine the use of Chinese communication methods, such as word of mouth, blackboards outside the dining hall, and the occasional general meeting with Western methods such as memoranda and minutes. The Chinese methods, which tended to be more personalized, had the merit of simplicity and speed, while the Western methods, which were more formal and impersonal, were used to follow up with precise details. The operation of the joint venture benefited from the technical contributions of each culture's approach, and the relationship between the two partners was also strengthened because each had in this way treated the other's culture with respect.

The idea of synergy is that the whole is greater than the sum of its parts. The key idea of this policy is that the 'positive aspects of the various cultures are preserved, combined, and expanded upon to create a new whole' (Tung 1993: 465). The achievement of synergy requires that each partner organization and its staff understands and appreciates the contributions that the other's culture can offer to the cooperation. Like the process of 'integration' advocated by Mary Parker Follett for making constructive use of conflict (Graham 1995), the synergy option does not ignore or suppress differences between partner cultures but requires that time and effort be devoted to discussing these openly in a spirit of mutual respect. Such discussion is, in turn, conducive to an exploration of how each culture can contribute to the progress of the alliance and how these contributions can progressively be combined in what emerges as a new alliance culture.

As with situations of asymmetric learning between alliance partners (see Chapter 13), synergy may be rejected as an approach to managing cultural diversity in alliances where it is accepted that one partner has a general superiority in technical and managerial know-how and that both the alliance and the other partner(s) will therefore benefit from adopting this approach wholesale along with its cultural foundations. Indeed, dominance by one partner in areas of its key competence, where it is particularly anxious to safeguard its proprietary knowledge, may be a condition for its entering into an alliance at all. In these circumstances, a policy of *domination* will be adopted, a policy aiming at integration on the basis of dominance by one partner's culture.

Many Japanese international joint ventures adopt a *domination* policy—they are managed primarily by the Japanese partner (Peterson and Shimida 1978; Wright 1979). In the case of some Japanese firms operating in the USA, one method of achieving this is by removing American managers from involvement in major decision-making.

Domination can also be a necessary basis for cooperation in those host countries for foreign investment which insist on a majority equity holding by the local partner and/or that local practices be followed in the management of an alliance. This limitation on equity share remains the case in China for foreign investment in strategic industries, where the local partner will also normally be a large state-owned enterprise with a strong internal Communist Party organization concerned to preserve local practices, especially in the area of HRM.

Another situation in which a policy of cultural domination by one partner is acceptable can be found where the other partner prefers to invest only a limited amount of capital, perhaps regarding royalties from technology transfer as a more secure future income stream. It may be quite content for its partner to manage the alliance according to its cultural norms, subject perhaps to the introduction of certain technical standards. These standards, and the training to support them, do of course introduce elements of the partner's own culture, but these may constitute a limited component within the alliance's management and organization as a whole.

Domination is a policy that gives rise to cultural fit in the sense that all the partners accept it and are prepared to work within its terms. However, the foundations for this acceptance can prove to be fragile over the longer term. While cultural dominance by one partner may be accepted by the weaker partner as a basis on which a desired alliance can proceed and achieve its economic goals, it could cause some resentment once those initial conditions have passed. This is particularly likely if the culturally dominated partner perceives that it is thereby placed in a position of subordination. As Tung (1993: 466) comments:

On the surface, while the organization appears to function effectively, in reality, when members of a subordinate group unilaterally adapt to the dominant culture, with no reciprocal effort on the part of the dominant group to understand and/or accommodate to members of the subordinate group, it can be counterproductive in the long run, generating misunderstanding and feelings of mistrust.

Segregation is a policy which aims at an acceptable balance between the cultural inputs of alliance partners but does not attempt any integration or synthesis between them. An example is when, in an international joint venture, one partner introduces its systems for production and quality control, while the other (particularly if it is the host-country partner) continues to manage external transactions in the field of supply, distribution, and government relations according to its customary manner. This form of inter-cultural accommodation does not offend the sensibilities of either partner, but clearly it can be a suboptimal solution in other respects. Cultural segregation between partners entails a corresponding separation of the tasks which each partner will manage within the scope of the cooperation, and this approach obviously reduces the opportunities for mutual learning between them to a very low level. It is, moreover, likely to lead to a poorly integrated and inefficient management system for the alliance, with continuing problems due to limited communications, and a sense of rivalry, between different functions within the organization. It is a policy of differentiation without the corresponding integration.

Segregation will probably give rise to personal problems for people who are seconded to work in the alliance, especially if they are expatriates. It can create difficulties for an expatriate to acquire the local language or understand the behavioural norms of the country where the alliance operation is located. The expatriate and his or her family will tend to be isolated, possibly in a foreign 'ghetto', with a high chance of family stress and personal failure in the role.

Most cases of cultural segregation within alliances occur in the early days of their operation, especially when one partner can offer expertise but the other needs to handle a difficult and not easily accessible local environment. Some joint ventures established by foreign firms in Russia have adopted a high level of internal segregation, in a situation where supplies can be problematic and even conditional on achieving understandings with local mafia. Hertzfeld (1991), an experienced consultant, has also suggested that a segregation is necessary for foreign joint ventures in Russia in order to avoid disputes over their leadership. If an alliance is to prosper, however, segregation must normally be regarded as an initial rather than a longer-term solution to the challenge of managing inter-cultural diversity.

The fourth possibility is one of *breakdown*. This is, of course, hardly a viable policy option, but it is a situation that can arise if one partner attempts to pursue a policy of domination against the wishes of the other partner(s) to an alliance. It is a condition in which the different groups in the alliance or joint venture are incapable of working with each other, and considerable tension and conflict will ensue so long as the alliance is kept in existence. Needless to say, the alliance's performance is likely to suffer badly from this state of affairs. Breakdown can develop out of a situation of segregation which one partner regards as not functional for the progress of the alliance and attempts to resolve through unilaterally introducing the norms and practices which follow from its culture. If segregation is handled with sensitivity, there is a good chance that it can be transformed into a state of inter-cultural synergy, or perhaps domination if the non-dominant partners believe that they will secure sufficient benefit from the change. If it is handled badly, then breakdown is the more likely outcome.

IMPROVING CULTURAL FIT

Deciding on a policy

Much of the responsibility for improving cultural fit within an alliance falls upon its chief executive and other senior managers. As several of the preceding chapters have noted (especially Chapters 3 and 8), the general managers of an alliance occupy a pivotal position both in terms of managing the relations between partner companies and in terms of generating a sense of common purpose within the alliance's own organization. In deciding how to proceed, and which policy option to take as a guideline, they have to weigh up two major contingencies. The first concerns the substantive *content* of the cultures which are present within the alliance. The second concerns the *flexibility* that may be available for modifying or developing each culture in relation to the others.

The content of cultures within an alliance needs to be assessed with regard to (1) how they differ and (2) to what degree. Each culture has an impact on people's attitudes and behaviour, and an assessment of the practical corollaries of each culture forms the basis for an analysis of the advantages and problems it brings from the standpoint of achieving the alliance's objectives. This provides the groundwork for addressing the challenge of cultural 'selection'; in other words, how to harness the resources offered by each culture selectively, deciding which to retain and integrate or harmonize together.

The more the cultures differ, the more difficult it is likely to be to achieve a cultural 'fit' between the elements of each that it is desired to integrate. The greater the difference, the more that inter-cultural reconciliation poses a challenge. If reconciliation proves problematic, the decision may be made either to work with one culture (the domination option) or to permit cultural segregation, at least in the early stages of a cooperation.

The gap between cultures is one consideration when deciding on a management policy for a multicultural management alliance. Another is the potential flexibility of each culture in relation to the others. This concerns the extent to which the cultures brought to an alliance are deeply embedded and therefore difficult to modify in a process of integrating or reconciling them with the other cultures. The question here is how long-standing and deep-rooted the cultures are, and the nature of the 'cultural webs' sustaining them. The cultural web of an organization, according to Johnson (1990) consists of the structures of power and authority, control systems, routines and rituals, symbols, stories, and myths which represent the reality to which the members of that organization have become accustomed, and which in turn act to maintain and reinforce its dominant cultural paradigm (see Chapter 5). A similar analysis applies to the political structures, institutional bodies and their regulations, the routines and rituals, symbols, historical legends, and so forth which comprise the surrounding 'web' of a national culture.

The point of present relevance is that, the more entrenched the web sustaining a culture, the greater will be the resistance on the part of its members and the groups to which they belong (like shareholders, professional associations, labour unions, and nationalities) to any attempt at changing that culture. The longer the history of a culture and the more it is perceived by those who hold it to serve their personal interests well, the more entrenched it is likely to be. It is therefore vital to understanding the bases on which the cultures in an alliance are rooted when deciding on the policy to adopt towards them. An assessment of how the cultural webs are made up will indicate which contextual factors need to be addressed as part of the process of bringing cultures together within the alliance. For example, some members of the alliance may resist identification with the alliance because they perceive it is the partner organization from which they have been seconded, not the alliance's management, which continues to determine their long-term progression in terms of career and remuneration. With this reward system, the partner in question is continuing to enmesh its staff within its own cultural web through what is in effect a control system.

Clearly, in order to arrive at an assessment of the content of cultures which have to be managed in an alliance, it is incumbent on each partner, and the alliance's own managers, to gain sufficient understanding of the other's organizational and (where relevant) national culture. This understanding can be used to develop a tolerance for the other's culture by understanding its historical genesis and the rationales behind it. It will help to identify those aspects of the partners' cultures which provide potential strengths to the cooperation, or which indicate the necessity for one partner to alter its standard practices in the light of the local context. This identification can also point out those aspects of the partners' cultures which are not consistent with the effective operation of the alliance, so enabling attention and effort to be concentrated on a focused effort to change them. An example of this might be the culture of recruiting staff primarily on the basis of family connections. Last, but not least, it can offer some insight into the embeddedness of a partner's culture, particularly those aspects which are likely to be most resistant to change.

Specific Issues

Assisting personal cultural adjustment

There are three issues which have to be managed in any inter-cultural strategic alliance: (1) the problem of personal cultural adjustment; (2) inter-cultural communication; and (3) the effectiveness of multicultural teams.

The scale of the problem of personal cross-cultural adjustment is indicated by the fact that a large proportion of expatriates end their assignments early. Black and Mendenhall (1990: 114) have summarized the extent of the problem: 'Studies have found that between 16 and 40 per cent of all expatriate managers who are given foreign assignments end these assignments early because of their poor performance or their inability to adjust to the foreign environment . . . and as high as 50 per cent of those who do not return early function at a low level of effectiveness.' While these figures include expatriates working in branches and subsidiaries as well as international alliances, they nevertheless clearly point to personal cross-cultural adjustment as an issue which alliance partners cannot afford to ignore. In addition to the fact that a manager who is failing to work well with colleagues from a different culture is very likely to generate misunderstanding and perhaps react aggressively, the simple financial costs of expatriate failure are also very high. To quote from Black and Mendenhall's review again, 'studies have estimated that the cost of a failed expatriate assignment is $50,000 to $150,000 . . . [it has also been] estimated that the direct costs to US firms of failed expatriate assignments is over $2 billion a year, and this does not include unmeasured losses such as damaged corporate reputations or lost business opportunities' (1990: 114). Since these are studies published in the 1970s and 1980s, the costs will have risen substantially as, of course, has the general scale of international business as well.

It is widely assumed that the selection of people with previous experience of working in international or inter-organizational contexts, and the provision of 'anticipatory training' before sending people to new assignments in unfamiliar cultural environments, are two measures which can help reduce the adjustment problem. The assumption is that both will provide for realistic expectations which facilitate a person's anticipatory adjustment to a new assignment. In fact, evidence as to the effectiveness of either measure is rather mixed.

As with any prior experience, much depends on whether it was positive or not. There are, for instance, two forms of cultural adjustment which do not constitute particularly good experience for future assignments of the same nature. One is when adjustment to an unfamiliar cultural environment has been achieved through withdrawal into an expatriate community. Some Japanese expatriates in the USA experience little culture shock because they avoid contact with their American colleagues, a closed-minded mode of adjustment that does little to build a solid basis for inter-partner collaboration or learning (*Training* 1993). The other is the attempt to cope by denigrating the other culture and aggressively insisting that things are done according to the expatriate's own national cultural norms, or those of his/her own organization. It is usually easy to find apparent confirmation for this negative and inflexible stance from other, disgruntled members of the expatriate ghetto. The selection of suitable staff is an important condition for successful intercultural adjustment. An organization must choose people who have open minds and flexible personalities, as well as those who have demonstrated a positive approach during their previous experience in alliances and/or international business.

Anticipatory training can assist adjustment to a different national culture if it is realistic, up to date, and offers language proficiency. Otherwise it may convey inaccurate knowledge and engender a false sense of confidence, which can actually impede the adjustment process. The trainer should therefore be someone who is from the country concerned and who has maintained regular contact with conditions in that country. Communication skills are a prerequisite both for effective collaboration within an alliance and for an individual to cope with the new local environment. For this reason, proficiency in a relevant language should be developed in anticipatory training, or looked for when selecting suitable candidates.

The provision of anticipatory training as comprehensive as this in its coverage of culture, environment, and language is somewhat of a tall order. It is costly and time-consuming. Some international alliance partners therefore seek to reduce the need for such training by appointing people to key alliance positions who have a cultural and linguistic affinity with members of the other partner's organization. For example, US firms with joint ventures in China often appoint Chinese–Americans, or even American-trained Chinese, as senior managers of those ventures. Also when first implementing a joint venture, the partner providing technology and managerial expertise may send in a strong team of expert expatriates for a limited period, such as six months, with assistance from colleagues who are familiar with the local language and culture. The idea is that the teams will get the alliance's operations and systems up and running as quickly as possible and then withdraw. The members of these teams in this way receive some protection from culture shock and their exposure to problems of cultural adjustment is limited. This approach is only available to a large well-resourced alliance partner, and, if not carefully explained to the other partner and implemented with its agreement, can create serious offence and loss of mutual confidence.

Ng (1996) highlights a different, but increasingly numerous, group of business people who are experiencing the challenge of personal cultural adjustment. In their case, the challenge arises from the fact that they are in a sense experiencing a massive input of anticipatory preparation for conducting international business outside their original cultures, and have to find ways of coping with the cultural duality this creates. These are the children of successful overseas Chinese entrepreneurs who are being sent, unaccompanied, to the West for their education, often at an early age. Others are going abroad to acquire a Western MBA which will give them the organizational and managerial know-how that their expanding companies require. When they return to succeed their fathers in running their businesses, they will have acquired a very different cultural make-up. Ng comments that 'what is ironic is that a western education may cause complications to the unaccompanied minor's succession to the family businesses, to the extent that succession may never take place due to cultural differences between the parents and unaccompanied minors' (1996: 6). As he points out, the extent to which these successors can become biculturally competent, maintaining their personal identity while at the same time developing another positive identity and competence with another culture, will be vital for effective succession within the overseas Chinese family business.

Ensuring adequate inter-cultural communication

The importance of good communication in pursuing a cooperative strategy has been stressed throughout the preceding chapters. This refers to communication between the partners, between their personnel working in the joint organization, and between that organization and the parent's offices. Each of these lines of communication crosses boundaries of organizational and, often, national cultures. Referring to the latter, Mishler (1965: 555) notes that 'the greater the cultural differences, the greater is the likelihood that barriers to communication will arise and that misunderstandings will occur'.

A key to ensuring that these communications within alliances are placed on a good footing lies in the role of what Newman (1992*a*, *b*) calls the inter-cultural 'boundary-spanner'. Describing the successful establishment of a Sino-US joint venture, the Nantong Cellulose Fibers Company (NCFC), Newman comments that the venture 'owes its existence and operating performance to skilful boundary spanning'. He defines this as follows:

The process of boundary spanning builds a bridge between two different organizations or between two or more people coming from different cultures. Boundary spanners— the persons who perform the bridging activity—need several talents: (1) An empathetic understanding of the customs, values, beliefs, resources, and commitments of people and organizations on each side of the boundary; (2) understanding of the technical issues involved in the relationship; and (3) ability to explain and interpret both (1) and (2) to people on both sides of the boundary. Single persons who can be effective boundary spanners in foreign joint venture situations are rare. So often a person with technical knowledge has to be teamed up with one or two people who know local languages and cultures. (1992*a*: 149)

In the case of the NCFC, the key boundary-spanner was a young bilingual and bicultural woman who was the daughter of American parents but had grown up in China; she had also worked for ten years on China trading matters and was very knowledgeable about Chinese government and business practices. She was therefore able to provide the US partner with perceptive insights about Chinese culture and institutional arrangements, and was a trusted interpreter of issues to both partners. Many other examples point to the key role that inter-cultural boundary-spanners play in assisting the creation and development of alliances either, as in the NCFC case, as externally appointed advisers or facilitators or as alliance general managers. Sir Alastair Morton's ability as chief executive of Eurotunnel to mobilize the cooperation of British and French partners in achieving one of the world's major engineering feats is an example of the latter. As Christopher Lorenz (1993: 12) commented:

[Eurotunnel] had to overcome a legion of differences between the French and British ways of doing business, Sir Alastair told a conference in London. These ranged from contrasting approaches to the control of capital expenditure, to an entirely different attitude to meetings. Whereas British managers attended them to thrash out decisions, he said, 'the French go to find out what the boss has decided to do'. That Eurotunnel has bridged such gaps is due, above all, to the openness and trust which Sir Alastair and his opposite number established early in the venture.

The key to adequate inter-cultural communication lies in a mutual willing-ness to understand why colleagues in an alliance may act in unfamiliar ways. This is where the availability of boundary-spanners and people with relevant experience, together with relevant anticipatory training, can make an impor-tant contribution. They will not, of course, make good a poor strategic fit or fundamental conflict of interests between the partners, but they can help to realize the potential of an inherently sound cooperative strategy.

The effectiveness of multicultural teams

A great deal of the cooperation between partners actually works itself out in what may broadly be termed the 'multicultural team'. This refers to meetings between managers and staff in the alliance, called to make decisions and solve problems, as well as the groups in which some of these personnel work together everyday. The dynamics of such teams is, therefore, of crucial signifi-cance for the success of the alliance.

Jane Salk (1992) conducted a particularly close and insightful study of bicul-tural management teams within three joint ventures: British–Italian, German–US, and French–German. While all of the teams experienced an ini-tial period in which cultural differences and stereotyping were important motivators of behaviour and relations among their members, as time went on relations within the teams evolved in different ways from this similar starting-point. After the initial phase, different contextual factors appeared to affect behaviour within the teams. Thus, external threats tended to heighten ten-sions between members of the different nationalities, even though initially they were a unifying factor. Teams which focused on equality of numbers and influence rather than on level of experience or seniority also tended to display more conflict and lower trust, though what is cause and effect here must be in some doubt. Third, leadership by the joint-venture general manager appeared to have some potential for pushing teams towards accepting a set of working practices and defusing different cultural identities. General managers were in a better position to exercise this influence if they could manage their own rela-tions with parent companies so as to avoid frequent absence from the joint venture and so have time to interact with team members.

Salk (1993) draws out several practical implications from her research. The initial design of an alliance should adopt career and reward systems, office layouts, and other provisions which help members to identify with the alliance team. General managers should be sensitive to the ways in which their actions, pronouncements, and other symbolic behaviours foster expectations in team members. They should also look for ways to use features, such as overarching goals, external threats, different skills and contributions by team members, to foster identification with the team and mutual attraction among its members. It is particularly important for the framers of an alliance and its general manager to look for ways to create strong superordinate goals for the management team early in its life. Vehicles for doing this include the setting of performance goals and capitalizing on opportunities offered by market or other external conditions, so that external opportunities and threats remain unifying rather than become divisive factors.

Drummond's (1997) conclusions on the facilitators of learning within multicultural teams broadly support these recommendations. He found in two branches of Toshiba, one in Brazil and the other in the UK, that the setting of goals, the establishment of a framework for control and feedback (including performance goals), and office layouts that facilitated close contact between team members, all assisted the progress of such teams.

SUMMARY

Culture is an elusive yet consequential phenomenon. The distance between partners' organizational and national cultures impact on the ease with which they can cooperate. As Chapter 5 noted, while achieving strategic fit is more fundamental to the viability of an alliance, a good cultural fit optimizes the potential of the alliance and helps to avoid the threats to its continuation which arise from misunderstanding and antipathy. Cultures, together with the institutional systems which regulate countries' economic, social, and political systems, give rise to differences in typical management practices and policy orientations. It is these differences which have to be accommodated when partners come together to form an alliance.

Cultures display themselves at different levels, ranging from rather superficial mannerisms to fundamental values. People are unlikely to change their underlying values, except as the result of personal or societal trauma. Nevertheless, there is evidence that people can become sensitive to their own cultures and how these differ from others, and that they are prepared to adapt their customary behaviour within clearly defined situations, such as their place of work, when they accept this is a worthwhile thing to do. There are, then, possibilities for achieving adaptation and accommodation between partners who come from different cultural traditions. Culture does not have to impose an insuperable constraint upon cooperation.

In addition, a mix of national or organizational cultures is not simply a problematic feature of alliances; it can also bring positive benefits to cooperating organizations. The managerial and organizational practices which stem from different cultures represent competences from which each partner can beneficially learn. Cultural diversity creates an opportunity to use the intrinsic worth of each partner's culture for the benefit of the alliance.

We identified three ways of accommodating cultural differences and the practices which stem from them. It is possible to adopt one partner's culture as the dominant mode. Alternatively, the partners' cultures and practices can coexist, but they are applied to different spheres of the alliance's operations. A third approach is the attempt to integrate partner practices and to derive synergy from this integration. This third approach is the most challenging but also the one likely to produce most benefit. We also set out guidelines for improving cultural fit. These are aimed at assisting personal adjustment to different cultures, promoting better communication between personnel from different cultures, and improving the effectiveness of teams composed of members from different cultures.

REFERENCES

Black, J. S., and Mendenhall, M. (1990), 'Cross-Cultural Training Effectiveness: A Review and a Theoretical Framework for Future Research', *Academy of Management Review*, 15: 113–36.

Boisot, M., and Child, J. (1996), 'From Fiefs to Clans and Network Capitalism: Explaining China's Emerging Economic Order', *Administrative Science Quarterly*, 41: 600–28.

Brown, A. (1995), *Organizational Culture* (London: Pitman).

Casson, M. (1995), *The Organization of International Business: Studies in the Economics of Trust* (Aldershot: Edward Elgar), ii.

Child, J., Faulkner, D., and Pitkethly, R. (1997), 'Foreign Direct Investment in the UK 1985-1994: The Impact on Domestic Management Practice', paper presented at British Academy of Management Annual Conference, London, September.

Deal T. E., and Kennedy, A. A. (1982), *Corporate Cultures: The Rites and Rituals of Corporate Life* (Reading, Mass.: Addison-Wesley).

Drummond, A., Jr. (1997), 'Enabling Conditions for Organizational Learning: A Study in International Business Ventures', unpublished Ph.D. thesis (Judge Institute of Management Studies, University of Cambridge, Feb.).

Dubin, R. (1956), 'Industrial Workers' Worlds: A Study of the "Central Life Interests" of Industrial Workers', *Social Problems*, 3: 131–42.

——Champoux, J. E., and Porter, L. W. (1975), 'Central Life Interests and Organizational Commitment of Blue-Collar and Clerical Workers', *Administrative Science Quarterly*, 20: 411–21.

Ebster-Grosz, D., and Pugh, D. (1996), *Anglo-German Business Collaboration* (Basingstoke: Macmillan).

Graham, P. (1995) (ed.), *Mary Parker Follett: Prophet of Management* (Boston, Mass.: Harvard Business School Press).

Hampden-Turner, C. (1990), *Corporate Culture: From Vicious to Virtuous Circles* (London: The Economist Books).

——and Trompenaars, F. (1993), *The Seven Cultures of Capitalism* (New York: Doubleday).

Hertzfeld, J. M. (1991), 'Joint Ventures: Saving the Soviets from Perestroika', *Harvard Business Review* (Jan.–Feb.), 80–91.

Hickson, D. J., and Pugh, D. S. (1995), *Management Worldwide: The Impact of Societal Culture on Organizations around the Globe* (London: Penguin).

Hofstede, G. (1980), *Culture's Consequences: International Differences in Work-Related Values* (Beverly Hills, Calif.: Sage).

—— (1991), *Cultures and Organizations: Software of the Mind* (Maidenhead: McGraw-Hill).

—— (1996), 'Riding the Waves of Commerce: A Test of Trompenaars' "Model" of National Culture Differences', *International Journal of Intercultural Relations*, 20: 189–98.

—— and Bond, M. H. (1988), 'The Confucious Connection: From Cultural Roots to Economic Growth', *Organizational Dynamics*, 16: 4–21.

Johnson, G. (1990), 'Managing Strategic Change: The Role of Symbolic Action', *British Journal of Management*, 1: 183–200.

Keesing, R. M. (1974), 'Theories of Culture', *Annual Review of Anthropology*, 3: 73–97.

Kroeber, A. L., and Kluckhohn, C. (1952), *Culture: A Critical Review of Concepts and Definitions* (New York: Vintage Books).

Lorenz, C. (1993), 'An Affair which Refuses to Become a Marriage', *Financial Times*, 19 Feb., p. 12.

Martin, J. (1992), *Cultures in Organizations: Three Perspectives* (New York: Oxford University Press).

Mishler, A. L. (1965), 'Personal Contact in International Exchanges', in H. C. Kelman (ed.), *International Behavior: A Social-Psychological Analysis* (New York: Holt, Rinehart & Winston), 555–61.

Newman, W. H. (1992a), *Birth of a Successful Joint Venture* (Lanham, Md.: University Press of America).

—— (1992b), 'Launching a Viable Joint Venture', *California Management Review*, 35: 68–80.

Ng, D. W. N. (1996), 'Succession in the "Bamboo Network"', *Financial Times: Mastering Enterprise*, no. 6, 20 Dec., pp. 6–7.

Peterson, R. B., and Shimada, J. Y. (1978), 'Sources of Management Problems in Japanese–American Joint Ventures', *Academy of Management Review*, 3: 796–804.

Ralston, D. A., Stewart S., and Terpstra, R. H. (1995), 'A Profile of the New Chinese Manager', unpublished paper (Management Department, University of Connecticut).

Salk, J. E. (1992), 'International Shared Management Joint Venture Teams: Their Development Patterns, Challenges, and Possibilities', unpublished Ph.D. dissertation (MIT Sloan School of Management, Cambridge, Mass.).

—— (1993), 'Behind the State of the Union: How Design and Social Processes Affect the Functioning of Shared Management Joint Venture Teams', unpublished manuscript (Fuqua School of Business, Duke University, Durham, NC, Mar.).

Sathe, V. (1985), *Culture and Related Corporate Realities* (Homewood, Ill.: Irwin).

Schein, E. H. (1985), *Organizational Culture and Leadership* (San Francisco, Calif.: Jossey-Bass).

Shane, S. (1994), 'The Effect of National Culture on the Choice between Licensing and Direct Foreign Investment', *Strategic Management Journal*, 15: 627–42.

Tajfel, H. (1982) (ed.), *Social Identity and Intergroup Relations* (Cambridge: Cambridge University Press).

The Economist (1996), 'Cultural Explanations: The Man in the Baghdad Café', 9 Nov., pp. 25–30.

Training (1993), 'Japanese Expatriates: Never Leaving Home?' (Nov.), 12–14.

Trompenaars, F. (1993), *Riding the Waves of Culture: Understanding Cultural Diversity in Business* (London: The Economist Books).

Tung, R. L. (1993), 'Managing Cross-National and Intra-National Diversity', *Human Resource Management*, 32: 461–77.

Whitley, R. (1992*a*), *Business Systems in East Asia* (London: Sage).

—— (1992*b*) (ed.), *European Business Systems* (London: Sage).

Williamson, O. E. (1979), 'Transaction-Cost Economics: The Governance of Contractual Relations', *Journal of Law and Economics*, 22: 3–61.

Wright, R. (1979), 'Joint Venture Problems in Japan', *Columbia Journal of World Business*, 14: 25–31.

12

Emerging Economies

THE IMPORTANCE OF EMERGING ECONOMIES

Developing countries contain almost 80 per cent of the world's consumers, and almost all of the world's population-based market growth will occur in them during the twenty-first century. From an economic point of view, the most significant developing countries are those whose economies are 'emerging' both in terms of market opportunity and in the sense that they are coming out from the constraints of state administration and restrictions on foreign trade. These economies are now seeking to modernize rapidly with the assistance of foreign governments and companies.

Whereas the economic growth rates of developed industrial economies have settled around an annual norm of 3 per cent or under, and their markets have become increasingly mature, the rates of annual growth in the so-called emerging economies of East and South Asia, Latin America, and East-Central Europe are typically double that figure. In some cases, like China, economic growth has been sustained at an annual rate of around 10 per cent. The annual growth rates of *industrial* production in many emerging economies are between 10 and 20 per cent. The differential in emerging economy growth rates is likely to continue despite the economic crisis experienced by South-East Asia.

The faster rate of growth in emerging countries starts from a less-developed economic base, which means that they manifest a high level of demand for both consumer and industrial products and services. Their economies therefore offer the most significant opportunities for companies from the developed countries to expand their markets. This potential, coupled with the policies of economic liberalization and reform which many emerging countries have now adopted, has led to an increase in the share of worldwide foreign direct investment (FDI) going to these countries during the 1990s, with China in the lead. On the other side of the coin, the East Asian economies in particular are themselves growing in competitive significance and they are becoming increasing providers of FDI as their companies expand overseas (UNCTAD 1997).

While acquisitions are generally the favoured mode of expansion into developed-country markets, cooperative forms such as joint ventures tend to be the most prevalent in emerging economies. This is partly a result of host-government preferences for local firms to share in the ownership of foreign-funded ventures in the expectation that such participation will increase their opportunities to acquire new technology, management skills, and other expertise. It also reflects a frequently found preference among foreign investing companies, at least in the early years, to reduce their exposure to risk, and to co-opt the assistance of a local partner in navigating through an unfamiliar environment.

Previous chapters have commented on the fact that the formation and management of cooperative ventures in emerging economies present their own particular challenges. In the first place, the cultural and institutional features of the emerging economy are normally quite different from those of the foreign partner's home country and this creates additional complexity for that partner. Secondly, the nature of partner objectives and the achievement of complementarity between them differs from those applying to most alliances between partners from developed countries. Thirdly, the differences between emerging and developed countries in culture and environment, together with the fact that in some cases the emerging economy has a colonial legacy with the sensitivities attaching to this, can give rise to special difficulties in the process of managing alliances. This chapter examines these three key challenges.

KEY EMERGING ECONOMIES

There are a number of dimensions along which the environments of emerging economies differ from those in developed countries. As Kohn and Austin (1996: 2690) comment, 'developing countries' contexts are complicated, continually in flux, and highly diverse'. This is due to a number of factors including (1) their transition from traditional and bureaucratic modes of industrial governance and business transacting, (2) the intrusion of politics into business affairs in conditions where there is often political instability at the macro-level and uncertainty because of corruption at the micro-level, (3) distinctive cultural norms attached to rigid social structures, (4) rapid population growth and large flows of population into urban areas, (5) a high proportion of young people in the age structure often with different attitudes and motivations to their elders, (6) weak infrastructure and limited technological sophistication, (7) capital scarcity, and (8) exchange-rate volatility and/or restrictions. Moreover, in large countries such as China, India, and Brazil, there are considerable differences along several of these dimensions within the one nation.

These factors create a high level of complexity facing a company which seeks to invest in an emerging economy. Gell-Mann (1995) makes a distinction between two types of complexity which it is helpful to apply to the emerging economy context. These are 'crude complexity' and 'effective complexity'.

Crude complexity is a function of the number of elements in a system and the number of connections between them. It is in these terms that most management and organization theorists have referred to 'complex' organizations and 'complex' environments. Modern information technologies now provide considerable assistance towards coping with this kind of complexity, which does not therefore in principle pose a major problem for corporations. Effective complexity, by contrast, is a function of the irregularity and hence unpredictability of a system of elements and relationships. Some management theorists have referred to this type of complexity with reference to 'variability' or turbulence in organizational environments. It is a much more potent source of uncertainty.

Emerging economies tend to be complex environments in both of these respects. Because they typically have a mixture of traditional and modern institutions, and often a combination of bureaucratic and market-based economies as well, these economies are complex in the 'crude' sense. There are usually more authorities, organizations, norms, and rules to cope with in order to get things done. A large, well-resourced multinational corporation can, nevertheless, deploy the staff and other resources to manage this kind of complexity.

It is much more difficult, however, to cope with the high level of effective complexity that also tends to characterize emerging economies. This arises from factors like the absence of a clear legal framework, uncertainty about the interpretation of the laws that do exist, vacillation in the policies of governments torn between the aims of attracting foreign investment and protecting local industries, the part played by personal connections and relationships in business transactions, the widespread presence of corruption, and the vagaries of transportation, power, and other parts of the infrastructure. These features can make it quite difficult both to interpret and to predict the conditions under which business can be carried on. The difficulty is amplified by the rapid rate of change that most emerging economies are currently experiencing. It is obviously attractive for new entrants to this kind of environment to find a local partner who can help to manage the high level of uncertainty.

China

China is the largest emerging economy, with a population of 1.2 billion, and by 1995 it stood second only to the USA as a global destination for FDI. It is a country that exhibits both types of complexity. The existence of different industrial ownership systems—state, collective, and private—varying degrees of marketization (Boisot and Child 1996), many contrasting regions (Child and Stewart, 1997), and significant generational differences in people's attitudes (Ralston *et al.* 1995) are aspects of China's 'crude' complexity. The challenges they present are those initially of understanding China as a business context and then taking account of the additional complications it poses for decision-making. However, once recognized and understood, it is possible to assess their implications with reasonable certainty.

Other characteristics of the Chinese context, on the other hand, generate 'effective' complexity in the system which is far more difficult for foreign companies to handle. These include the need to negotiate with many government agencies who are closely involved in business affairs, continuing political uncertainties, and the persistence of resource limitations. Governmental bodies are heavily involved in land use, labour administration, banking, and licensing. Laws and regulations are formulated centrally but administered locally, thus giving rise to ambiguity about what exactly the impact of government policy will be. Another area of ambiguity lies in the property rights Chinese government bodies enjoy over enterprises. Despite the objectives of the economic reform, many state and collective enterprises are beholden to governmental bodies including banks, especially for working capital and the enforcement of transactions. This dependence, which adds to uncertainty, can extend to the joint ventures which Chinese enterprises form with multinational companies.

There are long-term general uncertainties about the future development of Chinese politics. Also, government policies towards foreign investing companies are changing, and the authorities' long-term intentions in this area are not clear. More specific areas of political uncertainty include the lack of transparency of many Chinese laws and/or their uncertain enforcement, as is the case with intellectual property rights. Local governmental agencies have powers to interpret regulations, issue licences, and impose taxes, which furnishes ample scope for negotiation and corruption. Moreover, the attitude and flexibility of government bodies can vary between different locations.

The basic logic by which the Chinese economic system is ordered has idiosyncrasies which also engender uncertainty for foreign companies. The system is characterized by low levels of codification, so that transactions contain tacit and implicit conditions (Boisot and Child 1996). The interpretation of the terms of transacting, and reliability of transactions, depend on personalized criteria and understanding which can readily give rise both to a distortion of economic rationality and to corruption. The investment in cultural sensitivity required, and in time to develop the necessary relationships, are themselves not easy to ascertain in advance, and this adds yet further uncertainty. The law in this milieu has limited coverage and is itself subject to uncertain interpretation.

Although many foreign investors find China a profitable investment environment, with good longer-term prospects, others nevertheless face considerable difficulties in managing their ventures in China, according to investigations conducted in the 1990s (e.g. Vanhonacker and Pan 1993; Shan 1995; Lu *et al.* 1997). Changes in government laws and regulations, plus the vagaries of their interpretation at the local level, are a major headache for most foreign managers in China. The still considerable governmental bureaucracy, combined with regulatory ambiguity, generates legal and business risks. There have, for example, been major and unexpected policy changes on matters such as import duties and VAT rebates for joint ventures.

On the resource side, there continues to be a shortage of two key business resources—namely, domestic working capital (much of it being administratively redirected to propping up ailing state-owned enterprises), and high-quality, well-trained managers. When neither the availability of working capital, nor the loyalty of key local managers, can be taken for granted, significant elements of uncertainty are injected into the business environment.

Logistical problems also continue, and these create further uncertainty. They include poor infrastructure (especially in the transportation of goods), limited services, low-quality suppliers, and an insufficiency of market information. Although the Chinese government is according high priority to infrastructural development, this struggles to keep up with the pace of growth. There are problems in establishing distribution and service networks, while supplies can be unreliable and of poor quality. These problems arise partly because of the infrastructural problem, but also due to the shortage of technically trained staff and appropriate equipment. Other frequently mentioned concerns are bad debts, rising costs, and difficulties in local currency financing. These come on top of rising competition in many Chinese markets.

Companies in the consumer-goods sector, marketing international brands, face the problem of counterfeiting and copyright piracy. While this has received most attention in connection with compact disks and computer software, the CEO of one large US soap and toiletries corporation told John Child that he considered it to be the most serious problem his company faces in China today. The authorities have taken some steps to reduce the problem—for example, it had registered some 460,000 trademarks by the end of 1994—but enforcement at the local level continues to be variable.

Human-resource issues also present a significant challenge, and were the difficulties most frequently mentioned by expatriate managers in a recent study of sixty-seven joint ventures (Lu *et al.* 1997). Problems of relationships between Chinese and foreign personnel are often mentioned. Indeed, the major frustration experienced by Chinese joint-venture managers concerns the behaviour of their foreign colleagues and how this can sour the relationship between them. For example, many expressed the view that foreign managers were arrogant and insensitive, and failed either to understand the Chinese environment or to consult them about this and other matters. Such problems can normally be overcome if efforts are made to create trust, improve interpersonal communication, and encourage shared decision-making.

A less tractable problem is the shortage of competent local managers available to the rapidly growing numbers of Sino-foreign joint ventures and foreign subsidiaries. Local managers who are bicultural, bilingual, bi-educational (PRC and Western), and bi-functional (business and technical) are the key to success, but very difficult to find and retain (Shan 1995). This has brought to the fore issues of motivation and human-resource development, against a backdrop of extreme labour mobility between companies which are bidding for good Chinese managers with high salaries and other benefits. This competitive bidding for high-quality local managers can involve foreign companies in practices they may prefer to avoid elsewhere, such as the transfer of housing rights to staff after a given number of years of satisfactory service.

India

India is another of the world's largest countries, with a population estimated at 973 million in 1997, second only to China's. After its independence in 1947, India embarked on a long period of planned inward-looking development which bred a byzantine system of controls that became known as the 'permit-raj' (Wolf 1997a). As a result, India fell seriously behind the economic progress of other developing countries. For example, in 1947 India's per capita income was roughly the same as China's, but by the mid-1990s China's was approximately double.

India introduced economic reforms in 1991, aimed at liberalizing the market and opening up the country to foreign investment and competition. Foreign firms may now own up to 51 per cent of an Indian company's assets, except in a few consumer-goods industries, and they are officially granted considerable freedom in making strategic and operational decisions. Investment and production are now fed from licensing in most industries, while restrictions on capital markets and trade have been eased. More sectors have also been opened up to private investors.

India is, in some respects, a less complex country than China for foreign firms seeking to work with local partners. It exhibits crude complexity, which is relatively predictable, rather than effective complexity, which is less so. On the positive side, India has well-trained managers, uses English as the language of business and central administration, and has a relatively developed infrastructure which includes a large private sector and established financial institutions. These benefits are, however, somewhat offset by the considerable rigidities imposed by legislation, as in the field of employment, by a constraining government bureaucracy, and by cultural conservatism which is linked to a high degree of social stratification in society and centralization within firms (Tayeb 1996; Wolf 1997b).

Latin America

A third significant economically emerging region is Latin America, with an overall population of around 450 million. The region is as a whole experiencing growth, and improvements have been achieved in both inflation and the control of public finances. It is widely agreed that Latin America has the potential to transform itself into one of the world's most dynamic regions, and foreign companies are increasing their inward investment there. Again, however, the environment presents considerable effective complexity, indeed perplexity, to companies seeking to pursue a cooperative strategy there.

Unpredictability arises in large part from the tensions produced by the contradictions which characterize Latin American business environments (Rodrigues 1996a). Examples are the contradictions between a widespread fascination with novelty and the persistence of a traditional management style, between an excessive preoccupation with formal bureaucratic control within organizations and public life and decision-making being in reality influenced by personal relationships, between a professed concern with rules and norms and their disregard in practice. These contradictions would appear to have both reflected and contributed to the region's political instability, its oscillation between indigenous and modern Western values, and its excessive state intervention which has so far injected inconsistency as much as stability into the business context.

It is, of course, difficult to generalize across all the many countries which make up Latin America. However, we shall return later on to the largest, Brazil, and it is relevant to note here the cultural profile of the Brazilian that emerges from both local and comparative studies. These are a strong respect for authority and high-power distance, personalism, low individualism, openness to change and a lack of conservatism, and a relatively high avoidance of uncertainty (De Oliveira 1992; Rodrigues 1996b). The term 'personalism' signifies that Brazilians feel protected by ties of family and friendship, and tend to experience discomfort in impersonal and formal settings. It can readily extend to the bending of rules on the basis of personal favour. Another flexibility that characterizes Brazilian behaviour is an elastic view of time. The concept of time as a scarce resource to be managed has not yet been accepted even in urban life.

De Oliveira's comparison of decision-making in Brazilian and English organizations tends to confirm the implication, which Rodrigues has drawn for Latin America in general (1996a) and Brazil in particular (1996b), that foreign managers entering partnerships there would need to come to terms with the socially intensive nature of local management practice. This is liable to include the exercise of high influence by people in authority, the disregard of formal rules, and the intrusion of personal relationships into decision-making.

In the case of Brazil, Rodrigues (1996b) distinguishes certain characteristics of management in Brazil which derive from its history and culture, though she also cautions that these are relative as between the country's different regions:

Decision making in Brazilian organizations in general is concentrated around the chief executive . . . . As Brazilians do not make elaborate or systematic studies of alternatives or of the projected consequences of a decision, and do not spend much effort collecting information, decisions can be made more quickly than in European or Japanese organizations. But this can lead to unfortunate consequences. . . . Making and then reversing a decision is common in public as well as in private concerns. (p. 2678)

Brazilians do not dedicate their time solely to one thing or one person. People are usually late for meetings, conferences and other occasions. . . . Attention is given to problems and people as they come and go. . . . Long-term planning is considered a waste of time by many people. (p. 2678)

For the average Brazilian, the organization itself is not worthy of loyalty. Loyalty is given to a manager or superior, to a peer group or to those who can offer protection to the employee. (p. 2679)

In general, priority is given to social contacts rather than to tasks, and to personal rather than to formal communications. Informality and lack of structure result in inefficiency and the wasting of time and resources. However, Brazilians are good communicators on a personal level and do pay attention to what other people have to say. This allows quick communication and rapid diffusion of technology and information. It allows room for creativity and unobstructed change. (p. 2680)

Eastern Europe

Another major emerging economic region is that of 'Eastern Europe', which is a misleading designation because its component countries are far from homogeneous. In particular, it is necessary to make a distinction between the nations of East-Central Europe (especially the Baltic States, Croatia, the Czech Republic, Hungary, Poland, Slovakia, and Slovenia) and the others belonging to the former COMECON bloc. The former experienced a shorter period of Communist rule than did the nations of the former Soviet Union and they had previously formed part of the central European cultural tradition with at least some urban development and its accompaniment of bourgeois institutions.

The East-Central European nations have taken economic and political reform much further and they are now benefiting from economic growth. They do exhibit manifestations of their former management style, such as a reluctance to assume individual decision-making responsibility and an excessively dependent attitude, and these can lead to problems in relations with foreign business partners (Child and Markóczy 1993; Child and Czeglédy 1996). Nevertheless, these countries are also producing their own successful entrepreneurs and the state has already withdrawn considerably from both economic ownership and direct economic governance (EBRD 1996). The situation in the former Soviet Union (excluding the Baltic States) and in those Eastern European countries which have not been part of the West-Central European tradition, such as Bulgaria, Romania, and Serbia, is far less encouraging both from a market-growth perspective and from that of building a business environment based on the rule of law and dependable regulations affording would-be foreign partners an acceptable level of risk. Russia, for instance, has consistently been awarded the highest political risk rating among major emerging economies. This has arisen largely because the transformation away from central economic planning and governance led to an institutional vacuum in the absence of any alternative model in the country's living memory. For this reason, as Puffer (1995: 3019) has commented:

Managers [in Russia] must feel their way and operate by trial and error until an appropriate economic, political and social infrastructure is created. New institutions, such as banks, industry associations and regulatory bodies need to be created, new laws on taxation, environmental protection, business ethics and labour standards need to be passed and enforced and a new work ethic and a retrained labour force must be achieved.

PARTNER OBJECTIVES

When one of the partners in an alliance comes from an emerging country and the other from a highly developed economy, their configuration of objectives for adopting a cooperative strategy will almost certainly differ from that in the case of partners from two developed countries. Alliances between developed-country partners tend to be based upon expected economies, reductions of risk, opportunities for mutually increasing market power, and learning. Very often, both partners seek, and expect to obtain, quite similar benefits from their cooperation. In cooperation agreements between companies from emerging and developed countries, the difference in the nature of their respective objectives in forming an alliance is generally much greater.

In this latter case, the partner from the developed country will typically regard an alliance as an opportunity to enter, or more effectively develop, a new market with high growth potential and with good prospects of profitability in the medium to long term once early set-up and learning costs have been absorbed. Sometimes, the availability of lost-cost raw materials and/or low-cost labour may be an important incentive, but in the main the demand-side attractions tend to be foremost. Tax and other incentives which may be offered by the emerging country's authorities are welcome, of course, but not usually of basic significance in the decision to form an alliance. The choice of alliance form, particularly the decision whether to commit capital or not, is likely to depend on the partner's assessment of risk in relation to potential return from the investment, on its requirements to possess control rights in the alliance, and on the host government's policies and regulations.

The partner from the emerging economy is likely to place opportunities to transfer technology and expertise from the foreign partner high on its list of objectives for adopting a cooperative strategy. It, and even more its government, will also almost certainly value the employment and up-skilling opportunities offered by the foreign investment. Indeed, in many cases the injection of foreign capital may be the life-saver for ailing uncompetitive local firms, which may, ironically, have been forced into difficulties by the very opening-up and liberalization of their economies.

The main area of conflict between partners in the emerging–developed economy combination is likely to be over the alliance's net contribution to the emerging country's foreign trade. Many emerging country companies are eager to use cooperation with internationally experienced firms as a means to learning how to export on the world market, with the benefit of combining lower-factor costs with the technological and managerial advantages supplied by the foreign partner. The developed-country partner, on the other hand, is normally most concerned about the alliance as a means of penetrating, and building up a strong position in, the domestic market of the emerging economy. In some cases, this conflict can be avoided because the developed-country partner shares an export objective, and has the intention of using the cooperation as a base for exporting out to other countries in the region.

The mix of partner objectives can be illustrated from recent research involving respectively China and Brazil. In the case of China, we can refer to the objectives held by Chinese and foreign joint-venture partners. In the case of Brazil, interesting evidence is available from the case of a putative, and largely unsuccessful, attempt to establish joint ventures between Brazilian and Chinese enterprises. This second source of evidence also throws light upon Chinese objectives.

China: local partner objectives

In so far as most foreign joint ventures in China are with state-owned enterprises and joint-venture contracts require the approval of the Ministry of Foreign Economic Relations and Trade (MOFERT) or local government authorities, the objectives of their Chinese partners are those of the state. While Chinese managers have often been motivated to seek a foreign joint venture for specific local advantages of greater managerial autonomy, higher salaries, and operating privileges, the fundamental Chinese criteria for entering foreign joint ventures are (1) to absorb foreign capital, advanced technology, and management skills and (2) to gain better access to export markets. The favourable terms granted to foreign-funded enterprises with advanced technology and a high export capability reflect these objectives clearly.

Research conducted by Child and his colleagues during 1994 and 1995 found that among sixty-seven Sino-foreign joint ventures the average priority order of the Chinese partners' top five objectives was:

1. to enable technology transfer;
2. to learn management expertise;
3. to obtain a foreign cash investment;
4. to gain a strategic position *vis-à-vis* its own competitors;
5. the opportunity for profit (with a long-term emphasis among Northern China partners and a short-term emphasis among those located in Guangdong Province).

The study of negotiations between Brazilian and Chinese enterprises to establish alliances found that the latter were interested primarily in capital investment, forming a joint venture to give them more autonomy from higher governmental authorities (they were all state-owned enterprises), technology transfer, and opportunities to export (Rodrigues 1995).

The following are examples of Chinese goals for adopting a strategy of cooperating with foreign partners. In one case a Chinese government ministry initiated the venture and was attracted by the international standing of the US partner's unique photo-imaging technology. In another case, a US company's soft-drinks partner was seen to offer the means of achieving considerable improvements in production technology and product quality, as well as being willing to export from a China-based joint venture. In a third case, a joint venture with a Japanese construction-materials manufacturer, the Chinese partner's main goal was to achieve greater efficiency through acquiring a good management system from its partner. In a fourth example, a joint-venture hotel, the Chinese partner's objective was to generate foreign earnings through gaining acceptance by an international clientele, via the reputation and know-how of its Swiss partner.

In the past, many Chinese joint-venture partners had a strong interest in achieving short-term profits, in contrast to the longer-term orientation of most foreign partners. As Pearson noted (1991: 204), local government officials were keen to show quick results from joint ventures within their purview, since profitable projects brought in tax revenues and prestige to the municipality. Many state-owned enterprises which became partners in foreign joint ventures were not in sound financial health and a speedy attainment of profitability was also welcomed by the Chinese side as a means of underwriting such enterprises. These local pressures for quick returns from foreign investment encouraged the levying of charges which many joint ventures regarded as quite unreasonable, a problem which the 1986 Provisions endeavoured to mitigate. By the mid-1990s, the picture became rather more mixed, with indications that a stronger profit orientation in general, and a short-term one in particular, are more likely among Chinese partners from the south of the country (Child and Stewart, 1997).

Daniels, Krug, and Nigh (1985) investigated eleven Sino-US joint ventures established between 1979 and 1983. They noted that, from the perspective of the Chinese partners, technology transfer through a joint venture as opposed to, say, a licensing agreement offered assistance in the use and management of the technology and also the prospect of further learning if a joint research and development unit were established as part of the joint venture. The handling of export marketing by a foreign partner could also facilitate access to overseas markets and so build further on the advantage of improvements which a joint venture might bring.

China: foreign partner objectives

The dominant motive for Western and Japanese corporations to invest in China has been the prospect of gaining access to what they perceived as a huge domestic market. There was some early euphoria following the declaration of the open-door policy which then gave way to a more realistic appreciation of the technical difficulties of operating in China and the determination of the governmental authorities to protect their own local industry and to avoid a drain on foreign exchange. However, most Western investors have taken a long-term view that an early presence in China's market might lay the basis for a substantial market share and at the same time prevent international rivals from squeezing them out. Moreover, the protection of domestic industry and avoidance of imports did not apply equally to all foreign firms. Some introduced products or services which were new to China and/or also used local materials; examples are hair cosmetics and express document delivery.

Surveys of US firms investing in China (Daniels *et al.* 1985 and A. T. Kearney and ITRI 1987) found that the great majority wanted to establish a long-run position in China as a potentially strong growth market and as a base within the Asian region. They did not see short-term profit as a major objective and even less emphasis was placed on low-cost sourcing. Even firms like Nike footwear which invested in China primarily as a lowest-cost supplier could not but help note at the same time the potential market of 'two billion feet'. By contrast, many investors from Hong Kong and Macau, together with some Japanese firms, have looked for more immediate profits through low-cost unskilled labour and (in the case of Hong Kong and Macau) land which had become a scarce resource in their own territories. Much of the investment from Hong Kong and Macau has been in small low-technology processing and assembly plants catering for simple goods such as television antennas, toys, textiles, and porcelain figurines. In keeping with the greater emphasis of these foreign investors on short-term profits and their limited technological commitment, the average contract term of joint ventures with Hong Kong/Macau partners tends to be less than that for those with Western and Japanese investment (cf. Child *et al.* 1990: 16).

The pattern of priority objectives held by the foreign partners of the sixty-seven joint ventures mentioned above confirmed this picture. Partner firms from Western Europe, Japan, and the USA all tended to include in their top three objectives an expectation that the cooperation would gain them a strategic position in China *vis-à-vis* their competitors, give them access to the Chinese market, and afford a good opportunity for long-term profit. Some of the Japanese partners also attached high importance to the low labour costs which an alliance in China would offer, particularly in relation to the levels prevailing in Japan itself. Partners from Taiwan and Singapore also generally conformed to this pattern on priority objectives for their China ventures. Hong Kong partners, however, generally held a different configuration of top objectives, placing low labour costs first, followed in priority by low-cost sourcing, the chance to make a quick profit, and access to the Chinese market.

Sino-foreign joint ventures are among the most successful firms in China and many of them have been able to match their partner's objectives to the satisfaction of all concerned. The willingness of foreign investors to commit capital and transfer technology to China, and to use local resources, is quite compatible with Chinese objectives. The foreign desire to produce for the Chinese market may present few problems if the joint venture's products are new to the country and/or if the market is growing rapidly. Equally, many foreign companies are happy to use China as a production base from which to export, particularly to developing countries and those of the former Soviet Union.

On the other hand, the foreign partner's intention to safeguard its proprietary technology, to control the management of its investment, and to import
components or materials (whether for reasons of quality or of profiting from
transfer pricing) could clearly conflict with Chinese interests. Access to markets can also be the cause of serious dispute when this threatens the position
either of Chinese producers or of the foreign partner's existing pattern of
international business. The foreign wish to have access to China's domestic
market and the Chinese wish for joint ventures to facilitate the access of their
Chinese partners to international markets have in practice been the most fundamental difference of interest between Sino-foreign joint-venture partners.
Disputes about the quality standards offered by local suppliers and achieved
by the joint venture as a potential export producer, and about the foreign
restriction of access to proprietary technology which had therefore to be
imported or paid for through royalties, are also endemic to this issue. In addition to intrinsic conflicts of this kind, other difficulties arise because of the mix
of Chinese and foreign management traditions and the dynamics of adjustment and learning between the joint-venture partners—these problems have
been considered in previous chapters.

The Brazilian firms seeking to form joint ventures with Chinese partners
failed largely because their objectives were not compatible with those of the
Chinese (there were inter-cultural problems as well). They sought to pursue a
low-risk strategy, and were unwilling to invest much capital, if any, in China.
Most preferred to export their products to China and were therefore seeking a
local distributor rather than a manufacturing partner, with the aim of obtaining immediate profits and sales. They had a short-term perspective whereas
the potential Chinese partners had a longer-term perspective, at least in their
preferred role of being the recipients of technology, investment, and other
resources. Some of the Brazilian companies were also reluctant to transfer
their technology, or at least the most advanced type, for fear of leakage
through a Chinese partner. Finding the basis for complementarity when both
sets of emerging economy companies are reluctant to invest much capital is
clearly a substantial problem.

The process of mutual discussion and negotiation was also hampered by
the fact that most of the Brazilian firms were quite small with little previous
international experience. Following a visit to China organized by a Brazilian
ministry, they found it difficult to maintain communications by impersonal
means both because this was not their culturally preferred way of communicating and also because their Chinese contacts were reluctant to respond
(Rodrigues 1996).

Sometimes it is not so much the maximization of economic returns from the
operations of the joint venture *per se* as associated benefits and even the fulfil-
ment of political objectives which primarily motivate the formation of a Sino-
foreign joint venture. Aiello (1991: 50–1) concludes from his analysis of the
Beijing Jeep Corporation, a joint venture between Chrysler and the Beijing
Automobile Company, that this particular joint venture does not conform to the

normal assumption in international business economics that the partners have chosen to enter into this organizational form because it offers an attractive transactions governance structure for revenue-enhancing and cost-reducing activities. Rather, he argues, the maximization of dividend income from the venture was not a top priority for either partner. The US partner, while seeking an adequate return from its capital invested, was actually reaping much richer rewards from selling knockdown kits as well as spare parts and manufacturing equipment to China for payment in hard currency. The Chinese partner, in effect the Beijing Municipal Government, appears to have entered into the joint venture for reasons that were to do with politics as well as economics. It wished to prevent Beijing from being excluded from the national automotive market, in response to the central government's plan to make plants elsewhere into China's primary automotive producers. The development of modern productive capacity with the aid of US capital and know-how was also seen by the Beijing municipal authorities as a basis for building up local suppliers and an export base. The joint venture was, moreover, expected to bring in advanced manufacturing technologies and Western management techniques.

The Beijing Jeep joint venture, in Aiello's view, served therefore to provide a 'platform' from which both partners can extract what they want from the other party. In this case, the foreign partner was not particularly interested in developing the joint venture as a self-standing successful economic unit, while the Chinese partner was not interested in retaining a foreign connection once it had outlived its usefulness.

There may be a number of instances where one or both partners is using a joint venture primarily as a platform from which to extract gains rather than looking necessarily to its long-term development as a viable enterprise in its own right. In the case of a glass manufacturing joint venture, for example, the foreign minority investor is receiving a return primarily through sales royalties, levied as a fee for its closely guarded proprietary technology, rather than from the operating profits of the venture. It would like the venture to earn good returns on its capital, but it does not regard these as its main source of profit and has therefore been reluctant to inject further capital even when good investment returns were in prospect. The platform approach is obviously a perspective that foreign investors can adopt towards establishing a joint venture in China, though it is not one which promises a long life for the partnership. It may also be the case that the foreign investor acquires doubts about Chinese intentions to continue the joint venture over the long term and it must then decide whether to go along with this approach.

SPECIFIC MANAGEMENT ISSUES

It has become abundantly clear during the course of reading this book that managing the alliances which put cooperative strategies into practice is a difficult task. Some difficulties arise from features which alliances anywhere have in common, such as tensions between the different partners' objectives and contrasts between their approaches to management. Other problems are likely to be more prevalent for alliances located in emerging economies.

This is well illustrated in the management of Sino-foreign joint ventures. The managerial difficulties these ventures tend to experience fall into three main categories. The first comprises problems which arise because of differences between the objectives which the partners attach to their alliance. Problems of this kind had occurred in under one-quarter of the sixty-seven Sino-foreign alliances studied by Child and his colleagues in 1994 and 1995 (Lu *et al.* 1997). Chinese managers mentioned the problem of divergent objectives more often than their foreign counterparts, probably because in most joint ventures the foreign partner was in reality occupying the driving seat and steering their policies. Overall, however, divergence between partner objectives was not such a salient source of difficulty, and we have seen that there is often a high degree of complementarity between such objectives in developed–emerging economy partnerships. A thorough examination of strategic issues during the negotiations to form an alliance should, in fact, identify and resolve any significant incompatibilities between partner objectives, unless one side has a hidden agenda, which can sometimes be the case.

The second category comprises problems caused directly by the emerging-economy environments in which the alliances operate. Two main aspects are prominent in the case of China—the institutional and the infrastructural. Problems connected with the institutional environment were attributed to ambiguous laws and regulations, and to the ineffective and/or corrupt workings of the government bureaucracy. As might be expected, it was the foreign joint-venture managers who overwhelmingly experienced these as frustrating problems, with about one-third singling them out as major difficulties. Nevertheless, it is fair to say that their Chinese colleagues also find external bureaucratic rigidities quite frustrating, and they are aware of losing face when they are unable to deal with them. Infrastructural problems are a continuing feature of the Chinese environment, but considerable improvements have been made in recent years and they were not among the most frequently mentioned sources of difficulty. Unlike the other two problem categories, the deficiencies in emerging-country environments are not necessarily a source of division between the partners and their staff in the venture; indeed, to a large extent they present both parties with a common challenge.

The third, and most frequently mentioned, area of difficulty concerned problems in the internal process of joint-venture management. About two-thirds of the Chinese managers had experienced problems arising from what they saw as the unacceptable behaviour of their foreign colleagues. This unacceptable behaviour included arrogance, an unwillingness to listen, the lack of consultation, and a poor understanding of the Chinese environment and how things had to be accomplished within that context. Other related problems were attributed to specifically cultural differences between the partners' managers, particularly with respect to ways of conducting business. Here the main complaint was made by foreign managers, who were seeking to move the joint venture away from traditional norms and practices. Similarly, the area of human-resource management tended to be identified as a difficult area more frequently by foreign managers, many of whom were seeking to make changes to HRM practice. Language and communication barriers were also mentioned, but only in about one-quarter of the joint ventures.

The sensitivity of Chinese managers to what they perceive as the arrogance of foreign counterparts in an alliance, and the feeling of threat that arises when foreign companies enter emerging economies with a mission to bring modern management with them, are echoed in some of the experiences reported from Eastern Europe. For example, Simon and Davies (1996) examined the process of knowledge transfer from foreign investing firms to their joint ventures with local firms in Hungary. They found that a major barrier to learning among the Hungarian managers stemmed from the threat that the foreign partnership, and the way in which it was being implemented, posed to their social identities. In the unsettling conditions of radical organizational change, and with expatriate managers often being perceived as arrogant and controlling, the knowledge transfer that actually took place amounted to reluctant compliance rather than acceptance and learning. Local managers used the metaphor of 'colonization' quite frequently to express how they felt in this situation.

Quite apart from the loss of goodwill and motivation which arises in this kind of situation, knowledge of potential value for the alliance to adjust to its emerging economy conditions was likely to be withheld and lost:

foreign managers themselves may have much to learn about these local factors. Culturally and institutionally-specific knowledge falling into this category has a vital bearing on many important aspects of management both in terms of organizational systems and strategy. These include organization and human resource management within a firm, and marketing, strategy and public relations looking outward from the firm. . . . The remarks just made suggest that Eastern European managers should unlearn less than might be assumed either by Western advisors or the members of foreign companies which have located in Eastern Europe. Presumptions that Eastern Europe has failed, and that its managers therefore have little to offer and should be regarded simply as 'learners', are likely to mislead on the matter. Tacit knowledge deriving from close familiarity with the Eastern European context could be of the utmost value for Western partners who lack this familiarity and sureness of touch, yet it could easily be unrecognized or dismissed as inappropriate by those who assume that their competence is necessarily superior.   (Child and Czeglédy 1996: 173–4)

The unfamiliarity of most emerging-economy environments to the managers of international investing companies indicates a need to keep open both their minds and the channels of communication with their partners, each of which is vital if they are to learn about those contexts. The temptation is to do neither and, instead, to act on the assumption that their know-how, technologies, and products or services are sufficiently 'advanced' to mean that the challenge should be defined as one of how to get their emerging-economy partners to accept and understand these supposedly advantageous inputs rather than one of learning anything significant from them. This approach can overlook the valuable contributions that local partners can offer, such as a deeper understanding of host-country people's motivations, the contribution local brands may make to market penetration, and the flexibility that local entrepreneurs can offer an alliance in sectors with a high turnover of local firms and fluid conditions.

Beamish (1988) presents a comparison of two North American joint ventures established in the Caribbean region which points to the limitations of this one-sided policy. Each had formed its joint venture with well-established local private firms which had had previous experience with multinationals. Beamish describes (1988: 71) how, despite the fact that both joint ventures were doing well in terms of return on equity, the failure of one ('Beta') to encourage local participation threatened the future of the cooperation:

The Alpha joint venture was entered into voluntarily by the foreign MNE. It wanted a partner with local knowledge; it maintained regular communication with the partner; and it shared the decision-making and the profits. Both partners were satisfied with Alpha's performance and its prospects for continued success.

The Beta joint venture was entered into pre-emptively by the foreign MNE. It wanted a local partner only because of a perception that it would be better off with the local government if it had one. No contribution was expected from the local partner for local market knowledge or managers. No specific need for, or commitment to, the local partner was demonstrated by the MNE. The local partner was dissatisfied with this arrangement. This joint venture had significant problems to resolve in order to survive.

These arguments in favour of encouraging local participation in emerging-economy ventures are, however, strenuously challenged by the view that such participation is often only helpful in the early stages when foreign firms need local support to set up in an unfamiliar environment, or when they are 'forced' into joint ventures by the policies of host governments. Such firms, it is argued, will go through a period of initial dependence on the help of local partners. However, this dependence will progressively reduce as they acquire their own knowledge of the environment and form their own relationships within it. This implies that their need to wrestle with the difficulties of partnership progressively reduces. Vanhonacker (1997) advances this argument for foreign firms entering China, a context in which there is a strong trend towards establishing wholly owned foreign enterprises (WFOEs) rather than alliances with Chinese partners: 'pioneering companies, frustrated by the limitations and underperformance of EJVs, have begun experimenting with WFOEs. . . . foreign investors are finding that WFOEs, because of the flexibility and managerial control they deliver, make an excellent fit with China's competitive situation today' (p. 131). Vanhonacker reports that foreign investors in China are finding that the expectations of Chinese partners do not match theirs in several respects. First, Chinese companies do not have the experience to keep up with the speed and scope of change in the Chinese market.

Secondly, they expect their foreign partners to share advanced, proprietary technology which those partners are reluctant to give away for fear that it will be copied. Thirdly, Chinese partners look for a much shorter-term profit return than do most foreign partners who often wish to reinvest joint-venture profits to fund further expansion.

Prahalad (1997), in rather similar vein, takes the view that all joint ventures in transitional economies are inherently unstable, and that one partner is going to buy out the other eventually. He cites India's experience since the mid-1980s. When India moved away from a protected market and opened to foreign investment in 1983, multinational companies looked to local partners to serve as 'escorts' through the bureaucratic maze of the 'permit-raj'. At this stage, the local partner was needed to offer a lever on the government bureaucracy, and the MNC was interested in production for the local Indian market. Following the economic reforms of 1991, MNCs had progressively less need for their local partners and were able to move to majority ownership. They had by this time often established their own direct relations with the bureaucracy and also acquired good knowledge of the local market. Now they were willing to invest large sums into India, and were beginning to use that country as a source of competences to produce for the world market. Indian firms could not match the large investments made by foreign partners, they had no knowledge of the world market, and with the reform their connections with an in any case less-interventionist bureaucracy became less relevant. Prahalad's prediction for India and many other emerging economies is that (1) many joint ventures will be dissolved, (2) MNCs will see joint ventures with local partners as temporary arrangements, and (3) MNCs will compete with local firms in their domestic markets.

These predictions are being made for China and there appear to be similar developments in Eastern Europe as well. They clearly raise a significant political issue of MNC power for the host-country governments. This raises questions as to the long-term acceptability of moves away from cooperation towards unilateral dominance. Indeed, host governments may plan to reduce eventually the role of foreign companies in their economies, and may succeed despite globalization if their economies are sufficiently large. For instance, China's official plans for developing its main industrial sectors acknowledge a period of dependence on foreign companies for introducing advanced production capabilities and subsequently R&D competences, over a period of ten to fifteen years—following which, it is not clear that foreign firms are intended to retain a significant role. It therefore remains a matter for debate as to whether the best way for foreign firms to ensure a continuing role is to establish a position of dominance in their China sectors or to develop partnerships which both sides value and wish to maintain.

The point noted earlier also remains—namely, that policies of go-it-alone or domination over local partners eschew the assistance that a successful cooperative strategy can offer, given the uncertainties in emerging-economy environments. They assume that the foreign investor is large or confident enough not to share the risks of operating in such environments with chosen partners, and this clearly will not always be the case.

SUMMARY

Emerging markets are clearly attractive for companies from mature economies, and cooperation with local firms offers an entry route into them. The environments they present to business are, however, usually complex and in flux. They often lack well-developed legal systems and market infrastructures. Their cultures and institutions are distinct from those of the highly industrialized countries, and so correspondingly are their business practices, even though some convergence may now be under way. These features obviously add to the difficulties of getting the process of cooperation with local firms under way, especially for small and medium-sized firms which may not have the resources to spend the time and effort to do this on their own.

The objectives of prospective partners from developed and emerging economies are, nevertheless, often reasonably compatible—at least in the short to medium term. Initially, there is usually a strategic fit between the foreign partner's wish to develop markets and the local partner's desire to acquire competence, to underwrite financial survival, and to share in market expansion. There are, however, liable to be issues of access to and control over proprietary resources, especially advanced technology and local distribution networks. In the longer term, it is not clear that foreign investors will necessarily regard a strategy of cooperation with local emerging-economy firms as desirable or even necessary, especially as they absorb the country into their global market strategies and production networks. Equally, the authorities in some countries, such as China, may eventually seek to eliminate their reliance on foreign firms.

REFERENCES

A. T. Kearney and the International Trade Research Institute (ITRI) of the PRC (1987), *Manufacturing Equity Joint Ventures in China* (Chicago: A. T. Kearney).

Aiello, P. (1991), 'Building a Joint Venture in China: The Case of Chrysler and the Beijing Jeep Corporation', *Journal of General Management*, 17: 47–64.

Beamish, P. W. (1988), *Multinational Joint Ventures in Developing Countries* (London: Routledge).

Boisot, M., and Child, J. (1996), 'From Fiefs to Clans and Network Capitalism: Explaining China's Emerging Economic Order', *Administrative Science Quarterly*, 41: 600–28.

Child, J., Li, Z., Boisot, M., Ireland, J., and Watts, J. (1990), *The Management of Equity Joint Ventures in China* (Beijing: China–EC Management Institute).

——with Czeglédy, A. (1996) (eds.), 'Managerial Learning in the Transformation of Eastern Europe', *Organization Studies*, 17/2, Special Issue.

—— and Markóczy, L. (1993), 'Host-Country Managerial Behaviour and Learning in Chinese and Hungarian Joint Ventures', *Journal of Management Studies*, 30: 611–31.

—— and Stewart, S. (1997), 'Regional Differences in China and their Implications for Sino-Foreign Joint Ventures', *Journal of General Management*, 23: 65–86.

Daniels, J. D., Krug, J., and Nigh, D. (1985), 'US Joint Ventures in China: Motivation and Management of Political Risk', *California Management Review*, 27: 46–58.

De Oliveira, Carlos A. A. (1992), 'Societal Culture and Managerial Decision Making: The Brazilians and the English', unpublished Ph.D. dissertation (University of Bradford Management Centre).

EBRD (1996): European Bank for Reconstruction and Development, *Transition Report 1996* (London: EBRD).

Gell-Mann, M. (1995), *The Quark and the Jaguar: Adventures in the Simple and the Complex* (London: Abacus).

Kohn, T. O., and Austin, J. E. (1996), 'Management in Developing Country Environments', in M. Warner (ed.), *International Encyclopedia of Business and Management* (London: Routledge), 2690–702.

Lu, Y., Child, J., and Yan, Y. (1997), 'Adventuring in New Terrain: Managing International Joint Ventures in China', *Advances in Chinese Industrial Studies*, 5: 103–23.

Pearson, M. M. (1991), *Joint Ventures in the People's Republic of China: The Control of Foreign Direct Investment under Socialism* (Princeton: Princeton University Press).

Prahalad, C.-K. (1997), presentation (no title) to Conference on 'Strategic Alliances in Transitional Economies', William Davidson Institute, University of Michigan Business School, Ann Arbor, Michigan, May.

Puffer, S. M. (1995), 'Management in Russia', in M. Warner (ed.), *International Encyclopedia of Business and Management* (London: Routledge), 3015–20.

Ralston, D. A., Stewart, S., and Terpstra, R. H. (1995), 'A Profile of the New Chinese Manager', unpublished paper (Management Department, University of Connecticut).

Rodrigues, S. B. (1995), 'Local Rationalities in the Formation of Strategic Alliances: The Case of Emerging Economies', Research Papers in Management Studies, WP21/95, University of Cambridge, September.

—— (1996a), 'Management in Latin America', in M. Warner (ed.), *International Encyclopedia of Business and Management* (London: Routledge), 2936–50.

—— (1996b), 'Management in Brazil', in M. Warner (ed.), *International Encyclopedia of Business and Management* (London: Routledge), 2673–82.

Shan, W. (1995), 'Investing in China, New Business Strategies', notes from an unpublished presentation.

Simon, L., and Davies, G. (1996), 'A Contextual Approach to Management Learning: The Hungarian Case', *Organization Studies*, 17/2: 269–89.

Tayeb, M. (1996), 'Management in India', in M. Warner (ed.), *International Encyclopedia of Business and Management* (London: Routledge), 2875–80.

UNCTAD (1997): United Nations Conference on Trade and Development, *World Investment Report* (New York: United Nations).

Vanhonacker, W. R. (1997), 'Entering China: An Unconventional Approach', *Harvard Business Review* (Mar.–Apr.), 130–40.

—— and Pan, Y. (1993), 'The Impact of Country of Origin, Business Scope and Location on International JV Operations in China', working paper (INSEAD, Fontainebleau, France).

Wolf, M (1997*a*), 'Reforms Stir Hopes for Era of Prosperity', *Financial Times Survey: 'India 50 Years of Independence'*, 24 June, p. 1.

—— (1997*b*), 'Success, with More to Come', *Financial Times Survey: 'India 50 Years of Independence'*, 24 June, p. 3.

IV

THE MATURING RELATIONSHIP

This final part of the book deals with what is perhaps ultimately the most important factor in the creation of a lasting mutually beneficial cooperative arrangement between companies—namely, how to cause the relationship to evolve and mature and how to ensure that organizational learning remains its primary purpose.

Chapter 13 deals with the whole area of organizational learning and how it differs from individual learning. It stresses the importance of learning in an alliance as opposed to merely finding a partner to buttress one's weaknesses. It notes that, of the various cooperative forms, only alliances have learning as their primary object. The other forms, from networks to virtual corporations, have the objective of linking together enterprises with different skills, and learning, if it happens, is incidental to the main purpose of the cooperation.

Chapter 14 discusses the evolution or mature development of cooperative arrangements as a condition for their success. It stresses that alliances in particular that do not evolve into something greater than was envisaged at their initial establishment are likely to atrophy into arrangements of little abiding importance to the partners or indeed break up altogether.

13

Organizational Learning

THE NATURE OF ORGANIZATIONAL LEARNING

It has long been recognized that successful strategies are those which adapt organizations to the opportunities and threats in their environments, and which enhance their internal capacities. Adaptation to external developments and internal enhancement both involve 'organizational learning'. The term has since the 1970s come to be used to emphasize that organizations, just as individuals, can acquire new knowledge and skills with the intention of improving their future performance. It has indeed been argued that the only competitive advantage the company of the future will have is its managers' ability to learn faster than its rivals (De Geus 1988: 740). Organizations often adopt cooperative strategies with the specific intention of acquiring new knowledge and know-how. Successful cooperation itself requires a learning process by the partners (Inkpen 1995a).

Despite the large amount of discussion and writing on the subject, there is not a generally agreed model or even definition of organizational learning, and there has been a lack of synthesis and cumulative work (Fiol and Lyles 1985; Huber 1991). Most writers, however, agree that organizational learning consists of both cognitive and behavioural elements. Villinger (1996: 185) suggests that it is 'the process of developing a potential to improve actions (behaviours) through better knowledge and understanding (cognition)'. While learning is clearly a process, some would go further and include its outcomes within the scope of the term as well. This extension is helpful, because it serves as a reminder that an organization does not necessarily benefit from the acquisition of knowledge and understanding unless these are applied, so that the 'potential to improve actions' is actually realized.

Villinger prefers to use the term 'learning in organizations' because of the uncertainty over whether organizations themselves can actually be said to learn. The idea of 'organizational learning' does not resolve the paradox that 'organizational learning is not merely individual learning, yet organizations learn only through the experience and actions of individuals' (Argyris and Schön 1978: 9). As Nonaka and Takeuchi (1995) recognize, in a strict sense

knowledge is created only by individuals and an organization can only support creative individuals or provide suitable contexts for them to create knowledge. Their description of 'organizational knowledge creation' provides an
indication of how this individual learning can become available, and retained,
within the organization as a whole: 'Organizational knowledge creation . . .
should be understood as a process that "organizationally" amplifies the knowledge created by individuals and crystallizes it as part of the knowledge network of the organization. This process takes place within an expanding
"community of interaction" which crosses intra- and inter-organizational
boundaries' (p. 59).

This touches on the very practical question of how learning by individuals,
or groups of individuals, can become transformed into an organizational
property. The challenge here is partly one of how to make explicit, codify, dis-
seminate, and store the knowledge possessed by the members of an organization in ways that convert it into a collective resource. It is also partly a problem
of how to reduce the barriers which organizational structures, cultures, and
interests can place in the way of knowledge-sharing and learning.
Paradoxically, although cooperative strategies are usually intended to
enhance the learning of partner organizations, the fact that the strategic and
cultural match between them may be less than complete can seriously impede
the process.

The nature of the knowledge contributed by the members of an organization, or an alliance of organizations, is of considerable significance for the
process of learning. An important requirement for converting knowledge into
an organizational property is to make it sufficiently explicit to be able to pass
around the 'knowledge network'. Polanyi (1966) distinguished between tacit
knowledge and explicit knowledge. The former is usually regarded as personal, intuitive, and context-specific. It is therefore difficult to verbalize, for-
malize, and communicate to others. Explicit knowledge, by contrast, is
specified and codified. It can therefore be transmitted in formal systematic
language. To make tacit knowledge available to an organization at large in a
form which permits its retention for future use, it has to be converted into a
codified or programmable form. It may not be possible to accomplish this,
either for technical reasons or because the people with tacit knowledge do not
wish to lose their control over it. If this is the case, then the only way to put
tacit knowledge to organizational use may be to delegate responsibility for
action to the persons concerned and/or to persuade them to share their
knowledge with other experts on an informal basis.

The tacit nature of much useful knowledge can pose two problems for a
strategic alliance or other form of inter-organizational cooperation, depending on the intention of the partners. If the partners are looking to learn competitively from one another, then the retention of knowledge in a tacit form
can be a defensive measure, because it means that only their members have
access to it. If both or all partners adopt this tactic, then they are likely to face
major difficulties in converting the knowledge held tacitly or covertly by each

partner into a form usable for cooperative activities. This can, obviously, become counter-productive to the success of the cooperative venture, which almost certainly requires mutual learning in order to achieve other strategic objectives as well. The other problem is more likely to arise when one partner is gaining market access in return for providing superior knowledge to the other—a typical situation for alliances between organizations from developed and developing countries respectively. When the tacit knowledge held by the members of one partner organization is superseded by new knowledge and practices brought in by another partner, the consequent threat to the group identity of the former may generate considerable resistance to internalizing the new knowledge.

Another distinction which has important implications for practice is that between the different levels of organizational learning (see Table 13.1). Both theorists (summarized by Pawlowsky 1992) and those writing more pragmatically with reference to developments in joint ventures (CIBAM 1993; Child *et al.* 1994) have identified three main levels of organizational learning, in a broadly parallel way. The theoretical approach identifies *routine improvements* within the boundaries of existing organizational knowledge as the 'lowest' level. The middle level involves changes to the boundaries or structures of existing knowledge bases, which imply a *'reframing' of organizational systems and perspectives.* The highest level is *learning how to learn* through reflexive cognitive processes; it is proactive and generative. These three learning levels

Table 13.1. *Levels of organizational learning*

Levels	Theoretical approach	Pragmatic approach
Higher	*Learning—'deutero learning'* Learning how to learn so as to improve the quality of the organizational learning process itself.	*Strategic learning* Changes in managerial mindsets, especially in understanding the criteria and conditions for organizational success.
Middle	*Reframing—'double-loop'* Changes of existing organizational frameworks. Involves questioning existing systems. Oriented towards survival in changing environmental conditions.	*Systemic learning* Changes in organizational systems, with an emphasis on learning how to achieve better integration of organizational activities.
Lower	*Routine—'single-loop'* Improvements and adjustments to optimize performance within the limits of existing organizational frameworks and systems.	*Technical learning* The acquisition of new specific techniques such as more advanced production scheduling, or managerial techniques such as more advanced selection tests.

correspond to the terms 'single-loop learning', 'double-loop learning', and 'deutero-learning' coined by Argyris and Schön (1978).

The more pragmatic approach distinguishes between technical, systemic, and strategic levels of organizational learning. The *technical* level refers to the acquisition of new, specific techniques, such as for quality measurement or for undertaking systematic market research. This corresponds to routine learning. The *systemic* level refers to learning to introduce and work with new organizational systems and procedures. The focus here is on an integrative type of learning involving the restructuring of relationships and the creation of new roles. This parallels the notion of organizational reframing. The *strategic* level involves changes in the mindsets of senior managers, especially their criteria of organizational success and their mental maps of the factors significant for achieving that success. The emphasis on vision here is somewhat different from that on 'learning how to learn', but there is a parallel in the reflexive cognitive processes involved with a view to generating new insights and being proactive. The level of learning to which a collaborative venture aspires will depend on its purpose, and the involvement and needs of its partners. Higher levels of learning are likely to be more difficult to achieve, a point to which we return later.

Andreu and Ciborra (1996) point to the dynamic processes which link these three levels of learning together by means of three equivalent 'loops'. Their scheme is reproduced in Fig. 13.1. At the lower level is the *routinization learning loop*. This level of learning is aimed at mastering the use of standard resources and gives rise to efficient work practices. Most of the learning at this level will be technical in nature. Andreu and Ciborra cite as an example 'mastering the usage of a spreadsheet by an individual or a team in a specific department, to solve a concrete problem'.

New work practices can be internalized by the firm in the form of routines, and in this way they become part of its capabilities. This gives rise to a *capability learning loop*, in which new work practices are combined with organizational routines. The learning process is systemic in character because it involves generalizing work practices and techniques and placing them into a wider context. This defines not just what the practices do and how they work, but also the circumstances under which it becomes appropriate to use them and who has the authority or competence to apply them.

The third and highest learning loop is the *strategic loop*. In this learning process, capabilities evolve into core capabilities that differentiate a firm strategically, and provide it with a competitive advantage. Capabilities can be identified as core—having strategic potential—both by reference to the firm's mission and to what will give it a distinctive edge in its competitive environment.

While the Andreu and Ciborra framework depicts a primarily internal process of upward learning cycles within a single firm, cooperation with partner organizations offers a potential to learn at all three levels. It may provide direct and fast access to improved techniques and specific technologies. It can

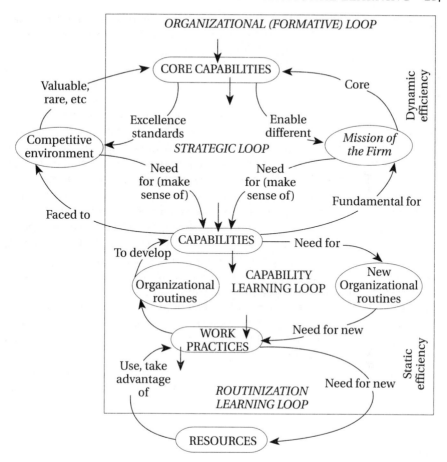

Fig. 13.1. Organizational learning loops at three levels
Source: Andreu and Ciborra (1996: 126, fig. 6.2).

facilitate the transfer and internalization of new systems, such as lean production and TQM. Cooperation can in these ways enhance a partner's capabilities, and these may assume greater significance if the cooperation also opens a door to new strategic possibilities through, for example, assisting market entry.

SIGNIFICANCE TO ALLIANCES

The ability to learn is probably the most important intangible asset that a company can possess. Its enhancement is frequently the main motive for entering into collaboration with other companies. Alliances create learning opportunities, especially if the partners possess somewhat different experiences or capabilities. Different experiences would, for example, come from operating in different geographical, cultural, and political environments. Different capabilities would be evident when, say, one partner has a particular strength in research and the other has a highly developed competence in production.

Many cooperative alliances and networks are formed between organizational partners who perceive that they can benefit from their complementarities (Geringer 1991). This gives them a common interest in learning how to extract the potential synergies between their respective competences. If their goals are also complementary they can collaborate in order to compete better, if they are business firms, or to provide a better service, if they are organizations in the public domain such as universities (Bleeke and Ernst 1993).

Competitors whose goals and interest diverge may also collaborate to benefit from learning opportunities. Opportunities to learn are, in fact, generally greater between competitors, but, of course, they will be wary about sharing their knowledge. The balance between the contributions each partner makes to the alliance and benefits each is able to extract from it will be a sensitive issue. It is subject to negotiation, and to the ability of one partner to outsmart the other. In this kind of situation, the cooperation is often relatively short-lived and the partners may well revert to competing with each other, if and when their alliance breaks up.

So, there are two possible learning situations within an alliance. One is based on an underlying spirit of *collaboration* between the partners, the other on an underlying attitude of *competition* between them.

Collaborative learning

There are two main ways in which alliances between organizations can enhance their learning (Inkpen 1995a: 53–4). One involves learning *from* a partner; the other involves learning *with* a partner. In the first case, collaboration provides access to the partner's knowledge and skills. These can include product and process technology, organizational skills, and knowledge about new environments, including an introduction to key relationships within them. The transfer of knowledge is a frequent and important motive for entering into a collaborative strategy. The process has come to be known as the 'grafting' of new associates who possess knowledge not previously available within the organization. Huber (1991: 97) cites, as an example, General Motors' acquisition of Ross Perot's corporation, EDS, in order to graft on its information-systems expertise.

In the case of some alliances which set up a new unit for a specific purpose, such as a joint venture, the knowledge sought from partners may only be relevant to, and embodied in, the outputs of that unit. Such learning may not have any general value outside the scope of the particular collaboration, though, as we shall see, there is always a danger of underestimating the value for the partner organization as a whole of knowledge acquired in this way. Like any graft, it has to take and faces the risk of possible rejection.

The example of Olivetti (see Box) demonstrates, however, that cooperation can open up important opportunities for organizational learning which were not envisaged or given much importance when the alliance was first formed.

Unexpected learning opportunities from alliances which do not necessarily achieve their stated objectives: The case of Olivetti

The Olivetti Corporation's main strategic alliance during the 1980s was its partnership with AT&T between 1983 and 1989. Only a few of the alliance's stated goals—such as forming a defence against IBM's dominance or imposing a new operating system (UNIX) in Europe—were achieved. Nevertheless, it had some positive, if unexpected, results as an exercise in learning. One was that the alliance accelerated internal learning and the acquisition and absorption of new knowledge through the broadening of Olivetti's management's horizons. Much the same was true of Olivetti's acquisition of Acorn, a small innovative British computer firm, during this period. While the original objectives of this acquisition, such as gaining a market share in the UK and a strong foothold in the education market, failed, there were unexpected benefits which enhanced Olivetti's knowledge. Acorn's wealth of skilled people and ongoing projects, for example, enabled Olivetti to become a leader in workstation technology.

Ciborra (1991: 66) comments of Olivetti's various collaborations that 'what seems to be particularly significant here is that in each alliance the elements of surprise and tinkering seem to have played a role in learning at least as important as the specific contractual arrangement'.

Source: Ciborra (1991).

The second way in which collaboration can enhance organizational learning is through the accumulation of experience and knowledge about how to manage alliances. This benefit is becoming increasingly significant in a world where more business activity is being organized through strategic alliances, including those whose management has to cope with cultural differences and unfamiliar environments. It falls primarily into the category of systemic learning, although it is also important for a successful collaboration that its members learn how to learn together (deutero-learning). Collaborative know-how might be used later in the design and management of other collaborations. Lyles (1988), for instance, found unanimous agreement among managers and staff of two US and two European firms, with a successful history of operating joint ventures in an international context, that there was a valuable transference of experience from previous ventures. This transference took place largely through the sharing of experiences, the continuity of top-management oversight, and the development of management systems. The companies were also able to use their experience as a credential which made it easier for them to form new joint ventures.

The collaboration between the Royal Bank of Scotland and the Banco Santander of Spain, announced in October 1988, is described by senior officials from both partners as having promoted organizational learning of mutual benefit. As the Box indicates, each partner was able to learn about and absorb improvements in banking operations as well as to learn over time how to deepen the process of working together.

Cooperation between the Royal Bank of Scotland and the Banco Santander of Spain

Initially, the major areas of cooperation between the two banks included access to branches, shared ownership of German and Belgian banks, offshore banking in Gibraltar, merchant banking, technology development, and acquisitions. As an act of faith and demonstration of commitment, a small percentage shareholding was exchanged at Group level.

The Chief Executive of the Royal Bank of Scotland commented later that:

We have been surprised by the intangible benefits from the alliance, as each side has got to know and observed the working practices of the other. Simple things like the differing ways in which we prepare and organize meetings; the nature and content of papers presented to internal audiences; and differences in structures and reporting relationships have all provided ample food for thought.

José Saavedra of the Banco Santander also remarked that:

We have learnt best how to launch an interest-bearing current account after having learnt what RBS's experience has been. We admire how they develop business by phone, even selling loans. At top-management level we are exchanging views on how best to handle credits, and geographical risks. On the Royal side, they look at our branch network with five people or less per branch, and compare it with their average of nine. Probably they will centralize the back office more. Also they are very good at serving customers, and we are very good at developing profitable customers. As time goes on something more consistent will come out of the cocktail shaker. But those are processes that are on going and enriching on both sides.

Source: Faulkner (1994).

As José Saavedra's words remind us, a cooperative alliance develops as a relationship over time. This has led to the notion of strategic alliance evolution in terms of a life cycle, corresponding to the concepts of product and technology life cycles (Lorange and Roos 1992; Murray and Mahon 1993). It is argued that, over time, a collaboration moves from initial contacts, through negotiations and start-up, to a phase of managed cooperation. This may, in turn, lead to an extension of the cooperation, a drift towards separation, or a more abrupt decision to divorce. Extension and deepening of the cooperation, based partly on learning how to work together and achieve synergies between complementary competences, could eventually lead to a free-standing entity with a sense of its own identity and independent management. Faulkner (1995a), from a study of sixty-seven cases, identifies a direct link between organizational learning and the alliance life cycle. He concludes that an underlying 'learning philosophy' is one of several conditions necessary for successful alliance evolution, along with strong bonding and regular new projects. To prevent the collaboration becoming dormant due to operational mismatches or over-dependence on one partner, constant adjustments will be needed.

Schacht (1995) studied the role of learning in the evolution of three international strategic alliances entered into by Hoechst. He distinguished between three types of learning which correspond to the categories of technical, systemic, and strategic already mentioned. These are learning new technologies, improvements in the organizational systems which supported learning, and learning about new strategic opportunities. Schacht found that the rates of these three types of learning over time varied as between the three cases. For example, in two of the cases the rate of learning about new strategic opportunities increased over time as the collaboration deepened, but in the third case it appeared to remain rather low. This latter was a collaboration which Hoechst had with Bayer on the development and promotion of an anti-AIDS drug. Although close informal communication developed between the companies' research scientists, which led to a rising rate of technology learning, the static rate of strategic learning appeared to result from the persistence of formal communication at higher organizational levels where goals were set for the collaboration and strategic issues discussed.

Schacht concluded from his research that the rate of learning was a key factor driving the evolution of the collaborations, and he identified management policies and provisions which contributed to effective learning. The evolution of collaborative relationships will also depend on the learning objectives which their partners attach to their cooperation. If they are committed to the idea of mutual learning within the partnership for an indefinite period, their relationship is likely to evolve progressively. If, on the other hand, they regard the cooperation as a one-off opportunity to access knowledge which they may subsequently turn to competitive advantage against their partners—an attitude of competitive learning—then clearly the scope for its evolution is limited.

Competitive learning

Competitive learning within a collaboration describes the situation where one partner intends to learn as much as possible from the other rather than adopting mutual learning as its priority. As Larsson et al. (1994) note, a dilemma for inter-organizational learning is that the endeavour by participating organizations to maximize their appropriation of the joint outcomes of collective learning undermines the conditions, such as mutual trust, for the generation of inter-organizational learning. This is the case of 'competition for competence' which Hamel (1991) reported from his investigations of international strategic alliances:

managers often voiced a concern that, when collaborating with a potential competitor, failure to 'outlearn' one's partner could render a firm first dependent and then redundant within the partnership, and competitively vulnerable outside it. The two premises from which this concern issued seemed to be that (1) few alliances were perfectly and perpetually collusive, and (2) the fact that a firm chose to collaborate with a present or potential competitor could not be taken as evidence that that firm no longer harbored a competitive intent vis-à-vis its partner.   (Hamel 1991: 84)

Hamel points to the possibility of asymmetric learning between alliance partners which derives from the fact that they have failed, or are unwilling, to transform their partnership into a fully cohesive organization. The lack of 'perfect collusion' is a failure by the partners to achieve total integration of their operations within the joint venture. The result is that organizational learning becomes a political football in the competitive process. Collaboration of this kind involves a race between the partners to learn from the other, to their own advantage rather than for the benefit of the alliance as an organization in its own right. Performance in this race is associated with inter-partner bargaining power. The partner with the greater bargaining power can, during the formation of the alliance, establish conditions favourable for it to achieve asymmetric learning by, for instance, insisting that the other partner's technology be made fully available. Successful asymmetric learning during the life of the alliance will in turn enhance that partner's bargaining power *vis-à-vis* the other to the point where the former dominates the alliance or where it breaks up under the strains that asymmetry generates.

Pucik (1991: 127) comments, with reference to technology transfer in strategic alliances, that the partners should approach the matter in a planned rather than a haphazard manner:

Organizational learning is not a random process, but a carefully planned and executed set of policies and practices designed to enlarge the knowledge base of the organization. Preventing an asymmetry (or creating an asymmetry in one's favor) in organizational learning is a strategic requirement for firms engaged in competitive collaboration, when technology is transferred between competitors. Win/win outcomes so fashionable in academic literature are not likely to occur with one of the partners placed at a bargaining disadvantage. Not providing a coherent strategy for the control of invisible assets in a partnership is a sure formula for failure.

The prisoner's dilemma applies to learning within the framework of an inter-organizational alliance. That is, when individual partners behave in an individually rational manner, attempting to maximize what they can extract from the cooperation at the expense of the other partners, the potential for all partners to gain is lost (Axelrod 1984). Organizations are therefore likely to learn the most together when they all choose collaborative learning strategies, involving high levels of openness ('transparency') and receptivity to new knowledge—the model of being a 'good partner' in strategic alliances (Larsson *et al.* 1994: 16). If, in the course of time, trust grows between the partners as their alliance evolves and demonstrates benefits to all partners, this should help to safeguard the collaboration against the temptation towards short-term maximization by any one of them.

REQUIREMENTS FOR ORGANIZATIONAL LEARNING

Even when partners undertake to collaborate with a view to mutual benefit, there are certain requirements for learning to take place. The first is that learning is included among a partner's intentions when it enters into a cooperative relationship and that it attaches value to the learning opportunities which arise. Secondly, the partner must have the necessary capacity to learn. Thirdly, the partner needs to be able to convert the knowledge into a collective property so that it can be disseminated to the appropriate persons or units within its organization, understood by them, and retained for future use. While these requirements all appear rather obvious, they are not so easy to achieve in practice.

Partner intentions

Hamel (1991) found from a detailed study of nine international alliances that the partners varied considerably in how far they viewed the collaboration as a learning opportunity, and that this was an important determinant of the learning which they actually achieved. For instance, several of the Western firms had not intended to absorb knowledge and skills from their Japanese partners when they first entered alliances with them. They appeared, initially, to be satisfied with substituting their partner's competitive superiority in a particular area for their own lack. In every case where this 'substitution' intent was maintained, the partners failed to learn in any systematic way from their collaboration.

Other companies, including many of the Japanese partners, entered into the alliances regarding them as transitional devices in which their primary objective was to capture their partner's skills. In several cases, partners undertook cooperative strategies for the purpose of learning the business (especially to meet international requirements), mastering a technology and establishing a presence in new markets. These are illustrations of a company's intention to use the learning opportunities provided by collaboration to enhance its competitive position and internalize its partners' skills, as opposed to collaborating over the long term and being content merely to access rather than to acquire partner skills. The threat posed by this strategy to an unwitting partner is obvious and it does not provide the basis for an enduring long-term cooperative relationship. In fact, when learning *from* a partner is the goal, the termination of a cooperation agreement cannot necessarily be seen as a failure, nor can its stability and longevity be seen as evidence of success. Hamel noted that a partner's ability to outstrip the learning of the other(s) contributes to an enhancement of that partner's bargaining power within the cooperative relationship, reducing its dependence on the other partner(s) and hence providing a gateway to the next stage of internalizing those partners' knowledge and skills. For these reasons, Hamel concludes that, in order to realize the learning opportunities offered by an alliance, a partner must both give priority to learning and consciously consider how to go about it.

Garrette and Dussauge (1996) found a significant difference in the apparent learning intentions of 'scale' and 'link' strategic alliances in the global automotive industry. Their conclusions were based on a study over time of 150 such alliances between thirty-six different car and truck manufacturers from Europe, North America, Japan, and Korea. Scale alliances are those in which the partners contribute similar resources pertaining to the same stage or stages in the value chain. These alliances may permit the achievement of scale economies or the reduction of excess capacity. They include joint R&D collaboration, the joint production of particular components or sub-assemblies, or even the co-production of an entire product. The PRV alliance established in 1971 by Peugeot, Renault, and Volvo to develop and manufacture a common V6 engine provides an example. Link alliances are those in which the partners contribute different and complementary capabilities relevant to different stages in the value chain. A common case is when one partner provides market access to products developed initially by the other firm, and an example is the alliance linking General Motors to Isuzu (Hennart 1988; Garrette and Dussauge 1996).

The scale alliances were formed between competitors with fairly similar production volumes, and it appeared that the partners were primarily seeking to benefit from economies of scale. Learning, in the sense of capturing the other partner's skills, did not appear to be a priority objective. On the other hand, link alliances were formed much more frequently by partners from different parts of the world, which creates more favourable conditions for transfers of knowledge to take place. The relative worldwide market shares of link-alliance partners varied more than in the case of scale alliances. This asymmetry, together with the complementary knowledge possessed by link-alliance partners, sets up conditions for learning and knowledge transfers to take place between them. Garrette and Dussauge take the fact that the link alliances tended to be reorganized more frequently as an indicator that skill appropriation between the partners was taking place.

Inkpen (1995*a*) provides an example of a US company which entered into a joint venture with a clear intention to learn (see Box).

An Example of a Clear Learning Intention

A US automotive supplier (Beta Corporation), like many others in its sector, was losing market share to Japanese companies in the early 1980s. Its management saw the formation of a joint venture with a Japanese company closely linked with one of the largest Japanese car manufacturers as an excellent opportunity to learn about Japanese management:

Beta concluded that purchasing Japanese technology was not the answer. The Japanese were using more expensive raw materials and were using the same equipment. In Beta's view, the differences had to be managerial. Beta had some idea of things like JIT and other techniques but senior management could not agree on what the real important differences were. They decided that a JV would help them learn from the Japanese. As a Beta manager commented, 'Our feeling was that we might not get rich from the JV but at least we could learn a lot about Japanese management.'

Source: Inkpen (1995*a*: 92–3).

Learning capacity

A partner's capacity to learn will be determined by a combination of factors:

- the transferability of the knowledge;
- how receptive its members are to new knowledge;
- whether they have the necessary competences to understand and absorb the knowledge;
- the extent to which the partner has incorporated the lessons of experience into the way it approaches the process of learning.

Transferability

Unlike the other three factors listed, this one refers to a quality of the knowledge itself rather than to a feature of the would-be learning partner. Transferability shows the ease with which the type of knowledge can be transferred from one party to another. Explict knowledge, such as technical product specifications, is relatively easy to transfer and to be absorbed. Tacit knowledge is far more difficult.

Receptivity

The more receptive people are to new knowledge, the more likely they are to learn. When the members of a collaborating partner organization adopt the attitude of students towards their counterparts from the other partner, they are being more receptive to insights from that partner than if they assume that they already possess superior techniques, organizing abilities, and strategic judgement. For example, some Chinese partners in joint ventures with foreign companies make the mistake of assuming that they cannot learn useful motivational practices from their foreign collaborators because they already have a superior knowledge of Chinese workers. Equally, some foreign partners unwisely disdain advice from their Chinese collaborators on the best ways to relate to external governmental authorities which wield an unusual degree of influence over the conditions for doing business.

Hamel (1991) found several influences on a partner organization's receptivity. Firms which had entered an alliance as 'laggards', in order to provide an easy way out of a deteriorating competitive situation, tended to possess little enthusiasm for learning from the other partner or belief that they could achieve it. They tended to be trapped by deeply embedded cultures and behaviours which made the task of opening up to new knowledge all the more difficult. In clinging to the past, they were not capable of 'unlearning' as a necessary prerequisite to learning (Hedberg 1981). Receptivity also depended on the availability of some time and resource to engage in the processes of gathering knowledge and embedding it within its own routines through staff-training and investment in new facilities. The paradox of deteriorating competitiveness as a pressure to learn and yet a constraint on being able to achieve it becomes critical for poorly performing partners. In some alliances, it may be resolved by the additional cash and other resources injected by the other partner. If a collaborator has, however, slipped far behind its partner(s) in the skills and competences necessary for it to absorb new knowledge, it may find it extremely difficult to close the gap.

Competence

Cohen and Levinthal (1990) argue that a firm's 'absorptive capacity' is a crucial *competence* for its learning and innovative capabilities. Absorptive capacity is a firm's ability to recognize the value of new, external information, assimilate it, and apply it to commercial ends. This competence is largely a function of the firm's level of prior related knowledge. Hence existing competence favours the acquisition of new competence, which implies that a partner entering an alliance with learning objectives should ensure that it does so with not only a positive attitude towards learning but also a minimal level of skills. If those skills are not available, the training of staff to acquire them should be an immediate priority.

Competence is required at all three levels—strategic, system, and technical—if a partner is to take advantage of the opportunities for learning offered by cooperation with other organizations. At the strategic level, a collaboration which is perceived as peripheral to a partner's overall strategy will probably yield fewer opportunities for the transfer of learning from the collaboration back into the partner's main organization. The lack of perceived strategic importance is likely to reduce the level of interaction between partner and the cooperative venture. Another problem can arise from a partner's failure to appreciate that it can derive broad strategic lessons from the cooperation rather than ones restricted to narrower issues. General Motors, for example, approached its NUMMI joint venture with Toyota with the expectation that what it could learn from Toyota would be confined to production skills in the manufacturing of small cars. As a consequence, although the lessons to be learnt were actually of general relevance, they were not applied to General Motors as a whole (Inkpen 1995*a*: 63)

Competence at the system level is required in order to make the most innovative use of new knowledge or technology which is acquired. For example, the introduction of mill-wide computerization in the paper and pulp industry opened up radical new possibilities for the constructive redesign of mill organization and the combined empowerment and enrichment of mill workers' jobs. This new technological development came about through close cooperation between paper manufacturers and system suppliers. The ability of UK paper manufacturers to take full advantage of the potential offered by the new systems depended on their organizational vision and competence, in terms of being able to envisage and accept radically changed roles and relationships (Child and David 1987).

The need for a partner to possess adequate skills for it to absorb and use new technical knowledge is a self-evident requirement. With the complex nature of many modern technologies, and the importance of deploying them in conjunction with the 'human' skills and motivations of employees, a multi-disciplinary technical competence is required. A particular technical skill the lack of which can cause problems in international alliances is competence in the partner's language. Hamel (1991) noted how the fact that employees in Western firms almost all lacked Japanese language skills and cultural experience in Japan limited their access to their Japanese partners' know-how. Their Japanese partners did not suffer from a lack of language competence to the same degree and benefited from the access this gave them to their partners' knowledge. Similarly, Villinger (1996) found that in East Central European firms acquired by Western companies, both Eastern and Western managers perceived language and communication deficiencies to be the main barriers to learning between the two parties, even though for the most part rather little priority was being given to improving language competences.

Previous experience

Experience is always a two-edged sword. Prior knowledge gained from an alliance which has been converted into an organization's routines can become a barrier to further learning, especially that of a discontinuous rather than merely incremental nature. Being good at single-loop learning may therefore become a handicap for double-loop learning (Argyris and Schön 1978). Having said this, it is expected that previous experience of cooperation will normally enhance the partners' capacity to learn because it gives them greater knowledge of how to manage, monitor, and extract value from their alliances. If partners enter alliances with the intent of learning to augment their competitive ability, then the benefits of previous experience will derive mainly from the extent to which it has developed their ability to extract value from the cooperation (Simonin 1997).

If there is an intention to collaborate for mutual benefit, and on a long-term basis, the experience of working together can in itself create relationship assets for the partners. They will have basic understandings about each other's capabilities and the qualities of confidence and trust in their relationship should have already been established. The fact that they have already overcome the hazards of the initial period of working together will have generated a degree of commitment to one another (Fichman and Levinthal 1991). These benefits of previous joint experience will tend to extend the openness shown by the partners towards each other, and hence add to the effectiveness of the learning process. Nevertheless, the value of previous experience as a capability which promotes learning in alliances between organizations will depend on the relevance of that experience. This is suggested by Inkpen (1995a: 65–6), who found that previous joint-venture experience on the part of the partners of ventures with Japanese companies did not lead to improvements in their learning process.

The learning process experienced by Rover in its alliance with Honda illustrates the interplay of conditions which we have identified, relating to the nature and level of the knowledge, and the partner's learning intention and experience (see Box).

Creating collective knowledge

Nonaka and Takeuchi (1995: 70), drawing largely upon cases of successful Japanese innovation, stress that the creation of knowledge for organizational use is a 'continuous and dynamic interaction between tacit and explicit knowledge'. For this process to succeed, in their view, there must be possibilities for four different modes of knowledge conversion:

1. *Socialization* (tacit knowledge → tacit knowledge): 'a process of sharing experiences and thereby creating tacit knowledge such as shared mental models and technical skills' (p. 62).
2. *Externalization* (tacit knowledge → explicit knowledge): 'a process of articulating tacit knowledge into explicit concepts' (p. 64). This form of knowledge conversion is typically seen in the creation of concepts which offers wider access to the knowledge and also links it to applications.
3. *Combination* (explicit knowledge → explicit knowledge): 'a process of systematizing concepts into a knowledge system. This mode of knowledge conversion involves combining different bodies of explicit knowledge . . . through media such as documents, meetings, telephone conversations, or computerized communication networks' (p. 67).

The Rover–Honda Alliance: Learning by Rover

In the alliance between Rover and Honda, Rover had a high intent to acquire technology and this technical learning was relatively easy to achieve. Also in the later stages of the alliance, Rover was receptive and keen to undergo technical learning. The nature of the technology transfer was clear and Honda was willing to provide the information in joint learning working teams.

Process-learning, involving knowledge about Honda's organizing systems, was more difficult, since by its nature it involves a lot of tacit knowledge as well as features related to Japanese cultural paradigms. This kind of knowledge was less transparent and less easily transferred, but as Rover's learning intention and receptivity grew, it became one of the success stories of the alliance from the Rover viewpoint. Processes such as 'just-in-time' were adopted and adapted to Rover's situation, and organizational innovations such as multifunctional teams and a flattening of the management hierarchy were introduced.

Once the cooperation had deepened by the mid-1980s to embrace the joint development of new automobile models, Rover's intent and receptivity to learning from Honda increased dramatically. The whole nature of Rover's attitude to itself, its personnel, and its way of working became transformed, so that a learning philosophy came to underlie it. By this stage, Rover's senior management had fully accepted the strategic value of the alliance, though this was not so true for its parent company, British Aerospace, which ultimately sold the company to BMW and led to termination of the cooperation.

Source: Faulkner (1995*b*).

4. *Internalization* (explicit knowledge → tacit knowledge): This process is closely related to 'learning by doing'. It involves the embodiment of explicit knowledge into individuals' tacit knowledge bases in the form of shared mental models of personal technical know-how (p. 69).

Nonaka and Takeuchi emphasize that organizational learning depends upon the tacit knowledge of individuals, and upon the ability first to combine tacit knowledge sources constructively and then to convert these into more explicit forms which are subsequently combined. Tacit knowledge itself is enhanced by explicit knowledge, taking the form for example of training inputs. Theirs is an illuminating framework for understanding the processes which must be in place for new knowledge to become an organizational property and hence constitute organizational learning.

Even within single organizations, there are often obstacles in the way of the smooth operations of these processes which derive from lines of internal differentiation. These lines of differentiation are both vertical (creating hierarchical barriers) and horizontal (creating barriers between specialist and physically separated groups or units). Differentiation forms the basis for distinct social identities and perceptions of competing interests. When two or more organizations come together to collaborate, such barriers are typically augmented by their different corporate cultures and, in the case of international alliances, their different national cultures.

These barriers reduce what Hamel (1991) terms 'transparency'—namely, the openness of one partner to the other(s), and its willingness to transfer knowledge. Hamel found that some degree of openness was accepted as a necessary condition for carrying out joint tasks in an alliance, but that managers were often concerned about unintended and unanticipated transfers of knowledge—transparency by default rather than by design (p. 93).

BARRIERS TO ORGANIZATIONAL LEARNING

Pucik (1991) identifies a number of barriers to organizational learning in strategic alliances. These can arise from (1) misplaced strategic priorities, such as short-term objectives and giving low priority to learning activities; (2) unfocused organizational control systems, as when little or no reward is given for contributions to the accumulation of learning as an invisible asset, and the responsibilities for learning are not clear; and (3) inconsistent human-resource-management policies, such as surrendering responsibility for staffing to the alliance partner.

As well as these failures to plan and provide for learning in an alliance, other obstacles to the necessary transference of knowledge identified by Nonaka and Takeuchi (1995) are liable to arise because of the divergent ways of sense-making and associated with the social identities of the different parties which make up the collaboration.

When the members of different organizations come together to collaborate, they bring their own social identities with them. These social identities are sets of substantive meanings which arise from a person's interaction with different reference groups during his or her life and career. They derive therefore from belonging to particular families, communities, and work groups within the context of given nationalities and organizations (Tajfel 1982; Giddens 1991).

The receptivity of the members of a strategic alliance to knowledge transfer from their partners, and their ability to learn collaboratively from the knowledge resources they bring to the alliance, are bound up with their social identities. Social identities are likely to create the greatest difficulties for collaborative learning in alliances which are socially constituted by partners which are distinct organizationally, nationally, and in terms of the economic development level of the society from which they come. Learning in these circumstances is not a socially neutral process. Just as with knowledge that is offered in the learning process by one organizational speciality to others, so knowledge and practice transferred from a partner to the alliance impinge on the other members' mental constructs and norms of conduct. Their social identity derives from a sense both of sharing such ways of thinking and behaving, and of how these contrast with those of other groups. The process of transferring practical knowledge between different managerial groups will be interdependent with the degree of social distance that is perceived between the parties involved. So, if initially this distance is high, the transfer is likely to be impeded. If the transfer is conducted in a hostile manner or in threatening circumstances, then the receiving group is likely to distance itself from those initiating the transfer. There is a clear possibility of virtuous and vicious circles emerging in this interaction.

International cooperation presents a particular challenge for organizational learning which is intended to draw upon knowledge transferred between the partners, or the partners and the cooperative venture, and to build upon the potential synergies between their complementary competences (Child and Rodrigues 1996). While alliances and other types of international organizational networking are extremely important means for international knowledge transfer and synergistic learning, they introduce special sensitivities into the process. They may be uneasy with respect to accommodating the interests of their constituent groups and to managing the cultural contrasts between them. These differences contribute to a sense of separate social identity between staff who are attached or beholden to the respective partners.

Some types of internationally transferred knowledge impinge on group social identity more than others. This is particularly true of knowledge relating to new systems and strategic understanding. Resistance to the transfer of such knowledge is likely to heighten the separate identities of the partner groups, including those doing the knowledge transfer for whom persuading their recalcitrant colleagues may take on the nature of a crusade. The relation between social identity and international knowledge transfer is a dynamic one, in which contextual factors such as the performance of the joint venture also play a part through inducing changes in factors which condition the process, such as partner dominance and compatibility. By contrast, the sharing and transfer of technical knowledge are normally less socially sensitive, and indeed are likely to benefit from the common engineering or other occupational identity shared by the staff directly involved.

The cooperation of Western transnational companies with firms in Eastern Europe provides an instructive contemporary example of the problem. Western companies are expected to make a significant contribution to the transformation of the former Communist countries of Eastern Europe, not only as financial investors but also as agents for new organizational learning (EBRD 1995). This collaboration often takes the form of joint ventures which dramatically illustrate how social identities, stemming from the mixed social constitution of such ventures, impact upon the learning process. For example, Simon and Davies (1996) interpret and discuss barriers to learning by local managers working in international joint-venture companies located in

Hungary. They draw upon the self-reported experience of the managers, and on their own experience as process consultants in the Hungarian operation of a major multinational. They argue that managerial learning is concerned basically with role learning. Roles and the willingness or confidence to assume them are frequently linked to the social identities people hold within a particular cultural setting. The authors conclude that a major barrier to learning among Hungarian managers stemmed from the vulnerability of their social identities. In the threatening conditions of radical organizational change, and with expatriate managers often being perceived as arrogant and controlling, the learning that occurred mostly amounted to compliance, which was a strategy for survival. Their study illustrates how the social psychological conditions affecting learning are informed by a broader context of the meanings which Hungarian managers ascribe to the evolving conditions of transformation in which they find themselves.

The members of an organization will be reluctant to give up the beliefs and myths which constitute important supports for their social identity. Jönsson and Lundin (1977) write of the 'prevailing myth' as one which guides the behaviour of individuals in organizations, at the same time as it justifies their behaviour to themselves and hence sustains their identity. Beliefs and myths form an important part of the 'cultural web' (Johnson 1990) which sustains an existing paradigm and set of practices against the possibilities of their replacement through organizational learning. The social identities of those involved in joint ventures are likely to be tied up in this way with their distinctive and separate beliefs, rigid adherence to which may be sustained by their very proximity to their partners who comprise an 'other' or out-group. This proximity reinforces the sense of difference on which social identity thrives.

It is therefore perhaps not surprising to find Inkpen and Crossan (1995) concluding from their study of organizational learning in forty North American–Japanese joint ventures that it was a rigid set of managerial beliefs associated with an unwillingness to cast off or unlearn past practices which tended severely to constrain the learning process within the ventures. For example, American managers often failed to appreciate their Japanese partner's areas of competency. In line with the American belief in the appropriateness of formalization, these managers commonly expected that the knowledge associated with differences in skills between the Japanese and American partners would be visible and easily transferable (p. 608). Nonaka and Takeuchi (1995: 95) illustrate from Japanese cases how, if the senior architects of an alliance recognize this problem, they may be able to undermine this rigid and blinkered thinking by deliberately injecting a sense of crisis and engendering 'creative chaos'.

FORMS OF ORGANIZATIONAL LEARNING

It is now possible to draw together some of the preceding analysis by identifying different situations with respect to learning within cooperative relationships between organizations. We do so by referring to the basic distinction between cognitive and behavioural learning, and the motivational factors associated with intent and transparency.

The typology set out in Table 13.2 incorporates these distinctions. It is adapted from the one first used by Child and Markóczy (1993) to identify different kinds of learning processes experienced by host-country managers in international joint ventures between Western and Chinese or Western and Hungarian firms, and also incorporates further categories identified by Inkpen (1995a: 74).

The first situation shown in Table 13.2 is the case of *forced learning*. Here there is no change of cognition and hence understanding, but new behaviour is acquired under some pressure. It could be argued that this is a case of adaptation rather than learning, because of the lack of cognitive internalization. A common example of forced learning in collaborative ventures arises when one partner insists on the unilateral introduction of new organizational routines or systems without the other either accepting the rationale for them, or indeed being offered adequate training to understand it. Although the term 'forced' refers here to how the acquisition of new behavioural practices is brought about, and not necessarily how the process is perceived by those on the receiving end, it is likely to meet with some reluctance on their part. Forced learning can readily arise in a situation where there is an asymmetry of power

Table 13.2. *Forms of organizational learning in cooperative relationships*

Form of learning	Change in:		Motivation to learn
	Cognition	Behaviour	
Forced learning	x	+	low
Imitation or experimental learning	x	+	moderate
Blocked learning	+	x	high
Received learning	+	+	high but asymmetric
Integrative learning	+	+	high and mutual
Segmented learning	part	part	low
Non-learning	x	x	low

Source: adapted from Child and Markóczy (1993).

Note: x = change absent; + = change present.

between the partners and a low motivation to learn by members of the less powerful partner.

A second possibility also results in the adoption of new practices (behavioural change) but without any appreciable learning of the rationale behind them (cognitive change). This is learning by *imitation*. It is likely to arise in the earlier stages of collaboration and may represent a phase of experimentation before practice can engender understanding, or knowledge extend to 'know-how'. There is probably at least a moderate level of motivation to learn in this situation, but the fact that the learning takes the form of imitation might indicate some limitation in the quality of training offered to support the learning process.

There were several cases of imitation arising in joint ventures in both China and Hungary. For example, in some Chinese joint-venture hotels local staff displayed positive attitudes towards learning new routines for customer service, in large part because they were well rewarded for this. It was doubtful whether they really acquired an understanding of the thinking behind the new approach since its execution was often wooden and repetitive. John Child is reminded of the occasion when he had to go in and out of one hotel several times in succession with various packages, being greeted on each entry by the same commissionaire with 'welcome to our hotel' and on each exit with 'have a nice day, sir'! In several Hungarian joint ventures with Western partners the previous dependence of managers on higher government authorities was transferred to a new dependence on the foreign 'expert' partner in which its instructions were followed but without much apparent new understanding (Markóczy and Child 1995).

The two situations mentioned so far are ones in which, at most, behaviour and practices have changed but without any significant increase in know-how or understanding. However, the opposite can also occur, when the members of an organization undergo changes in cognition that are not reflected in their behaviour. This could be due to inadequacies of resourcing which prevents implementation, an over general or theoretical formulation of the new knowledge, or the over-riding of the situation by other strongly held beliefs. These factors cause the translation of new understanding into revised behaviour to be *blocked*. In the context of an alliance between organizations, blocked learning can arise when staff from one partner receive training from those of another partner but are not accorded the appropriate positions and/or budgetary resources to put what they have acquired at the cognitive level into practice. Their motivation to learn may well be high and the intentions of the other partner towards their learning may be positive, but the organization of the training may, for example, not be matched to that of the responsibilities and resources allocated under the collaboration. This is, in fact, often the complaint of executives who attend off-site courses and are then frustrated in the application of their new learning when they return by superiors and colleagues who do not understand the change in competence that has taken place.

Another possibility is that the participants in an alliance learn both cognitively and behaviourally. This could be a unilateral process of *received learning* when one partner willingly receives new insights from another. If both parties endeavour to express and share their knowledge and practices, the level of *integrative learning* may be attained. This latter exhibits the potential of a cooperative strategy for organizational learning in its most advanced form, in which innovative synergy is attained between the different contributions and approaches which the partners bring to their alliance. Integrative learning involves a joint search for technical, system-building, and strategic solutions to the needs of the alliance. It means that partners are receptive to the concepts and practices brought in by their counterparts, and are willing to modify their own ways of thinking and behaviour in the light of these.

Two further possibilities are included in Table 13.2 for purposes of comparison. In both cases the motivation to learn from cooperation is low and little learning actually takes place. The first is a situation in which, at best, very limited learning takes place because the partners to a collaboration choose to allocate separate responsibilities between them for different areas of cooperative activity. It is appropriate to call this *segmented learning*, and it often arises when the mutual trust between partners is low or when restrictions are imposed by governments on the exchange of technology, as occurred under the COCOM rules. Hertzfeld (1991), an experienced consultant, has for instance suggested that a segmented mode of learning is necessary for foreign joint ventures within the former Soviet Union in order to avoid disputes over their leadership.

The other possibility is that of *non-learning*, in which no learning takes place at all. This is likely to arise when the motivation to learn is low because the partner concerned accords a low (or even negative) priority to learning from the cooperation and/or because there is low transparency of knowledge between the partners. The case of a Sino-European joint venture, reported by Child and Markóczy (1993: 626), illustrates a negative learning priority. The Chinese partner attempted to resist the reconfiguration of production and support functions along more effective lines because it saw this as reinforcing the power of the European management over the running of the venture's facilities and over the labour force.

There is an evident parallel between these forms of organizational learning and the options for managing cultural diversity in alliances discussed in Chapter 11.

MANAGEMENT OF ORGANIZATIONAL LEARNING

This closing section outlines a number of provisions that can be made towards facilitating the process of learning within cooperative ventures. It assumes that the partners share a genuine wish for integrated learning, and that their prospects for cooperation are not vitiated by the strong competitive intent of one or more partners to exploit their collaboration for short-term ends. We have seen, of course, that these assumptions do not always apply. We look first at overcoming the cognitive and emotional barriers to learning, then at reducing organizational barriers, and finally at fostering the intensive communication and circulation of information required for effective learning. These issues overlap to a considerable extent, and the provisions for tackling them should therefore be mutually supportive.

Overcoming cognitive and emotional barriers

A lack of intent to learn can be an important cognitive barrier in the way of realizing the learning potential of collaboration with other organizations. This can arise because a partner enters into an alliance for reasons other than learning, such as to spread the risks of R&D or to achieve production economies of scale, and does not appreciate that it has something valuable to learn until it becomes more familiar with that partner's capabilities. Inkpen (1995*b*: 13) found several examples of North American firms which did not have a learning intent when entering a collaboration with a Japanese partner, and developed this only when they became aware of their inferior levels of skill. Ways of reducing lack of intent to learn due to inadequate prior knowledge include programmes of visits, and (better) secondment, to prospective cooperation partners, and close examination of their products and services. The highly successful Korean *Chaebol* have, for example, learnt a great deal through reverse engineering of other companies' products, and investigations along such lines can enhance an intent to learn through collaboration by signalling technical and other skill deficiencies.

Drummond (1997) studied projects or programmes involving Japanese and local participants within Toshiba's consumer-products subsidiary in the UK and the Semp-Toshiba joint venture in Brazil. Each project succeeded in creating new organizational knowledge. A high level of managerial commitment to the projects, signifying an intention to generate knowledge through them, was one of the consistently important factors facilitating the learning process.

The emotional barriers to learning within a collaboration often boil down to a problem of mistrust. As we have seen in Chapter 3, there is no short cut to establishing trust. It is, nevertheless, possible to identify conditions which promote trust and therefore to derive practical guidelines to that end. Commitment to the relationship, and a degree of direct personal involvement by the partners' senior managers, are again important here. If the principals take the time and trouble to establish a close personal relationship, this gives confidence and a signal for other staff from each partner to regard one another in a positive light. The conditions for reducing emotional barriers to learning within a collaboration require a long-term view of the cooperation and sufficient managerial commitment, especially from the top (Faulkner 1995*a*).

Reducing organizational barriers

Serious organizational barriers are created if the senior managers of alliance partners do not know how to benefit from the opportunity to learn from their collaboration. Inkpen found that a major problem arose because of the inability of the North American parents of joint ventures with Japanese partners to go beyond recognition of potential learning opportunities to exploitation of these opportunities. They did not establish organizational mechanisms to assist this exploitation. In some cases they even resisted the idea that there was something to learn from the collaboration, so contributing to a situation of blocked learning where joint-venture managers could not get their improved understanding carried over into practical actions (Inkpen 1995b; Inkpen and Crossan 1995).

The role of senior managers in an alliance is again critical, as a lever for reducing organizational barriers to learning. Managers and staff will take their cue from the senior levels. Senior managements are in a position to establish organizational procedures and provisions which foster the learning process within their cooperative ventures. Inkpen and Crossan (1995) identify ways in which provisions can be designed, or practices encouraged, by senior managers that facilitate links across organizational boundaries to promote the learning process. In the case of joint ventures, these include '(1) the rotation of managers from the JV back to the parent; regular meetings between JV and parent management; (2) JV plant visits and tours by parent managers; (3) senior management involvement in JV activities; and (4) the sharing of information between the JV and the parent' (p. 609).

Control is a further organizational feature which facilitated learning in the Toshiba experience. There are two main aspects to this: (1) establishing limits to the actions of participants in the learning process and (2) assessing outcomes. Control is not usually regarded as a facilitator of learning. Indeed, learning is normally associated with autonomy and creativity, which are considered as opposites to control. However, as Drummond points out, this is to adopt a naïve view of organizational politics—a belief that those participating in learning projects will not try to direct their process towards their own objectives rather than those which benefit the alliance as a whole. Control, then, seems to be a very important condition for a learning intention to be given clear direction. Secondly, the systematic assessment of outcomes should ensure that these are recorded and so entered into the organization's memory. It also provides feedback on the effectiveness of the learning process which should enable the alliance and its partners to improve their capacity to promote learning. This capacity was identified in Table 13.1 as deutero learning.

When the collaboration takes the form of a separately established joint venture, the leadership provided by its CEO in terms of building trust and a shared identity between staff from the two partners is critical. This means that the CEO should forcefully articulate a long-term view of the collaboration and its development. Among more specific provisions, the venture's CEO must establish adequate communications between staff who need to work together to pool their knowledge and skills, and must ensure that meetings are held to discuss views, including differences, openly. He or she must also see that there is an adequate circulation of information, sufficient personal contact between managers and staff seconded by the partners, and adequate resources of time and funding invested in activities oriented towards learning. Not least, the CEO has to generate a sense of common learning objectives through a shared identity with the collaboration, based among other things on an understanding that its members enjoy real possibilities for career progression within it.

This focus on the facilitation of learning by the people who are placed in charge of alliances or joint ventures derives from their critical position in the middle of the vertical system between the partners, on the one hand, and the staff working within the alliance, on the other hand. It echoes the conclusion reached by Nonaka and Takeuchi (1995) that what they term the 'middle-up-down' style of management can make a crucial contribution to fostering knowledge creation. Managers in the middle can reduce the gap that often otherwise exists between the broad vision coming down from top management and the hard reality experienced by employees. In the case of alliances, the manager in the middle is the venture CEO, who has the additional tasks of articulating the objectives for learning within the collaboration and providing the practical means to facilitate it.

The aim of the organizational provisions just mentioned is to promote the conditions for integrated learning within alliances. Another requirement, which the techniques of organizational behaviour can facilitate, is to break down the hostile stereotypes which partner groups may hold of one another, and which if allowed to persist will militate against the development of trust and bonding. Many of the techniques first developed by practitioners of 'Organization Development' can be used to advantage in this situation, though one must remain sensitive to the cultural mix when deciding on specific methods. The 'confrontation-meeting' approach which often works well with North American personnel could, for instance, cause grave offence if tried with staff from East Asia. Once stereotypes are recognized and diffused, various techniques for team-building are available to promote a collaborative approach to learning between members of the alliance.

Open circulation of information

A climate of openness can also facilitate organizational learning. It involves the accessibility of information, the sharing of errors and problems, and the acceptance of conflicting views. Drummond found that Japanese managers particularly stressed the need to share problems and make information accessible in their UK subsidiary. They insisted on the importance of documenting problems when they occurred so as to avoid them in the future. The availability of information also stimulates an awareness of new needs and concepts. It requires mechanisms to encourage the circulation of such information to the persons or groups who need it. These mechanisms are obviously more effective if the barriers to learning just described are not a serious impediment.

The idea of 'redundancy' expresses an approach to information availability which is positive for organizational learning. Redundancy is 'the existence of information that goes beyond the immediate operational requirements of organizational members. In business organizations, redundancy refers to intentional overlapping of information about business activities, management responsibilities, and the company as a whole' (Nonaka and Takeuchi 1995: 80).

For learning to take place, information or a concept available to one person or group needs to be shared by others who may not need the concept immediately. It may, for example, be information on how a particular problem was tackled creatively in another one of a partner's alliances. If that information is circulated, it is accessible to others should a comparable problem arise. Redundancy also helps to build unusual communication channels, and it is indeed fostered by the melding of horizontal with the more usual vertical channels for reporting information. In this way it is associated with the interchange between hierarchy and non-hierarchy or 'heterarchy' (Hedlund 1986) which helps to promote learning on the basis of procedures which are different from those officially specified by the organization and hence based on the solutions to old problems (Nonaka and Takeuchi 1995).

Modern information technology makes a very significant contribution to the promotion of information redundancy, through its capacity for information storage and more importantly through its ability to transmit that information to virtually all points within an organization. E-mail in particular, offers access to information and the facility to communicate in ways which are not constrained by boundaries of time, geography, or formality. So long as the partners to an alliance link up their e-mail systems, these provide an excellent vehicle to circulate non-confidential information and to encourage creative commentary around it.

The case of PepsiCo, summarized in the Box, illustrates how information redundancy and modern information technology are used to promote learning within the company. Open and fast communication is coupled with an encouragement of local managers to act upon the information circulated to them, including initiatives to contact others within the company worldwide from whom they might usefully learn.

SUMMARY

This chapter has made the following key points:

- There are three levels of organizational learning: technical, systemic, and strategic. Cooperation with partner organizations offers a potential to

PepsiCo's Approach to Creating Information Redundancy

PepsiCo is one of the world's largest global food and beverage corporations, ranking nineteenth among US companies by market capitalization in 1996. It operates through many local alliances, and stresses the value of open communication both within its corporate systems and with its partners. An illustration of open communication with its partners is the fact that, in PepsiCo's China joint ventures, all the general managers speak Mandarin Chinese, and its Asia-Pacific budget meetings are conducted entirely in Mandarin.

Despite its size and scope, PepsiCo does not operate with organization charts or many formal procedures, but instead prefers to encourage informal communication flows and to promote the empowerment of its constituent units. As one corporate officer recently said, 'at the end of the day the most relevant information for me, and the job I have to do, is going to come from the people who are closest to the project . . . so the lines of communication are open at all levels'. Senior officers of the corporation stress the benefits of this approach for encouraging learning.

PepsiCo circulates information within its corporate network to the point of redundancy. Its internal e-mail system is an important vehicle for this circulation. It overcomes international time differences, permits simultaneous communication with several people, is very fast, and encourages an open, informal expression of views. Consolidated reports for different countries and regions are also widely circulated. If, as a result, managers wish to learn more about developments elsewhere in PepsiCo's worldwide operations, they have access to all the company's telephone numbers and are encouraged to make direct contacts and to decide whether to travel to the location, subject only to their travel and entertainment budgets. Many examples are told of how this rich circulation of information, and the ability to act upon it, have promoted learning and the transfer of beneficial practices throughout the corporation. For instance, it facilitated the transfer from their Hungarian operation to their China joint ventures of knowledge about ways of curbing theft on distribution runs.

Source: John Child, personal interviews.

learn at all three levels. It can provide access to techniques, facilitate the transfer of new systems, and enhance a firm's ability to undertake new strategic initiatives.

- The underlying attitude behind an alliance can be collaborative or competitive. The former allows for joint learning by both partners and is likely to be more productive over the long run. The latter creates a situation in which one partner intends to learn as much as possible from the other, while at the same time offering as little knowledge as possible.

Organizational learning becomes a political football in the competitive process between the firms and this is not a sustainable situation in the long run.

- There are several requirements for learning to take place within an alliance. The partner must have an intention to learn. It must have the necessary capacity to learn. It must also be able to convert any knowledge it gains into a usable organizational resource.
- There are various forms of learning within cooperative relationships: forced learning, imitation, blocked learning, received learning, and integrative learning. Each of these is associated with different degrees of change in understanding and in behaviour.
- The successful promotion of organizational learning within cooperative ventures requires (1) the surmounting of cognitive and emotional barriers, (2) the reduction of organizational barriers, and (3) openness of communication and an effective circulation of information.

REFERENCES

Andreu, R., and Ciborra, C. (1996), 'Core Capabilities and Information Technology: An Organizational Learning Approach', in B. Moingeon and A. Edmondson (eds.), *Organizational Learning and Competitive Advantage* (London: Sage), 121–38.

Argyris, C., and Schön, D. (1978), *Organizational Learning: A Theory of Action Perspective* (Reading, Mass.: Addison-Wesley).

Axelrod, R. (1984), *The Evolution of Cooperation* (New York: HarperCollins).

Bleeke, J., and Ernst, D. (1993) (eds.), *Collaborating to Compete: Using Strategic Alliances and Acquisitions in the Global Marketplace* (New York: Wiley).

Borys, B., and Jemison, D. B. (1989), 'Hybrid Arrangements as Strategic Alliances: Theoretical Issues in Organizational Combinations', *Academy of Management Review*, 14: 234–49.

Child, J., and David, P. (1987), *Technology and the Organization of Work* (London: National Economic Development Office).

—— and Markóczy, L. (1993), 'Host-Country Managerial Behaviour and Learning in Chinese and Hungarian Joint Ventures', *Journal of Management Studies*, 30: 611–31.

—— Markóczy, L., and Cheung, T. (1994), 'Managerial Adaptation in Chinese and Hungarian Strategic Alliances with Culturally Distinct Foreign Partners', *Advances in Chinese Industrial Studies*, 4: 211–31.

—— and Rodrigues, S. (1996), 'The Role of Social Identity in the International Transfer of Knowledge through Joint Ventures', in S. Clegg and G. Palmer (eds.), *Producing Management Knowledge* (London: Sage), 46–68.

CIBAM (1993): Centre for International Business and Management, 'The Role of International Strategic Alliances as Agents for the Improvement of Management Practice and Corporate Performance—An Outline Proposal for Research', unpublished internal paper (Judge Institute of Management Studies, University of Cambridge).

Ciborra, C. (1991), 'Alliances as Learning Experiments: Cooperation, Competition and

Change in Hightech Industries', in L. K. Mytelka (ed.), *Strategic Partnerships: States, Firms and International Competition* (London: Pinter), 51–77.

Cohen, W. M., and Levinthal, D. A. (1990), 'Absorptive Capacity: A New Perspective on Learning and Innovation', *Administrative Science Quarterly*, 35: 128–52.

De Geus, A. P. (1988), 'Planning as Learning', *Harvard Business Review*, 66/2: 70–4.

Drummond A., Jr. (1997), 'Enabling Conditions for Organizational Learning: A Study in International Business Ventures', unpublished Ph.D. thesis (Judge Institute of Management Studies, University of Cambridge, Feb.).

EBRD (1995): European Bank for Reconstruction and Development, *Transition Report* (London: EBRD).

Faulkner, D. O. (1994), 'The Royal Bank of Scotland and Banco Santander of Spain', in J. Roos (ed.), *European Casebook on Cooperative Strategies* (Hemel Hempstead: Prentice Hall), 157–73.

——(1995a), *International Strategic Alliances: Co-operating to Compete* (London: McGraw-Hill).

——(1995b), 'Strategic Alliance Evolution through Learning: The Rover/Honda Alliance', in H. Thomas, D. O'Neal, and J. Kelly (eds.), *Strategic Renaissance and Business Transformation* (Chichester: Wiley), 211–35.

Fichman, M., and Levinthal, D. A. (1991), 'Honeymoons and the Liability of Adolescence: A New Perspective on Duration Dependence in Social and Organizational Relationships', *Academy of Management Review*, 16: 442–68.

Fiol, C. M., and Lyles, M. A. (1985), 'Organizational Learning', *Academy of Management Review*, 10: 803–13.

Garrette, B., and Dussauge, P. (1996), 'Contrasting the Evolutions and Outcomes of "Scale" and "Link" Alliances: Evidence from the Global Auto Industry', *Cahiers de Recherche* (CR580/1996; Jouy-en-Josas, France: Groupe HEC).

Geringer, J. M. (1991), 'Strategic Determinants of Partner Selection Criteria in International Joint Ventures', *Journal of International Business Studies*, 22: 41–62.

Giddens, A. (1991), *Modernity and Self-Identity: Self and Society in the Later Modern Age* (Oxford: Polity Press).

Hamel, G. (1991), 'Competition for Competence and Inter-Partner Learning within International Strategic Alliances', *Strategic Management Journal*, 12: 83–103.

Hedberg, B. (1981), 'How Organizations Learn and Unlearn', in P. C. Nystrom and W. H. Starbuck (eds.), *Handbook of Organizational Design* (New York: Oxford University Press).

Hedlund, G. (1986), 'The Hypermodern MNC—A Heterarchy?', *Human Resource Management*, 25: 9–35.

Hennart, J.-F. (1988), 'A Transaction Cost Theory of Equity Joint Ventures', *Strategic Management Journal*, 9: 361–74.

Hertzfeld, J. M. (1991), 'Joint Ventures: Saving the Soviets from Perestroika', *Harvard Business Review* (Jan.–Feb.), 80–91.

Huber, G. P. (1991), 'Organizational Learning: The Contributing Processes and the Literatures', *Organization Science*, 2: 88–115.

Inkpen, A. (1995a), *The Management of International Joint Ventures: An Organizational Learning Perspective* (London: Routledge).

——(1995b), 'The Management of Knowledge in International Alliances' (Carnegie Bosch Institute Working Paper, No. 95-1; Pittsburgh, Pa.: Carnegie Mellon University).

——and Crossan, M. M. (1995), 'Believing is Seeing: Joint Ventures and Organizational Learning', *Journal of Management Studies*, 32: 595–618.

Johnson, G. (1990), 'Managing Strategic Change: The Role of Symbolic Action', *British Journal of Management*, 1: 183–200.

Jönsson, S. A., and Lundin, R. A. (1977), 'Myths and Wishful Thinking as Management Tools', in P. C. Nystrom and W. H. Starbuck (eds.), *Prescriptive Models of Organizations* (Amsterdam: North-Holland), 157–70.

Larsson, R., Bengtsson, L., Henriksson, K., and Sparks-Graham, J. (1994), 'The Interorganizational Learning Dilemma: Collective and Competitive Strategies for Network Development' (Working Paper 1994/22; Institute of Economic Research, School of Economics and Management, Lund University, Sweden).

Lawrence, P. R., and Lorsch, J. W. (1967), *Organizations and Environments* (Boston, Mass.: Harvard Business School Press).

Lorange, P., and Roos, J. (1992), *Strategic Alliances: Formation, Implementation and Evolution* (Oxford: Blackwell).

Lyles, M. A. (1988), 'Learning among Joint Venture-Sophisticated Firms', in F. Contractor and P. Lorange (eds.), *Cooperative Strategies in International Business* (New York: Lexington Books), 301–16.

Markóczy, L., and Child, J. (1995), 'International Mixed Management Organizations and Economic Liberalization in Hungary: From State Bureaucracy to New Paternalism', in H. Thomas, D. O'Neal, and J. Kelly (eds.), *Strategic Renaissance and Business Transformation* (Chichester: Wiley), 57–79.

Murray, E. and Mohon, J. (1993), 'Strategic Alliances: Gateway to the New Europe', *Long Range Planning*, 26: 102–11.

Nonaka, I., and Takeuchi, H. (1995), *The Knowledge-Creating Company* (New York: Oxford University Press).

Pawlowsky, P. (1992), 'Betriebliche Qualifikationsstrategien und Organisationales Lernen', in W. H. Staehle and P. Conrad (eds.), *Managementforschung 2* (Berlin: De Gruyter), 177–237.

Polanyi, M. (1966), *The Tacit Dimension* (London: Routledge & Kegan Paul).

Pucik, V. (1991), 'Technology Transfer in Strategic Alliances: Competitive Collaboration and Organizational Learning', in T. Agmon and M. A. von Glinow (eds.), *Technology Transfer in International Business* (Oxford: Oxford University Press), 121–38.

Schacht, O. (1995), 'The Evolution of Organizational Learning in International Strategic Alliances', unpublished M.Phil. dissertation (Judge Institute of Management Studies, University of Cambridge).

Simon, L., and Davies, G. (1996), 'A Contextual Approach to Management Learning: The Hungarian Case', *Organization Studies*, 17: 269–89.

Simonin, B. L. (1997), 'The Importance of Collaborative Know-How: An Empirical Test of the Learning Organization', *Academy of Management Journal*, 40: 1150-74.

Tajfel, H. (1982) (ed.), *Social Identity and Intergroup Relations* (Cambridge: Cambridge University Press).

Villinger, R. (1996), 'Post-Acquisition Managerial Learning in Central East Europe', *Organization Studies*, 17: 181–206.

14

The Evolving Alliance

PATTERNS OF ALLIANCE EVOLUTION

Alliances do not stand still, at least if they are to survive. As partnerships, often formed in response to challenging competitive conditions, they are founded upon relationships that have a dynamic of their own and are subject to the influence of external changes bearing not only directly upon the alliance but also on the parents separately. They have to transform and adapt with a sense of direction. The main exception are those partnerships, such as oil-exploration consortia, which are designed for one-off purposes rather than to evolve into long-term relationships. Thus, only 4 per cent of these partnerships in the petroleum industry normally last longer than five years, according to a 1995 survey published in the *Oil and Gas Journal* (cited in De Rond and Faulkner 1997).

For most alliances, however, the choice appears to be to evolve or to fail. How cooperation evolves is a question that scholars have tended so far to ignore (Ring and Van de Ven 1994; Doz 1996). The evolution of alliances can proceed along different paths and lead to quite different outcomes. It can incur periodic crises and often leads to termination of the cooperation. Experience of joint ventures with US partners suggests that there are two critical periods in their existence. The first comes at about two or three years of life, by which time an unsatisfactory relationship should have become evident. The second comes after about five or six years of alliance life, by which time one partner may be ready to move onto another arrangement. This could be disengagement from, or take over of, the other partner. It has been estimated that the median life span for alliances is only about seven years and that nearly 80 per cent of joint ventures eventually end in a sale by one of the partners (Bleeke and Ernst 1995).

This chapter begins with the idea of evolution as applied to alliances, and it notes a number of evolutionary schemata suggesting the stages through which alliances develop. It then considers some of the possible outcomes to which the evolutionary paths of alliance development can lead. A third section examines the predominantly internal factors which can affect the patterns of alliance evolution, and which are therefore relevant to management policy.

Evolution phases

Evolution in relation to strategic alliances needs careful definition. As a scientific term evolution calls to mind, most prominently, the Darwinian/Lamarckian debate over the possibility of passing on acquired characteristics genetically. Lamarck believed this to be possible. So, if someone were to develop a particular skill, such as piano-playing, his heirs would be more genetically disposed to be good piano players. Darwin denied this, claiming that species evolved by natural selection such that the animals with the best fit with the environment were the ones which survived and continued the species through their progeny. Clearly genetic change, if it were possible, would come about far more rapidly if Lamarck were right than under Darwinian rules. However, the scientific debate was won by Darwin.

Evolution in this sense can, of course, be used only as a metaphorical term in the study of management, since companies do not breed in a genetic sense. As such, the scientifically discredited Lamarckian theory returns as a useful concept. It is perfectly possible to conceive of companies learning, adapting, and then passing on their knowledge or know-how to future generations of managers, thus giving their company a competitive advantage. The Darwinian process may, however, take place in populations of companies (Hannan and Freeman 1989), as those with the best environmental fit survive in markets requiring companies with certain characteristics, and those without them go bankrupt.

When the term 'evolution' is applied to cooperative arrangements like strategic alliances, the term is not normally used with much scientific rigour. Here the definition offered by the *Oxford English Dictionary* is probably most appropriate, namely, 'any process of gradual change occurring in something, especially from a simpler to a more complicated or advanced state'. In this sense, the evolution of alliances may be taken to mean merely that they develop in scale, scope, or form over time. Since this development takes place in relation both to the partners and to the environment of their cooperative operations, evolution is a dynamic rather than simply an additive process. The most effective alliances seem to be those that show evolution over time, rather than merely a competent pursuit of their objectives agreed at set-up.

Achrol, Scheer, and Stern (1990) describe the four stages of alliance development in their schema as *entrepreneurship, collectivity,* and *formalization,* leading to *domain elaboration.* Thus alliances are typically fluid and creative at the outset. This stage is followed by one of the integration of alliance personnel to its purpose, where a defined sense of mission is developed. The formalization stage involves the development of systems and procedures; ultimately the domain-elaboration stage is one of self-renewal, where the alliance's flexibility is renewed, its scope redefined, and a new and expanded quest embarked upon.

Lorange and Roos (1992), who distinguish three main phases in the development of alliances—formation, implementation, and evolution—stress that evolution is far more important to an alliance than control by its partners. Moreover, 'we see a need to change the control emphasis of a strategic alliance as it evolves from the hands-on physical control mode to a more decentralized financial control form. It goes without saying that the executives involved in the management of the strategic alliance from the two parents' sides must be sensitive to how they should shift their emphasis on control over time' (Lorange and Roos 1992: 121).

Evolution will vary in the form it takes, and this is dependent on, *inter alia*, the initial alliance form adopted. A joint venture is set up in the form of a hierarchical company and, with the support of its founding parents, may evolve like any other company. Lorange and Roos describe the generic evolution of a successful joint venture as commencing with responsibilities firmly in both partners' hands, developing into a situation in which the venture claims more responsibilities for itself. At this stage, one partner may become the more dominant. The third stage will be achieved as the venture becomes a freestanding entity with its own independent management. The joint venture may, like Unilever, ultimately come to dwarf its parents in power and commercial strength. It may acquire new shareholders, extend its role, recruit staff unconnected with the parents and in fact do anything within its articles of association. The same applies to a consortium that is given a separate corporate existence. Airbus Industrie, having been formed in 1970 as a *Groupement d'Intérêt Économique* under EU regulations with profits and losses accruing to the four partner companies rather than to the consortium itself, was in 1997 being reformed into a limited company.

Lyles and Reger's (1993) study of how a joint venture developed illustrates a number of these points: different phases in alliance evolution, the conditions affecting its degree of autonomy *vis-à-vis* parent companies, and eventual absorption by one of the parents. The outlines of this case are given in the Box. The case also exemplifies the most common end-point of joint-venture evolution—namely, an outright purchase by one of the partners.

Collaborations are different in that, lacking a corporate structure, issues of autonomy are unlikely to arise in the way that they are liable to do with joint ventures and subsidiaries. Collaborations are destined to remain just that or to evolve into another form. They may, of course, as did the Royal Bank of Scotland and the Banco Santander, also create both consortia and joint ventures as part of their overall collaboration. Since the relationships are directly between the partners rather than via a third, jointly created organization, they can be very complex and require a level of intimacy not present in most joint ventures. The 'gatekeepers' for each partner are likely to play an important role in shaping the evolution of the collaboration. The effectiveness with which they perform that role will depend on the standing they enjoy within their respective companies and the quality of their personal relationships, as well as their personal ability and vision.

Evolution of a the ACE Consortium

This joint venture was established in 1946 and evolved over a period of thirty-two years. It was formed, to produce speciality industrial machine tools, by seven firms, two from the USA and the others from five different European countries. One of the American firms, ACE, wanted to enter the European market with its existing speciality industrial machine tools, while the other firms were interested primarily in finding a reliable supplier of machine tools produced locally in Europe under licence from the second American partner.

The alliance passed through three main phases. The first lasted ten years and was one of slow and rather unfocused development under a senior management supplied by three of the partners. The second phase lasted a further twelve years under an entrepreneurial CEO supplied by one of the American partners. This period saw the redesign of the American partner's products for the European market, and an expansion of both supporting functional activities and new plant locations. During this phase, the joint venture was highly profitable and expanded successfully. Indeed, it developed a superior product to ACE's own which brought the joint venture into conflict with that parent. The joint-venture CEO was able during this period to increase the joint venture's autonomy through several sources of upward influence: his successful entrepreurial leadership, the seeking of support from the parent company's customers, differentiation of the joint venture's product, and informal relationships with parent-company managers. Four years into this second phase of evolution, ACE increased its equity position to 75 per cent. This appears to reflect its desire to strengthen overall control, as well as to invest further into success.

The CEO's retirement led into a third phase of evolution. The replacement CEO was less entrepreneurial. During this phase, the joint venture's product line was reduced and it now reported directly into the relevant product division within the dominant parent company. Ten years on, the joint venture was completely acquired by the majority parent company.

Source: Lyles and Reger (1993).

More loosely structured cooperative arrangements are less likely to evolve very far. *Ad hoc* pools reflect collaborative arrangements that require no more than a bare minimum of resourcing, usually for a limited period of time. They are normally based purely on contractual agreements and do not return any surplus funds into the alliance itself. Therefore, the prospects of an *ad hoc* pool evolving are small. A successful *ad hoc* pool may, however, provide the basis for more intensive arrangements in the future, in the form of a consortium. Evolution is more likely to take place in a consortium, as the partners' interests and capabilities synchronize, and they learn as a result. However, the evolution in this case is frequently limited to the re-creation of complementary roles in a new follow-up consortium rather than developing into more sophisticated forms of cooperation (De Rond and Faulkner 1997).

As Bleeke and Ernst (1995) point out, the various alliance forms are frequently likely to end up as a sale of one partner to the other, or of one partner's joint-venture holding to the other, in the dissolution of the alliance, or in the agreement of the partners to extend or contract the range of activities they carry out together. There is ample evidence for all these possible outcomes, and no one particular outcome is inevitable. Outcomes depend crucially upon the ongoing relationships between the partners and the partners' changing strategic imperatives. Murray and Mahon (1993) depict alliances as exhibiting a life cycle as illustrated in Fig. 14.1.

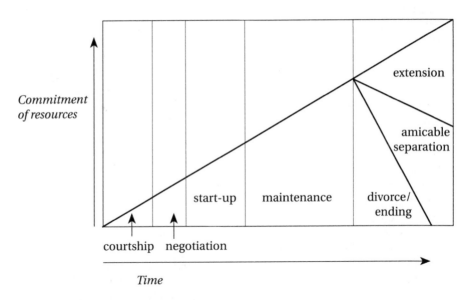

Fig. 14.1. A life-cycle model of alliance evolution
Source: Murray and Mahon (1993).

The two axes of the figure indicate time and commitment of resources by the alliance partners. Alliances begin with a courtship stage, as does any relationship. If this goes well, detailed negotiations follow to develop an agreement. Then follows stage three, the start-up phase, in which joint activity begins, and substantial resources are committed. Murray and Mahon describe the next stage as the maintenance phase, which involves the routinization of operations and reporting relationships, as the organizations continue to work together on an operational basis. This is, of course, the phase when the ultimate success of the alliance will be tested, as it gains in responsibilities, continues in steady mode, or declines in importance and becomes marginalized by the partners. The fifth stage of the life cycle is described as the ending, which can take a number of forms:

1. the end of the specific relationship with extensions into other areas of mutual interest;
2. an amicable separation with no immediate further joint activity;
3. a hostile parting, inhibiting the likelihood of any future joint activity.

The time line for the fourth stage may, of course, be short or extended to an infinite length, depending on circumstances.

Schacht (1995) takes issue with Murray and Mahon's view that the options for the ending phase of an alliance are limited to extension, separation, or divorce. Continuing at reduced levels, for instance, is a real possibility. Schacht argues that neat classifications of alliance evolution are oversimplified. Instead, he seeks a more complex and contingent prognosis of alliance evolution, tying it more closely to organizational learning. 'A more comprehensive international strategic alliance life cycle model . . . would have to recognize that, when new projects are initiated within ISAs, prior progress along the various learning curves need not be lost. Subsequent projects could start at higher levels of organizational knowledge about technologies, opportunities and systems/procedures' (Schacht 1995: 62). Schacht emphasizes the need for an active stance towards managing the life cycle of an alliance and relating it to the possibilities for organizational learning, if a required pattern of alliance evolution is to be achieved. He also stresses the role of organizational politics in influencing the evolution of organizational learning. The existence of the 'not-invented here' syndrome, for example, may have a strong impact on reducing the achievement of organizational learning, and thus inhibit the evolution of the alliances.

Ring and Van de Ven (1994) view the evolution of alliances, or, as they call them, Cooperative Inter-Organizational Relationships (IORs), 'as consisting of a repetitive sequence of negotiation, commitment, and execution stages, each of which is assessed in terms of efficiency and equity . . . the duration of each stage varies according to the uncertainty of issues involved, the reliance on trust among the parties to a cooperative IOR, and the role relationships of the parties' (Ring and Van de Ven 1994: 97).

In the *negotiation* stage, the intended partners develop joint expectations and make sense of the mission they are to embark upon. Through formal negotiations and informal sense-making they assess the various uncertainties associated with the deal, and form views on trust, commitment, respective roles, equity, and efficiency. In the *commitment* stage, the terms and governance structures of the alliance are established. The degree of legal formality with which this stage is endowed varies with the nature and culture of the partners. In the *execution* stage, the commitments and rules of action are put into effect and business actions are initiated, such as the purchasing of materials, the production of goods, and the administration of the agreement towards an agreed set of objectives.

Although the first cycle of the IOR's activity will no doubt be the most involved and protracted, owing to the high level of uncertainties involved in partners who have not worked together before, further proposed projects that cause the alliance to take on further responsibilities and hence evolve will, in Ring and Van de Ven's view, go through the same three-stage process. This process was very clearly visible in the 'five trades' described by Roland Bertodo that characterized the successive projects of the Rover–Honda collaboration (see Box).

The Evolution of the Rover–Honda Alliance

The evolution of the Rover–Honda alliance took the following path. At the commencement there was a limited licensing arrangement for Rover to manufacture the Triumph Acclaim from Honda 'knocked-down' kits. The next phase was the development of the Rover 200, which was a Japanese-designed car with Rover fenders, wheels, bumpers, and interior. There was also an agreement at this time for Rover to make cars for Honda. Rover provided the missing European values in terms of styling that Honda needed. In 1986 the alliance evolved further with the launch of the Rover 800 and the Honda Legend. This involved the two companies working together in joint design and manufacturing teams. In 1989 the next project—the Rover 200/400 with its twin the Honda Concerto—was embarked upon. This involved further development of the alliance, as it was the product of joint development and co-production plus cross-sourcing of components. In 1990 the two companies embarked on further integrated production and development and carried out a 20 per cent share exchange. The alliance had evolved from a simple arm's-length licensing agreement in 1979 to a situation in 1990 with joint design teams working on new models, joint production of each other's cars, joint sourcing of components, and shared R&D, yet the companies retained their separate identities.

Source: Faulkner (1995*b*).

Evolution in alliances also depends upon the development of personal relationships between those involved in the cooperation. In its absence, role behaviour predominates and the alliance is unlikely to evolve. As Ring and Van de Ven (1994: 103) put it:

Through repeated interactions over time . . . these formal role relationships and expectations become socially embedded in an incremental and escalating progression of socialization, accommodation, and normative expectations that mutually arise among cooperative IOR parties. Qua persona behaviour substitutes for role behaviour as personal relationships build and psychological contracts deepen.

Whereas some commentators ascribe the evolution or dissolution of alliances over time to the degree of matching they are able to achieve with the exogenous factors prevailing in the external environment, Ring and Van de Ven concentrate on the internal behavioural factors and governance structures that develop between the executives of the alliance partners. They conclude (1994: 113), 'As the uncertainty, complexity, and duration of economic transactions within and between firms increase, it becomes increasingly important for scholars and managers to understand developmental processes of how equity, trust, conflict resolution procedures, and internal governance structures emerge, evolve and dissolve over time.'

Outcomes of evolution

Bleeke and Ernst (1995) conclude from their experience with over 200 alliances, mainly those in which a separate entity like a joint venture is created, that the way alliances evolve is crucially dependent on the relative bargaining power of the partners. This, in turn, relates to the initial strengths and weaknesses of the partners, how these strengths and weaknesses change over time, and the potential for competitive conflict between the partners. In the light of these factors, these authors identify six patterns of alliance evolution (1995: 103):

1. *Collisions between partners.* These alliances are inherently unstable. They involve the core businesses of two strong direct competitors. Owing to competitive tensions, these alliances tend to be of short duration and fail to achieve their strategic and financial goals. Most 'collisions between competitors' end in dissolution, acquisition by one partner, or merger. An example was the alliance between General Electric and Rolls-Royce which broke up in 1986 with accusations that Rolls-Royce had introduced a directly competitive aero engine. The motives for establishing such alliances can include an exploitation of market power, or a period of trial marriage prior to a merger.

2. *Alliances of complementary equals.* These alliances are, by contrast, potentially stable and long-lasting. They involve two strong and complementary partners which remain strong during the course of the alliance. Because they are building on each other's strengths rather than trying to plug gaps, the partners obtain mutual benefit from their cooperation, which is likely to last much longer than the five-to-seven years' average lifespan for alliances. The alliance between Rover and Honda exemplifies this kind of alliance, as well as its potential to broaden and deepen over the course of time. This potential means that the partners should concentrate on assessing ways in which the alliance should evolve so as to enhance the value of their stake in it.

3. *Alliances of the weak.* This is the case where two or more weak companies join forces in the expectation that this will improve their market power. It was clearly an important motive for the formation of Airbus Industrie. Bleeke and Ernst argue that in such alliances the weak usually

grow weaker, the alliance then fails, followed quickly by dissolution or acquisition by a third party. Airbus Industrie shows that this is certainly not an inevitable prognosis, though clearly, if a partner to this kind of alliance sees it simply as a refuge from competition, it will very soon become a lame duck which pulls down the whole cooperative enterprise.

4. *Bootstrap alliances*. This is the case where a weak company tries to use an alliance with a stronger one to improve its capabilities. This strategy can be successful in a minority of cases, resulting in the strengthening of the weaker partner. The partnership then develops into an alliance of equals, or alternatively the partners separate after the weak partner has achieved a capacity to compete on its own. The weaker partner must have a clear intention and plan to learn, and the stronger partner must be willing to provide such help, if this strategy is to succeed. Bootstrapping is often the hope of partners from developing countries, who view alliances with stronger foreign companies as an opportunity to acquire technological and other expertise which they need to become internationally competitive. The trend, as noted in Chapter 12, is, however, for the stronger foreign partners to acquire increasing control over the weaker ones and eventually to buy them out. Bleeke and Ernst themselves conclude that this is the usual outcome of alliances falling into this category.

5. *Disguised sales*. In these alliances, a weak company becomes the partner of a strong company, often one with which it is, or will become, in direct competition. The weaker partner remains weak and is eventually acquired by the stronger one. Disguised sales rarely last more than five years. The problem is that alliances are often pursued as a second-best strategy when their management is unwilling to sell a weak company.

6. *Evolution to a sale*. In this case, the alliance starts with two strong and compatible partners. However, competitive tensions develop and/or bargaining power shifts, and one of the partners ultimately sells out to the other. Nevertheless, because of the complementarity between the partners, these alliances often succeed in meeting their initial objectives and provide value to the partners. For this reason, they may well survive beyond the average life span for alliances.

Bleeke and Ernst argue that it is dangerous for companies to ignore the high probability that any alliance will end up in a sale by one of the partners to the other(s). If managers do not appreciate that an alliance will probably end up in a sale, they run the risk of ending up with an unplanned sale which fails to secure maximum shareholder value. Their point is that managers should always bear in mind that alliances quite often turn out to be transitory arrangements which, nevertheless, serve an important strategic purpose. The implication is that an alliance can be a good vehicle for acquisition, divestiture, or other goals, so long as its evolution is planned. In order to be in a position to plan for a particular path of alliance evolution, an initial evaluation is critical: 'Such evaluation can help companies avoid disastrous partnerships and unanticipated sales of important businesses. It can help managers choose corporate partners that will advance their organization's long-term strategic plan. And it can help reveal opportunities in which an alliance may be used as a low-risk, low-cost option on a future acquisition' (Bleeke and Ernst 1995: 97).

Bleeke and Ernst conclude that categories 1 and 3 in their typology—collisions between partners and alliances of the weak—almost always fail and should be avoided. This requires some qualification. If competing partners decide to merge, following a trial period, then the merger may well be more effectively planned and managed because it was preceded by a period of cooperation. Secondly, alliances of the weak can succeed if a productive division of labour is worked out between the partners, and if as a result the deployment of scarce resources (such as technical staff and R&D facilities) can be optimized and economies of scale realized. They also assert that type 5, disguised sales, are based on shaky grounds.

Child and Rodrigues (1996) also identify four different paths in the evolution of international alliances, with particular reference to knowledge transfer between the partners. They suggest that alliance evolution depends both on the balance of power between the partners and on the distance between their respective social (cultural) identities. Their analysis has the merit of bringing to attention the part that cultural distance (versus fit) may play in determining whether alliances evolve towards a more intensive, mutual form of cooperation or not. There are several conditions which enhance this positive evolution of alliances.

NECESSARY CONDITIONS

Alliances are normally set up for specific purposes. They may be focused on the synergies available from the fusion of key competencies from the partners directed towards a specific target, or the interaction may be more complex. In successful alliances new projects and responsibilities are given by the partners to the alliance over time. If the initial purpose or relationship scope remains the only one, the alliance may be unlikely to enter the dynamic category. Lorange and Probst (1987) emphasize that many alliance failures are due to the fact that they have not had sufficient adaptive properties built into them to cope with evolutionary pressures. Some redundant resources must, they believe, be committed to the alliances to achieve sufficient flexibility for development. This is also emphasized by Nonaka (1989). The combating of entropy is seen by Thorelli (1986) as the key reason for pursuing the path of evolution, and a feeling that where there is no longer growth the onset of decay may not be far away.

Dynamic alliances like ICL–Fujitsu show a flow of new projects, additional areas of cooperation, and flexible adjustment to change. What started as a technical support alliance between ICL and Fujitsu in 1981 has since led to a far-ranging technology, product, and marketing alliance. It culminated in Fujitsu's acquisition of ICL and its incorporation into the Fujitsu 'family'. Fujitsu has, however, maintained ICL's identity and stressed its continuing role as a partner rather than as a subsidiary.

Less successful alliances may also go through substantial developments, but exhibit major limitations. Courtaulds and Nippon Paint, after a period in which the alliance ceased to evolve having achieved its initial objectives, then pursued the new-projects trail with a coil-coating joint venture into Continental Europe, and closer R&D cooperation. However, mutual understanding between these partners required substantial reinforcement following a difficult period and the realization by Courtaulds that Nippon was becoming a world-class player and a potentially serious competitor.

Alliances rated only limitedly successful show little sign of evolution. ICI Pharma was set up with an arrangement that proved insufficiently attractive to ICI for it to wish to put more new projects through the venture. As a result the venture continues during the life of its existing product portfolio, but may have few prospects beyond that.

Flexible adjustment

Flexibility in the relationship between partners is obviously an important success factor, since it implies that, when circumstances change, the alliance is allowed to reflect this in a sensitive way. Dynamic alliances tend to show considerable flexibility during their life. ICL–Fujitsu, for example, had to cope with a changing relationship as Fujitsu moved into the position of a majority equity-holder and then sole owner, and suppress any possible risk to the relationship from that development. It seems to have achieved this with sensitivity. The Rover–Honda alliance moved through different levels of activity, each of them placing different requirements and levels of strain on the people involved in the relationship. They coped well owing to a willingness and ability on both sides to adapt to changing circumstances.

In less successful alliances, lack of flexibility may be a major problem. ICI Pharma, for example, was somewhat inflexible not to have renegotiated the troublesome Sumitomo agreement, as was Courtaulds with Nippon Paint for some while.

Balanced development

The idea of balanced development suggests that a key condition for the success of an alliance is that one partner does not move strongly ahead of the other in its strategic and other benefits. However, it may be hypothesized that, so long as one partner feels itself to have done well from the alliance, it will not be too concerned if the other partner has done even better. Such matters are, at all events, difficult to judge objectively, and are highly dependent upon perception. The ICL–Fujitsu alliance, for example, is very dynamic, yet clearly ICL is very dependent on Fujitsu for its future. Yet ICL executives professed themselves very happy with the alliance, even when Fujitsu had moved to a position of owning 80 per cent of their company. However, Killing's (1983) findings that alliances where one partner is dominant are often the most successful may well be relevant here, for they suggest that a dominant partner removes much of the ambiguity from a relationship, and introduces some of the advantages of hierarchy. Clarity of authority may then lead to improved performance, as the inefficiencies of consensus-building (Kanter 1989) are replaced by clear leadership.

Recriminations over relative benefits are more likely in relatively unsuccessful alliances than in successful ones. ICI, for example, reported unbalanced benefits to the partners, presumably reflecting their view that Sumitomo struck a deal at the outset that was clearly more profitable to the Japanese company than to ICI. It does not seem therefore that the condition of balanced benefits is a key one in alliance development, although at the extreme it may become a source of contention if other matters are going wrong. The failed alliance between AT&T and Olivetti is a case in point.

De Rond and Faulkner (1997) point to another aspect of balanced development or 'symmetry'. This stems from evidence that firms are vulnerable to dissolution either if a partner shuts down or if partners form a collaborative relationship with a new partner (Singh and Mitchell 1996). Consequently, companies are advised to identify potential new partners, even while cooperating with their current partners, and to develop and retain some proprietary skills. This may, of course, offend current partners and threaten to undermine their trust in the alliance, if it is not pursued wisely. Nevertheless, a careful balance between maintaining independent strength and cooperating with others appears unavoidable, especially in industries experiencing high levels of technological change.

Trust and bonding

Chapter 3 indicated how mutual trust between the partners can, as it develops through various stages, nurture the further evolution of their cooperation. The process of establishing trust between the partners can be provided with an initial foundation if they arrive at a clear specification of their mutual contributions and obligations, and assess the strength of the inducements or threats that remove or offset advantages to the other partner in reneging on the agreement. These conditions permit a calculation to be made of the advantages of cooperation and of developing the cooperative relationship.

If initial difficulties can be avoided or overcome, and if the alliance proves to be an economic success, it is likely to mature into an organization with an increasing sense of its own identity and culture. Unless the alliance is established for a one-off or temporary purpose only, or as a stepping stone for one partner to absorb the other, the partners may well not place any time limit upon its potential life. The very success of an alliance will tend to encourage the partner/parent companies to grant it an increasing measure of autonomy, and also provide the management of the alliance with the legitimacy to take its own decisions (Lyles and Reger 1993). This evolutionary process permits stable, ongoing relationships to develop, relationships both between people in the partner organizations who have a responsibility for (or interest in) the alliance and between people working on an everyday basis in the alliance's own organization. They are in a position to accumulate knowledge about each other, and this tends to reinforce the relationship. Moreover, the success of the alliance in meeting partner interests also preserves the initial and fundamental basis for their relationship which lies in calculation.

As relationships develop over time within the context of a successful collaboration, so there is a natural tendency for those concerned to identify increasingly with one another's interests as well as for emotional ties to grow. In this way, 'bonding' can form between partners, which Faulkner (1995a) has identified as being, in turn, a significant requirement for alliance success. Thus a virtuous cycle may be established, which reinforces both trust and the cooperation which it nurtures. This cycle can, of course, be broken and reversed.

Bonding may occur if the trust and cooperation between partners reaches a stage at which it is underpinned by a strong mutual identification based on shared norms and even a degree of affection. Thorelli (1986) has argued that alliances which do not consciously evolve and create bonding mechanisms are affected by entropic forces, and gradually either cease to be important, or even move towards dissolution. Three possible bonding mechanisms have been identified as means whereby alliances may achieve effective bonding. Clearly all three do not need to be present in all alliances, and there may be other mechanisms. However, if no bonding mechanisms are present, the prognosis for the alliance may be poor, as the partners may be regarding it more as a specific resource or skill substitution mechanism, rather than as an interactive collaboration.

Important bonding mechanisms are:

1. successfully going through an external challenge together;
2. exchanging personnel at a number of levels on a regular basis;
3. developing a culture that is a combination of the partners' cultures.

Clearly bonding will be easier to achieve in a joint-venture company, where the staff are all working together, than in a collaboration, where typically they are not. Personnel exchange may be in the form of secondment to the joint venture, which has a very different impact on the individual to personnel exchange to the partner companies in collaborations.

Bonding is a more difficult task within collaborations, since the companies relate at an overall corporate level, but still only a part of the partner's personnel have close exposure to the personnel of the other partner company. Thus Rover manufacturing, design, and technology staff had close relationships with Honda personnel, but sales and marketing personnel did not. In these circumstances, bonding strength varied considerably. It was high, and deliberately so, in Rover–Honda and ICL–Fujitsu, who claimed to have surmounted an external challenge successfully together, to exchange personnel regularly and to be in the process of developing a combined culture. Neither Imperial–Wintermans nor Courtaulds–Nippon Paint made any substantial claims to bonding in any of these areas. Of the limited category of alliances, lack of bonding is frequently a problem. ICI Pharma, for example, made no claims to bonding with its partner.

Bonding appears, therefore, to be significant for successful alliance development, but to present different challenges for joint ventures and non-joint ventures. For joint ventures, bonding within the venture seems relatively straightforward, but the relationship between the partner companies themselves, and between the partner companies and the joint venture, is more complex and difficult. In collaborations, the challenge is to develop a mutually effective culture that spreads outwards even to personnel not directly involved with alliance matters. In the absence of this, the cultural interface merely moves from that between the partner companies back into the partner companies themselves, where different cultures develop between those who are and those who are not actively involved in the alliances.

We emphasized the fact that, while the success of cooperation between organizations requires the presence of clear net benefits to each of them, the quality of that cooperation and its ability to evolve constructively depends in turn to a considerable extent upon the relatively few individuals who are the active links between the organizations. The ability to achieve bonding is very much in the hands of those primary actors. As well as gatekeepers and the other staff from each partner who are regularly working together, top partner managers must also be included in this category. Chapter 8 noted how top-management commitment to alliances has emerged as a major factor in their success, partly because bonding at that level strongly encourages cooperation lower down.

Sometimes the process of bonding begins remarkably soon and actually assists the clarification of economic possibilities and the partner's willingness to commit the investment of time and money to realize these. For example, a medium-size British company producing advanced electronic equipment acquired a relatively small American company which possessed technology that would enable it to enter a new and potentially significant product domain. The American company had, as one of its customers, a very large fast-moving consumer-goods manufacturer, based in the USA but with a global scope. It was a very minor supplier to this consumer-goods giant, but the British acquirer appreciated the possibility of developing an important bridge via the customer into a large potential market. According to our informants in the British company, its senior management consciously cultivated

the vice-president in charge of procurement for the consumer-goods corporation to establish a personal relationship between him and its own CEO. Within
eighteen months, a genuine friendship grew between them to the extent that
their two families were spending their holidays together. This bonding
between the two executives has been instrumental in enabling the two companies to collaborate, with a minimum of legal formalities, in developing suitable applications of the new technology. As they continued to collaborate,
both parties increasingly appreciated the economic benefits that could derive
from the successful application of the new technology and which will doubtless build the 'hard' foundation for their future partnership.

Organizational learning

As described in Chapter 13, organizational learning is an important key to the
successful evolution of alliances (see also Doz 1996). The example just cited
could be regarded as one in which the willingness of partners to learn was initially assisted by personal bonding and where the learning then led to a deepening appreciation of the economic potential of further collaboration.
Alliances in which partners actively learn from each other are likely to appreciate the value of the alliance more strongly than others. This is particularly
likely in relation to the skills in which they felt deficient when seeking a partner, but it also extends to other unexpected spin-off learning.

If an alliance in which learning has been achieved should suddenly terminate, the partners will be able to count the benefits in terms of the development of their competencies. For those alliances where partners merely engage
in mutual skill substitution rather than corporate learning, the loss of a partner is inevitably more damaging. Nothing may have been learnt and there is a
sudden gap in the provision of the functions carried out by the former partner.
As the previous chapter noted, alliance partners bent on evolution through
learning should ensure that this learning is disseminated throughout their
organization and not just to the personnel directly interfacing with the
alliance partner. They should also set up a system for regularly reviewing what
they have learnt as a result of the alliance, and set targets for the next phase of
learning.

SUMMARY

This chapter takes note of a number of life-cycle evolutionary schemata that
have been proposed by commentators, and suggests that such cycles may be
conditioned to move from one stage to the next in the process of evolution
predominantly by internal factors that emerge within the alliance. Important
amongst these are the development of personal relationships between execu-

tives in the partner companies such that they enhance the trust, bonding, and commitment which provide the cement for all relationships, balanced development, and flexibility. Emphasis has been placed on the close relationship of alliance evolution, as exemplified by new projects and new responsibilities accruing to the alliance, to the achievement by both partners of clearly identifiable organizational learning. It could even be argued that, when partners in the alliance cease to learn together, this will be a sign of the onset of a terminal stage in alliance evolution—namely, dissolution or acquisition by one partner.

REFERENCES

Achrol, R. S., Scheer, L. K., and Stern, L. W. (1990), *Designing Successful Trans-organizational Marketing Alliances* (Report 90–118; Cambridge, Mass.: Marketing Science Institute).

Bleeke, J., and Ernst, D. (1995), 'Is Your Strategic Alliance Really a Sale?', *Harvard Business Review* (Jan.–Feb.), 97–105.

Child, J., and Rodrigues, S. (1996), 'The Role of Social Identity in the International Transfer of Knowledge through Joint Ventures', in S. R. Clegg and G. Palmer (eds.), *The Politics of Management Knowledge* (London: Sage), 46–68.

De Rond, M., and Faulkner, D. O. (1997), 'The Evolution of Cooperation in Non-Joint Venture Strategic Alliances', paper presented to the Fourth International Conference on Multi-Organizational Partnerships and Cooperative Strategy, Oxford, July.

Doz, Y. L. (1996), 'The Evolution of Cooperation in Strategic Alliances: Initial Conditions or Learning Processes?', *Strategic Management Journal*, 17: 55–83.

Faulkner, D. O. (1995a), *International Strategic Alliances: Co-operating to Compete* (Maidenhead: McGraw-Hill).

——(1995b), 'Strategic Alliance Evolution through Learning: The Rover/Honda Alliance', in H. Thomas, D. O'Neal, and J. Kelly (eds.), *Strategic Renaissance and Business Transformation* (Chichester: Wiley), 211–35.

Hannan, M. T., and Freeman, J. (1989), *Organizational Ecology* (Cambridge, Mass.: Harvard University Press).

Kanter, R. M. (1989), *When Giants Learn to Dance* (London: Simon & Schuster).

Killing, J. P. (1983), *Strategies for Joint Venture Success* (New York: Praeger).

Lorange, P., and Probst, G. J. B. (1987), 'Joint Ventures as Self-Organizing Systems: A Key to Successful Joint Venture Design and Implementation', *Columbia Journal of World Business*, 22: 71–7.

——and Roos, J. (1992), *Strategic Alliances: Formation, Implementation, and Evolution* (Oxford: Blackwell).

Lyles, M. A., and Reger, R. K. (1993), 'Managing for Autonomy in Joint Ventures: A Longitudinal Study of Upward Influence', *Journal of Management Studies*, 30: 383–404.

Murray, E. A., and Mahon, J. F. (1993), 'Strategic Alliances: Gateway to the New Europe?', *Long Range Planning*, 26: 102–11.

Nonaka, I. (1988), 'Toward Middle–Up–Down Management: Accelerating Information Creation', *Sloan Management Review* (Spring), 9–18.

Ring, P. S., and Van de Ven, A. H. (1994), 'Developmental Processes of Cooperative Interorganizational Relationships', *Academy of Management Review*, 19/1: 90–118.

Schacht, O. (1995), 'The Evolution of Organizational Learning in International Strategic Alliances', unpublished M.Phil. dissertation (Judge Institute of Management Studies, University of Cambridge).

Singh, K., and Mitchell, W. (1996), 'Precarious Collaborations: Business Survival after Partners Shut Down or Form New Partnerships', *Strategic Management Journal* (Summer), 99–116.

Thorelli, H. B. (1986), 'Networks: Between Markets and Hierarchies', *Strategic Management Journal*, 7: 37–51.

15

Conclusion and the Future

AN OVERVIEW

This book has covered a wide range of issues relevant to the creation and management of cooperative strategy in the present age. This concluding chapter begins by drawing these topics together in an overview. It then goes on to argue that important benefits could arise from bringing cooperation further into the mainstream of management thinking and practice, and it focuses on two ways forward. The first is to give more attention to the challenge of managing cooperation and developing it to a mature and fruitful condition. The second is to appreciate the key role that cooperative strategies can play in enabling organizations to cope with the uncertainties of new highly complex business environments. These themes reflect the emphasis in this book on the *process* and *context* of cooperation.

Perspectives

An overview of the main perspectives which can be brought to bear on cooperative strategy and the management of alliances indicates that they provide numerous insights. Most of these are still underdeveloped in two respects. First, there are still potential synergies which could come about from combining some of them. For example, both the iterated form of game theory and work on trust-based relations should, if brought together, offer valuable understandings on how cooperation can be strengthened as a cumulative process over time. In so doing, it would be useful to combine the rational calculative approach of game theory with the more sentient and normative features of social interaction which are given a prominent place in theories of trust. The second area of underdevelopment is the drawing-out of practical guidelines from the essentially academic insights offered by the various perspectives. We have seen how such insights bear upon both the formulation of cooperative strategy and its implementation. Market-power theory, transaction-cost economics, game theory, and strategic-management theory are all oriented towards cooperation as a strategic choice. Transaction-cost economics and game theory also address certain aspects of ongoing cooperative relationships, which are the primary concern of agency theory and organization theory.

There are several implications for the practice of cooperative strategy which can be drawn from these perspectives. From the economic perspective, cooperative strategies can enhance market power. Furthermore, one of the considerations in choosing whether to cooperate with other firms, and the form of that cooperation, is the level of transaction costs involved, and, in the absence of common interests and mutual trust, an alliance needs to provide each partner with adequate incentives not to take advantage of the other and with systems to monitor their respective contributions.

From a game-theory perspective, there is a need to balance and reconcile cooperation and competition between partners. Highly self-interested behaviour in business relations tends to become self-defeating. If cooperation between partners is established according to clear principles such as 'firm but fair', there is a good possibility that their relationship will become progressively self-strengthening.

In strategic-management theory, executives need to be clear about their motives for adopting a cooperative strategy in general and for entering into specific alliances in particular. The selection of a suitable partner is of fundamental importance and likely to have a major bearing on the success of the alliance. In this regard it is important for alliance partners to work out a good mutual strategic fit, and then to optimize the process of their cooperation by improving cultural fit.

From the perspective of organization theory, the ability of a partner to exercise control over an alliance will be significantly determined by its dependence on the other(s) for the provision of non-substitutable resources which are crucial for the alliance's operations. This implies that the formal rights inherent in equity share or contracts may not be sufficient to ensure control. Alliances are hybrid organizations which combine some features of conventional hierarchical management with those of networks. Their organization has to recognize and support a number of dilemmas which stem from this hybrid nature, such as the tension between the ability to control an alliance and to learn from it.

Trust

Cooperation between organizations creates mutual dependence and requires trust in order to succeed. This comes down to trust between the individuals who are involved in the alliance. Uncertainty about partners' motives, and a lack of detailed knowledge about how they operate, require that a basis for trust be found for cooperation to get under way in the first place.

We have suggested that there are identifiable stages in the evolution of trust.

Calculation, then understanding, and then bonding progressively provide the foundations on which trust can develop. Trust is seen to develop gradually as the partners move from one stage to the next. This is consistent with the view that trust can be strengthened by the partners building up the number of positive exchanges between themselves. As the partners become increasingly aware of the mutual investment they have made in their relationship, the benefits they are deriving from it, and the costs of reneging, they have more incentive to carry it forward. In this sense, the trust between the partners will benefit from the 'shadow of the future' (Axelrod 1984). The view of trust as an evolving process provides valuable clues about the way in which cooperative relationships can be developed both within and between organizations.

While alliances between firms do sometimes arise on the basis of already existing personal friendships, they usually start off on impersonal terms. In other words, the partners have to calculate that, under conditions of limited knowledge, the potential benefits of cooperation outweigh the risks of partners reneging on their commitments. Once an alliance is being implemented, the growing body of shared information and mutual knowledge should enhance trust between the partners, because it increases their ability to understand each other better, and hence predict each other's actions. Eventually, the experience of working together may produce a sense of shared identity and personal friendship. In short, the partners develop trust through the repeated experience of working together, making joint decisions, and other contacts which generate familiarity and then bonding.

The conclusion that trust between partners can develop over time through continued interaction between them, from an initial basis that is purely calculative, is consistent with the experimental findings from iterated games—namely, that the probability of cooperation may be improved initially by providing mutual hostages and then progressively reinforced by the benefits it is seen to provide. The experimental evidence of empirical game theory suggests that, although non-cooperation emerges as the dominant strategy in single-play (i.e. initial) situations, under iterated conditions the incidence of cooperation rises substantially.

The potential advantages of promoting trust between partners and their employees are considerable, for they offer an opportunity to relieve (though not necessarily resolve) the dilemmas of control, integration, and learning which are inherent in organizing alliances. So far as control is concerned, trust can avoid the managerial costs of second-guessing the other partner's intentions and ways of doing things. It is likely to facilitate agreement on common control and information systems. Trust will break down some of the more intractable barriers to integration between the partners and their personnel, barriers which are usually far more difficult to deal with than, say, differences in technical skills or language. The development of trust should also promote the conditions necessary for a cooperative strategy to achieve its learning objectives, by making its members more willing to share information and ideas.

These insights are fundamental to an understanding of cooperative strategy, its rationale, and its management. They also help to identify the policies and practices which can be taken to promote trust as a condition for effective cooperation. Some policies are geared towards creating a clear calculus for mutual benefit; others are aimed at enhancing shared information, especially to resolve conflicts and to open up communication; while yet others assist the growth of mutual bonding.

Motives

Alliances need for their initial stimulus a challenge from a changing external environment. If then an organization develops a feeling of resource deficiency in relation to such an external change, or if it wants to spread risk, or needs to get into a market fast, and/or believes that the transaction costs of an alliance would be less than those incurred from internal development or acquisition, then the motivation to find a cooperating partner exists. If a partner can be found with a similar and complementary motivation and set of capabilities, then the circumstances for the conclusion of an alliance are in place.

So runs the economic argument for the establishment of alliances. However, such explanations need to be supplemented by the identification of motivations that stem from political agendas within firms. The economic arguments may be necessary but they are not always sufficient. Ultimately neither transactions costs, the extent of risk, nor future economic benefits can be known at the time the decision is taken to set up an alliance. There must, therefore, also be a political motive for the alliance, perceived by a coalition of the company's key decision-makers. Political agendas are many and varied within a corporation, and, in the absence of corporate champions able to focus such a coalition towards cooperative action, the motives for the formation of strategic alliances or other forms of cooperation may be insufficient to lead to their creation.

Finally the motivation to cooperate remains high even when the alliance has exposed the partners to the temptation to steal each other's secrets and run, so long as the alliance is of indeterminate length, the penalties for defection are high, and reputations matter.

Partner and form selection

Important criteria for partner selection are the need for the partners' assets to be complementary, and for the identification of potential synergies between the prospective partners. It has been observed that, whilst strategic fit is normally carefully assessed prior to concluding an alliance, the extent of cultural compatibility is frequently neglected. Yet culture clashes are the most commonly cited reason for alliance failure.

There are several forms of alliance, joint ventures, collaborations and consortia being the most common forms. The conditions under which each of these forms might appropriately be adopted can be identified. Joint ventures are most appropriate for distinct businesses with distinct assets; collaborations are best where flexibility is the key requirement, and consortia where two partners are not enough to ensure competitive advantage. These forms refer only to strategic alliances, however, and also ignore the other ways of looking at form—namely, the scale alliance (cooperation between competitors to realize scale economies) and the link alliance—cooperation between firms at different stages of the value chain.

Networks

There are a number of different forms of network, notably the equal-partner network and the dominated network. There is also the virtual corporation. This is similar to outsourcing, but with electronic information controls and communication. The growth of the predilection for creating firms around key competences with outsourcing has led to the corresponding growth of virtual-corporation theory. This differs from strategic-alliance theory in that the virtual corporation does not have inter-company organizational learning as its prime objective, whereas strategic-alliance theory does. Virtual corporations are concerned with creating a variable configuration company from existing companies with excellent specific skills. Inter-company learning is likely to play little part in this.

However, outsourcing can be excessive when the nature of the core company becomes unviable. Even the core competences may be inadvertently outsourced—for example, R&D or design. Competitive advantage may well then be lost. As more functions are taken over by people outside the firm, loyalty to the firm and commitment tend to disappear. Indeed a study of several hundred UK companies by PA Consulting in 1996 revealed that they outsource over a quarter of their total budgets for what they regard as their key business processes. There were only three activities that more than 35 per cent of the companies in the survey regarded as 'core'—business strategy, information-technology strategy, and new-product development. This meant that everything else, including R&D, customer service, finance and accounting, and manufacturing, was regarded as non-core by two-thirds of the companies surveyed.

Indeed it may be very possible to set up a virtual corporation by identifying a strategically vital centre, outsourcing everything else, and linking the whole by IT packages, with the central core representing the brain, owning the brand name, and maintaining the motivation even amongst the outlier partners by sophisticated relationship development. But it is quite different to cut back an existing integrated corporation and transform it into a virtual corporation. The demotivation resulting from being cast into the outer periphery, or from fear that one will be the next to go, makes such a transformation very difficult to achieve successfully. However uncertain the future of the virtual corporation may be, that of networks in general is probably much more assured, as they have the robustness to withstand high levels of economic volatility.

Negotiation

As is very apparent from the case studies described in this book, the valuation of the contribution of each partner to a strategic alliance is a very inexact process, and depends heavily on corporate politics and the respective attitudes of each partner to their future work together. Some strike a very hard bargain, and others a very easy one in the interests of future goodwill and cooperation. Some principles, however, apply universally:

1. The creation of a perceived win–win situation leads to a more effective alliance, even if it means negotiating in a less hard-nosed way than is customary in company negotiations.
2. The benefits and not just the costs should be considered in valuing assets to be put into or used in the alliance.
3. The strength of need of the partners will influence the values that are negotiated, especially where a good market-price benchmark is not available.
4. The uniqueness of a particular asset, e.g. brand name or technology, creates a premium value determinable only by negotiation.
5. The valuation range of an asset will be somewhere between its existing value and the assessed NPV of the future benefits to the alliance accruing from its use.
6. The position in that range will depend upon the relative strength of the partners, their possible alternative courses of action to the alliance, the uniqueness of the assets and the negotiating ability and forbearing or hard attitude of the partners.

General management

The general management of alliances is more challenging than that of integrated firms, because it involves maintaining active cooperation between two or more partner companies whose agendas are overlapping rather than identical. In addition, many alliances today are international in scope, and this means that their general managers may find themselves having to take account of the expectations of various groups, such as governmental regulators and community organizations, in an unfamiliar national environment.

The importance of managing external relationships concerning the partners, and internal relationships within the alliance itself, is indicated by the factors that are associated with alliance success. Positive partner attitudes, especially trust and commitment, are the major external factors, while clear organizational arrangements and the management of information flows are important internal factors. To be more specific: the most important factors necessary for the development of a successful alliance would seem to be contained in the concept of a close relationship between the partners—that is to say, flexibility, trust, and committed attitudes towards each other. An alliance general manager can do much to facilitate the development of this relationship through helping the partners to make sense of the alliance in terms of their own expectations, and to reach a shared understanding of the context in which it operates. Good organizational arrangements, especially in relation to information dissemination, and dispute resolution—for example, the establishment of 'gateways'—enable the inevitable and difficult problem of managing an enterprise by consensus to be carried out with a good chance of success.

The essence of a successful alliance must be to learn from one's partner, and not just to use the partner's skills to substitute for one's own deficiencies (although this may be the aim in other collaborative forms). Adoption by both partners of a learning philosophy, but within a situation in which personal and inter-company bonding has taken place, is a likely sign of an enduring alliance.

Of the factors identified above, by far and away the most important seems to be the commitment, mutual trust, and flexibility in the relationship between the partners. Given positive attitudes, frictional problems can normally be resolved. However, in the absence of flexible and trusting relationships any problem encountered places the relationship in jeopardy. Managing the relationship between the partners, to foster both their strategic and personal motives for cooperation, seems to be the key to a successful alliance, and a top priority for its general management.

Control

Control is a critical issue for the successful management and performance of cooperative ventures. It can also become an extremely sensitive matter. If partners compete for control and do not arrive at a mutually acceptable solution, this can jeopardize their relationship and inhibit its potential for realizing complementarities and achieving learning. A subtle balance may have to be struck between the need for control and the equal need in an alliance to maintain harmonious and constructive relationships between the partners.

Control is a complex multidimensional feature of management, and the complexity is increased when the activity to be managed comes under the purview of two or more separate organizations. Three of these dimensions are key as they apply to alliances. These are the extent of control exercised by partners over their alliance, the activities and decisions which they control (focus), and the mechanisms by which control is exercised. The extent of control available to a partner does not necessarily rest upon its formal rights through ownership and contractual agreement. It may depend quite considerably on informal practices, such as a partner company maintaining close personal links with managers and staff working directly in the alliance. It may also be enhanced by a partner's initiatives, such as offering to provide new techniques and training for members of the alliance which lay down a set of practices and a culture that is consistent with the partner's own. In these ways, the extent of control can be conditioned by the mechanisms that are adopted, and the activities to which these are applied. Control of a collaboration, which may be based on little or no contractual foundation, will depend very largely upon the relationship between the partners' respective gatekeepers, and the accord they can work out.

Control is also a subtle phenomenon. In some circumstances it is accepted and regarded as legitimate, in others not. The paradox is that resistance by one partner to the exercise of control by another may diminish the overall control that the former can exercise. Genuine cooperation in a non-zero-sum relationship enables the partners together to exercise greater control, through the fact that they each have greater influence than is the case if the alliance is beset with conflict and low trust.

Although it is a basic tenet of managerial wisdom that adequate and appropriate control is a requirement for satisfactory performance, the evidence on this issue for alliances does not offer clear guidelines on the key issue of whether it is advantageous to share control or to have one leading partner. A partner's control policy should be worked out with a consideration of its goals in forming an alliance and the nature of its dependence on the partner for realizing these. In this respect, it is important for the partners to distinguish between strategic and operational levels of control. Cooperation between firms will usually work best if they each perceive that they have a sufficient voice over the strategic direction it will take. Within an agreed set of long-term goals and priorities, it may then be quite acceptable for one partner to take the lead in controlling certain operational areas in which it clearly enjoys superior expertise, experience, or knowledge.

Human-resource management

A carefully considered set of human-resource-management (HRM) policies and practices can make a significant contribution to the success of alliances. They can assist the adjustment of corporate cultures and practices to the needs of the partnership, offer mechanisms of control, promote organizational learning, and foster the selection and development of staff who are capable of working effectively in a milieu of inter-organizational collaboration. In these and other ways, HRM can help to enhance the productivity of alliances, as well as the ability of partners to benefit from them.

HRM should have a central role in an organization's cooperative strategy. It needs to be brought into the planning and negotiation of alliances, when many of the relevant parameters, such as staffing and the allocation of managerial rights, are being decided. The quality of cooperation will be enhanced by selection, training, and staffing policies which focus on communication competencies (including relevant language skills) and which promote cultural understanding. Consideration also needs to be given to organizational procedures which facilitate adjustment and bonding between partners, such as the wide reporting of progress made through the cooperation.

Central HRM procedures for selection, training, appraisal, and compensation need to be aligned with a partner's policies on control and learning within its alliances. HRM procedures can contribute to the realization of these policies as they are applied to the particular circumstances of the partnership.

The potential benefits which can be realized from closely aligning HRM activities to a company's cooperative strategy point to the desirability of having this function represented at the highest level in the meetings and other discussions which formulate the strategy. If HRM is confined to the periphery of cooperative strategy formulation, as is quite often the case in practice, then its ability to facilitate the successful implementation of the strategy will be correspondingly limited.

Culture

Culture is an elusive yet consequential phenomenon. The distance between partners' organizational and national cultures impacts on the ease with which they can cooperate. While achieving strategic fit is more fundamental to the viability of an alliance, a good cultural fit optimizes the potential of the alliance and helps to avoid the threats to its continuation which arise from misunderstanding and antipathy. Cultures, together with institutional systems which regulate countries' economic, social, and political systems, give rise to differences in typical management practices and policy orientations. It is these differences which have to be accommodated when partners come together to form an alliance and to a lesser extent other forms of collaboration.

Cultures display themselves at different levels, ranging from rather superficial mannerisms to fundamental values. People are unlikely to change their underlying values, except as the result of personal or societal trauma. Nevertheless, there is evidence that people can become sensitive to their own cultures and how these differ from others, and that they are prepared to adapt their customary behaviour within clearly defined situations, such as their place of work, when they accept this is a worthwhile thing to do. There are, then, possibilities for achieving adaptation and accommodation between partners who come from different cultural traditions. Culture does not have to impose an insuperable constraint upon cooperation.

In addition, a mix of national or organizational cultures is not simply a problematic feature of alliances; it can also bring positive benefits to cooperating organizations. The managerial and organizational practices which stem from different cultures represent competences from which each partner can beneficially learn. Cultural diversity creates an opportunity to use the intrinsic worth of each partner's culture for the benefit of the alliance.

There are three basic ways of accommodating cultural differences and the practices which stem from them. It is possible to adopt one partner's culture as the dominant mode. Alternatively, the partners' cultures and practices can coexist, but they are applied to different spheres of the alliance's operations. A third approach is the attempt to integrate partner practices and to derive synergy from this integration. This third approach is the most challenging but also the one likely to produce most benefit. We also set out guidelines for improving cultural fit. These are aimed at assisting personal adjustment to different cultures, promoting better communication between personnel from different cultures, and improving the effectiveness of teams composed of members from different cultures.

Emerging economies

There is an obvious attraction of emerging markets for foreign investing firms. These business environments are, however, typically complex and fluid, often with underdeveloped legal systems and markets. Their cultures and institutions are distinct from those of the highly industrialized countries, and so correspondingly are their business practices, even though some convergence may now be under way.

The objectives of prospective partners from developed and emerging economies are, nevertheless, often reasonably compatible—at least in the short to medium term. While they may compete for the same scarce resources, especially advanced technology, there is usually a strategic fit between the foreign partner's wish to develop markets and the local partner's desire to acquire competence, underwrite financial survival, and share in market expansion What is less clear is whether foreign investors will necessarily regard a strategy of cooperation with local emerging economy firms as desirable or even necessary in the long run, especially as they absorb the country into their global markets and production networks.

Organizational learning

There are three levels of organizational learning: technical, systemic, and strategic. Cooperation with partner organizations offers a potential to learn at all three levels. It can provide access to techniques, facilitate the transfer of new systems, and enhance a firm's ability to undertake new strategic initiatives.

The underlying attitude behind an alliance can be collaborative or competitive. The former allows for joint learning by both partners and is likely to be more productive over the long run. The latter creates a situation in which one partner intends to learn as much as possible from the other, while at the same time offering as little knowledge as possible. Organizational learning becomes a political football in the competitive process between the firms and this is not a sustainable situation in the long run.

There are several requirements for learning to take place within an alliance. The partner must have an intention to learn. It must have the necessary capacity to learn. It must also be able to convert any knowledge it gains into a usable organizational resource.

There are various forms of learning within cooperative relationships: forced learning, imitation, blocked learning, received learning, and integrative learning. Each of these is associated with different degrees of change in understanding and in behaviour.

The successful promotion of organizational learning within cooperative ventures requires (1) the surmounting of cognitive and emotional barriers, (2) the reduction of organizational barriers, and (3) openness of communication and an effective circulation of information.

Evolution

A number of patterns of evolution have been suggested by writers. Some patterns have been driven mostly by internal forces within the alliance—often principally by the development of close personal relationships between alliance members, which have brought about increased trust, bonding, and commitment, and led to overall balanced development and high flexibility. This may lead to new projects for the venture and increased responsibilities, and continuing organizational learning often ensues. Other patterns of evolution may be driven by the recognition of external opportunities, but even here internal propitious conditions and close personal relationships will be needed to make the alliance evolve.

THE FUTURE

This book has been motivated by the belief that there will be important benefits from bringing cooperation further into the mainstream of management thinking. There are two directions in which progress needs to be made.

The first requirement is to give more attention to the process of managing cooperation and how it can be developed to a mature condition. This need arises from the fact that, so far, more attention has been given to the antecedent conditions and desired outcomes of cooperation rather than to the process of making it work and fostering its development. Consideration of the managerial process should reveal how the full potential of cooperation between firms can be realized. We have endeavoured to make a start along this road by devoting Parts III and IV of this book to managing cooperation and maturing the relationship.

The second requirement looks to the changes that are being experienced in the business environment and the positive role that cooperative strategies can play in that context. The need here is to explore more fully the contribution that cooperation can make as a mode of business organization under conditions of increasing complexity. We now consider these two avenues for development in turn.

The maturing of cooperation

Discussion of cooperation between firms has so far been dominated by a static, short-term, and instrumental perspective. This has focused primarily on the calculus involved in establishing alliances and other forms of cooperation, including their anticipated economic outcomes. We have noted its evidence in work on the motives to form alliances, in applications of transaction-costs analysis to the choice of cooperative form, and in analyses of strategic fit. At issue here are the conditions bearing upon the decision of whether and in what form to cooperate. These conditions and the calculus arising from them are undoubtedly critical for the underlying viability of any cooperation. Nevertheless, they constitute the platform for cooperation rather than the process itself. The subsequent management and evolution of cooperation presents a further important strategic and operational challenge. It offers the opportunity to realize the full benefits of cooperation. These benefits may indeed lead the partners to modify their initial evaluations of the cooperation in the light of the experience and learning it brings.

Considered arguments have, of course, been advanced in favour of a short-term and purely calculative approach to cooperation between firms. These are grounded on the assumption that competition is the natural order of business. One example is the view taken by writers such as Hamel and Prahalad that cooperation is an inherently unstable arrangement in an essentially competitive world of global business. This implies that most companies entering into partnerships should reckon on them having a short life, and that they should plan to disengage from the cooperation once it has met the specific objectives that they attach to it. The previous chapter noted the argument of McKinsey consultants Bleeke and Ernst that, if the great majority of joint ventures end up in a sale after five years or so, the partners should plan for this right from the start and enter it into their initial calculus.

It is also pointed out that cooperation is often used as a limited-duration device to acquire key competencies from competitors. In which case, companies had better beware of over-cooperation with actual or potential competitors. Otherwise they may find that cooperation has given their competitors access to their proprietary technology or core tacit knowledge. This view, then, justifies a focus on the entry and exit conditions for alliances. It tends to confine any attention that is given to the cooperative process between entry and exit to the need to safeguard against reneging or exploitation by one partner at another's expense. It adopts a cautionary, and essentially negative, attitude towards cooperation. Cooperation, according to this opinion, can be dangerous to a firm's health.

These cautions can be substantiated by experience, but taken by themselves they project a slanted and limited light on inter-firm cooperation. When companies have entered alliances on naïve or false pretences, this indicates that cooperation was inappropriate to the circumstances, or that inadequate safeguards were built into the relationship. It does not follow that cooperation *per se* is unproductive. Indeed, we noted in earlier chapters that, for productive cooperation to develop, the partners should be assured that they will not be betrayed by the other party. In particular, the trust between partners which is intrinsic to genuine cooperation, and the creation of conditions for mutual learning by the partners, both rely upon an adequate specification of terms and conditions for the cooperation at the outset.

The factors which promote and enhance cooperation remain insufficiently explored, as do the ways whereby cooperation can be managed effectively. The 'soft' and processual side of cooperation management requires more attention. Nevertheless, we can already identify the main ingredients for effective business cooperation:

1. *A realistically worked-out basis for a relationship.* This should assure the partners that the mutual benefit they expect to obtain from cooperating will outweigh the investments they have to make, the risks of the partner's failure to deliver on its obligations, and the opportunity costs arising from alternative policies such as simple market trading. The extent to which reliance can be placed on formal contractual conditions is a very relevant contextual condition here.

2. *Selection of a cooperative form which suits the contingencies relevant to the cooperation.* These might include partner motives, whether an alliance is of a scale or a link nature and the capital requirements associated with this, the extent and nature of resourcing by partners, the balance of global and local needs to be met by the alliance, and the legal and political conditions in its environment.

3. *A conscious policy of open communication and effective flows of non-sensitive information between the partners and their cooperative unit* (if one has been established). This build-up of information will help to promote each partner's understanding of the other. The interpretation of information, as well as propagation of the merits of cooperation, can be facilitated by the appointment of alliance managers from the senior echelons of each partner who are given sufficient time and resource to carry out this role.

4. *Evident public commitment to the cooperation on the part of top executives from each partner.* This should include regular personal visits to

each other. The senior personnel from each partner, and the alliance managers or coordinators, are in a position to activate another requirement for continuing business cooperation—namely, that thought must always be given to how that cooperation can fruitfully progress beyond its initial objectives. In other words, some redundant resources need to be committed to evolving the alliance.

5. *The creation of trust between the partners.* This should be based on the honouring of agreements and the development of close ties between the personnel from each partner firm who work together within the cooperation.

This list of ingredients for effective cooperation points to the ties which have to be sustained and developed in the process. Ebers and Grandori (1997: 270) identify three kinds of ties which exist between cooperating organizations, each of which require active management during the course of the cooperation:

1. *Flows of resources and activity links.* Agreement on the broad outline of resource flows and activity links may well be reached at the outset of an alliance or other form of inter-firm cooperation. They generate an interdependence between the partners. It is, however, impossible to plan the details of these flows and links a priori, and the organic development of the cooperation will modify them over time. They therefore have to be managed and coordinated actively.

2. *Information flows.* These must be kept open not only to achieve an effective management of joint activities, but also to encourage the growth of mutual confidence and trust between the partners.

3. *Flows of mutual expectations and evaluations.* These flows among the partner members influence their perceptions of the opportunities and risks of the cooperation, and hence help to shape their evaluations of the partnership and its future. It is important that arrangements are in place to permit the partners to compare and discuss their expectations and evaluations of the cooperation on a regular basis.

The importance of providing for adequate ties between partners and their cooperative unit cannot be understated, and it is often neglected in practice. For example, the case study by Lyles and Reger (1993), summarized in the previous chapter, illustrates the significance of keeping policy-makers aware of the benefits arising from cooperation. If partner companies are receiving feedback which demonstrates the positive value to them arising from the cooperation, they are likely to encourage its further development through providing appropriate resourcing and/or granting it the autonomy to secure its own support. Learning is likely to be another important feedback loop, and to have two types of content. The first is evidence of substantive learning, such as ways in which the other partner is providing access to new techniques. The second is evidence that there has been learning how to cooperate, such that problems are being successfully ironed out. This second type of positive feedback will in turn help to promote trust between the partners.

The combination of experiments with repeated two-partner games and insights from the study of trust is beginning to indicate how the quality of cooperation can be enhanced over time. It appears to be critical to ensure that each partner believes it worthwhile at the outset to give cooperation a chance. This belief might be facilitated by (1) a sustained period of initial negotiation, conduct of feasibility studies, and other joint 'work'; (2) a recognition that, once transactions have commenced between the partners, it will be difficult to withdraw from them and that therefore one partner will have to live with the consequences of any cheating by the other partner; and (3) safeguards against the risk of reneging. These safeguards may be local to the cooperation in terms of hostages given up by the partners, such as the investments they have sunk into the joint operation. They can also be institutional: either in the form of effective laws to protect contracts and property rights, or in the 'softer' form of effective social norms about honesty and the obligation to carry out commitments.

Once the process of cooperation is under way, it can be reinforced through positive feedback, as just indicated. Additionally, cooperation is a social process in which members from each partner will work together, at least from time to time. As Chapter 3 indicated, it is likely that the process of joint working will reinforce trust, especially if it meets with success, as the people concerned come to know each other better and perhaps eventually form some personal friendships. There is, of course, no guarantee that this accumulation of resources for trust will progress smoothly, and trust will always remain a fragile, readily disabused, phenomenon. Nevertheless, an understanding of the bases on which trust can be promoted provides valuable guidance to managers of cooperative business relations on how they can nurture such a delicate plant, yet one so essential to successful cooperation.

The key message from this book on the process of cooperation is that it can often be nurtured, very fruitfully, beyond its initial condition. It could therefore be extremely limiting to judge cooperation between firms solely in terms of that initial situation. Managed with some determination to make it succeed, the partners' evaluation of their cooperative strategy might well change in the light of their experience. They may come to attach greater value to cooperation, through this experience, than they did initially, and they may place it within a longer time perspective than was originally the case.

Looking ahead

Reference in this book to new forms of cooperation and the new emerging economies points to our need to understand better the benefits of cooperation under conditions of increasing complexity. This issue is of natural concern to large global multinational corporations, for it is linked to the question of whether they can sustain their dominant role in world business essentially through their present forms, adapting these at the periphery rather than transforming them substantially. Many MNCs appear to regard cooperation as a transitory expedient in circumstances, such as entry to a new market or operational location where an initial knowledge deficiency or absence of local political connections renders it necessary to work at first with a partner. At the back of their corporate minds is the assumption that, after a while, they should either reduce their dependence on the partner or absorb it. From this perspective, cooperation is not regarded as an enduring or fundamental condition for success in the modern world, despite the rapidly increasing number of alliances since the mid-1980s.

There are, however, good reasons to suppose that cooperation between organizations is going to become increasingly appropriate for coping with the emergent conditions of the global competitive economy. The world economy is becoming increasingly integrated so that changes in one region impact rapidly elsewhere. The rate of change is increasing, one example being the steady reduction of product development-to-market lead times. There is increasing technological crossover from one sector to another, as well as between countries. This conjunction of increasing interdependence and unpredictable combinations between players is creating complex adaptive systems which are inherently dynamic and evolutionary rather than static.

It is no longer sufficient to describe the relevant context for firms as one of globalization. Globalization in itself just creates a simple form of additive complexity, equivalent to Gell-Mann's notion of 'crude complexity' (see Chapter 12). In other words, globalization by itself adds extra elements into reasonably well-understood equations, such as those governing optimal logistics. Rather, the business environment is taking on characteristics of Gell-Mann's 'effective complexity' in which the relationships between components of the system are becoming less predictable and more subject to non-linear transformations. The equations and their interactions are no longer so easy to model or understand.

This transition also means that the new environment is no longer one that can be adequately characterized as a system of a 'punctuated equilibrium'. This is a system in which periods of relative stability are interrupted by stormy episodes of restructuring. The 'disturbances' in this type of system are reasonably predictable, and there are macroeconomic tools for mitigating them. By contrast, what we are now coming to experience is a state of affairs in which equilibrium cannot be taken as the norm (if, indeed, it ever could). The term 'dynamic disequilibrium' appropriately conveys the character of this system.

Indeed, in the newly recognized knowledge-based increasing-returns industries economists (Arthur 1989) now recognize that there are no inevitable equilibria. Being an early mover, operating in a dense ecology of alliance, path dependence, and lock-in of trained consumers seem to ensure a far surer route to success than the traditional one of producing something cheaper and better. In these industries the optimal product is not bound to triumph, and chance plays a major role. As Bettis and Hitt (1995) put it, strategic-response capability becomes the key to survival as it does in biology, and a network of alliances helps develop such a capability.

The challenge for firms in such a system is to optimize along more than one front simultaneously, rather than sequentially in the way they are used to doing. They have to retain the competitive and strategic strengths they have developed through sunk costs, yet at the same time be prepared to follow alternative avenues should these suddenly turn up. They must try to maintain competitive advantage while also adapting continuously. Even large multinational corporations are unlikely to possess all the competencies required for this, and their very own scale and internal complexity can cause their adaptability to be severely handicapped. As a result, firms will have to find new forms of organizing to suit the emergent business environment. These will need to be 'new organizational forms that help avert complexity catastrophes . . . or practices that promote a rich fund of ideas' (Beinhocker 1997: 38). This is where the necessity for cooperative strategies becomes evident.

Firms can choose to deal with this phenomenon of complex adaptive systems through one of two general approaches. The first is to attempt to *reduce the impact* of external complexity through using their own resources and negotiating positions to create conditions which will preserve value for their specific competencies and practices. The application of massive resources to R&D may enable a firm to generate a steady stream of advanced products that have high appeal to the market, including appeal to latent consumer needs. This may enable the firm to dominate its sector sufficiently to offset, at least for some years, the threat of competition to its profits. One sees examples in pharmaceuticals, such as Glaxo, and consumer electronics, such as Sony. However, as Beinhocker (1997: 35) notes, evidence suggests that in the new environment firms are finding it difficult to maintain higher performance levels than their competitors for more than about five years at a time. A 'go-it-alone' strategy is becoming increasingly difficult to sustain even for the largest, best-resourced firms. Most, of course, are not in that category in the first place.

Another facet of this 'reduction-of-complexity' policy can be seen in attempts by MNCs in emerging economies to use their international reputation and the financial resources they can offer for commercial and social investments. This 'clout' enables them to open up their own direct channels to the host government and its agencies without the use of local partners as intermediaries. They can then attempt to reduce environmental uncertainties by using these channels to negotiate their own preferred accommodations to the environment, backed by governmental intervention.

Cooperation between firms is not necessary to this approach. If it is used, this is likely to be for relatively short-term benefit, to plug resource gaps or to overcome barriers. If there are such gaps or barriers, acquisition rather than cooperation is the preferred solution. The firm attempts to ride through complexity relying on its own strength in order to preserve its cultural and structural integrity. This approach is, however, flexible only at the periphery and retains the rigidities of the corporate core. In a turbulent environment, it is subject to the dangers that La Fontaine correctly discerned 300 years ago in his fable of the oak and the reed.

Cooperation is, by contrast, integral to the alternative policy, which can be described as one of attempting to *absorb the uncertainties* of an effectively complex environment. Here the aim is to absorb the uncertainty generated by complex adaptive systems by means of working closely with one or more partners. In this approach, a firm relies on partners to enhance its capacity to adapt by providing competencies and resources that are complementary to, and extend, its own. It also endeavours to engage the active support of its partners in formulating policies that address the environment. The idea is to achieve a synergy not only of resource but also of thinking, which can help to generate more flexible strategies. Cooperation can, and does, extend to networks of alliances or collaborations. These, as we have noted in Chapter 6, permit a flexible adjustment to changing market and technological conditions by permitting different combinations between the partners to suit particular projects as well as by facilitating an ongoing exchange of information within the network.

If, as seems the case, success within the new business environment lies in having relevant information, an ability to learn, and the capacity to access and combine key competencies including technologies, then the potential value of a cooperative approach is indisputable. These requirements can, of course, be provided within a single organization, but with increasing difficulty. Firms are finding it more and more problematic to bear the cost and risk of technological development alone. Moreover, a single organizational culture can easily suppress the stimulus to learning and adjustment that comes from divergent thinking, especially at lower levels of the organization. It is also difficult to encompass an adequate understanding of different environments within the staff of a single company.

Many MNCs are today attempting to organize in ways that cope with their inherent paradoxes, trying to reconcile hierarchy with heterarchy, control with adaptation and learning, globalization with localization. To achieve this, they will have to learn how to establish federated enterprises, or internal alliances. This may well prove inherently more difficult for them than the alternative of adopting a cooperative strategy. Doubtless MNCs will continue to prosper in areas of advantage where, for example, global products or services have great appeal, but it is likely that they will increasingly have to secure the advantages of flexibility and accelerated learning which cooperation with other organizations can offer.

There is no denying the problems and pitfalls that can beset the new strategy. This book has identified many of them. At the same time, it argues that a cooperative strategy is relevant to the business environment of the twenty-first century, and that the means are available to manage it successfully.

REFERENCES

Arthur, W. M. (1989), 'Competing Technologies, Increasing Returns and Lock-In by Historical Events', *Economic Journal*, 99: 116–31.

Axelrod, R. (1984), *The Evolution of Cooperation* (New York: HarperCollins).

Beinhocker, E. D. (1997), 'Strategy at the Edge of Chaos', *McKinsey Quarterly*, 1997/1: 24–39.

Bettis, R. A., and Hitt, M. A. (1995), 'The New Competitive Landscape', *Strategic Management Journal*, 16: 7–19.

Ebers, M., and Grandori, A. (1997), 'The Forms, Costs, and Development Dynamics of Inter-Organizational Networking', in M. Ebers (ed.), *The Formation of Inter-Organizational Networks* (Oxford: Oxford University Press), 265–86.

APPENDIX. THE CASE STUDIES

A synopsis of the major (Faulkner 1995) case studies referred to in the text is set out below.

1. THE CABLE & WIRELESS CONSORTIUM

Cable & Wireless (C&W) is pursuing a strategy of becoming a global force in the telecommunications market. Given its limited size in global terms, this requires development through strategic alliances. The Japanese market is clearly important for this strategy, and C&W determined in 1986 to attempt to obtain the licence to become the second Japanese international carrier. In order to do this it decided that a consortium company needed to be set up including some major Japanese corporations in order to achieve credibility with the Japanese government. International Digital Corporation (IDC) was therefore founded in 1986 with C&W, Toyota, and C Itoh each holding 17 per cent of the equity and about twenty Japanese shareholders sharing the remainder. The consortium was, after a considerable battle with the Japanese government, successful in obtaining the international carrier licence.

The alliance has undoubtedly been a success in establishing itself in Japan. It has achieved a 16 per cent share of Japan's international telecommunications traffic. C&W has made strong Japanese friends, been accepted in Japan, and been able to set up a further joint venture, Fairway Networks, on the domestic front in Japan. Japan has gone from having the highest prices in international telecommunications in the Asian region to one of the lowest, and, from not being on the major networks of the world, it has in three years become the major hub centre for the whole area. Much of this is due to the stimulus provided by IDC. The capital value of IDC has increased to about 700 times its initial share value as at July 1992. Also Mercury, a C&W subsidiary company, now has about 30 per cent of the UK traffic with Japan, which it certainly would not have had without IDC, so for the £17 million invested by C&W the spin-off benefits have been immense, although remittable profits have been somewhat meagre.

There appears to be considerable trust, commitment, and bonding at least short term between the partners, brought about principally as a result of the difficult political birth of the company in the face of the Japanese government's chauvinistic inclinations. C&W admits that its shareholders all have different agendas, and it is very uncertain what will happen in the longer term, when the licence situation is again reviewed in Japan.

2. COURTAULDS–NIPPON PAINT

Courtaulds set up a collaborative alliance with Nippon Paint of Japan in 1976, because it needed a reliable Japanese company to service its and its customers' needs in Japan. Nippon for its part wished to rise in the league table of Japanese marine paint companies, and regarded an alliance with Courtaulds, the acknowledged world leader in the area, as a significant step in helping it achieve this aim.

The alliance has a mixture of good and limiting characteristics, leading to considerable difficulty in predicting its future. On the good side, the partners have both benefited substantially from the relationship, and show characteristics of trust, commitment, and growing sensitivity to cultural differences. However, overall objectives increasingly cease to be congruent as Nippon becomes more successful, and develops global ambitions. Courtaulds, however, required a territorial non-compete clause outside Japan and this was incorporated in the collaboration agreement. This was ultimately to cause Nippon problems.

There is also little evidence of bonding, or of organizational learning, although, after a period of stagnation, evolution took place. The alliance has endured for a long time, and its prospects for the future probably depend crucially on the level of bonding achieved by the new generation of senior executives in both companies, and on the partners' ability to reconcile their objectives, and achieve greater organizational learning. There is little doubt that both partners value the relationship greatly, although their respective objectives, and views of each other differ to some degree. To Nippon, Courtaulds are a very strong global marketing company with whom they are happy to share joint global development. They see themselves as stronger technologically, however. Courtaulds see Nippon as greatly improved technologically, and as a strong partner to represent them in Japan, but probably not as an equal global partner in the world-wide marine paints market.

3. DOWTY–SEMA

Dowty–Sema was set up as a joint venture in 1982 by the current partners' predecessor companies at the instigation of the Ministry of Defence, in order to provide an alternative tenderer to Ferranti in the specialized market of command-and-control systems for ships. Until its integration into Bae–Sema in 1992 it was 50 : 50 owned by the Dowty and Sema.

The joint venture was clearly a success in growth terms. It had been very successful in obtaining work from the MOD. From nothing in 1982, it grew in ten years to 110 staff and an annual turnover of £50 million. But as a company it suffered from its lack of independent assets with which to carry out the work. 90 per cent of the value of each contract was subcontracted back to the owning partners Dowty and Sema in the form of work to be carried out. Only 10 per cent remained with the prime contractor Dowty–Sema. The venture was, therefore, little more than a shop window for marketing and sales purposes.

All decisions of any importance followed only after lengthy committee meetings involving both the partners and the venture management. Owing to these cumbersome organizational arrangements, neither the partners nor the venture seem to have made much profit from the contracts landed by Dowty–Sema. Thus the flawed organizational arrangements made at set-up were compounded by inappropriate management behaviour which impeded the genuine flourishing of the venture.

There appears to have been little commitment or trust between the partners below Board level, and the concept of a learning organization was not in evidence to any appreciable extent.

However, a *deus ex machina* was to rescue the venture in 1993. The TI Group, having bought Dowty, did not want to be in the defence sector, so it sold its holding in Dowty–Sema to Bae–Sema. So Dowty–Sema is now a wholly owned subsidiary of Bae–Sema, with the ex-subcontracting division of Sema as the other subsidiary. However, the Bae–Sema joint venture is run as an integrated operation, with its own payroll, pension scheme, and profit responsibility, and Dowty–Sema may well prosper as a result of the transfer.

4. EUROBREK

The name Eurobrek is a fictitious one invented to represent the joint-venture company set up in 1989 by a major European and a major American food company to compete in Europe against Kelloggs in the breakfast-cereals market. A confidentiality agreement precludes the use of the real names. The joint venture operates from a base in the UK and, largely as a result of purchasing the cereal interests of another major UK producer, it already has in excess of 10 per cent of the UK market.

Overall the alliance is judged to be successful, as it is achieving its market-share targets, and is marketing new products successfully. For it to prove successful in the longer term, however, there may be attitude adjustments necessary to overcome problems, the seeds of which are only just beginning to

reveal themselves. The UK partner is traditionally uncomfortable in joint ventures, and Eurobrek has not been given true autonomy to do its job, since the
UK partner carries out the sales activity for it. Furthermore the characteristics
of an evolving learning organization cannot yet be clearly seen. There is also
only limited bonding and trust developing between the partners.
Commitment by the partners is strong to the achievement of success in the
sector and in relation to Kelloggs, but not necessarily to the joint-venture
form.

Ultimately, however, the success of the challenge to Kelloggs will be determined by the branded market—i.e. the consumer— and here it is difficult to
see any obvious advantage for Eurobrek, although Eurobrek's willingness to
provide own-label product to major retailers may give it some advantage over
Kelloggs, who currently will not do so. Retailers are concerned that both companies are committing large amounts of advertising expenditure in a mature
market. Whilst advertising may get the first sale, only consumer taste will
ensure the repeat sale, and here the future is still uncertain, as the sustainable
competitive advantage over Kelloggs is difficult to discern.

The future will then be awaited with considerable interest in the European
cereal market. Kelloggs currently has seven of the top ten brands in the UK in
its portfolio, and Eurobrek has only one. To become a successful joint venture
in its own right, it is probable that greater flexibility in attitude is needed by
the partners, and the ceding to Eurobrek of the assets needed to make it oper-
ationally self-sufficient.

5. EUROVYNIL CHLORIDE CORPORATION

EVC is a joint venture set up in 1986 by ICI and Enichem of Italy to rationalize
the production and sales of PVC in Europe. In order to do this it was judged
necessary to take up to 1 million tonnes of capacity out of the joint capacity of
the two partners. EVC is a 50 : 50 owned venture company based in Belgium,
with the remit to sell PVC and allied products based largely on ICI and
Enichem raw material and manufactured in plants still run by ICI and
Enichem respectively.

This joint venture has to be regarded as relatively successful, since it
achieved its primary objective of returning the area of activity for the partners
to profit in normal non-recessionary times, largely through capacity rationalization, and efficiency improvement. However, the fact that EVC was forced to
buy 90 per cent of its raw materials at above-market prices from the shareholders, and that production took place in factories owned by the partners
and not by EVC, has considerably constrained its developmental potential.

Basic organizational arrangements have been appropriate—i.e. a joint venture—but culture differences between the partners have made life somewhat
difficult for the EVC personnel. There is little commitment or bonding evident,

beyond that required for getting out of the over-capacity problem with as little financial burden as possible. No obvious learning philosophy has been adopted by either partner. Owing to the limited appreciation by the shareholders of the most appropriate principles to follow if a joint-venture company is to thrive and evolve over time, and the somewhat bleak prospects for PVC in the medium-term future, a prognosis for the longer-term future would suggest that the best solution for all parties would be a third-party sale, as was apparently in prospect in 1990. EVC cannot realistically expect to achieve this until it has ownership of its manufacturing, and possibly raw-material-producing plants, so that the joint venture can present itself as a self-standing business.

6. ICI PHARMA

ICI Pharma is a joint venture set up in 1972 by ICI Pharmaceuticals (60 per cent) and Sumitomo Chemicals (40 per cent) to produce and market certain ICI pharmaceutical products in Japan. ICI provides the product specification, Sumitomo manufactures the product and achieved Japanese registration, and the joint venture ICI Pharma sells and distributes it.

The joint venture has achieved an acceptably high share of the small part of the Japanese pharmaceutical market that is not dominated by Japanese national companies. In the eyes of the partners the venture has met its measurable objectives, and achieved a good reputation in the industry in Japan. However, according to ICI, the lion's share of the profit has gone to Sumitomo.

Cultures also remain very separate. Trust and bonding have not developed appreciably, and commitment is not evident despite the venture's longevity. Although learning has clearly taken place, it has been largely opportunity learning rather than the adoption of the learning philosophy. The alliance is not evolving in a major way from its original boundaries. Indeed recently ICI has set up a production plant in Japan and is intent on removing the responsibility for producing ICI Pharma's products from Sumitomo.

The ICI side believes that, when the alliance was set up, Sumitomo got the best of the bargain, and has been insufficiently flexible to renegotiate the deal as this has become apparent. The existence of this somewhat strong view held by ICI is probably sufficient by itself to confine the alliance to the limited success category of alliances.

7. ICL–FUJITSU

The collaboration between ICL and Fujitsu came about in stages over a ten-year period. It began as technology cooperation in 1982, and then extended through Fujitsu buying a minority of ICL equity, to the situation where the Japanese partner owns more than 80 per cent of ICL, but is pledged to treat it as a partner rather than as a subsidiary, and to place a large part of its shareholding back on the market at an opportune time.

The alliance is judged both internally within the companies, and externally within the industry, as very successful. The only factor in the long-term prognosis that does not point in the right direction is that of balance. Clearly Fujitsu has the ultimate power, due to its 80 per cent ownership and overwhelming financial strength. This unbalancing factor could affect the alliance negatively, if the present colleagues in the operation of the alliance change over time, since many commentators suggest that the most durable alliances are those where there is an approximate balance between the respective strengths of the partners. However, Killing's research (1983) suggests that alliances with one dominant partner may well be most successful, as a possible source of power ambiguity is thereby avoided. In that event the prognosis for the ICL–Fujitsu alliance is good.

The alliance is a collaboration, and as such the points of contact between the companies are many. Organizational arrangements are flexible, and commitment, trust, and bonding are clearly in evidence. Differences in culture seem to be regarded as a positive factor rather than a potential problem, and, as is common in an alliance involving a Japanese partner, the learning aspect of the alliance is particularly strong.

8. IMPERIAL–WINTERMANS

The collaboration between Imperial and Henri Wintermans in the marketing of Wintermans' cigars in the UK is an alliance that exchanges UK market access, provided by Imperial for Wintermans, for technology transfer, provided by Wintermans to update Imperial's cigar-manufacturing technology. The alliance was formalized in 1989, and has been successful in that Imperial has met its target for sales of Wintermans' cigars, and Wintermans has transferred its technology.

The organizational arrangement has worked well. The two 'gateway' executives on either side relate well, and there is commitment and trust between Wintermans and Imperial. However, Wintermans are owned by BAT, a major rival of Imperial, and BAT is becoming increasingly interventionist in Wintermans' activities. Also the question of the limited possibilities for evolution of the alliance may place a limit on the alliance's capacity for growth. It may be that there is little more to go for in market share in the cigar market in the UK without Imperial and Wintermans attacking each other's share. On the technology side both companies are 'state of the art' since Wintermans' technology transfer to Imperial. Brand rationalization can probably go no further on the Imperial side, and not much further on Wintermans'.

Imperial talk speculatively of merging production units to achieve the greatest possible economies of scale, but this would be difficult to do without setting up a formal joint-venture company, and with Wintermans operating world-wide and Imperial only in the UK this would present difficulties. Finally, the position of BAT as Wintermans' owners represents a major potential conflict of interest which may ultimately destroy the alliance.

The alliance, therefore, having achieved its initial objectives with admirable effectiveness and positive attitudes, may be approaching the point when its strategic imperatives need to be reassessed, as these may no longer afford any obvious opportunities for evolution.

9. ROVER–HONDA

The collaboration between Rover and Honda was a very long-lasting one that led to the resurrection of Rover as a quality car-maker, and the effective entry of Honda into the European market. It started in 1979 as a simple arm's-length franchise for Rover to assemble a Honda car in the UK, badge it as a Triumph (a British Leyland marque), and market it, and subsequently developed into a very extensive alliance including joint manufacturing, sourcing, design, and R&D. Only marketing and distribution were handled separately in the UK.

The alliance was very fruitful from the viewpoint of both partners. Alone neither was a world-class motor manufacturer. Honda were strong in the USA and a medium-sized player in Japan. Its European presence was negligible. Rover was strong in Europe but nowhere else. In fact 95 per cent of its production in 1980 was for Europe including the UK. However, together Rover–Honda presented a powerful world force with a strong presence in Japan, USA, and Europe.

Rover moved steadily into profit in the mid-1980s largely as a result of its organizational learning from the alliance, and in 1990, as a subsidiary of British Aerospace plc, it contributed an annual profit in excess of £50 million to its parent, although the recession in the late 1980s inevitably damaged profits. However, if quality and a regenerated reputation were prime objectives, these have certainly been established as a result of the alliance. The 800, the 200, and the 400 series are all generally acknowledged to be first-class cars from a quality viewpoint, and Rover's reputation is reflected in its profit figures. It is estimated also that the inter-company business between the two companies is currently worth in the region of £500 million annually.

Honda, for its part, has grown from a medium-sized player in 1978 with a turnover of around £4 billion to one with a worldwide sales level of more than £12 billion, of which 66 per cent is earned outside Japan, and a net profit after tax of more than £500 million in 1990. In Europe Honda's sales of cars have increased from a negligible amount in 1978 to £700 million or 191,000 units in 1990. Not only has Honda raised its European direct sales, but it has also benefited from part of Rover's approximately 450,000 unit sales.

The alliance established loose organizational arrangements from the start, which worked well for it. It established gateway executives and resisted the temptation to set up a joint-venture company, thus allowing steady evolution of activities to take place without limiting boundaries.

After initial culture problems, the alliance developed trust, commitment, and at least adequate bonding between personnel from Rover and Honda. Unfortunately this trust and commitment did not extend to Rover's shareholders BAe, and the alliance was ultimately probably terminally damaged when BAe sold Rover to BMW, thus virtually bringing to an end one of the most successful strategic alliances in recent history.

10. ROYAL BANK OF SCOTLAND–BANCO SANTANDER OF SPAIN

The collaboration alliance between the RBS and the Banco Santander of Spain, set up in 1988, is a partial union of two medium-sized national banks in the face of the expected Europeanization of the banking industry. The partners own a small minority of each other's shares. The alliance operates on many fronts, including joint ventures in Germany and Gibraltar, and a consortium for money transfer covering a number of European countries. This consortium, named IBOS, has become the most successful part of the alliance, and was not foreseen as a significant project at the outset of the alliance, demonstrating the importance of allowing evolutionary forces to develop in successful alliances.

The alliance partners have learnt that, through the extension of IBOS, they can achieve most of what they wish to achieve on the European scene without the added expenditure and risk of acquisition.

Over the four years of the alliance's life there has been considerable evolution of the relationship. Most of the activity areas set out at the beginning are now well under way. The IBOS system is developing in a far greater fashion than had been envisaged. Staff are being exchanged on secondment to the other partner. The appropriate alliance attitudes of commitment, trust, and bonding are well developed between the personnel directly involved in the alliance, and organizational learning is evident on both sides.

The alliance is a very successful venture from the cooperation viewpoint, representing a considerable increase in the European standing of RBS and Santander, and as a by-product has considerably strengthened the ability of RBS to serve its customers in Central and South America. However, customers flow only one way at present. The propensity of UK investors to go into Spain is not matched by those of Spanish investors to invest in the UK, so Santander tends to gain from increased sales more than RBS.

Only the future will tell whether the mature development of the Single Market in financial services will leave the alliance partners strong enough to compete with the major European 'supermarket' banks, or whether adequate niches will develop to avoid the need for head-on competition. Furthermore, both banks are domestic banks in essence, and to put two domestic banks together does not create an international bank, as this requires different types of teams, possibly a wider range of services, and perhaps a different culture. The alliance always envisaged the partners staying as individual banks rather than creating a unified bank. So it must remain an open question, over the next few years at least, whether even a successful alliance could possibly still fall between the two stools of being not sufficiently specialist for a niche bank and not sufficiently large for a major Eurobank.

REFERENCES

Faulkner, D. (1995), *International Strategic Alliances: Co-operating to Compete* (Maidenhead: McGraw-Hill).

Killing, J. P. (1983), *Strategies for Joint-Venture Success* (New York: Praeger).

INDEX

Note: page references for chapters are shown in **bold**.